Albert Duvall Quigley

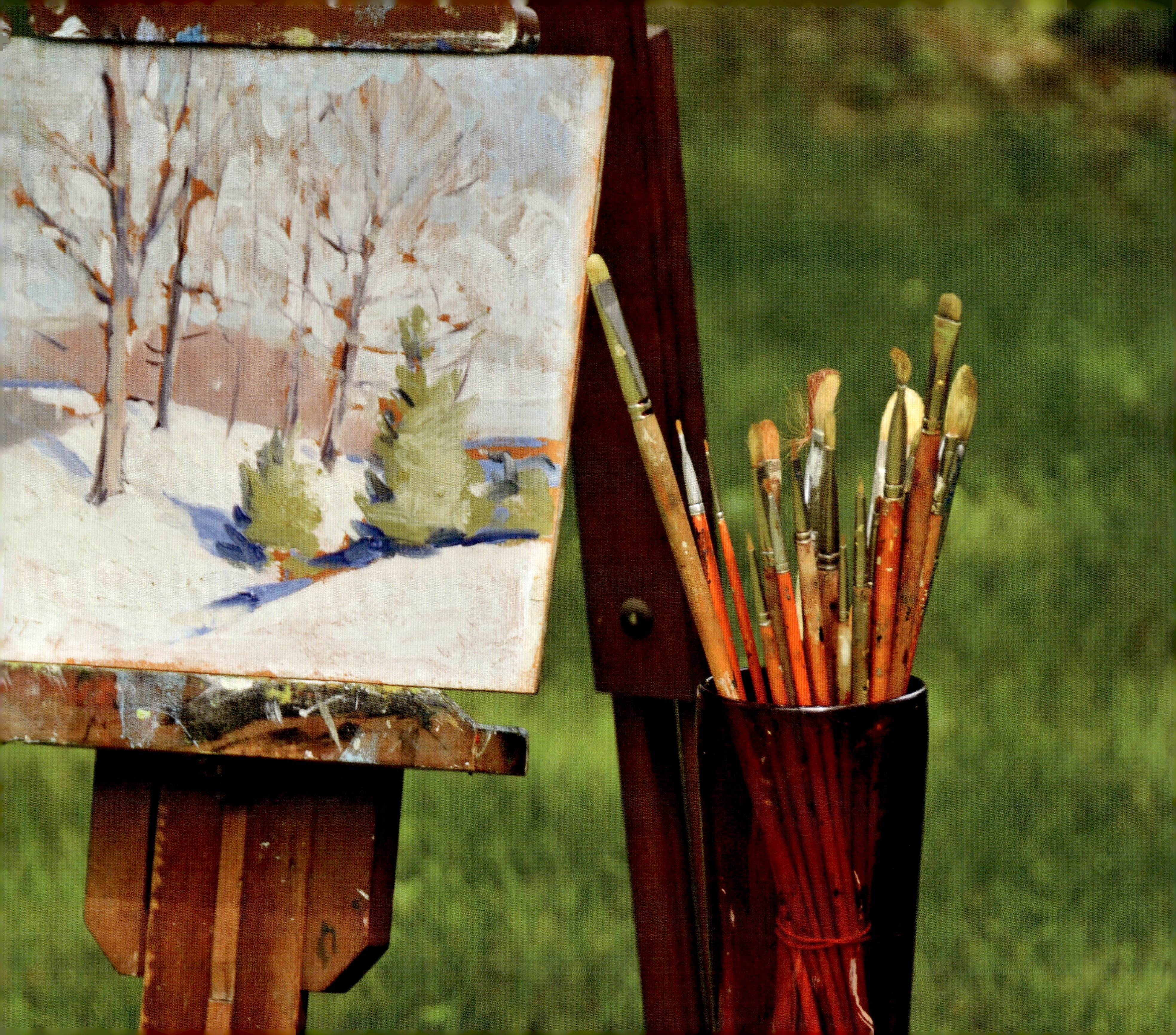

Albert Duvall Quigley

1891–1961

Artist, Musician, Framemaker

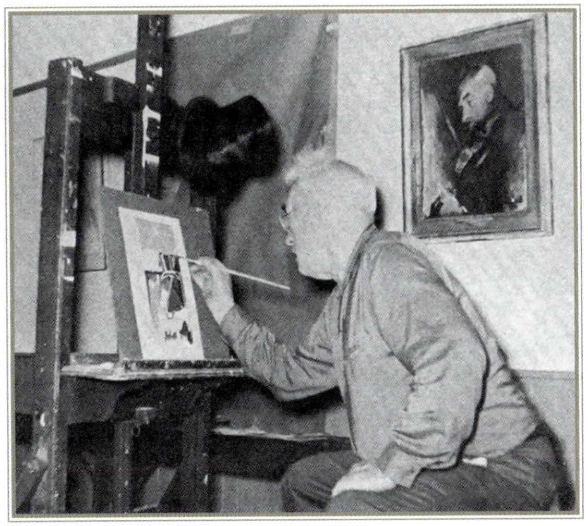

BAUHAN PUBLISHING
PETERBOROUGH, NEW HAMPSHIRE
2017

ISBN 978-087233-242-3

Library of Congress Cataloging-in-Publication Data
Names: Container of work: Quigley, Albert Duvall, 1891-1961.
Works. Selections. | Historical Society of Cheshire County.
Title: Albert Duvall Quigley : 1891-1961 : artist, musician, framemaker.
Description: Peterborough, NH : Bauhan Publishing, 2017. |
Catalog compiled for an exhibition celebrating Quigley's life and work, held May 2017,
Historical Society of Cheshire County (NH), and for the 250th anniversary celebration
of the town of Nelson, NH, where Quigley lived for many years. | Includes bibliographical references.
Identifiers: LCCN 2017011039 | ISBN 9780872332423 (softcover : alk. paper)
Subjects: LCSH: Quigley, Albert Duvall, 1891-1961--Exhibitions. | Nelson (N.H.)--Biography—Exhibitions.
Classification: LCC ND237.Q52 A4 2017 | DDC 759.13--dc23
LC record available at https://lccn.loc.gov/2017011039

BAUHAN PUBLISHING LLC
PO BOX 117 PETERBOROUGH NEW HAMPSHIRE 03458
603-567-4430
WWW.BAUHANPUBLISHING.COM

Historical Society of Cheshire County
P.O. Box 803, 246 Main Street
Keene, New Hampshire 03431
www.hsccnh.org

Cover: TEAM OF OXEN IN FIELD, oil on board, 27 x 69 in., private collection, mural set in pine frame, mounted into the wall over fireplace

Frontispiece photograph: Albert Quigley's easel and brushes, Harriet Wise, photographer

Title page photograph: Albert Quigley at work, courtesy of the Historical Society of Cheshire County

Contents page: Section of an untitled painting, oil on board, 18 x 21 in., private collection

Painting frames: Quigley's handmade frames are shown whenever possible. Where they are not shown, it is because of space considerations or because a painting was used to illustrate a point in the text.

Book design by Henry James. Body set in Electra, captions set in Seria Sans.
Printed by Versa Press.
All photographs of Quigley paintings by Lee Germeroth Photography except where otherwise noted.
Photographs of May Sarton on pp 23, 25, 27 from The Lotte Jacobi Collection, The University of New Hampshire. Used with permission.

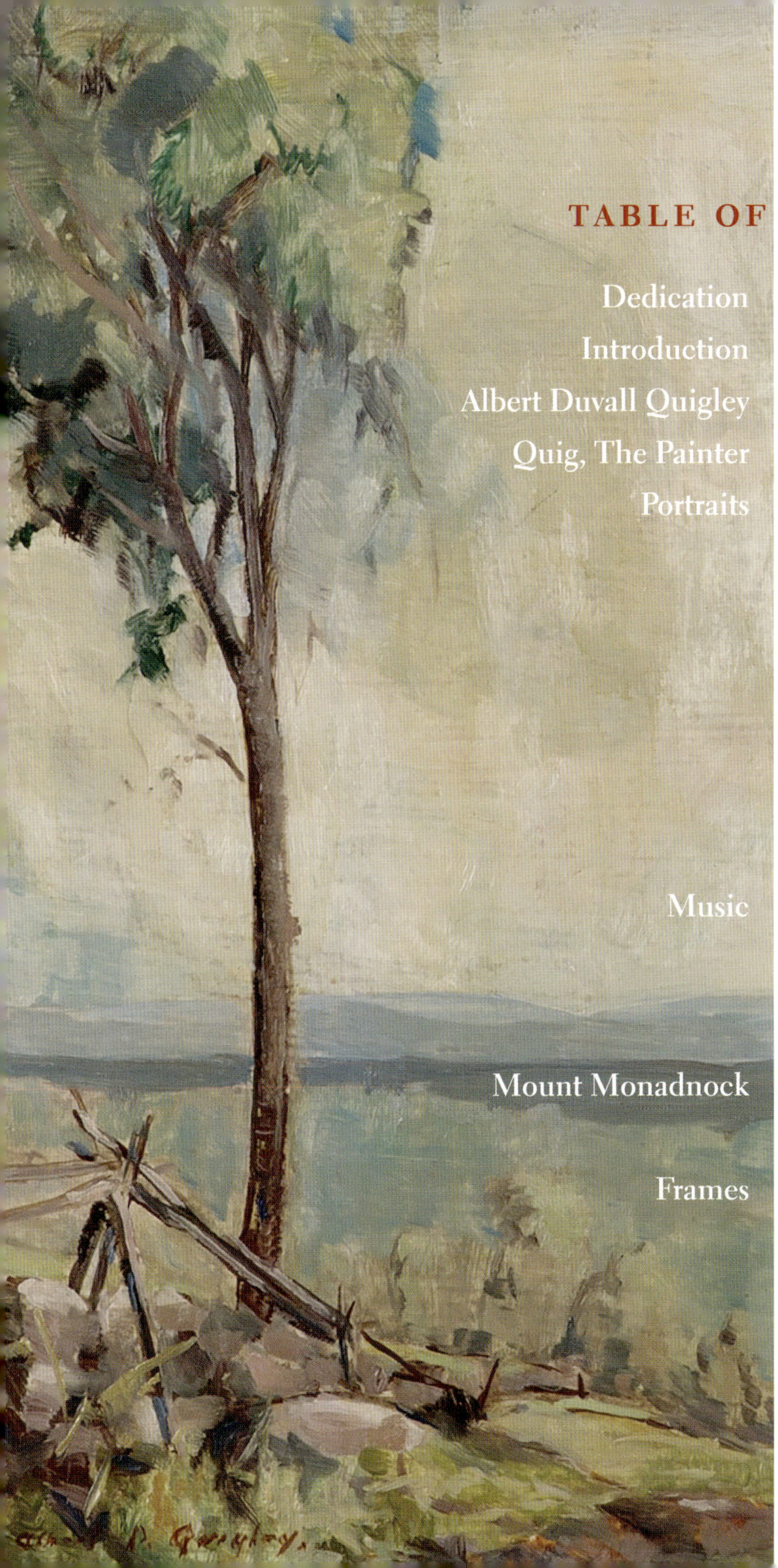

TABLE OF CONTENTS

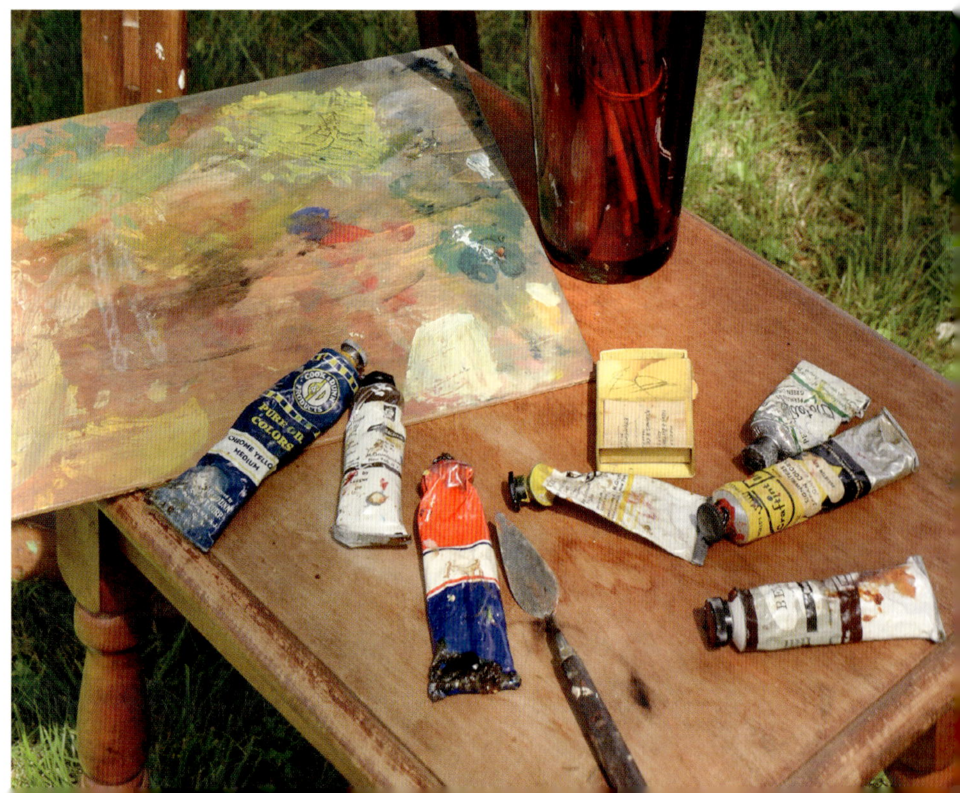

DEDICATION

Barnabas (Barney) Quigley

June 3, 1936–January 26, 2016

Barney Quigley, one of three children of Mildred and Albert D. Quigley (Quig), passed away on January 26, 2016, a little more than a year before the publication of this comprehensive catalogue of his father's work. His parents and two siblings died earlier.

Having grown up in Nelson, New Hampshire, Barney was very pleased when Teri Upton approached him a couple of years ago with a suggestion to compile a catalogue to honor Quig's work as artist, framemaker and musician; with a concurrent exhibit at the Historical Society of Cheshire County in Keene, New Hampshire. With Barney's encouragement, Teri established the Albert D. Quigley Exhibit Committee. They quickly developed plans to have this book and the exhibit coincide with the 250th anniversary of the founding of the town of Nelson.

Barney and his wife, Nancy, with their daughter Darcy, worked tirelessly with this committee—writing Quig's biographical essay and helping to locate and identify the impressive number of paintings that are reproduced here. At the time of Barney's death, the committee had already photographed over one hundred paintings as well as some of Quig's old tools—his easel, palette and brushes. They had also recorded several interviews about Quig, and retrieved audio files of his fiddle playing from the Eloise Hubbard Linscott 1944 collection of recordings held by the Folklife Center at the Library of Congress.

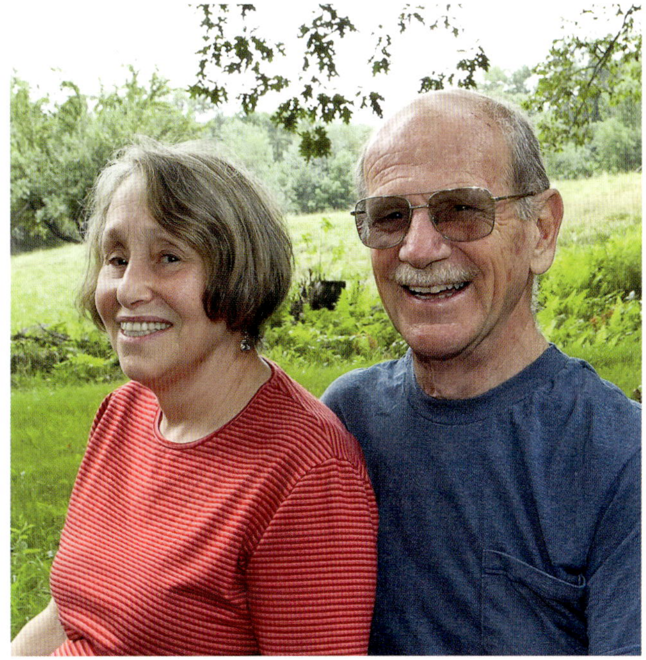

Nancy and Barney Quigley; Harriet Wise, photographer

Barney always claimed he never inherited his father's artistic and musical talents, but no one could ever match his rhythm and distinctive style, clogging on the floor of the Nelson Town Hall, dancing to the same tunes that Quig had played on his fiddle in that same hall. And later, living in New York, both he and Nancy took up the art of

OPPOSITE Albert Quigley's palette
Harriet Wise, photographer

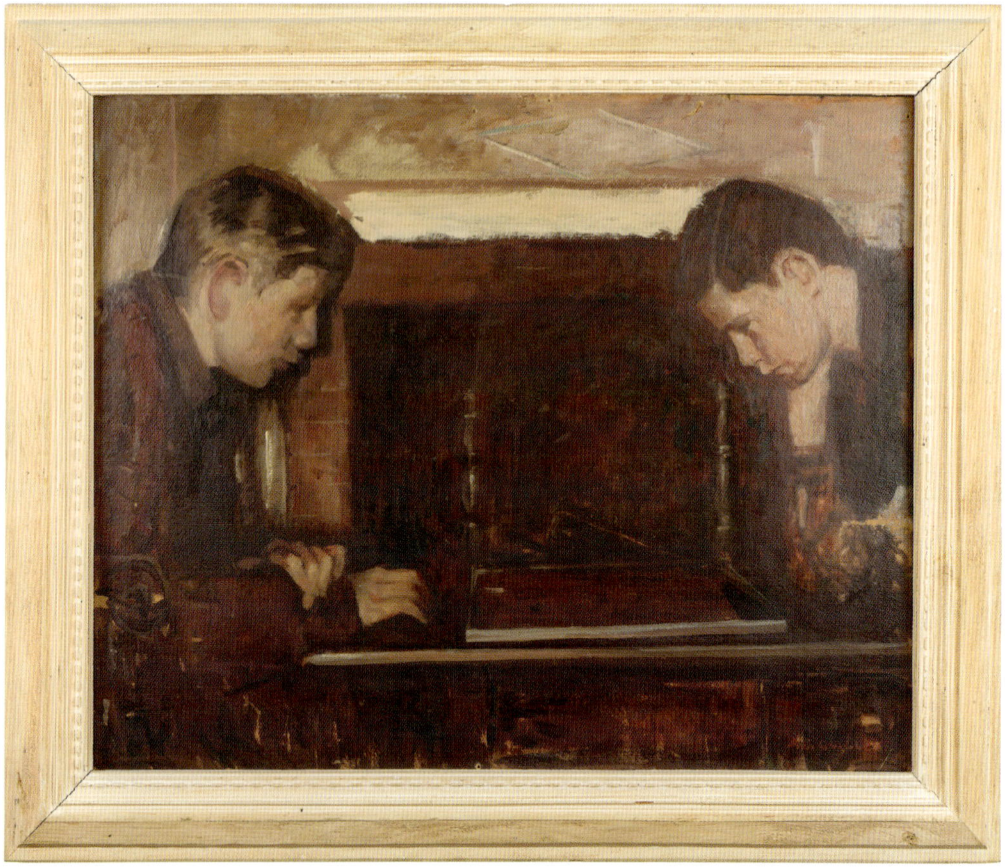

CHECKERS GAME PLAYED BY BARNEY QUIGLEY AND PHIL STACK
Oil on panel, Quigley frame, 30 x 36 in.
Barney and Nancy Quigley
Arnold Adler, photographer

pottery. Juried into many regional shows, Barney's work, sometimes whimsical, was often glazed with the same subtle hues that Quig frequently used in his paintings.

Barney attended the one-room brick schoolhouse in Nelson Village. He went on to Keene High School, the U.S. Navy, and New England College in Henniker, New Hampshire, where he met Nancy Marks, whom he later married. In 1969, having moved to Riverdale, New York, Barney commuted to his office in lower Manhattan to oversee the successful business that he built as a marine surveyor.

However, Nelson was never far from his mind. He visited when he could and thirty-five years ago he and his family became Nelson summer residents, maintaining a seasonal cottage on Lake Nubanusit.

Upon his return to Nelson in the summers, his old hometown friendships resumed with full intensity and new ones blossomed overnight. His irrepressible and puckish sense of humor, his storytelling, his gentleness and kindness, and the depth of his recall of all things Nelson are irreplaceable, and the memory of these things and of his special friendships will always remain with us. His obituary reads: "Above all the things he did in his life, it was the people he knew and loved that he treasured most."

We dedicate this catalogue to our treasured friend, Barney, knowing that, in spirit, he is immensely proud to join with us, his family and friends, in celebrating the work of his late father, Albert Duvall Quigley.

—Karen Tolman
on behalf of the Albert D. Quigley Exhibit Committee

INTRODUCTION

"painter of this landscape
and of all our faces"[1]

ALBERT DUVALL QUIGLEY was an important member of the Nelson, New Hampshire, community and a significant contributor to the artistic and cultural landscape of southwestern New Hampshire in the mid-twentieth century. Kind, hard-working, a great storyteller with abundant talents and a passion for life, Quig—as he was usually called—was a memorable personality. Yet, while we have some writings on his life, work and artistic relationships, Quig was modest and left behind very little autobiographical information. Though we are still able to learn about his life from people who knew him and his peers, many of these resources may not be with us for much longer. It is therefore important that we record their information now, to preserve their knowledge for the next generations; that has been one goal of this catalogue.

Gathering such information not only helps us better understand Albert Quigley and celebrate his work, it also provides an opportunity to locate additional information that will help illuminate the wider network of artistic talent in Southwestern New Hampshire of

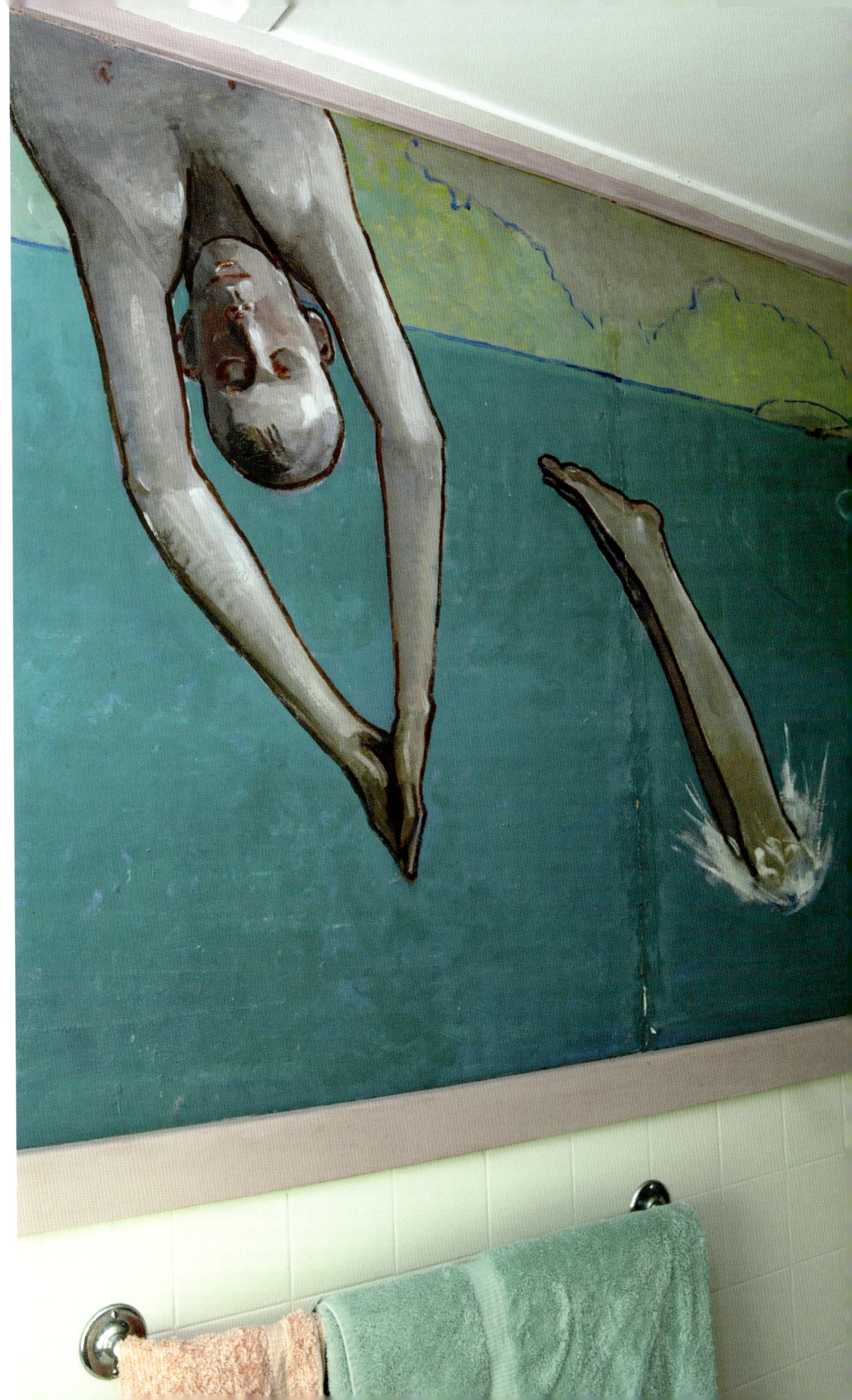

which Quig was a part. We know that he was close to Alexander (Alec) James and other important figures of the nearby Dublin Art Colony. Although he was on the periphery of the Colony as an artist, Quig made frames for many of those artists' work, and in fact Alec James' most important paintings are often completed by a Quig frame. Stylistically, Quig's own landscapes and portraits clearly share characteristics with those of James [lower right], Abbott Thayer [far lower right], Richard Meryman, and other Colony artists of this period. The origins of the shared style, technique and tone of the group's work are unclear, and this volume, together with the 2017 exhibit celebrating Quig's art, should generate discussion that may well help expand our knowledge of both artistic and personal connections among these artists.

In addition to the artists of the Dublin Colony, other New England artists also captured the essence of the Monadnock Region's landscape. Many of their paintings of the period share strong visual and stylistic ties to Quig's and the Dublin Colony artists' work, but again there is no knowledge whether personal connections existed. (We do know that Gouri Ivanov-Rinov, painter of dreamlike landscapes, was a close friend of Alec James.) Artists such as Stanley Woodward, Robert Emmett Owen, Frederick Rhodes Sisson and Charles Curtis Allen were all Quig's contemporaries; shared lineage from artistic mentors Abbott Thayer, Frederick Bosley and Frank Benson further extend the possible connections among the artists of the region. Many of them, including Quig, had studied in Europe during this period, but we know very little of whether or how they came to know one another while abroad.

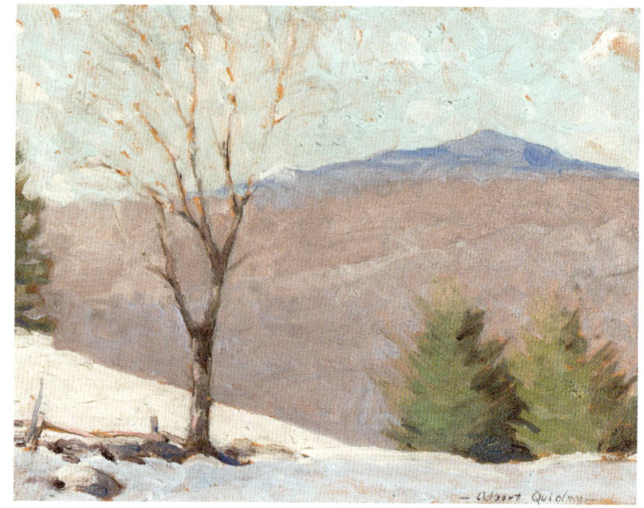

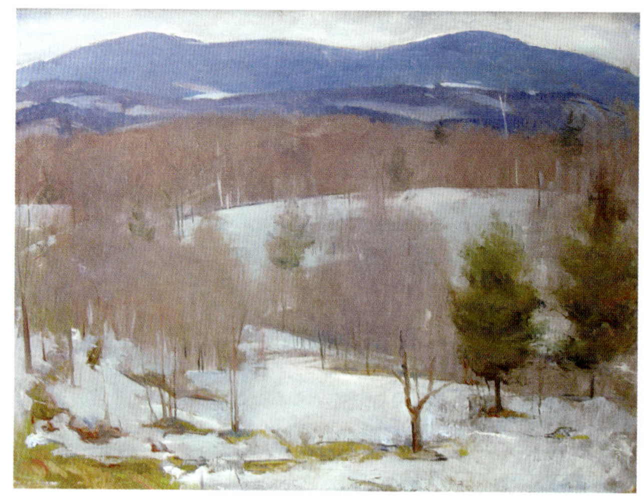

ABOVE **MOUNT MONADNOCK**
Oil on board, 16 x 13 in.
Earle H. Staples

BELOW **MONADNOCK SPRING LANDSCAPE** (1928)
Alexander R. James, 1890-1946
Oil on canvas, 25 x 36 in.
Private collection
Courtesy photograph

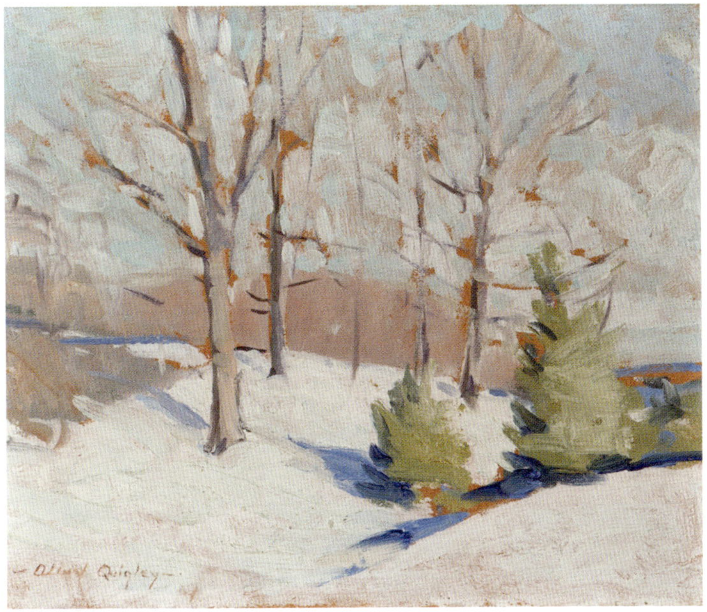

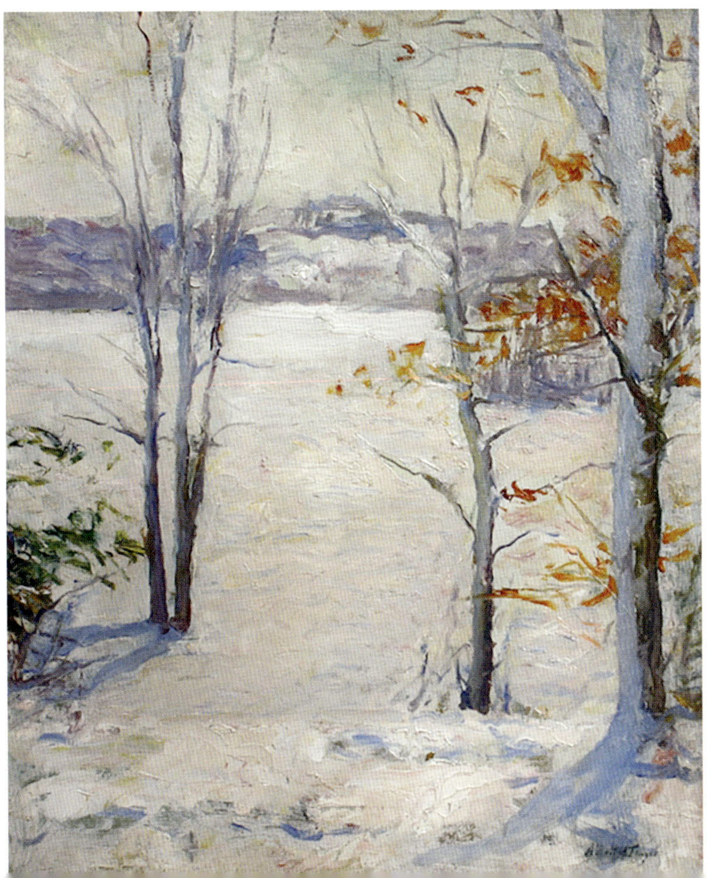

Much closer to home were Quig's neighbors John de Martelly and Marie Spaeth, significant artists of the period with ties to Nelson's Pennsylvania Settlement. A little further afield, the prolific artist William Lester Stevens painted from a small studio in Conway, Massachusetts, with a view of Monadnock in the distance.[2] His strong brushstrokes and palette appear related to Quig's, as do Massachusetts-born Charles Woodbury's magnificent winter scenes of Monadnock. Finally, Quig's beautiful Spofford murals evoke thoughts of muralist Barry Faulkner of Keene. Did Quig and Faulkner ever collaborate? We don't know.

Both this volume and the exhibit of Quigley's work have the potential to awaken interest in his work and that of his contemporaries. During two years of planning and preparation, many "lost" paintings have been found and others whose existence was unknown have come forth. People have shared their stories about Quig's life, work and friendships, and we hope this will continue until a fully-rounded picture of artistic life in the region emerges.

Though visual evidence links these artists' work to time and place, a Quig painting is almost always recognizable and what sets it apart can be summed up briefly: he painted as an intimate of the land he inhabited. The earth tones of his landscapes capture the land's look precisely, as do the shadows of winter snows. The portraits not only capture the faces of his subjects, but the lives behind those faces. Emotions are not hidden. The simple backgrounds are beautifully suggestive. The quality of the New England light cannot be separated from the subject, and the handcrafted frames are part of the total mood of the paintings.

ABOVE **UNTITLED**
Oil on board, 15 x 17 in.
Quigley frame
Private collection

BELOW **VIEW TO MONADNOCK**, ca. 1910
Abbott Handerson Thayer, 1849–1921
Oil on canvas, 23¼ x 19½ in.
Courtesy photograph

Quig understood his world, its people and the community, and his work reflects the depth of his knowledge.

One story illustrates this particularly well. In the 1970s another colorful Nelson figure, Frank Upton, was serving as an art broker of sorts for Quig's daughter, Tami, who was selling several of her late father's paintings. In the corner of Frank's barn, away from the paintings for sale, hung Quig's stunning painting of a Nelson church scene in winter. It was a deeply familiar scene to Quig, whose home was just across the road. The painting belonged to Frank and was not for sale, and Frank could identify each townsperson in the scene and tell his inimitable stories about each tiny figure. More than a landscape, the painting told a story of the village. Quig, as no simple rural painter and framemaker could have done, had not only captured that day and the scene: he had created a world.

Quig was also an accomplished musician and an important figure in the world of contra dancing and fiddle playing. His work with Ralph Page, Newt Tolman, Harvey Tolman and a host of other area musicians laid the foundation for strong regional music traditions. Many of us grew up contra dancing away our Saturday nights in Nelson to the tunes Quig created or made popular. These dances released weekly pressures, strengthened the fabric of community, and instilled a sense of pride as it allowed those of us with few artistic talents ourselves to participate actively in the art of others. The dances, now on Monday evenings, continue to the present day—a wonderful tradition.

By far the most detailed written information we have had on Quig, until his son, Barney, wrote a biographical

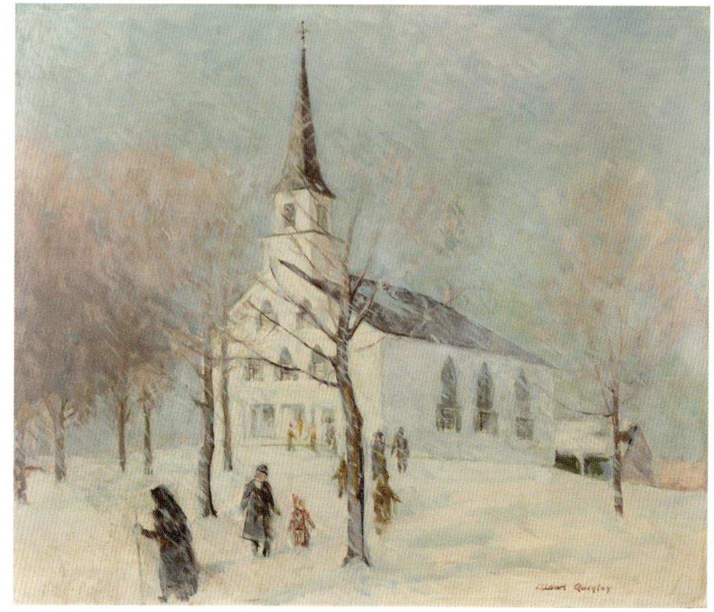

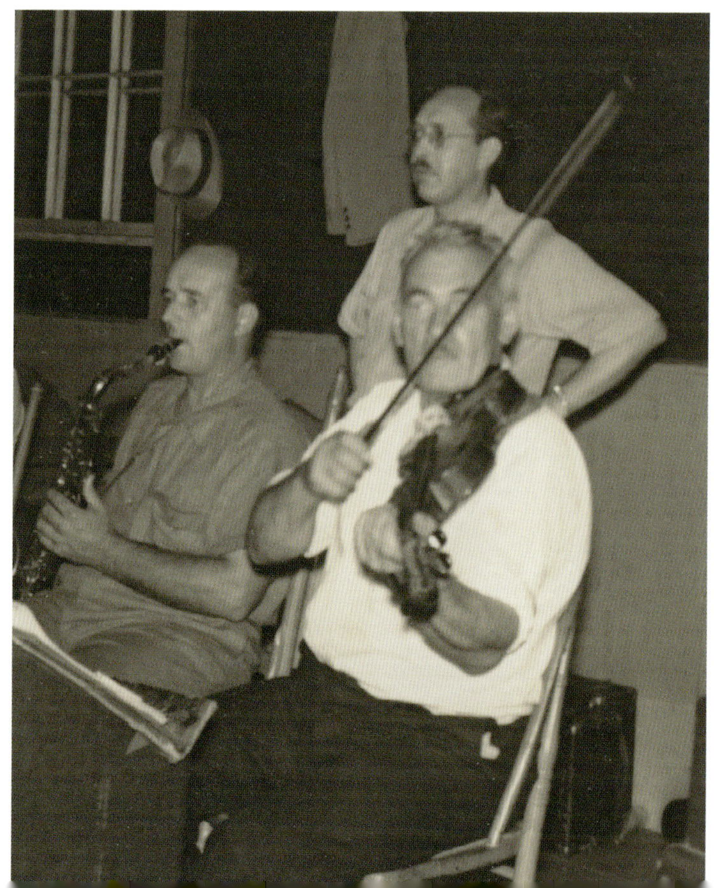

ABOVE NELSON CHURCH

BELOW Albert Quigley on fiddle

Ralph Page standing

Courtesy of Tolman Pond Archives

essay for this catalogue, came from his neighbor, the poet May Sarton. They became friends when she moved to Nelson in the 1950s, and their friendship is well-documented both in her memoirs, *Plant Dreaming Deep* and *World of Light*, which devote entire chapters to Quig, and in her poems. They were different people in many ways. Despite Quig's talents, he faced challenges and hardships in life and struggled to provide for his family. Unwilling to sacrifice his art, he did his best to balance the art and daily life while remaining true to his being. He approached each day with vigor, ready for the adventure that the next moment would surely offer.

Sarton, on the other hand, came from a very different set of circumstances. Her world was much more structured, formal and planned. Her writing was profitable and she never experienced economic hardship. With strong educational and cultural credentials, she could have fit in comfortably with Dublin's privileged. Yet it was Quig who intrigued her and whom she befriended. Sarton clearly saw the special soul and great talent within this man of meager means. She made no claim to understanding her good friend; she did understand, however, that there was a lot more to the sometimes quiet and pensive artist than others would ever realize. Upon Quig's death, she reflected on her loss to discover that he had challenged her as an artist to see the land and its people and life itself with an openness, a fervor, an appreciation, a sense of wonder.

> *[I am,] I think, more of a poet than I was before I knew him, if to be a poet means allowing life to flow through one rather than forcing it to a mold the will has shaped; if it means learning to let the day shape the work, not the work, the day, and so live toward essence as naturally as a bird or a flower.*[3]

Albert Quigley died in 1961. He is buried, with his beloved wife, Mildred, and their daughter Thomasa (Tami), in a plot next to his friend May Sarton's, in the peaceful, tree-shaded Nelson Cemetery. His life was measured in accomplishments, raw talent and perseverance. A vibrant member of the community, the door to his home was always open and welcoming. Children loved him and the wooden toys he'd craft for them.[4] Their parents cherished the tunes he played and the chance to dance to them. As we accept the role as caretakers of his art, his music and his history so that future generations may enjoy and partake of it, let us pause to celebrate. But when the celebration has ended, when we wander to the village past that old white church, when we forge across frozen lakes lighted only by winter's shadows, when we spy the granite blue of Monadnock through a sturdy set of pines, when our feet tread the floorboards in a dance, and when we embrace our neighbors with good conversation and shared meals, let us remember Albert Duvall Quigley and continue to learn from this man's gifts to us what he has taught us about our community, our land, our lives.

—Lance Tucker
on behalf of the Albert D. Quigley Exhibit Committee

---

1. From a May Sarton poem written on January 24, 1961, and first published as a eulogy to Albert Quigley in the *Keene Sentinel* editorial section on January 26, 1961.
2. From a biography of William Lester Stevens (1888–1969) by Charleston Renaissance Gallery.
3. May Sarton, *Plant Dreaming Deep* (New York: W. W. Norton and Company, Inc., 1968), 138.
4. Edie Clark, "Albert Duvall Quigley—Village Painter (1891–1961)," 2008. Originally written for the 1991 Quigley exhibit sponsored by the Community Church of Harrisville and Chesham, New Hampshire, this biographical essay appears on the website of the Friends of the Dublin Art Colony (www.monadnockart.org). Used by permission.

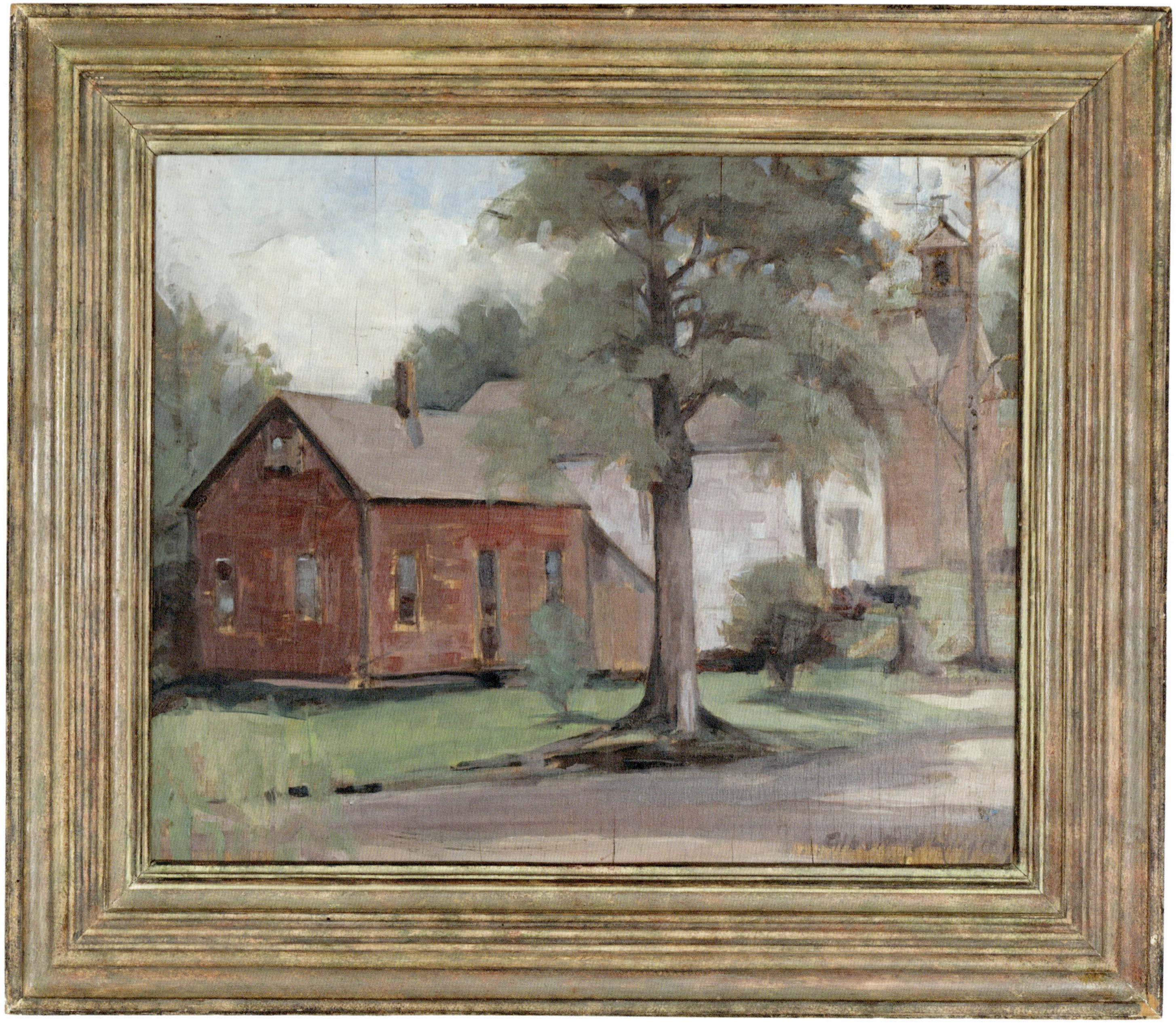

LITTLE RED HOUSE

Oil on board, Quigley frame, 22 x 26 in., private collection

The Quigley house in Nelson, New Hampshire

Albert Duvall Quigley

A BIOGRAPHICAL ESSAY

by Barnabas Quigley

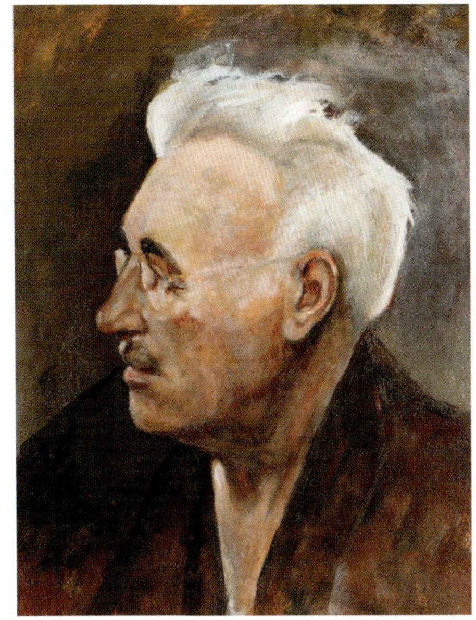

SELF PORTRAIT

MY FATHER, ALBERT QUIGLEY, was born in April 1891 in Frankfort, Maine, where he grew up and attended school. He showed artistic talent early on, first as an ornamental stonecutter in the Maine granite quarry where he went to work after graduating from high school, and then as a painter in oils, on canvas and panel. In this, he was following in the footsteps of his father and grandfather, who worked in the quarries and painted in their free time.

At the stone quarries, Allie—as my father was then known—met Alvah Batchelder, the blacksmith for the operation, who also served as the quarries' doctor. Coincidentally, Alvah was also called Allie, and the two Allies became good friends. They shared a lively interest in music and often attended concerts together. As their mutual interest in classical music developed, both apparently took lessons on stringed instruments, particularly the violin, and both played and made stringed instruments later in their lives.

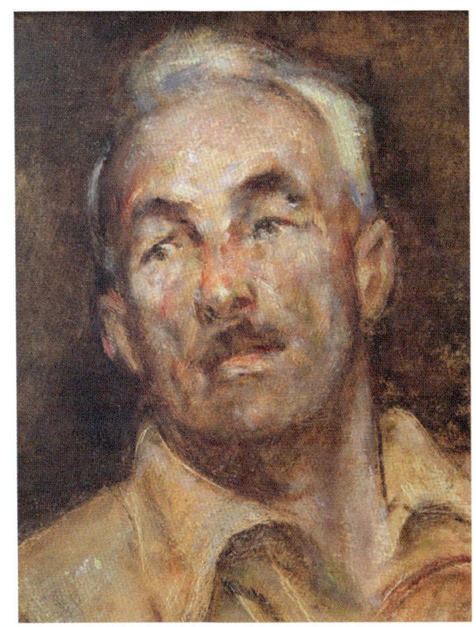

ALBERT QUIGLEY
by Alexander James

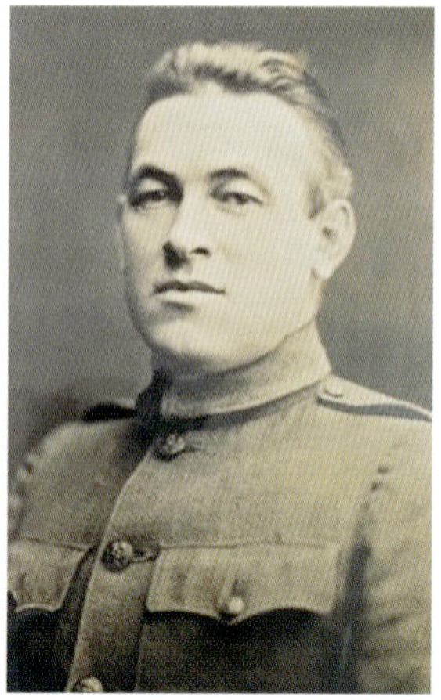

Albert D. Quigley in military uniform Courtesy of Lisa Quigley Valliere

My father once told me that Batchelder, who had been blessed with keen eyesight and a steady hand, was called upon frequently to remove sharp fragments of metal and stone from the eyes of the workers, a service he performed for my father several times during his days in the quarries.

As far as I know, my father began painting before being drafted into the US Army in 1917 during World War I, and he told me that one of his paintings hung in the Frankfort Town Hall while he was in the army. He also said that during his service in northern France, he was assigned to make drawings of enemy planes so gunnery squads could distinguish them from allied aircraft and avoid firing on our allies.

In 1919, after the war had ended, he was awarded an American Expeditionary Forces scholarship to study painting at the Isadora Duncan Pavilion in Bellevue, outside Paris. Whether this was his initial exposure to formal training is unclear, but his studies in France surely influenced the course of his life.

After leaving France, he returned to Frankfort briefly. Then, encouraged by service friends from the Keene, New Hampshire, area, he resettled there in 1920, hoping to improve his lot. He started painting again, and renewed his interest in music. I understand that at some point during the 1920s or early 1930s, Quig, as he was now known, played with a group of classical musicians in Keene.

During this time he went to work for the Tilden Company as a professional photographer, and met his future wife, Mildred. The prospects of earning a living in art were not very promising, but that didn't stop them from marrying in 1925. However, when a job became available at a quarry in Terryville, Connecticut, Quig reluctantly left his new bride in Keene and went back to stonework.

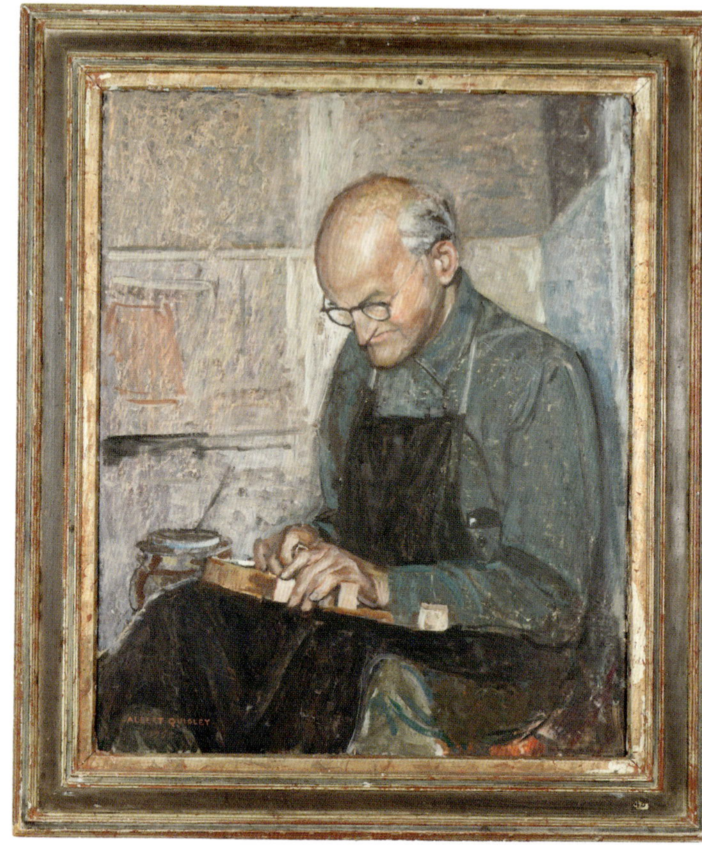

ABOVE **ALVAH BATCHELDER** (1959), oil on board, Quigley frame, 37 x 32 in. Thorne-Sagendorph Art Gallery at Keene State College

In a difficult economy, the quarry soon closed and he returned to Keene.

By then Quig had become acquainted with some of the area's artists and had formed a particular friendship with Dublin, New Hampshire, artist Alexander James, son of philosopher and psychologist William James and nephew of author Henry James.

Alec James became an informal patron and arranged for Quig and Mildred to move into the V-Lawn Inn while it was being renovated. The Inn was across the street from Alec's home in Dublin, giving Quig ready access to his friend's studio. The two often painted together, and Alec shared not only information and advice, but also art materials of a quality beyond Quig's means. In return, Quig created frames for many of Alec's paintings.

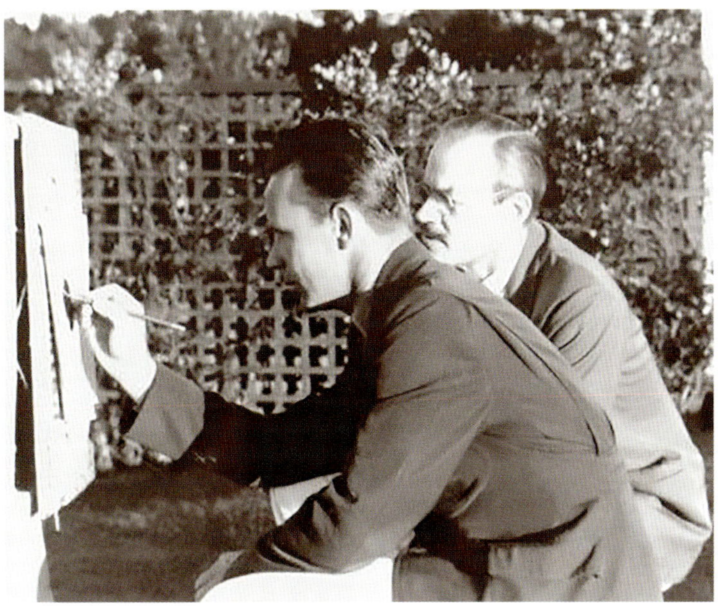

Fellow artists Gouri Ivanov-Rinov and Alexander James (ca. 1936)
Courtesy of the Dublin Historical Society

In 1931, at about this time, my brother Terrence (Terry) was born.

At the suggestion of their friends Fran and Newt Tolman of Nelson, New Hampshire, after the Inn's renovations were completed in 1934, Quig and Mildred rented a small red house and land on Nelson Common next to the town hall. The white, steepled Congregational Church across the street became a frequent subject of Quig's paintings, along with various local buildings and vistas.

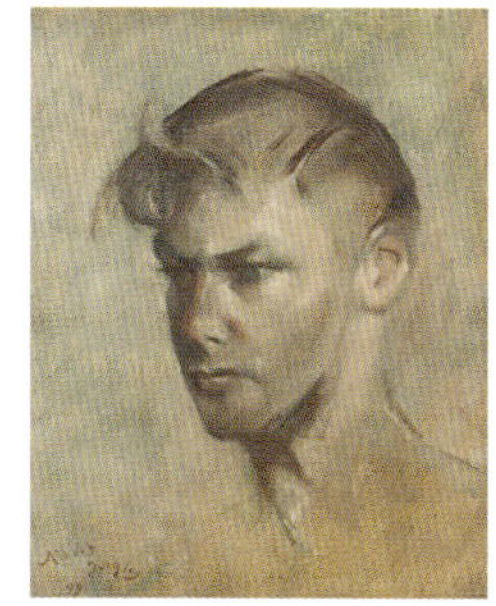

TERRY QUIGLEY

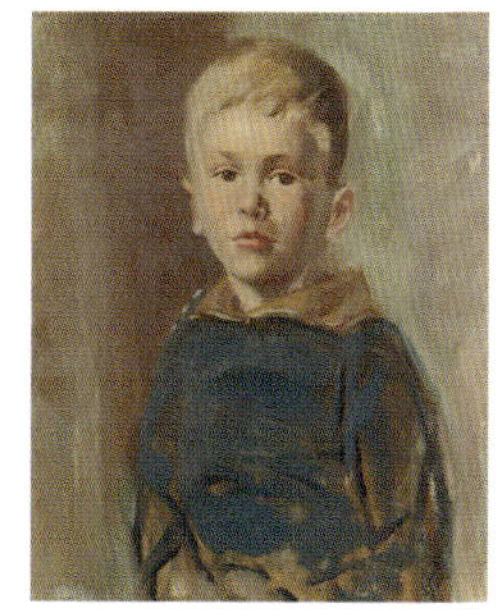

BARNEY QUIGLEY

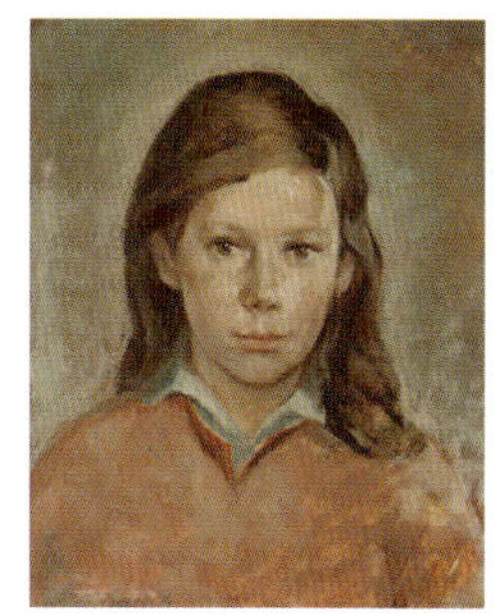

TAMI QUIGLEY

Soon after they moved, Quig was awarded a full scholarship to study art in Boston, as a Bartol Scholar at the School of the Museum of Fine Arts (SMFA). He studied drawing with Ture Bengtz, industrial design with Eleanor Barry, and painting and drawing with Alexandre Jacovleff, director of the Painting Department. He also studied with John Sharman and with Gouri Ivanov-Rinov, a member of the Dublin Art Colony.

Quig completed his studies at SMFA in 1935 and I was born the next year, followed by my sister Thomasa (Tami) in 1938. Although Quig was still painting with Alec James and other fellow Dublin artists, it was becoming more and more difficult to support a growing family near the end of the Depression.

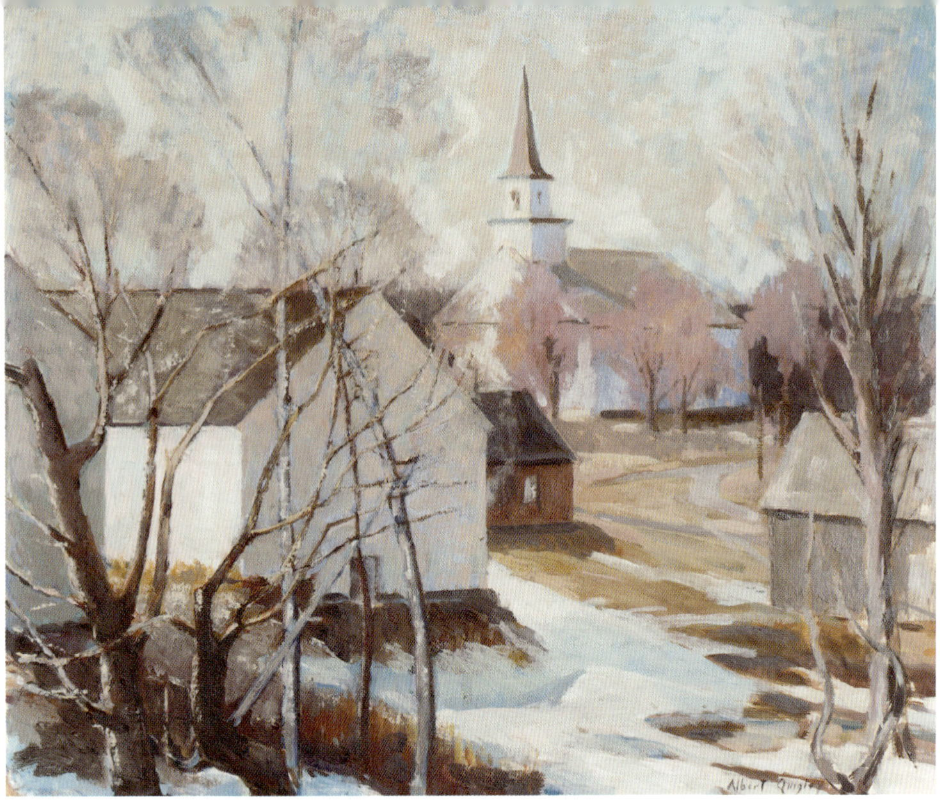

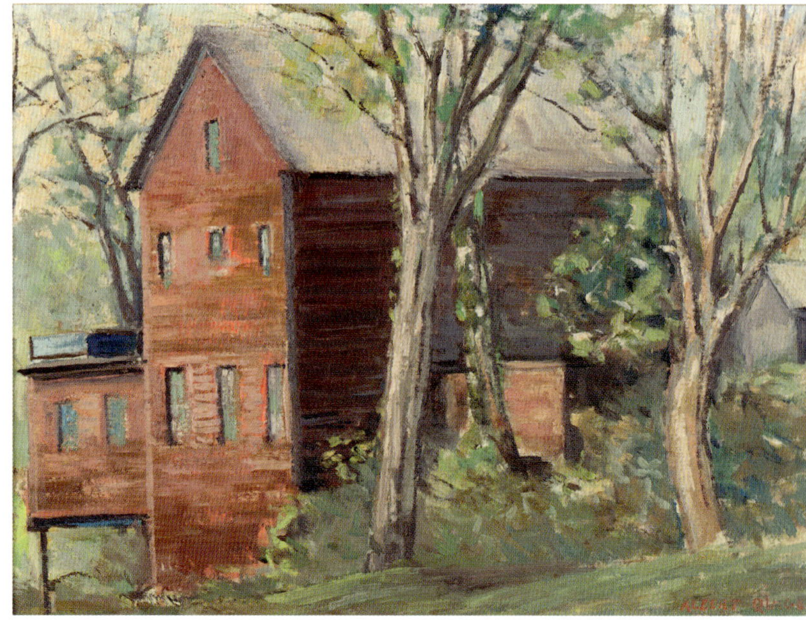

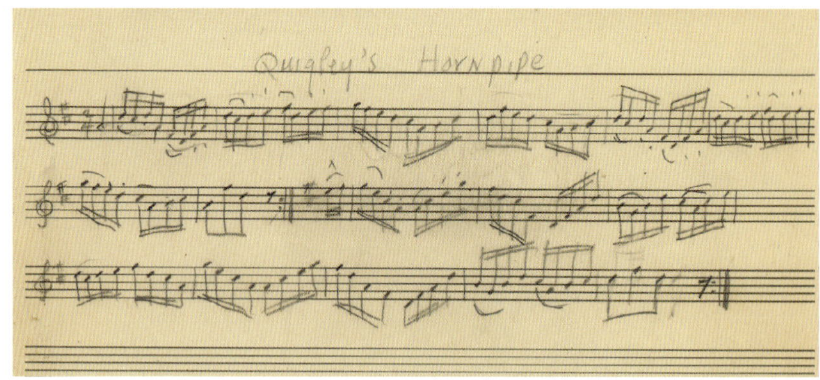

Meanwhile, my father's involvement in the musical life of the Monadnock Region had accidentally come about. He had bought an old cider mill on the Old Stoddard Road from Horace Upton, the local mailman, to use as a studio and framemaking facility. He and the Tolman brothers, Newt and Fran, also played square dance music there to avoid disrupting their families. As they were playing one night, they heard accompanying dance calls coming from outside. They went out and discovered Ralph Page standing in the road calling square dances to their music. After that evening, Ralph started organizing dances, hiring Quig as his first fiddle. My father's musical background enabled him to arrange or occasionally compose dance tunes that were played by Ralph and other dance orchestras. Quig was soon occupied with music every night, which meant it was too late to travel home afterward, so he often got back to Nelson only one day a week.

ABOVE **NELSON VILLAGE,** Oil on Renaissance Panel, Quigley frame 27 x 31 in., Lynne W. Russell-Johnson. Painting shows back of the Nelson Town Hall and the Quigley house with the church in the distance. Board was originally prepared on February 9, 1940.

ABOVE **CIDER MILL,** Oil on panel, Quigley frame, 22 x 28 in. Private collection. Arnold Adler, photographer

BELOW Fiddle tune, "Quigley's Hornpipe," in Albert Quigley's handwriting Courtesy of Harvey Tolman

I remember as a small child riding to Keene with Horace Upton one Saturday morning. He dropped me off at the hotel where my father was staying after the previous night's job. Feeling very grown up, I visited for about an hour, until Mr. Upton had to return to Nelson with the mail.

Quig bought a secondhand Model A Ford sedan, mainly to provide transportation for the Ralph Page square dance musicians and their instruments. This worked well for a short time, but with three young children at home, Mildred soon wanted more assistance, so Quig cut back on traveling to dance performances and went to work five nights a week at the Cheshire Mills in Harrisville, New Hampshire. He kept his days free to resume painting his landscapes and portraits and repairing violins. He also took over much of the child care, which enabled my mother to go back to work. He continued playing fiddle for lively Nelson dances in the town hall with, among others, Newt Tolman on flute and Fran Tolman on piano.

By the early 1940s, my father had established a reputation as a restorer of paintings for Boston art dealers. In those days, with no telephone or electricity, we would have no advance warning, just a Railway Express truck pulling up to deliver wooden crates of paintings to be restored. When the restoration work was done, Quig would send off a letter and the Railway Express truck would return to pick up the crated paintings. Eventually a check would arrive in the mail.

My father's paintings were often traded for goods and services. He painted a large mural in the pediatric ward of the Elliot Community Hospital in Keene to pay for the births of my brother, myself, and my sister. The murals in the summer home of Dr. Holmes on Spofford Lake in Chesterfield, New Hampshire, paid the bills for delivering me. My father also painted murals in several of the restaurants in Keene, as well as in some private homes. Toward the end of the Depression he was employed by the Works Progress Administration to paint murals in public buildings. One of these was in the Munsonville church on Granite Lake in Munsonville, New Hampshire. Unfortunately, all the murals except for those in Spofford have been destroyed or painted over. At the Holmes's house the murals, still maintained in pristine condition by the doctor's family, enliven the hall, ceiling, and rooms upstairs.

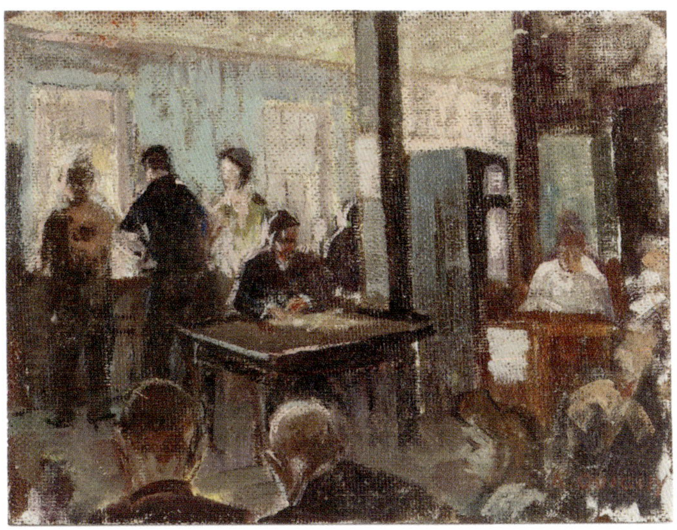

WELFARE OFFICE
Oil on board, unframed, 9 x 12 in.
Private collection

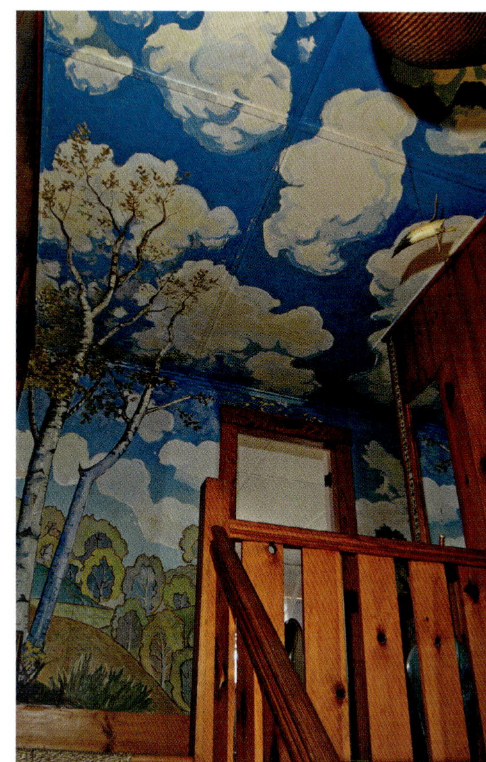

SPOFFORD LAKE MURALS

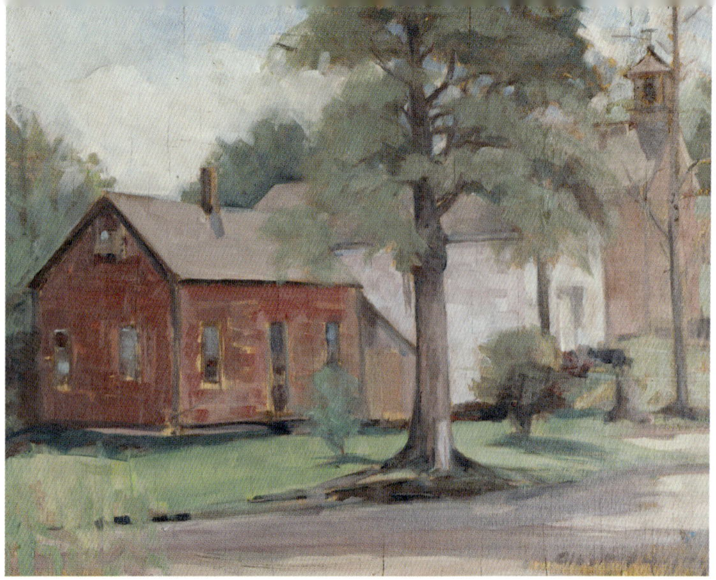

LITTLE RED HOUSE
Oil on board,
Quigley frame, 22 x 26 in.
Private collection

Gradually, the work accumulated. One of my fondest childhood memories is of going with my parents to the Davis farm in nearby Roxbury. The owner of the farm was a great friend of Quig's who invited him to come with the family at any time and paint his choice of the vistas there. For a while money was again flowing in at least as fast as it was flowing out. Paintings were selling with encouraging frequency, and Quig's work was featured in local area art shows. He was painting, working at other jobs, playing his fiddle, and, as always, making frames for his own paintings and those of Alec James. There were a few treasured fall painting trips to Woodstock, Vermont, with Alec and a group of mostly Dublin artists.

In the 1940s Quig purchased the Nelson house and property for $640 with a fifteen-year mortgage from the bank. Around this time it became obvious that his eyesight was failing. Apparently Alvah Batchelder's doctoring hadn't prevented scar tissue from forming on the corneas of his eyes, and as a result he painted much less during this time and the quality of his work was noticeably affected.

He continued to frame paintings, and although he made the frames and supervised the work to completion, my mother actually took over with the detailed work of finishing the frames, where better eyesight was required.

In 1945 my mother became the town clerk of Nelson, a job she held for ten years. She also attended to elderly residents in the village, who could not or would not be confined to a hospital or nursing home. Both brought in some extra income. She was also a trustee of the library and a member of the school board.

Alexander James died suddenly in 1946, and his death threw Quig into a depression; the combination of his failing eyesight and the loss of his close friend caused him to stop painting. His only work in the art field for some time after Alec's death was the framing of Alec's remaining paintings, a labor carried out by my parents together.

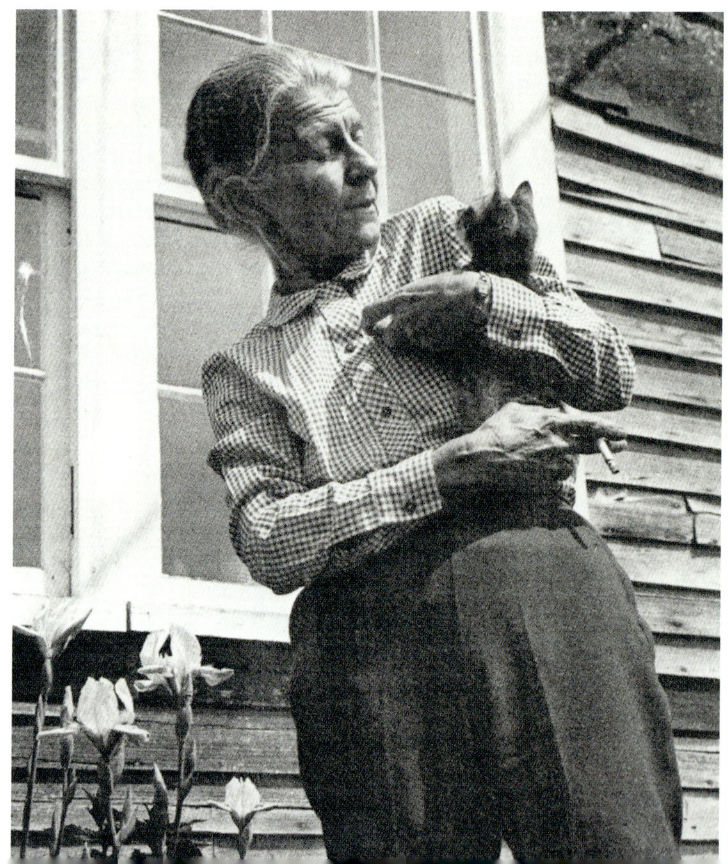

Mildred Quigley
Eric Sanford, photographer

The following year Gerald Cobleigh, their summer neighbor from across the town common, brought over an eye doctor friend who purchased some paintings. Dr. Dubé asked to see more of Quig's work, but my father explained that he had stopped painting because of his vision problems. Dr. Dubé set up—free of charge—a series of treatments, examinations, and fittings for glasses over the next year and a half. As a result, Quig claimed his eyesight was now better than it had been since childhood, and he resumed what he enjoyed doing most, to his great relief and pleasure.

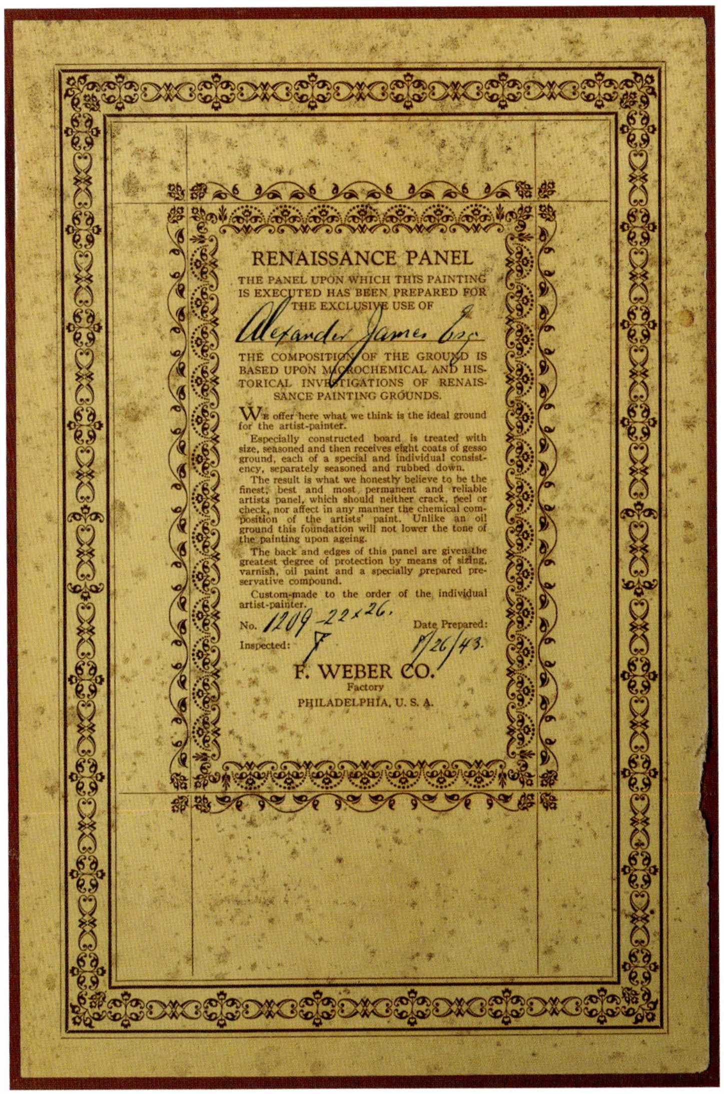

RENAISSANCE PANEL

THE PANEL UPON WHICH THIS PAINTING IS EXECUTED HAS BEEN PREPARED FOR THE EXCLUSIVE USE OF

Alexander James Esq.

THE COMPOSITION OF THE GROUND IS BASED UPON MICROCHEMICAL AND HISTORICAL INVESTIGATIONS OF RENAISSANCE PAINTING GROUNDS.

We offer here what we think is the ideal ground for the artist-painter.

Especially constructed board is treated with size, seasoned and then receives eight coats of gesso ground, each of a special and individual consistency, separately seasoned and rubbed down.

The result is what we honestly believe to be the finest, best and most permanent and reliable artists panel, which should neither crack, peel or check, nor affect in any manner the chemical composition of the artists' paint. Unlike an oil ground this foundation will not lower the tone of the painting upon ageing.

The back and edges of this panel are given the greatest degree of protection by means of sizing, varnish, oil paint and a specially prepared preservative compound.

Custom-made to the order of the individual artist-painter.

No. 1209 22×26. Date Prepared:

Inspected: F 8/26/43.

F. WEBER CO.

Factory

PHILADELPHIA, U. S. A.

Information on back of Renaissance Panel prepared for Alexander James

The James family very generously gave Quig full use of Alec's studio and the shop, plus framing and painting supplies, which Quig gratefully utilized. A supply of well-seasoned pine lumber, purchased for framemaking, provided both frames and some furniture. With my parents' increased income they were able to install electricity in the house, though indoor plumbing was still years away. On our kitchen wall hung Quig's portrait of Alvah Batchelder working on a violin, alongside several violins in various stages of repair.

With his renewed vision, Quig eagerly explored working in charcoal and Conté crayon, as well as his beloved oils. Alec had left some fine English art panels, which were given to Quig, and he used them for several paintings. We three children were sometimes required to pose, not always eagerly, for portraits. Quig also asked

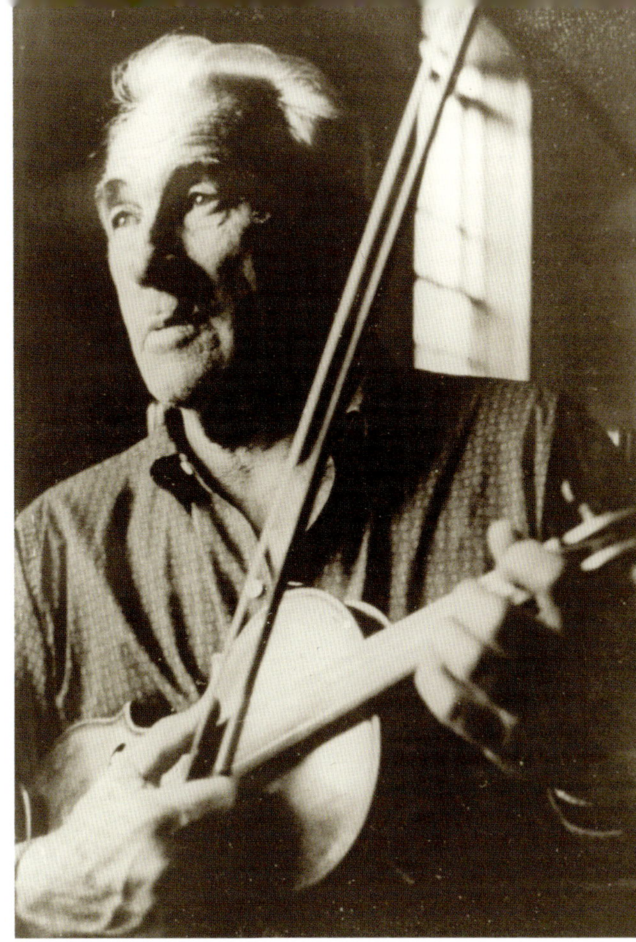

Albert Quigley
with his fiddle
Courtesy of Quigley family

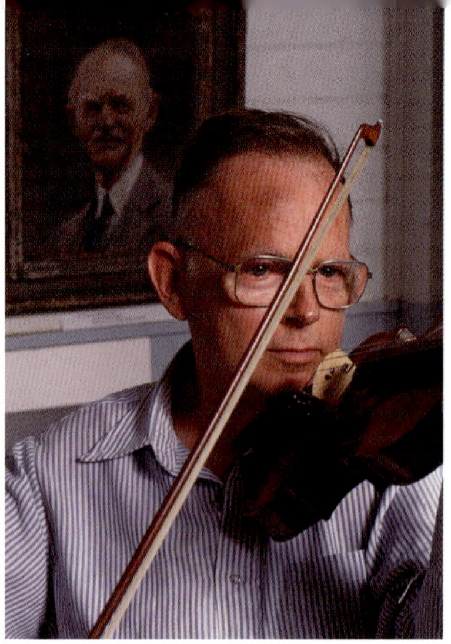

other children from Nelson village to sit for portraits, and he was commissioned to paint family friends. He began using the upstairs room of the schoolhouse, two doors away, as a painting studio.

During the 1950s our neighbors across the way, Morris and Cora Tolman, died. Their home was sold to the writer May Sarton, who moved into the house from Cambridge, Massachusetts. She and my parents quickly became fast friends. In particular, May later expressed in her writings the deep bond she formed with Quig, a fellow lover of art and life.

ABOVE Harvey Tolman in front of Quig's painting of his grandfather, Wilmer Tolman; Harriet Wise, photographer

RIGHT In the Quigleys' kitchen; Eleanor Blair, photographer

It was about this time that a greeting card company, Yankee Artists, opened in Keene. Quig and several other local artists were employed to paint watercolors, which were used to create silkscreen prints on balsa wood. Quig and the company owners consulted John de Martelly—Nelson artist, experienced lithographer, and printer—on the silk-screening process, and the cards were produced for some years. Quig also branched out into restoration, on sculpture and pottery brought back from Egypt by Joseph Lindon Smith, an Egyptologist whose home and studio were in Dublin.

My father began returning to his Maine hometown occasionally to visit family members and his old friend Al Batchelder. During one of the visits, Batchelder gave Quig one of the violins he had made. I remember that soon after he came home, Quig crated up a painting and sent it off to the Batchelders. Another time, my cousin Harold Quigley and his wife Dot were visiting Nelson

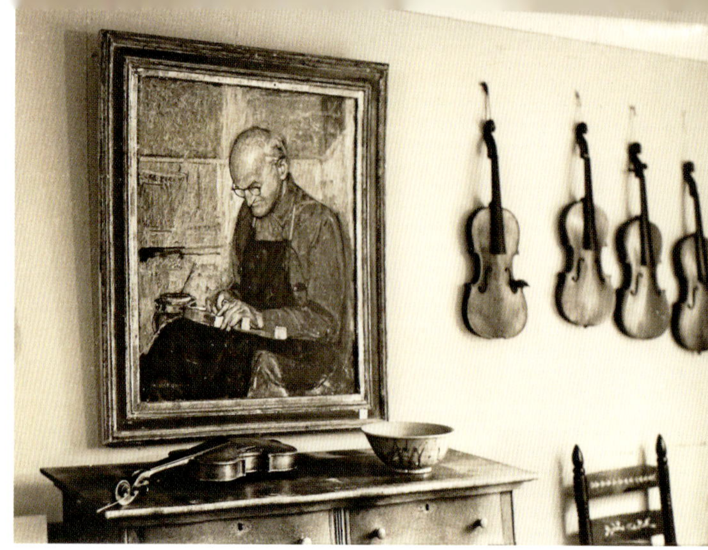

from Frankfort and when Harold admired a particular painting, my father gave it to him on the spot. Members of our Frankfort family have told me that some of my father's early works are still in town.

Around 1960 Harvey Tolman came to Quig and expressed an interest in fiddling. My father dug out an old fiddle, strung it up, and taught Harvey some of the rudiments of violin playing. Harvey went on to become a local fiddler extraordinaire and winner of several awards, including the New Hampshire Folk Heritage Award in 2007.

This was a contented time for us. But then, toward the end of 1960, we began to notice that Quig was not feeling well. Urged to consult a doctor, he said he would hear none of it until after the holidays, and none of us realized how ill he was. He spent Thanksgiving and Christmas with his family. On New Year's weekend he played for three different dances. On January 23, 1961, he died of cancer.

In the spring, after the snow had melted, Albert Duvall Quigley was buried in the Nelson Cemetery, just up the hill from our home.

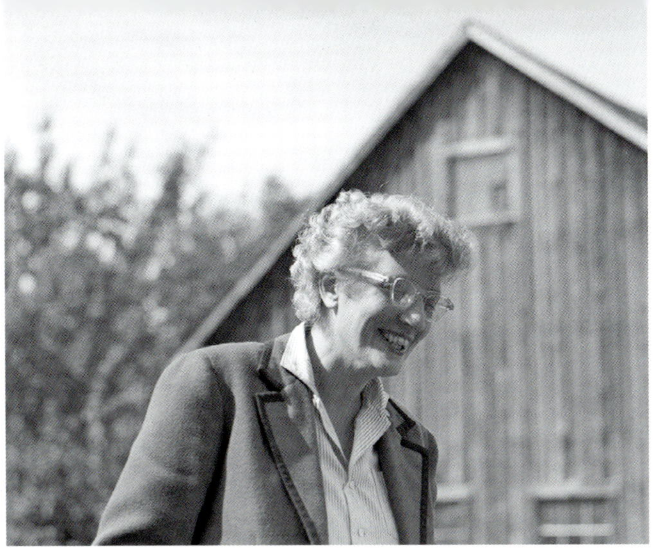

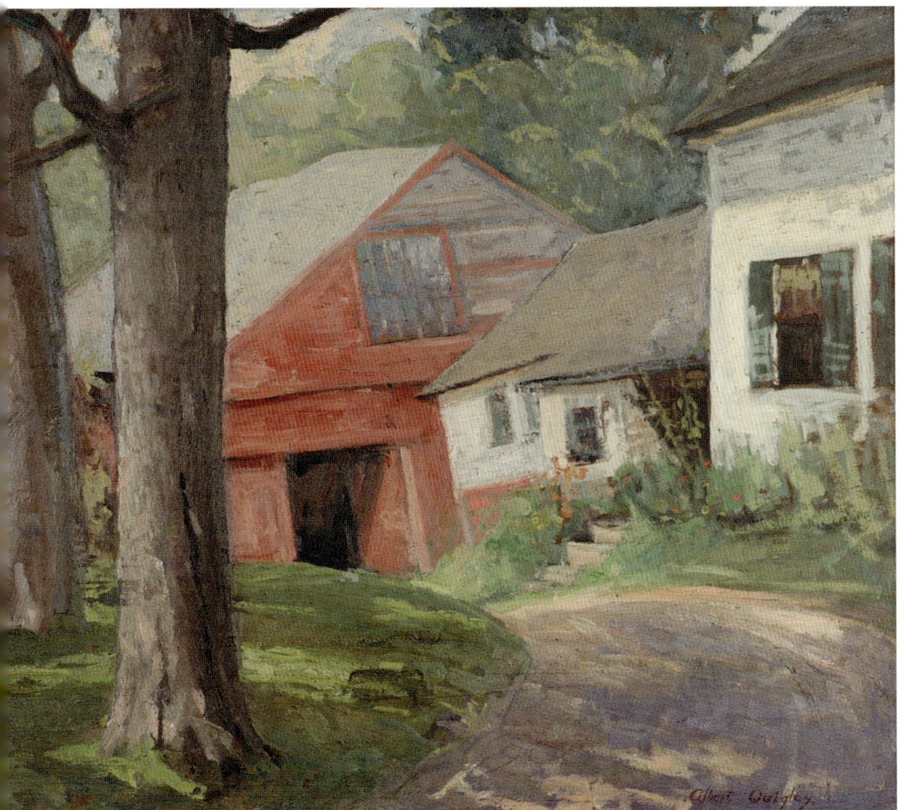

ABOVE May Sarton, 1967
Lotte Jacobi, photographer
Courtesy of the University of New Hampshire

BELOW MORRIS AND CORA TOLMAN'S HOUSE, (ca. 1942)
Oil on panel, 22 x 26 in., private collection
Arnold Adler, photographer
Also known as the Rand House, later owned by May Sarton

Quig, The Painter

by May Sarton

ALBERT QUIGLEY, or "Quig"—how well his nickname suited him! Even now, I cannot say it aloud without a feeling of warmth about my heart, a gaiety of spirit, as if a delightful breeze were rising, a sense of elation. When I moved to the remote village of Nelson, New Hampshire, not far from Monadnock mountain, I was after solitude, a rooted place where I could work in peace. I knew no one in the village and, at first, was far too absorbed in rebuilding my own house and in settling in to be conscious of my neighbors. The thrill was an oriole that I saw and heard singing at the top of one of my old maples.

But as I look back on this flight into solitude, and on all that the house and the village came to mean in the fifteen years I spent there, it seems to me that the first time I saw Quig, if I had had any prescience, I might have thought of the greeting lonely Bushmen give each other when they meet in their desert wilderness and the first one says, "Good day! I saw you from afar and I am dying of hunger." The stranger answers, "Good day! I have been dead, but now that you have come, I live again."

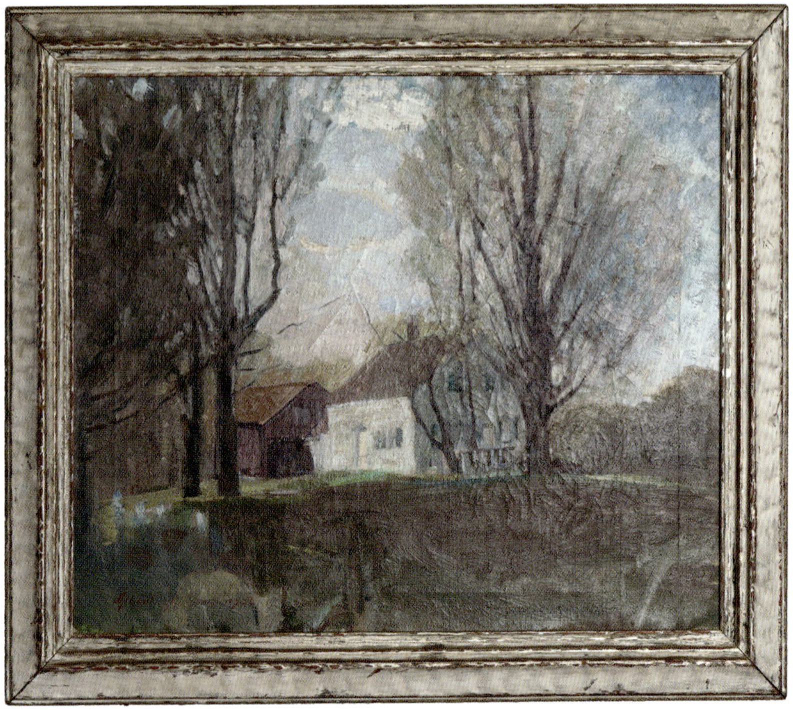

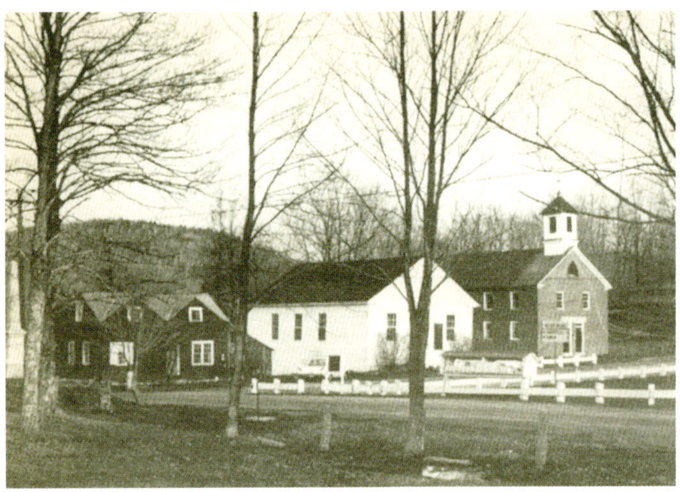

ABOVE **RAND HOUSE IN NELSON VILLAGE**
Oil on canvas
Quigley frame, 24 x 29 in.
Private collection
House later owned by May Sarton

RIGHT The Quigley house in Nelson Village at far left
Eleanor Blair, photographer

Quig was always hungry for companionship with someone who could understand what his life was all about. I had been through a grueling personal experience, and had come to Nelson to find my own life again, alone. We were both living on the edge of nowhere, with our backs against the wall. But the Quigs had been here in Nelson for thirty years, and I had only just arrived. It was October.

Almost at once I began to find out how much I had to learn. For at first glance the Quigley household seemed to be a general chaos; at that time Mildred Quigley was going every morning to cook for and nurse the postman's sick wife, get her up and dressed, feed her and the cats, and bring order out of that other chaos up the road, and she had little time for her own house. The trestle table Quig had made from one wide pine board might have unwashed dishes strewn about on it, but it also often had a broken violin he was mending, or parts of a picture frame he was putting together. He was also rebuilding the house itself, so there were piles of lumber lying about and one's eyes rested on an unfinished wall . . . it took a while for me to realize what richness of life all these half-finished things represented.

Meanwhile I had already begun to understand that Quig was an unhoped-for-friend, at a time when I needed just the particular friend he turned out to be. At first glance he looked like a countryman, dressed often in a plaid shirt and heavy boots, a crest of white hair and thick dark eyebrows over a rugged face—these suggested an outdoor character who would enjoy hunting and fishing. Only when one came to know him did the

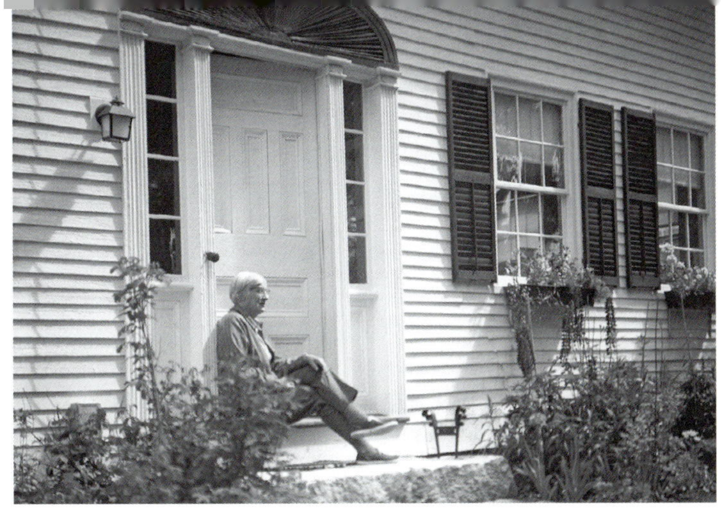

May Sarton at home in Nelson, 1967, Lotte Jacobi, photographer
Courtesy of the University of New Hampshire

extreme sensitivity of the man within his disguise come through. The eyebrows, for instance, were mobile. Did they actually tremble sometimes like the delicate furry antennae of a moth? As I grew to know him, I saw how sensitive he was to atmospheres, to textures, to every shade of color, to tones of voice, as sensitive as he was to the sound of his violin when he tucked it under his chin to tune it, his head cocked a little. I saw the tenderness in his dark eyes, their shyness, the way he tried to hide (but could not) the fact that feeling was always close to the surface. But no one could miss the humor in this face.

Soon after I moved in, I invited the Quigs over for a drink. I lit a fire in the big fireplace and had put some yellow chrysanthemums in a blue jar on the old table. I felt that the seventeenth-century heavy Flemish furniture which had found its way to this New England village from our old farmhouse in Wondelgem, Belgium, suited the house. But it was not exactly what people might expect. So I had been a little nervous before the arrival of these, my first guests from the village.

Mildred and I were soon launched on all sorts of talk about their children, about Cora Tolman who had lived there before me, about various neighbors. I noticed that Quig, holding his drink in one hand, was silent. After some time, he came back to us and said quite quietly, “I have been silent because I am looking. I am so moved by this furniture—it is so beautiful,” he said, glancing over at the great bahut, a Flemish cupboard with curved pillars built into the sides, which shines a deep chestnut color, rather rough and rather splendid. It was my first experience of what I liked to call “a fit of looking” on Quig’s part. He was as absorbed in what his eyes registered at such times as a person is whose ears are wholly absorbed in listening to music, and he had the same abstracted expression. I don’t suppose anyone ever came into the house who felt it more, and I was very much touched.

It is hard to remember; did we dive right into intimacy that first day, so no tentative approaches were necessary? At any rate I soon knew that I could talk with Quig about my work, as one can only talk to a fellow craftsman. Our crafts were different, but we had the same difficulties in getting started, the same despair sometimes at the end of a morning’s struggle when nothing had quite “come out,” the same hours of sudden triumph; it was wonderful to be able to share all this. Fairly often one or the other of us crossed the green

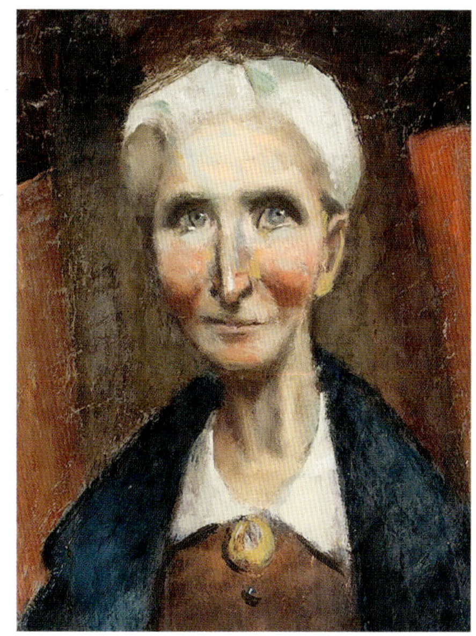

AUNT CORA

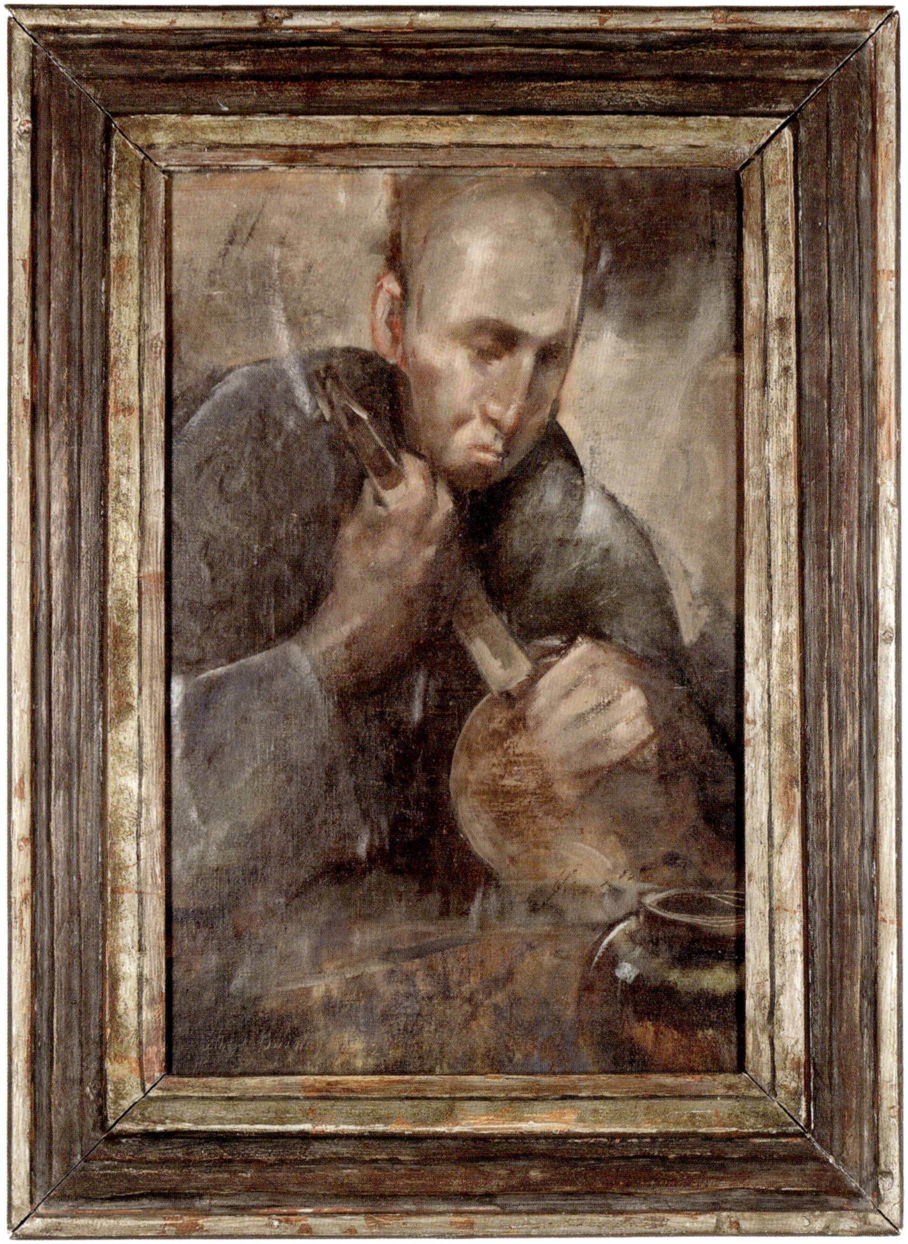

ALVAH BATCHELDER
Oil on board, Quigley frame, 25 x 19 in.
Private collection

about noon and exchanged not the time of day so much as "the state of the work." No one could come close to Quig without being aware of his warmth, the belief he poured out about art itself and the value of the artist's life, the way he entered into the problem. His own life had been a perpetual war with material circumstances to find time to paint at all, yet I never heard him complain about that. He blamed himself for not doing better and—in his sixties when I came to know him—attacked each new day with the anxious eagerness of a boy.

Little by little I was able to piece together what had made him the complex human being he was.

Albert D. Quigley, to give him his full name for once, was not a New Hampshire boy. He had come from Maine and had the sea in his blood; his father was of Irish descent, but had run away to sea rather than be confirmed into the Catholic Church (and Quig inherited this dislike of established religion). The elder Quigley was a stonecutter and taught his son the trade in a village where everything was owned by the firm, including the general store. But it must have been evident early on that Quig had other talents . . . he was musical and taught himself to play the violin, helped by the old violin maker, Alec Beckler [Alvah Batchelder], whose portrait he later painted and from whom he learned one of the many skills he had in his knapsack—rebuilding broken instruments and even making violins himself. Those years in Maine were rich in visual images which the young man stored up; how many of the later paintings are memories? I possess one of smelt fishers getting ready to set up their nets, all in smoky grays and blues, which change as the light changes in the room so that, as a painting to live with, it is inexhaustible. There was something large and dreamy about Quig that suggested the sea at the back of his mind. He was not one of the tight-lipped, reserved people of these hills. There was a distance in his eyes.

After his father's death, when Quig was in his mid-twenties, World War I came. He went to France in the Signal Corps, and when he came back, he was a changed man. He never talked in my presence about war experiences—what he talked about was the experience of France. When I met Quig it had been forty years since he had seen France, but it seemed as if he remembered every village, every tree and winding road, every plastered wall with a geranium on top of it, as if he had seen them yesterday. This crude Maine stonecutter in his mid-twenties was an unlikely doughboy: not for him the search for women or cafés. When he had had a few hours or a day off he set out on foot to explore the countryside, observing, noting with those eyes as retentive and piercing as a hawk's. And there in France the painter was born.

There was no GI bill in those days, but the AEF set up a school in Bellevue and there Quig studied after he was demobilized. One of my dreams was to take Mildred and Quig back to France for a few weeks. It never did happen, but we imagined what it would be like and often talked of it, and the imagining was so real for all three of us that we almost felt we had made the trip.

Of course it was out of the question for Quig when he came back from the war to think of earning a living as a painter, at least at first, and he went back to stonecutting, then photography. There in Keene,

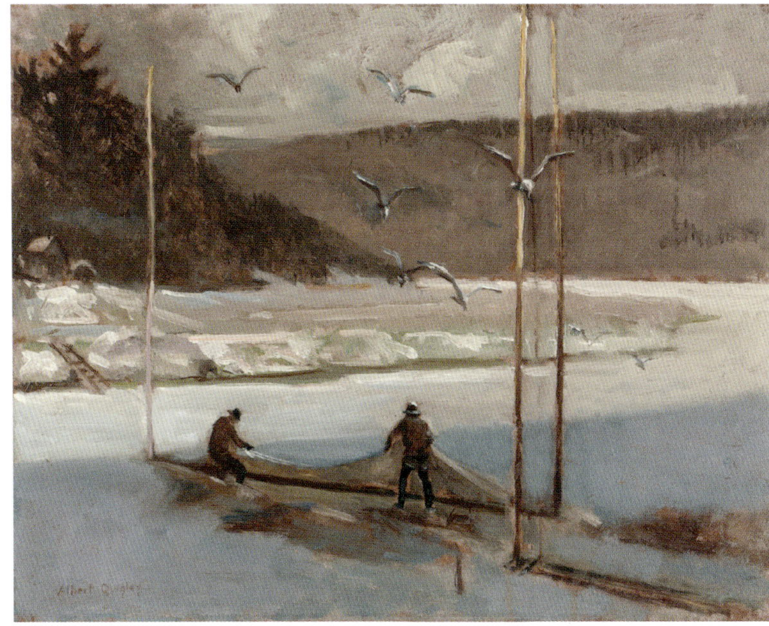

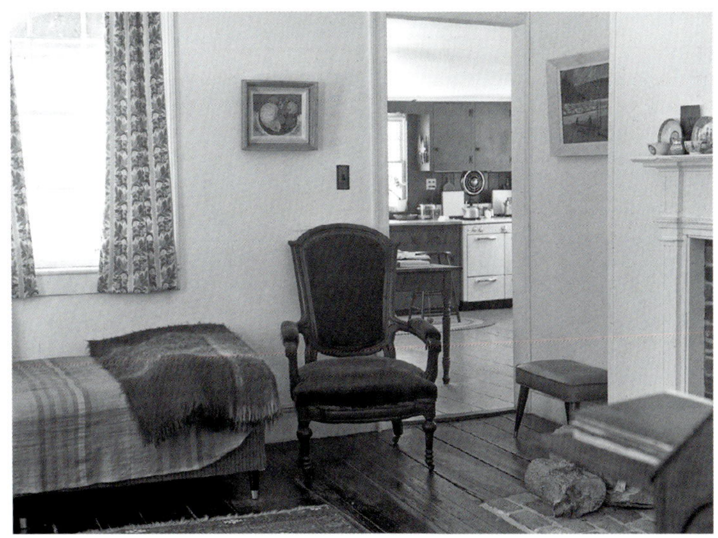

ABOVE **SMELT FISHING ON THE PENOBSCOT RIVER, MAINE**
Oil on panel, 18 x 22 in., private collection, Arnold Adler, photographer

BELOW May Sarton's living room with the same painting hanging to the right of the doorway, 1967, Lotte Jacobi, photographer
Courtesy of the University of New Hampshire

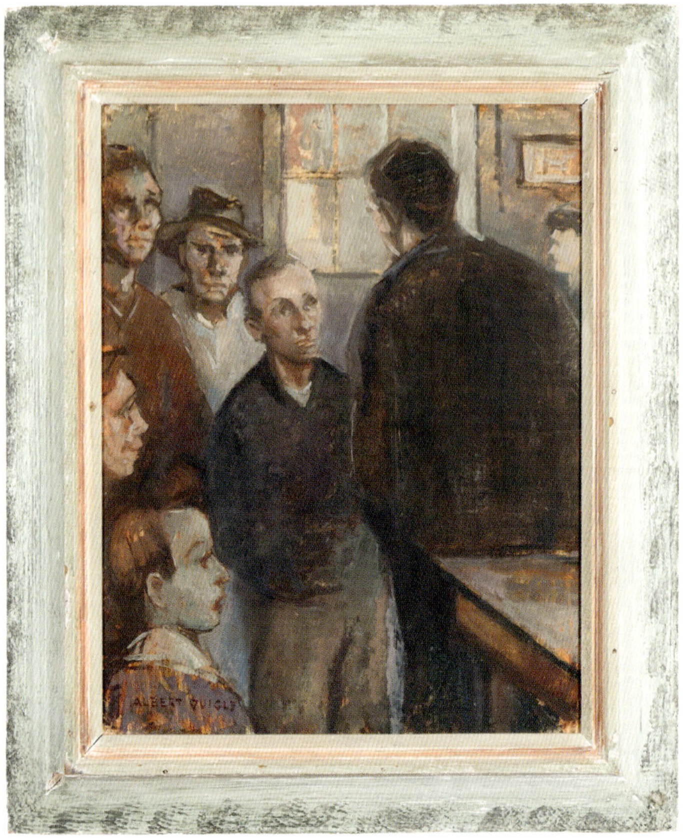

WELFARE OFFICE
Oil on board
Quigley frame, 24 x 20 in.
Rose Lape

New Hampshire, he met Mildred and there his real life began, for this was a "marriage of true minds" if I ever saw one. Quig never had an easy time . . . no man with his aspirations could have an easy time. But he had in his life two pieces of extraordinary luck. The first was when, at a table in a restaurant, he saw that haunting, intense, reserved face of a young woman whose own circumstances had made her if not morose, at least willfully determined to go it alone—come hell or high water. She was a piece of lonely bitterness, working as clerk, walking down the street (as she told me) with her hat pulled down over her eyes. It was like Quig to recognize her, when he was walking to work some days later, and like Quig to make the instinctive, natural gesture: he flipped the hat up so he could see her face. He said, "Let's go for a walk." That walk was the first of many that took them down every street in Keene to its end—sometimes miles and miles.

If ever a man needed a wife with the courage of a lion, it was Quig, and he found it in Mildred, so small that she looked as if a breeze might blow her away, so valiant that a hurricane would not budge her if she had decided to stay put. Their life was shared in its every aspect: how often I dropped in to find Mildred putting gold leaf on a frame—work Quig had begun but not gotten around to finishing. How often I found them under the circle of light of the green student lamp playing cribbage together. They were both great readers, avid for life in all its forms, lovers of children (they had three as the years went on) and of animals: there was usually a cat snoozing on the arm of a chair, and when I first knew them there was also an old spaniel called Honey.

It was not only that these two shared an arduous life, but they had so much fun together! When Quig was feeling merry, he liked to cook up braised beef, and on special occasions open a bottle of Chianti to go with it. He also liked to make jonnycakes and muffins, which did not always come out so well as he hoped they would. They were both great storytellers, so, when one found oneself in their company, the riches poured out on each side. They were—and Mildred is—people full of lore of all sorts. And they could match wits with almost anyone on almost any subject that came up.

But one has to envision all this rich life against a continual struggle to make ends meet. When they came to Nelson, Quig took over a shiplike piece of a house and rebuilt it with his own hands. These were the Depression years; Quig worked on the night shift at the Harrisville woolen mill as a tender from three to eleven at night. That meant that he could have his real life in the daytime—as a painter, as a maker of violins, as a frame maker, as a house-builder, as a father and husband. He also embarked on a new career as fiddler for the square dances—a fashion that swept the country in the late twenties and early thirties. The Nelson Town Hall has an exceptionally good floor for dances. On weekends Quig was often away in Fitzwilliam, Keene, or even as far south as Worcester or Boston, fiddling.

During all these activities the door of the old house was never locked; there was someone dropping in for a talk at almost any time of night or day. But Quig had a haven when the mood to paint was on him—he made himself a studio in the top floor of the unused brick schoolhouse next door. There he could take refuge from all the unfinished business at home and spend a spate of hours in front of a canvas, meditating and doing what he loved most to do and what he did best of all. Talking with him I realized freshly how much like writing a poem painting can be. It too cannot be done on will. The spirit must move. But when the spirit moved, this man who often seemed to be puttering about among a

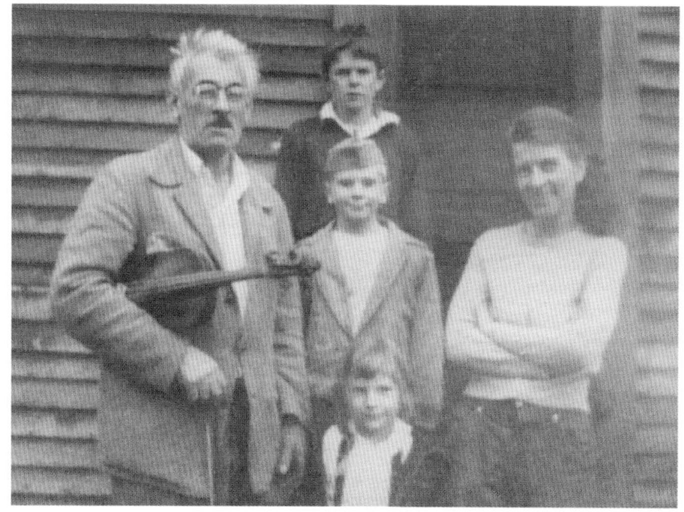

The Quigley family
ca. 1942
Courtesy of the
Quigley family

thousand and one unfinished tasks came wholly into focus. Then his concentration was absolute. There was a wonderful silence up in the old schoolhouse, such a living silence that it seemed more vivid than any word. There Quig knew who he was meant to be.

The second extraordinary piece of luck was connected with the artist in Quig. It was his friendship with Alexander James, who lived in nearby Dublin—Alec, son of William James, bawdy, fresh, nervy as a racehorse, a remarkable painter of portraits who was eaten up with conflict about his work. Alec and Quig fitted into each other's needs like brothers. As I write of them I evoke the long companionly silences as they painted side by side, then the break and the laughter as they rivaled each other in telling outrageous stories. Alec, of the New England aristocracy, rich by comparison, living in a beautiful house with an immense studio made out of a barn; Quig, stonecutter's son, mill worker, ex-doughboy, fiddler—their differences melted in the passion they shared for their craft and art.

For Alec, Quig was like an older brother, less volatile, sturdier, less conflicted, perhaps partly because he was not wholly committed to painting, not a professional with all the weight of reputation and competition in the market to burden him, as it did Alec. There was a wholeness and sturdiness about Quig that must often have worked as a balm. On the other hand, Alec taught Quig much about technique, about brushes, canvas, paint itself, taught him expensive tastes in these matters—and helped him to pay for these extravagant materials by using Quig as his own framer and getting him orders from other customers as well. "Dear old Quig" as Alec called him, represented perhaps the pure unadulterated person, the free man, above all the one person to whom he could talk freely about his own anxieties and problems. Like any real friendship—and this was a great one—it sprang out of mutual need and was nourished from mutual riches. And no one outside the two men will ever know the depth of it.

But without Mildred, who stayed home with the three little children, none of it would have been possible. It was her generosity and understanding that left Quig free, free to come and go into that other world, without the slightest stain of reproach on her side or of guilt on his. Even very good marriages indeed have their times of stress. It is the measure of the reality of this one that the intense "engagement" between Alec and Quig was allowed free play, without a shadow.

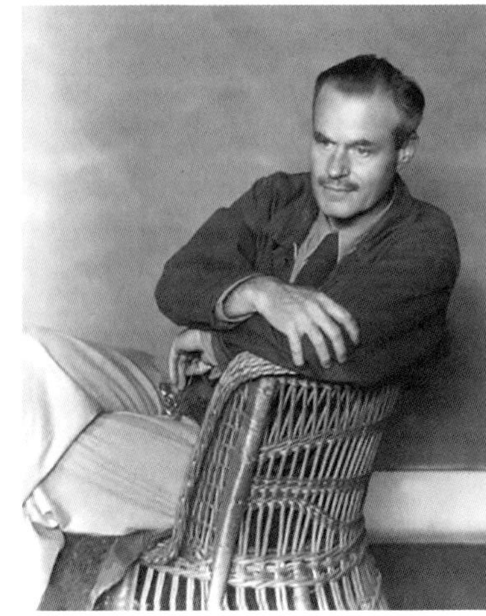

Alec James, 1938
Peter A. Juley & Son, photographer
Courtesy of the James family

When I met Quig, Alec was already dead—he died too young of a heart attack—but I don't suppose I ever talked seriously with the lonely survivor of that friendship without Alec's name coming up.

I have not spoken yet of one of Quig's salient characteristics, his love of ceremony. He was not a great drinker, but what he loved, as he often told me, was the ceremony: the fire lit, the enclosed peaceful hour when he and Mildred came to sit by my fire, the flowers, the talk, framed all in the "ceremony" of a cocktail. (I am amused at the juxtaposition of two unlikely words!) We never met, we three, for an hour at the end of the arduous day, without feeling that something of moment had happened between us; we never talked without the talk turning on "real things"—relationship and all its mysteries, art and all its mysteries, nature and all its mysteries.

For me, to be with the Quigs was in some deep sense to come *home*: come home to the values with which I had grown up, and which so often appeared to be anachronistic in life as it is lived in the United States. For one thing, the world we shared, in "ceremony," was completely uncompetitive. Status—social, professional—had no place here. We found ourselves conversing like three philosophers about the things that *really* matter. When I bought my house in Nelson, I had imagined solitude and peace, but I had not imagined this being restored to the values with which I had grown up, and which after the death of my scholar-father and my artist-mother I had begun to believe could be found only in Europe.

Ceremony, laughter, tenderness . . . Quig had them all in large measure, and all are exemplified in a story he told me about the time he was working in the mill. Among his fellow workers at that time was an old man who had periodic heart attacks, as everyone was aware. This old man remembered the folk dances of Nova Scotia and asked Quig if he would not bring his violin and play some of the old tunes at their lunch break. So one day they went down to the cellar with their sandwiches and coffee, and Quig played the jigs and reels buried deep in the old man's memory. So spirited was the playing and so spirited the memory, that the listener was moved to get up and dance; dance he did, old and sick as he was, in a delightful fling of restored youth. They parted to go back to work by different stairways. Later that day Quig heard that the old man had dropped dead on his way up.

But as he told it, Quig was well aware that if one had to die, as we all do, going out dancing is perhaps as good a way as any other. Was I imagining the tears that shone in Quig's eyes as he told this story? And did I tell him that it reminded me for some reason of Yeats? Yeats would have seen the point.

Quig did not "go out" fiddling, as perhaps he would have liked to do. He was much too busy building a big addition onto the house all that last year to know really that he was ill. He thought he was just tired. Single-handedly he added a new dimension to the living room and built on second-floor bedrooms above it. I am glad I lent him my new saw; maybe it helped. By late fall he had to admit that he was ill, and took to his bed. There he lay in the big room downstairs, a cat and a fiddle on the end of it; there he lay receiving callers with shy jokes about his condition, making a "ceremony" even of this last illness.

I saw him once more in a "fit of looking"—in the hospital before he died. I took him a pocket edition of Delacroix's *Journal* and he happened to open it to the stunning portrait of Chopin. While Mildred and I talked softly at the bedside, Quig disappeared into his world of joy, the world of the painter. I don't believe he heard a word we said, but I saw once more that concentrated light in his eyes, and he did not let the book go out of his hands while I was there.

Beside this I want to place another day, when he was well and himself. He had been working for weeks to make his first violin: delicate, absorbing, tense work. He had often mended broken instruments (people got to know that he could make something of what looked like a total wreck and brought him their broken violins as if broken human bones to a surgeon), but he had never embarked

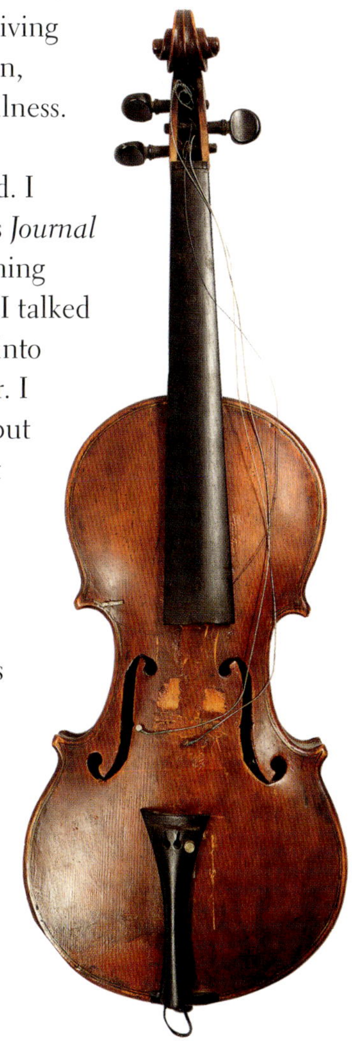

Albert Quigley's handmade violin
Brian and Jessie Quigley

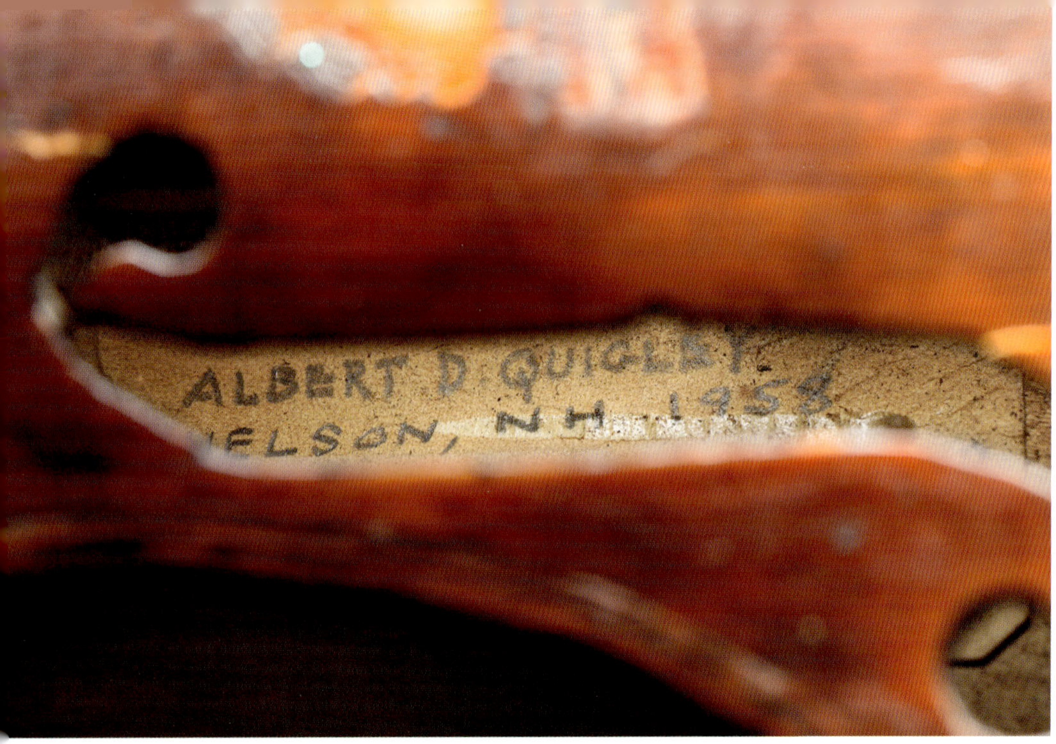

Verification of Albert Quigley's violin (inside box) Full inscription reads: "Albert D. Quigley, Nelson, NH, 1958. Aided by his old friend Alvah Batchelder, Frankfort, ME." Brian and Jessie Quigley

on the different adventure of starting from scratch. I happened to walk over at the end of a morning and heard the sound of a violin before I opened the door. Could it be? It was the birth of his new violin; he had lifted it to his chin and drawn a bow across the strings for the first time! For me it was a great moment to hear it sing, to hear it being given the breath of life.

Lives are framed by death. Quig had been so much a part of this landscape that perhaps we had come to take him for granted like some old tree which would surely outlive us all, its strong roots twined around granite. Then, quite suddenly, he was gone. People who had not expected to felt sharp loss—what? Quig not there? But he had always been there, always responsive, always caring. He just couldn't be dead! All sorts of people felt bereaved as if they had lost a parent, a brother, the best of friends. Somehow in the last months when he must have been feeling very ill, Quig had managed to paint the three [four] boys of the undertaker in Keene: rare indeed is the man whose death brings tears to the eyes of the undertaker! But this man mourned, as did the village idiot to whom Quig had been kind, as did a rich woman to whom he had taught all he could about painting, as did the poet across the green (myself), as did his fellow workers at the mill—and many, many others. How many we knew when the funeral unexpectedly drew a host of people, people the family hardly knew, people from far away, people whose lives Quig's had touched and touched deeply. Only Alec was not there.

Death frames. What was framed for us on that final day is hard to put into words. All the bits and pieces of a life which often seemed scattered among too many gifts suddenly came together, and we saw him whole. The wholeness was in the tenderness toward life itself, the power of joy, the liveliness of mind, the something like triumph of a man who had tasted no worldly success but had never ceased to create and to give. I sat down that morning and wrote what I felt, wrote it quickly, almost as one makes a death mask, to catch the total being before the winds disperse it.

How rarely as a poet does one feel useful and needed! But I have never felt so proud to be published anywhere as I was when the *Keene Sentinel* published my celebration of Quig on its editorial page, and when the minister (the same man who had come to bury Alexander James) read it at the funeral itself.

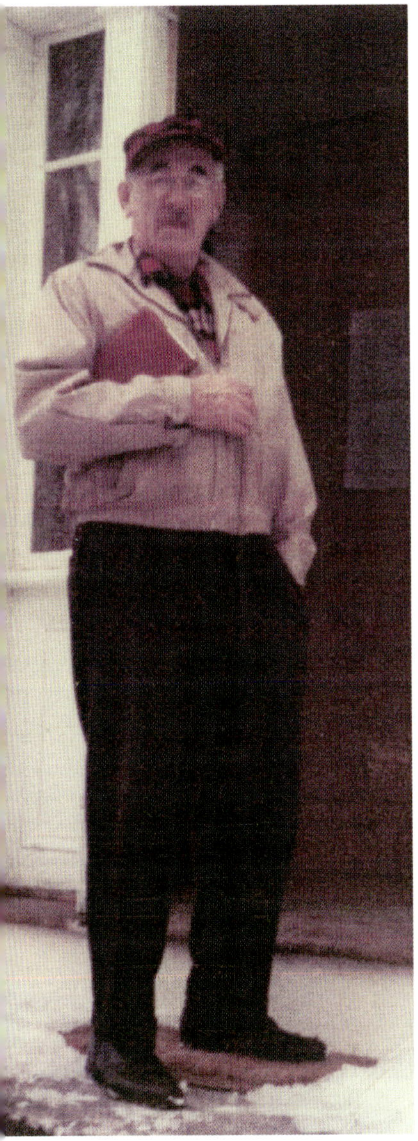

Albert Quigley
Courtesy of the Quigley family

Lately, he lay downstairs, a dying king,
His violin at the end of the bed like a couchant beast
In some old tapestry or heraldic painting,
The battered orange cat blinking by the fire,
The fat asthmatic dog snoring beside him—
Family, neighbors gathered there all day:

He kept his wit intact, though flesh had nearly left him.
And still he sparkled like a frost-touched leaf,
So withered now a breath might take him,
Accepting laughter as a final homage.

Before we could get used to the idea of death,
He had gone,
Before we could get used to it,
Had slipped away in the night,
Leaving this empty bag of a world—no Quig in it.
God, it's a lonely village now without him!
(Still beautiful in the snow and cruel cold—
Nelson, he animated with his warming presence.)

He was everyone's father, graced in the giving,
Prodigal of tenderness real fathers rarely give,
Enfolded us, believed, could weep like a woman,
Yet held fast to those values that stand up to death,
Kingly in this. Yet always a poor man, bills piling up,
Never out of the woods, never quite in the clear—
His last act to paint the portraits of four boys.
Somehow he did it, summoned himself,
and kept his promise.

Improvident, generous, his white hair in a crest
Said, "I'm cock of the world because I love it"—
Cock, not by possession, but by love.
Maker of violins, he held them in his hands
Because he wanted the true sound, the singing tone;
Painter of this landscape and of all our faces:
We have to see now and we have to try to hear
Without his accurate, intimate eye and ear.

(Remember how he loved the early spring, its redness,
Its feathery graces, remember how he loved Cézanne,
Renoir, Degas, in those last days held in his hands
A portrait by Delacroix, and would not be distracted:
Often I have seen him silenced by a fit of looking.)

Lover of ceremony, and all courteous graces,
He was one of the last fiddlers, jigs and reels,
And "swing your partners!" We'll dance in the old hall
A last dance for Quig, the fiddler, whose tunes kept
Our feet light, our eyes open, our hearts true.
I tell you his joys are with us. We are not alone.
(But, God, it's an empty village that we have to fill!)

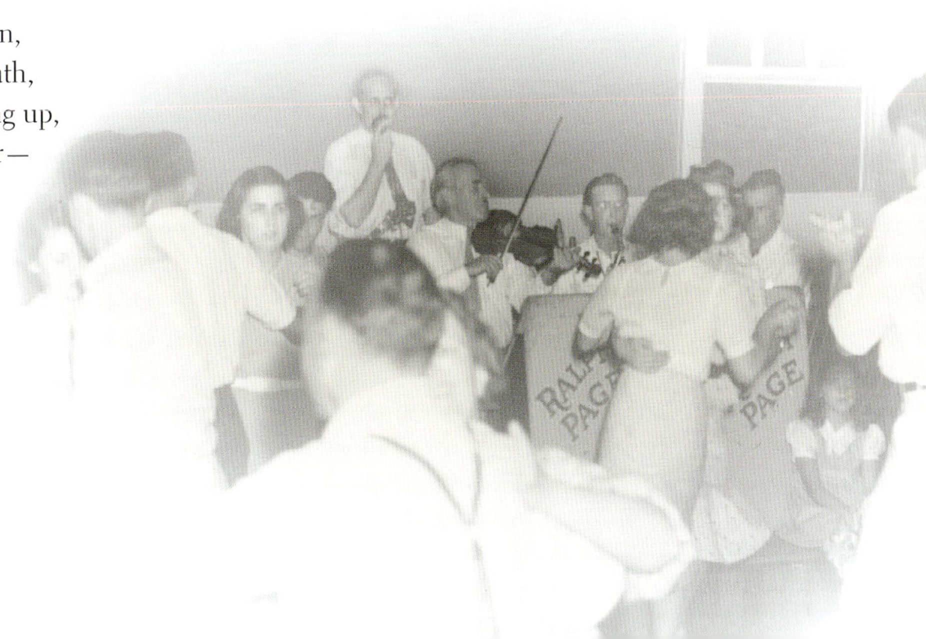

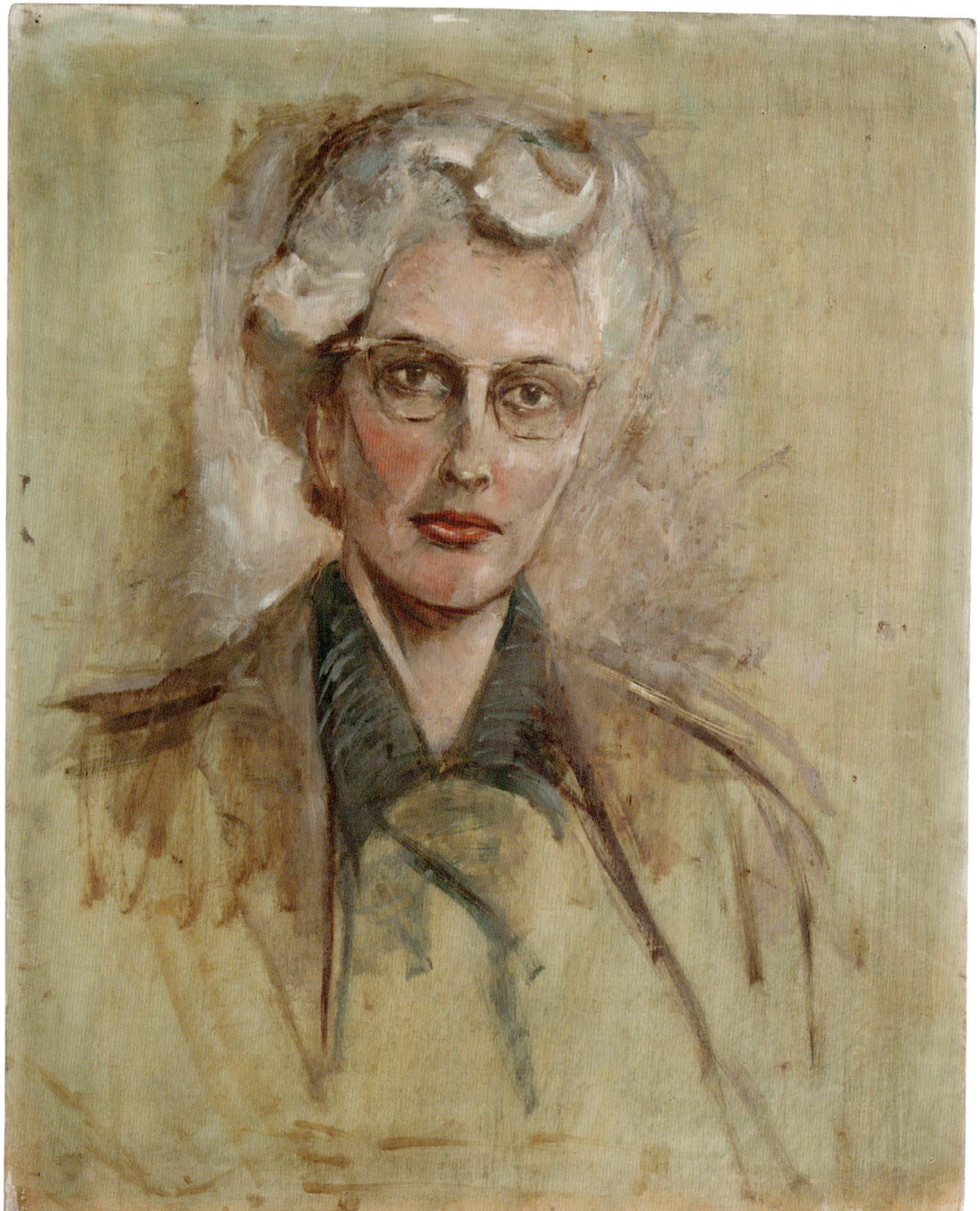

MAY SARTON
Unfinished oil on board
22 x 18 in.
Roberta Wingerson

Portraits

Subject matter for Quigley varied . . . . He often painted portraits, many of them from memory and most of them unsolicited. The portraits were often of local people whose faces interested him. Of his father's paintings, Barney says his favorites were the portraits which represent a small gallery of local characters who came alive to him through his father's studies.

—Edie Clark, author
written for the 1991 Quigley art exhibit sponsored by the Community Church of Harrisville and Chesham, New Hampshire

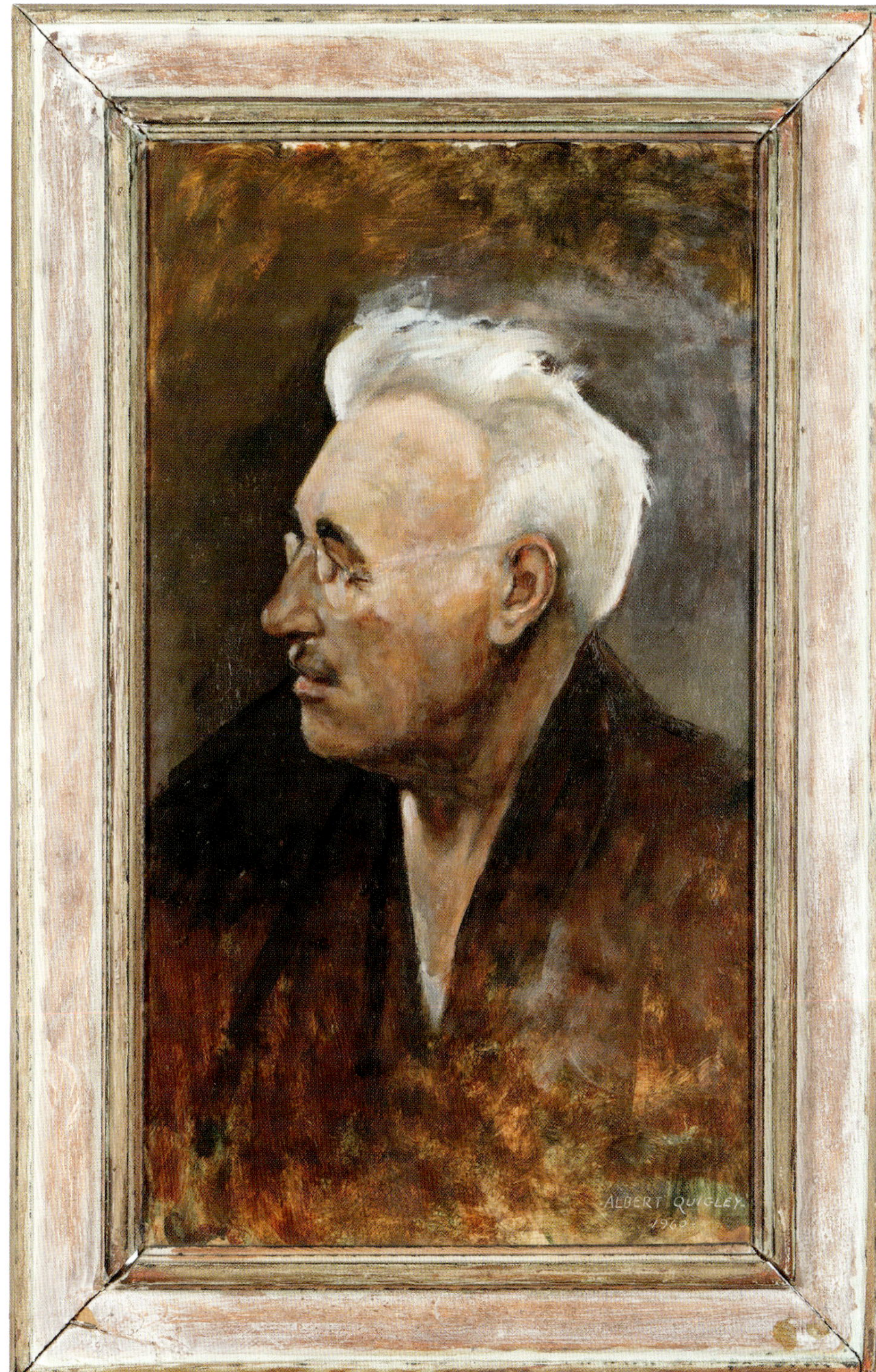

SELF PORTRAIT
Quigley frame, 29 x 19 in.
Thorne-Sagendorph Art Gallery
at Keene State College

The Quigley Children

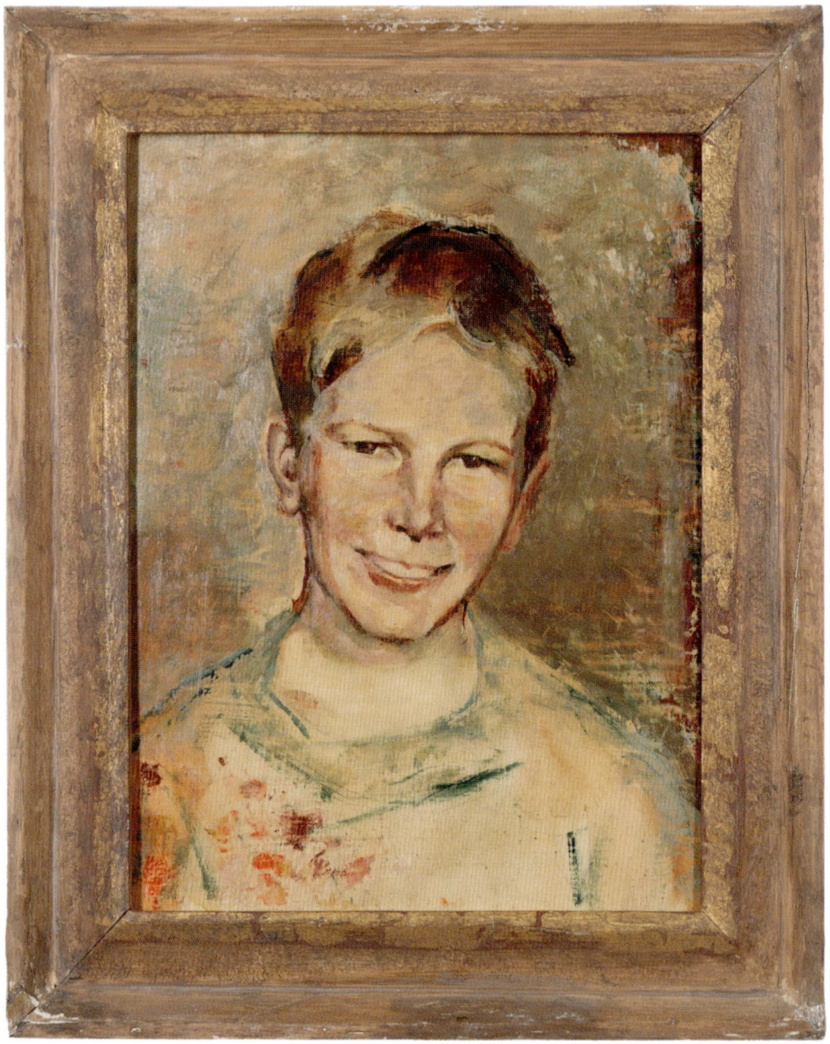

BARNEY QUIGLEY (ca. 1950)
Unfinished oil on board, Quigley frame, 23 x 19 in.
Private collection

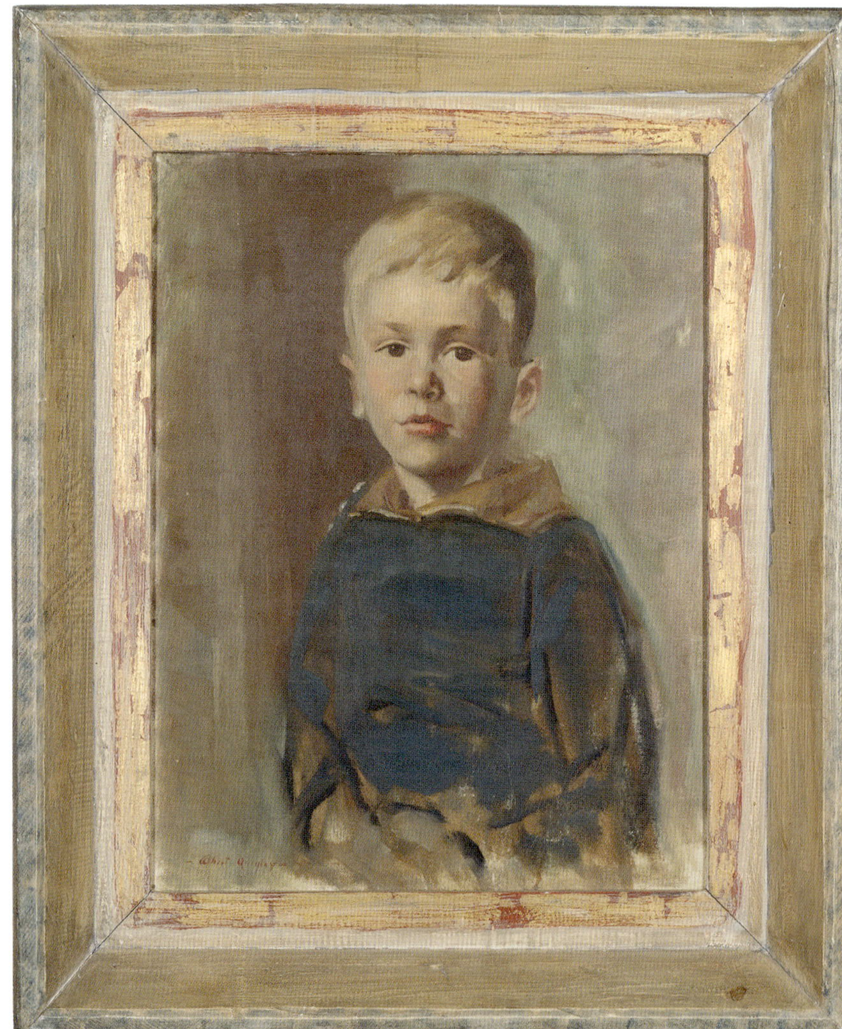

YOUNG BARNEY (1942)
Oil on panel, Quigley frame, 29 x 25 in.
Private collection

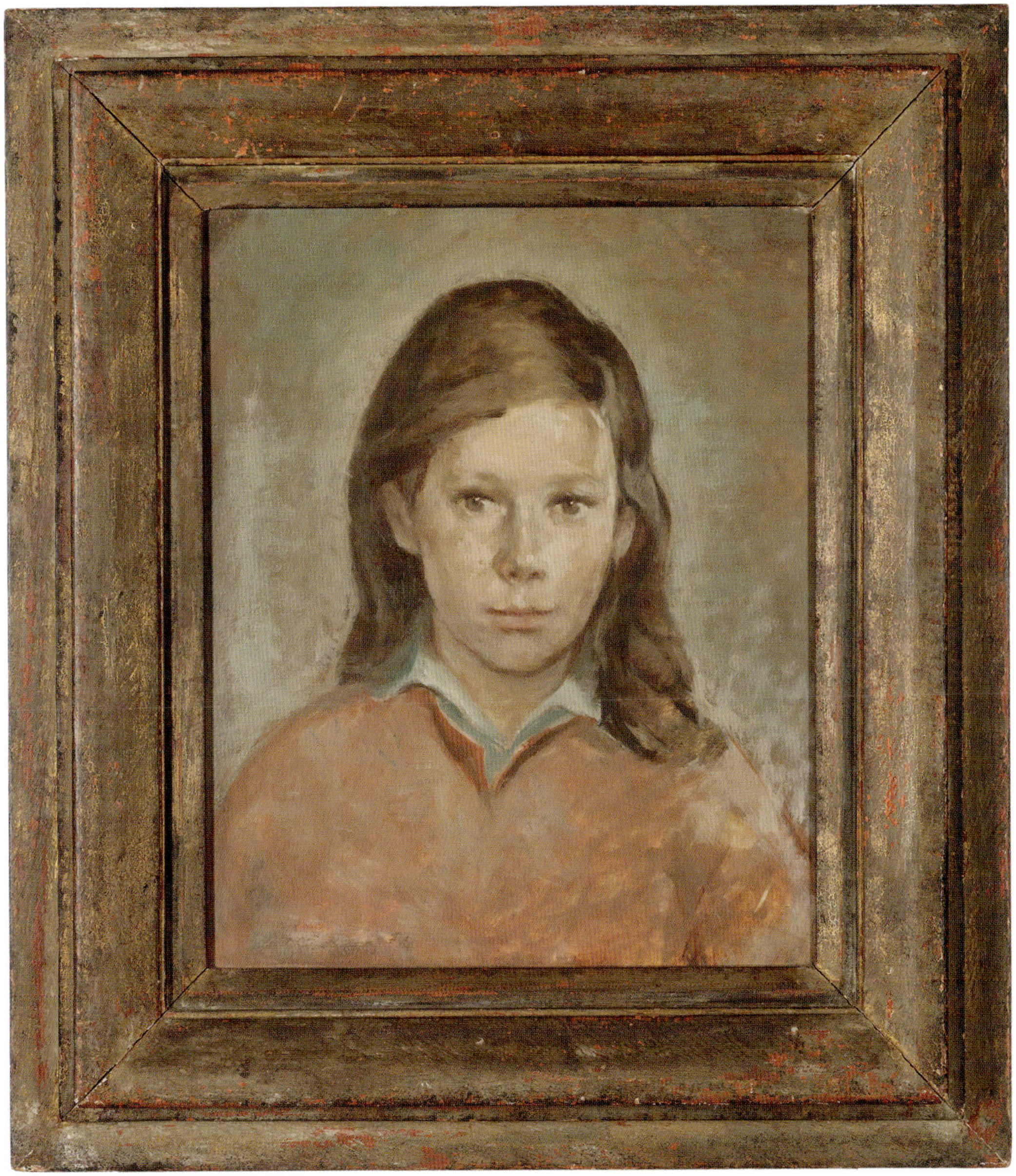

TAMI QUIGLEY (ca. 1950)
Oil on board, Quigley frame, 22 x 20 in.
Private collection

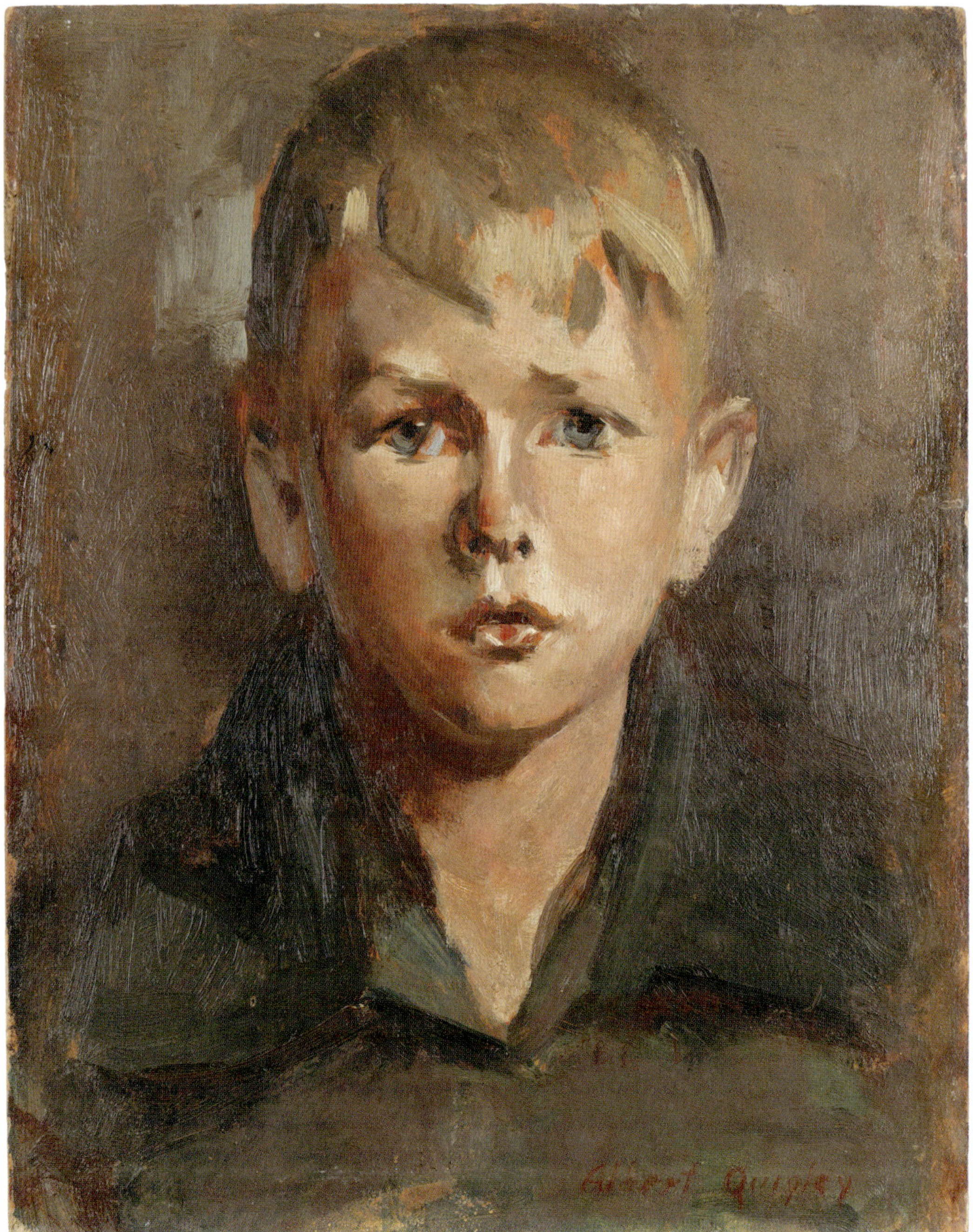

TERRY QUIGLEY AS A BOY
Oil on board, unframed, 14 x 11 in.
Brian and Jessie Quigley

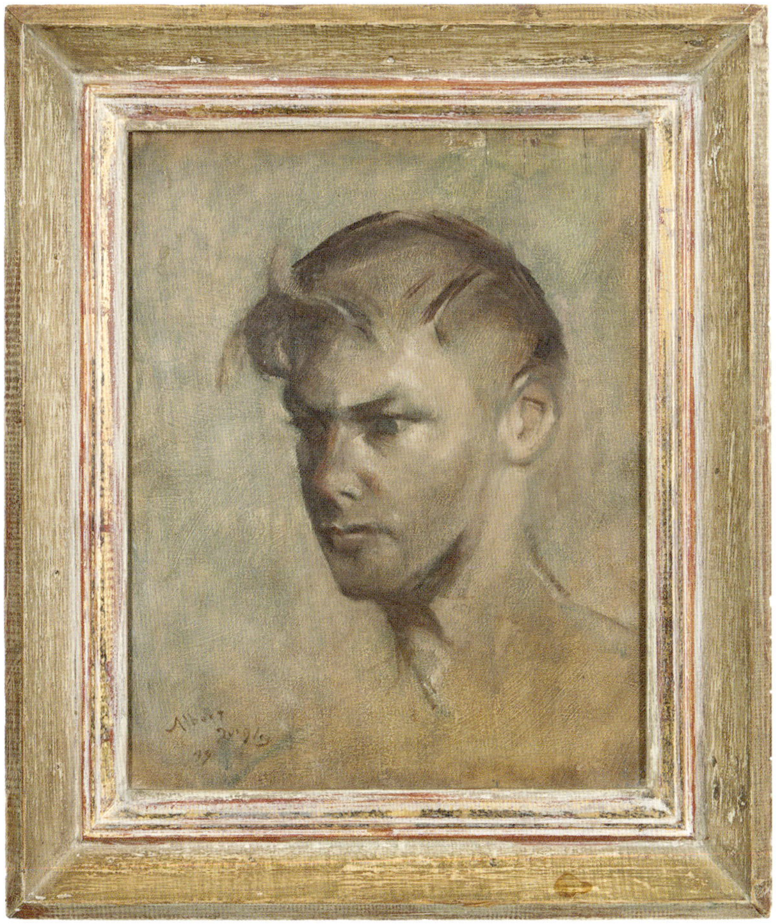

TERRY QUIGLEY (1949)
Oil on board
Quigley frame, 22 x 18 in.
Brian and Jessie Quigley

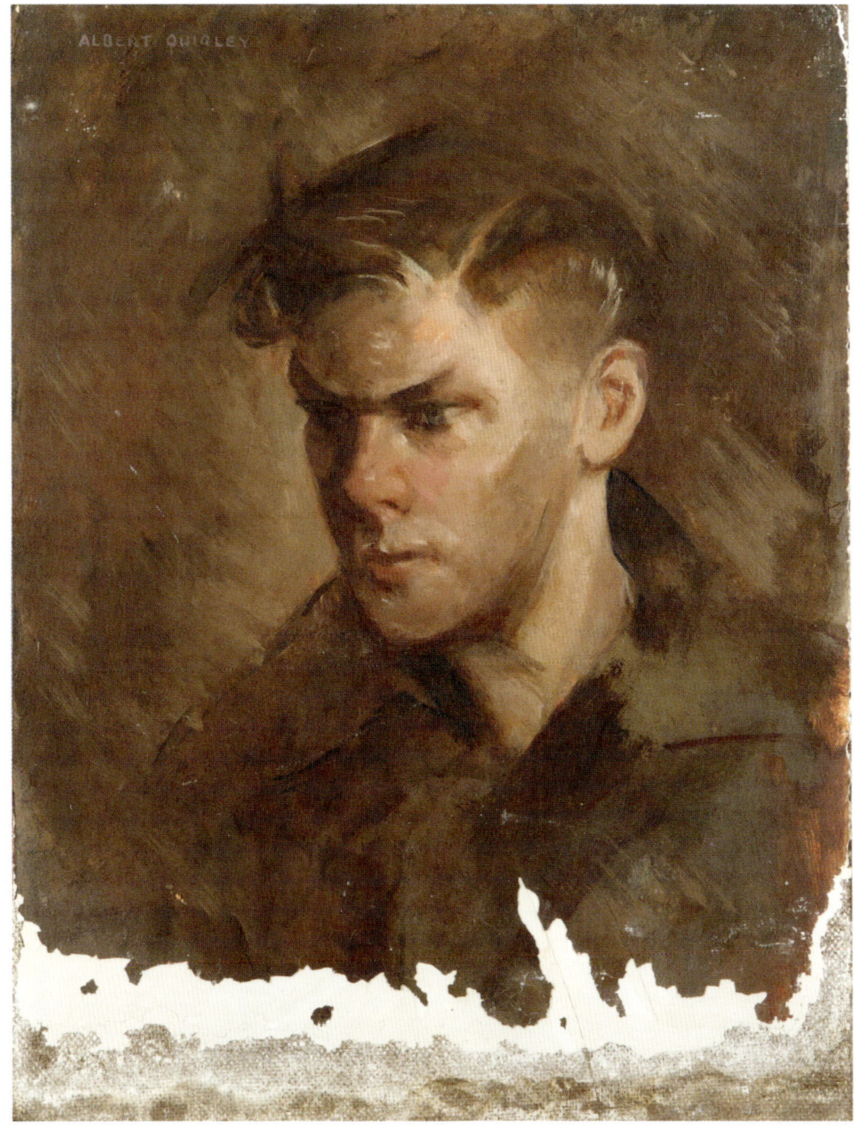

TERRY QUIGLEY AS A TEEN
Oil on board, unframed, 19 x 14 in.
Brian and Jessie Quigley

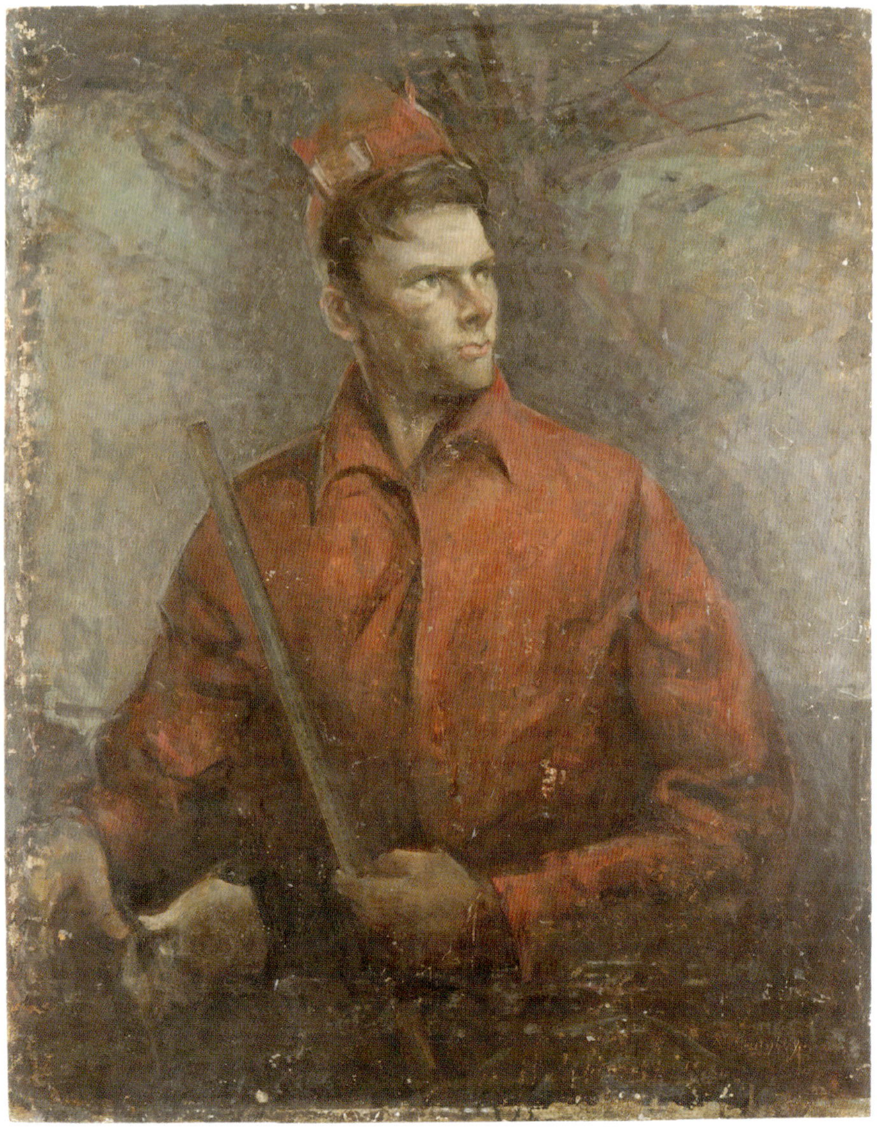

TERRY QUIGLEY
Oil on board, unframed, 30 x 24 in.
Brian and Jessie Quigley
Terry dressed for hunting with license in hat

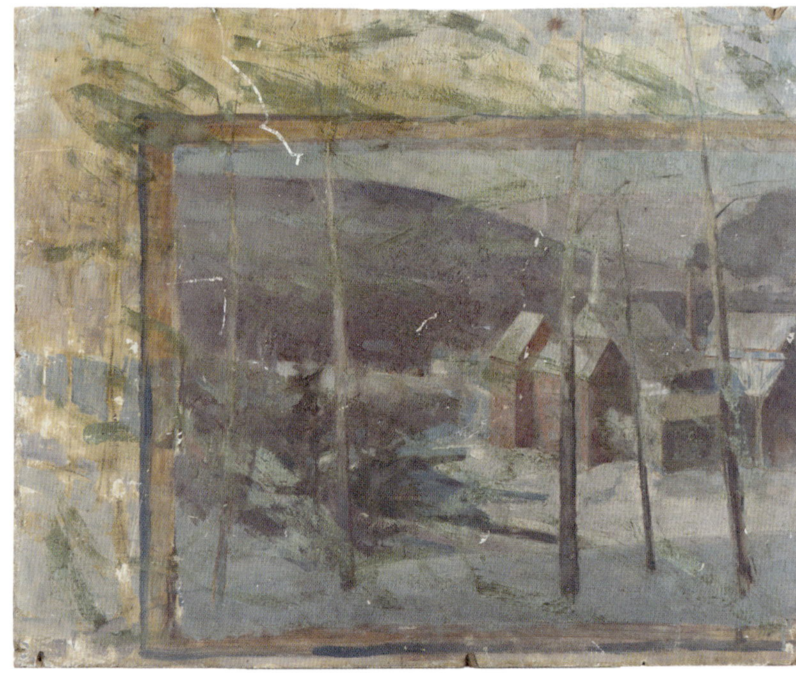

An unfinished work is painted on the back of the portrait of Terry.

The Foley Family

Celebrating Albert Quigley

In January 1960, my father, Frank J. Foley, contacted Albert Quigley about painting a portrait of his grandfather, Dennis J. Foley. DJ, as he was called, had been the proprietor of the Foley Funeral Home, our family business, for many years, as well as a fireman. He was well known in Keene and received much recognition upon his death in 1938. My father had a number of photographs of DJ. Albert Quigley painted the portrait from these, and it is astounding how well he captured the image and the spirit of my great-grandfather. The painting was hung prominently in the funeral home, and my father then asked Quig to paint a portrait of his father, Frank J. Foley, Sr. This Quig did from memory.

Both portraits were painted in Quig's home studio in Nelson, and I made several trips with my father to watch the artist at work. To me, Mr. Quigley (as I always called him) was large and imposing, larger than life. He

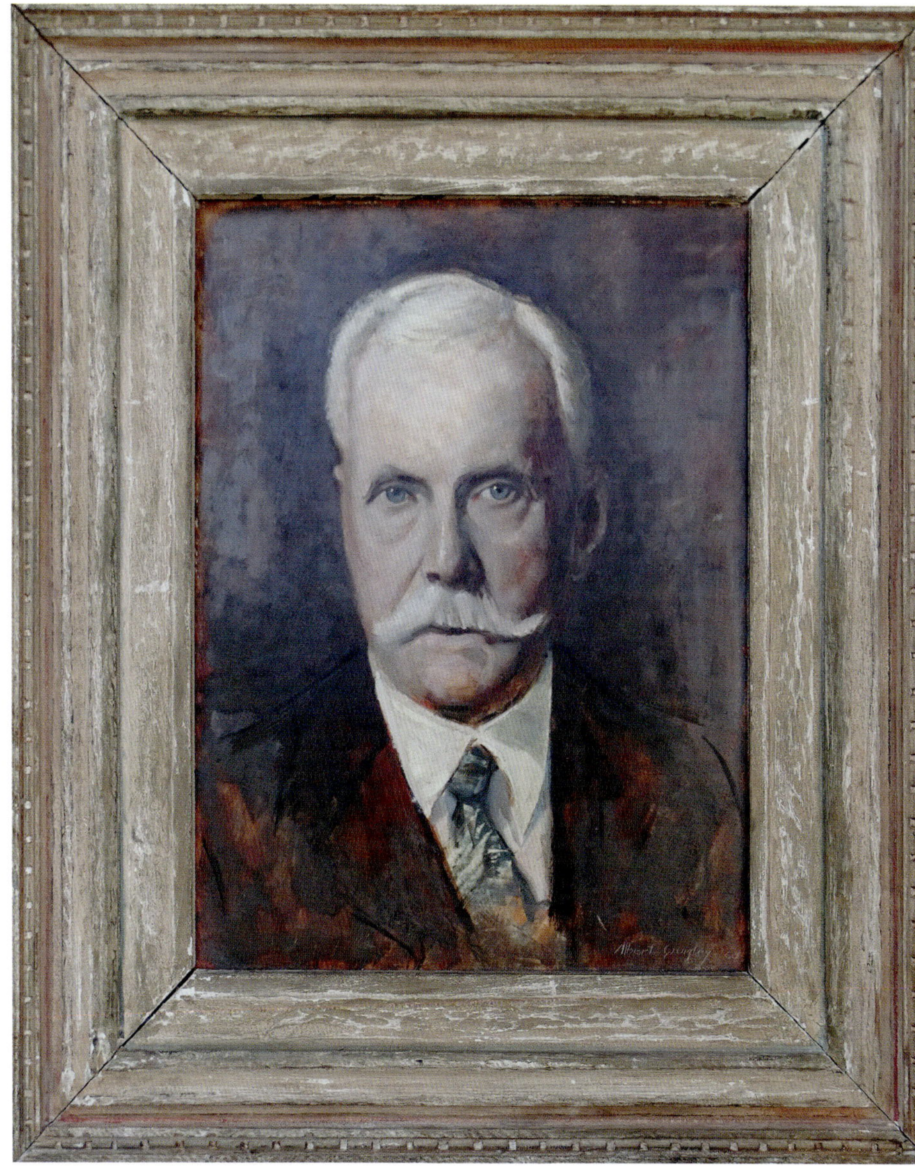

DENNIS J. FOLEY (1960), great-grandfather of Frank Foley
Oil on canvas, Quigley frame, 25 x 18 in.
Frank Foley
Courtesy of the Foley family

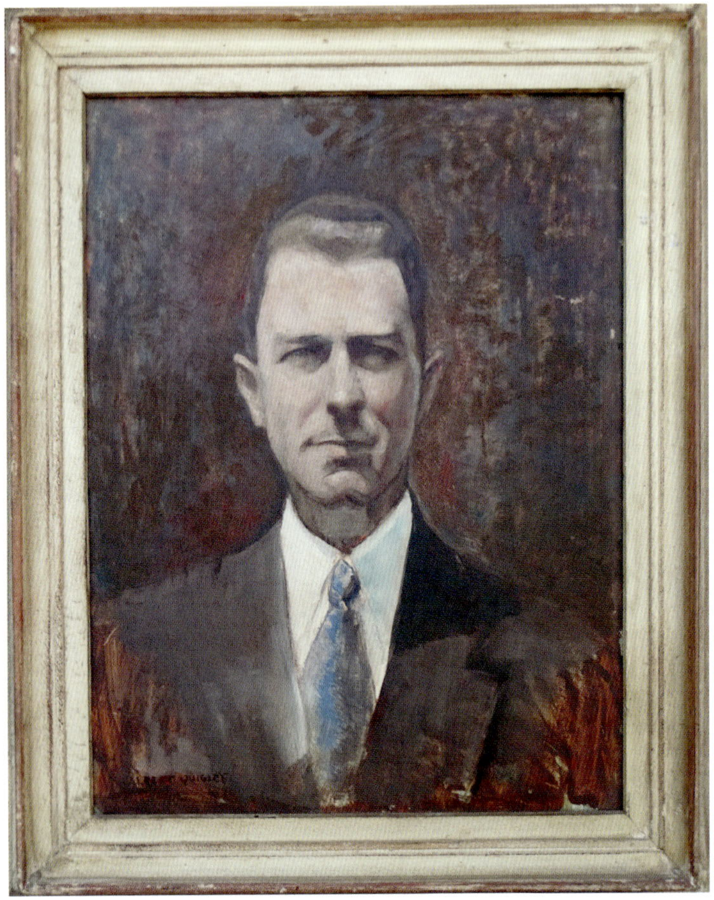

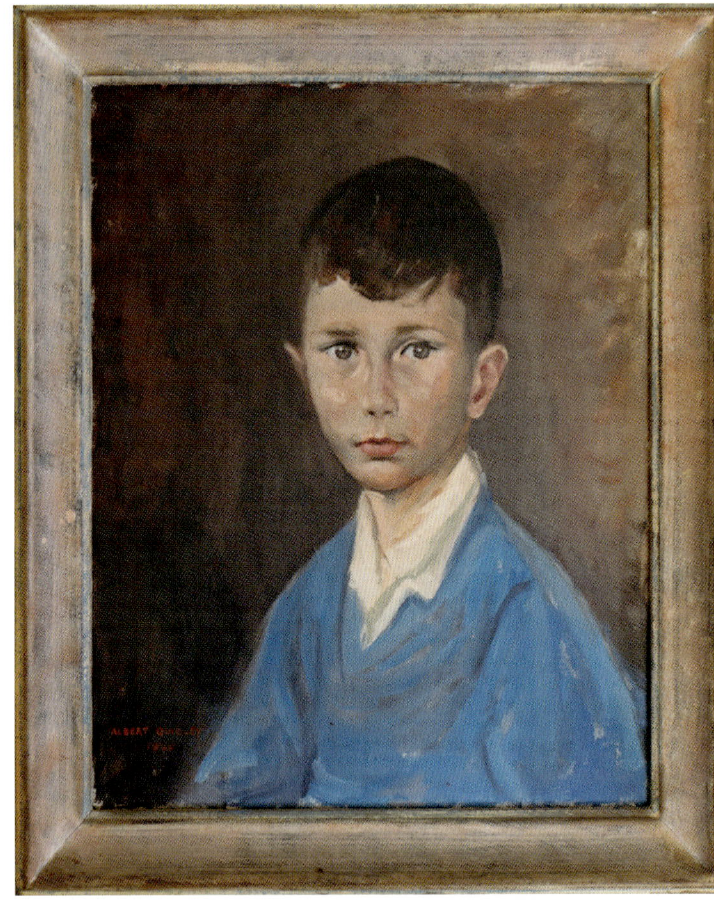

LEFT **FRANK J. FOLEY** (1960), grandfather of Frank Foley
Oil on canvas
Quigley frame
25 x 18 in.
Frank Foley
Courtesy of the Foley family

RIGHT **KEVIN FOLEY** (1960)
Oil on canvas
Quigley frame
24 x 20 in.
Karen Foley
Courtesy of the Foley family

was tall and broad, and he looked strong. He was a force that filled his studio. The studio itself reflected Quig's life. He was a musician as well as an artist, and fiddles hung on the walls. Of course, there were paintings, mostly landscapes, many not yet finished. Easels, some holding paintings and others unoccupied, stood on the floor. There were many of his beautiful frames, also unfinished, empty and waiting. I remember Mr. Quigley spending a lot of time on the frames, especially that of DJ's portrait.

My father and Mr. Quigley told lots of stories about people they knew. Even though I didn't know much about the people they talked about, I listened carefully and laughed a great deal, though I wasn't always sure why. I remember also thinking that this was the most animated

I had ever seen my father. He liked being there and Mr. Quigley seemed to revel in the company, even patiently answering my many questions. Almost always, Quig shared his studio with a large, healthy-looking cat, and both he and Mildred (Mrs. Quigley to me) made a big deal of feeding the cat raw milk. To this day, I can see in my mind's eye that cat happily lapping up its raw milk.

From the portraits of my grandfather and great-grandfather, my mother got the idea to have portraits done of my three brothers and me to give to my father for Christmas. Mr. Quigley painted our portraits in Keene, and the process took most of the rest of the year. My mother would take us to The Linen Shop, which was up an awful set of stairs above a store in Central Square. The back room of the shop was our makeshift studio. I remember it as less than ideal, with few windows and poor light. No matter, Mr. Quigley toiled away on my mother's commission. I remember that she was quite taken with the artist, and her presence seemed to cheer him up too. I did not know then that Mr. Quigley was not well, and those stairs had to have been a real challenge for him.

Everyone loved the portraits, which turned out to be his last commission. Mine was the last one he worked on, and it was never quite finished. He was not satisfied with the mouth and worked on it even after that final Christmas, until his illness worsened and he was unable to continue. There was great sadness in our house at Mr. Quigley's passing. My father had seen his father and grandfather brought to life through their portraits in ways he had never imagined. My mother had enjoyed the lively give and take with the artist, as he made my brothers and me look better than we actually were. I think of him often and know that my short time with Mr. Quigley enriched my life then as it still does today.

—*Frank Foley, 2017*

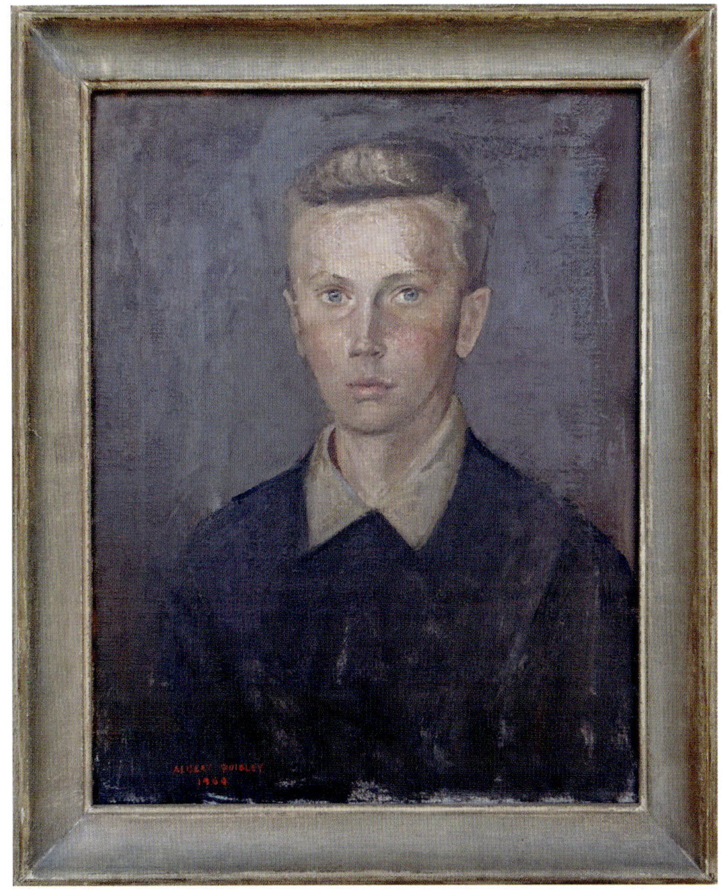

FRANK FOLEY
(1960)
Oil on canvas
Quigley frame
25 x 18 in.
Frank Foley
Courtesy of the Foley family

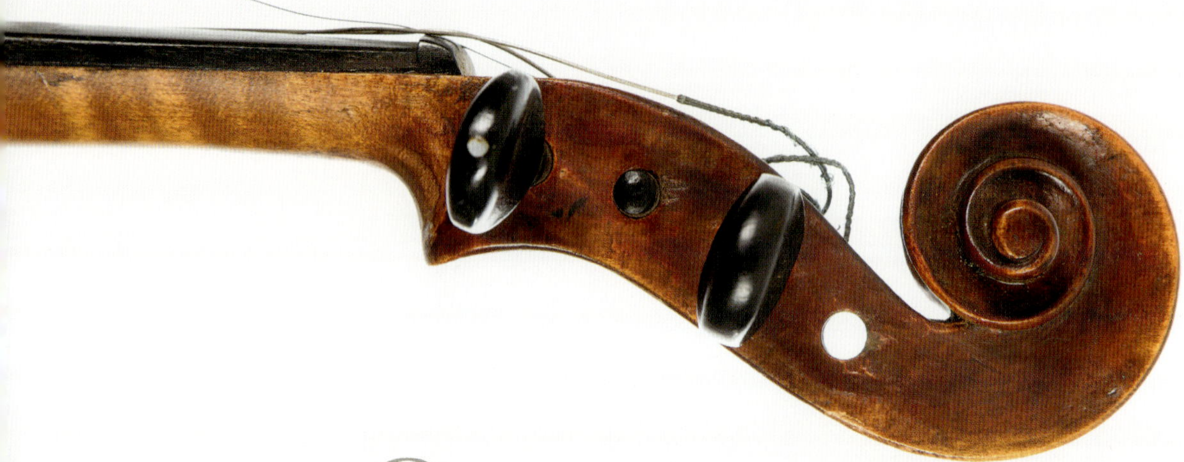

Quig's last contract was when he was approached by a funeral director in Keene, New Hampshire, who told him that he had been to several artists in New England and New York with photographs of his grandfather and asked to have an oil painting—a portrait of his grandfather done from the photographs—and he said that he hadn't found one that was satisfactory but somebody had recommended Quig. He said, "My deal is that I'll have you paint a portrait of my grandfather and if I don't like it, I won't take it, but I'll pay you for your time and your materials. And if I do like it, you name the price." He came back and took one look at the painting, the portrait, and he said, "My God, how did you do that? Nobody else came close." And Quig said, "Well, I knew your grandfather."

So then he came back and had his father's portrait painted, for which Quig was paid very well, and then unbeknownst to him, for a Christmas present, his wife had requested that Quig come and paint portraits of their four sons, which Quig finished just before Christmas and delivered. And that was just before Quig's demise.

But, right after Christmas, he also got three jobs playing for square dances on New Year's weekend. He went out and played every one of them. I know because I drove him to each of the jobs. And, three weeks later, he cashed it in.

—Barney Quigley
from an interview on March 23, 2014

In 1960, my father asked Mr. Quigley to do a portrait of his grandfather, Dennis John (DJ) Foley. My brother Frank now has the portrait, which Mr. Quigley painted in large part from memory with the aid of several photos. My father then asked the artist to do a second portrait, of his father, Francis J. Foley. I remember going to Mr. Quigley's farm in Nelson where I saw his studio, with fiddles and handmade picture frames hanging from the walls. The studio was in the barn, and numerous cats were around, drinking milk from large bowls.

Later in 1960, my mother, Pauline Foley, contacted Mr. Quigley and asked him to do portraits of me and my three brothers, Frank, Tom, and Kevin, as a Christmas present for my father. She told me she paid Mr. Quigley $100 for each painting. The portraits were done on the second floor of a store in Central Square near the old police station. I was twelve and in seventh grade at Keene Junior High School. I remember going there in late fall, and sitting on a wooden chair. Illumination came from a bulb overhead and one large window in the back of the room. The days were getting shorter, so there wasn't much light.

Mr. Quigley worked from a stool with his canvas held tight by nails on an easel. He wore gold-rimmed glasses and suspenders, and he rarely said anything. He sketched out my portrait in a light brown base paint and then started to fill it in. He finished all four portraits just before Christmas, though I believe he did some final touching up of my brother Frank's after Christmas. During the holidays, Mr. and Mrs. Quigley came to our house once for cocktails. I'd only seen him concentrating silently over his painting, but during the visit he was very different, smiling and talkative.

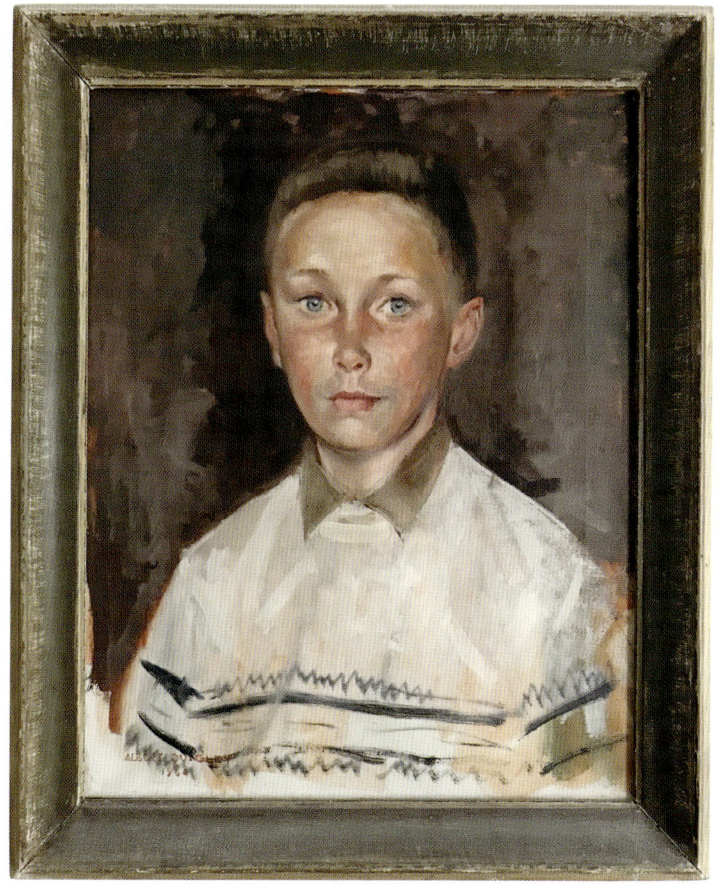

JOHN FOLEY (1960)
Oil on canvas
Quigley frame
John Foley
Courtesy of the
Foley family

—John Foley, 2017

Aunt Cora

AUNT CORA
Oil on board, Quigley frame
28 x 22 in.
Private collection

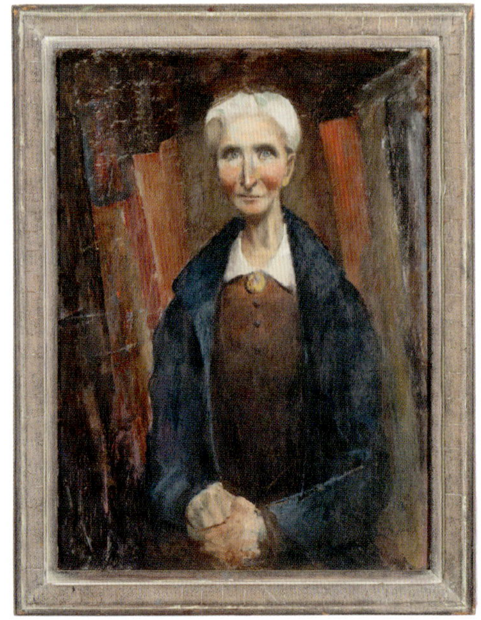

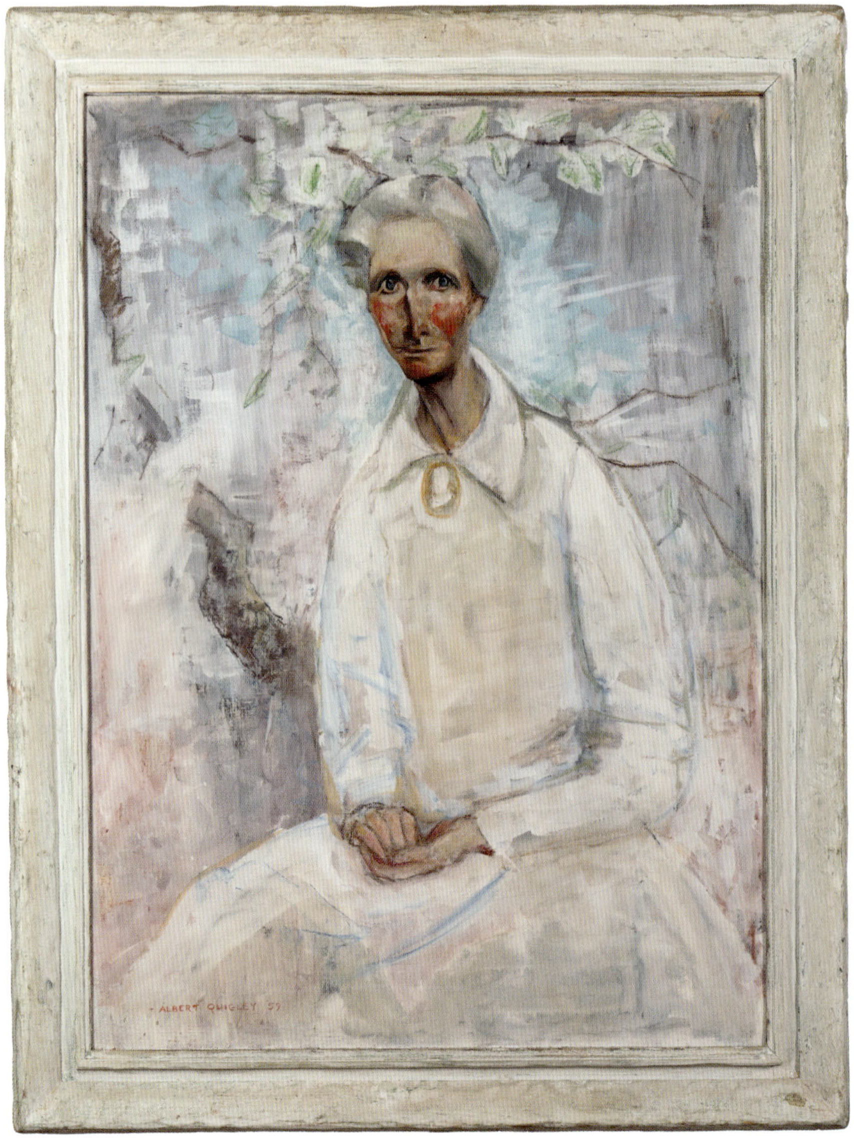

AUNT CORA
Oil on board, Quigley frame
39 x 29 in.
Private collection

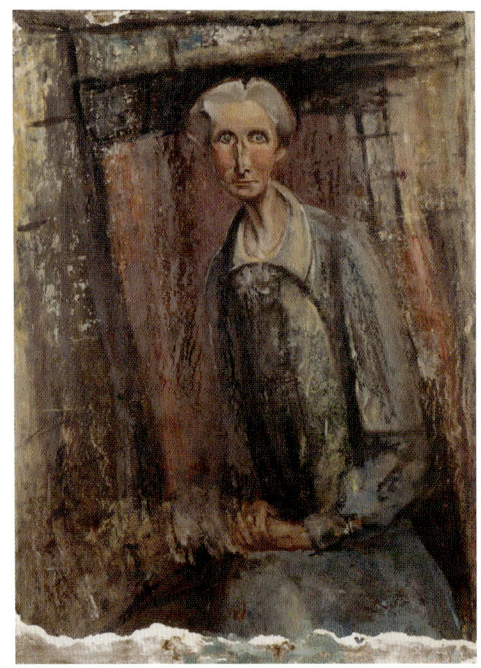

AUNT CORA
Oil on Masonite, unframed
40 x 30 in.
Private collection

Sandi Navish Patnode

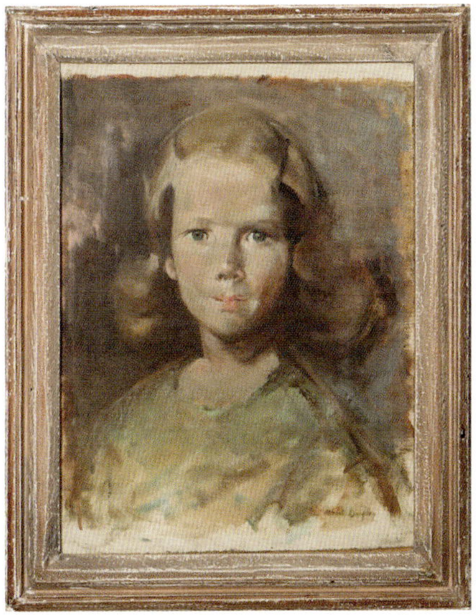

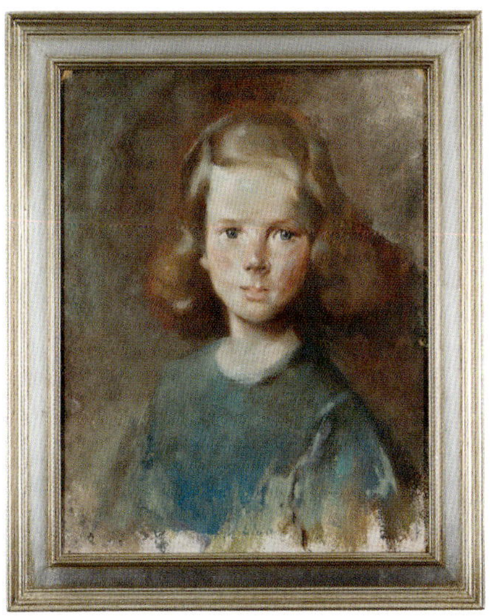

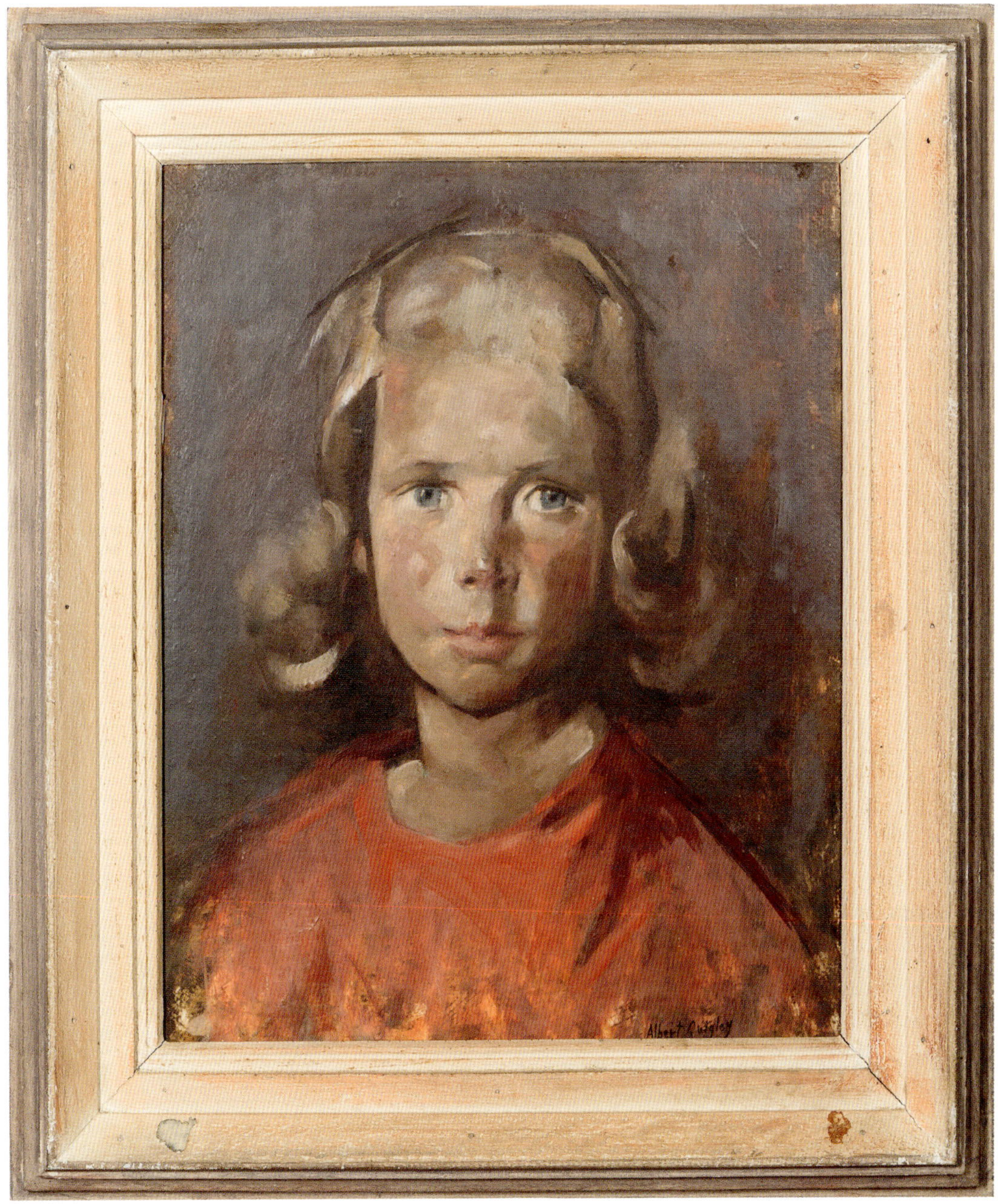

ABOVE **SANDI NAVISH PATNODE**
Oil on board, Quigley frame, 20 x 16 in.
Barney and Nancy Quigley

BELOW **SANDI NAVISH PATNODE**
Oil on board, 22 x 18 in.
Sandi Navish Patnode

SANDI NAVISH PATNODE
Oil on board, Quigley frame, 20 x 17 in.
Private collection

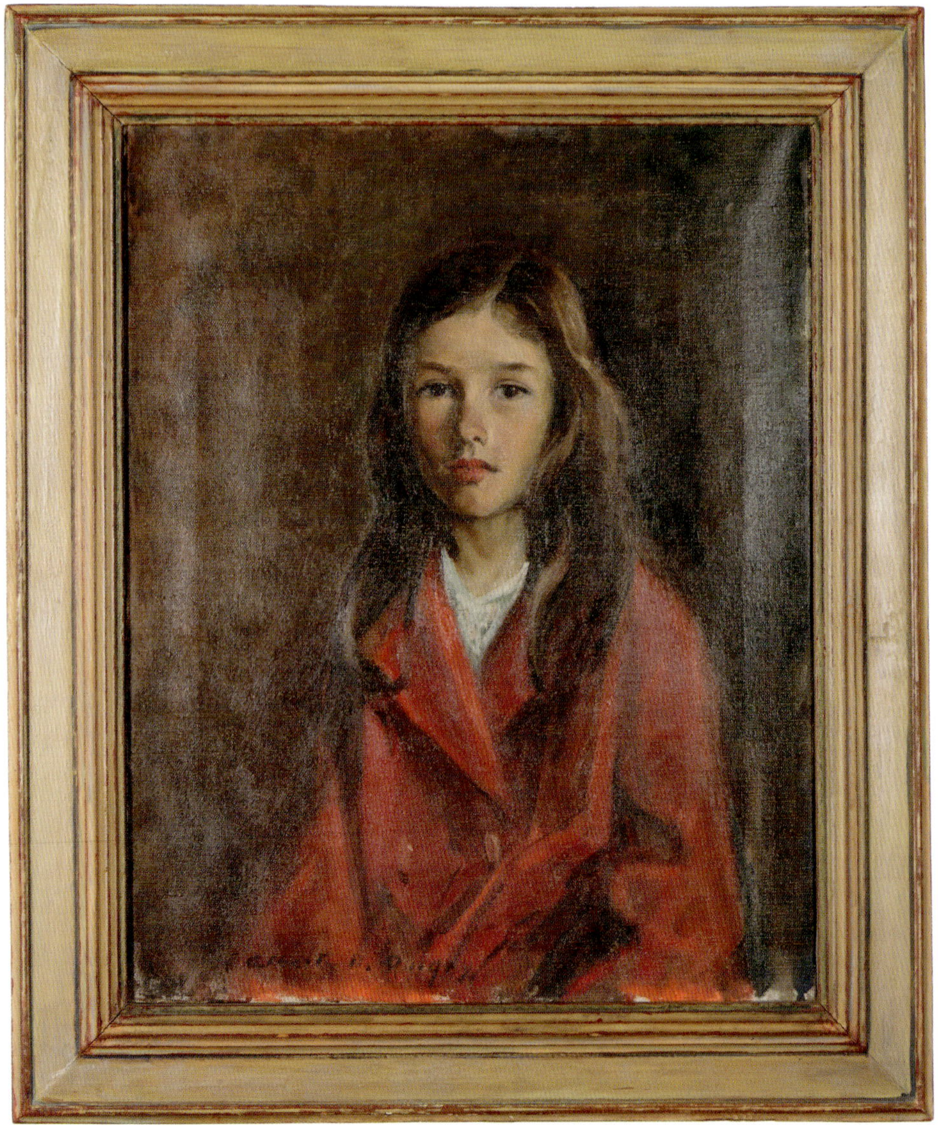

The Cobleigh Children

I sat three or four times for Quig when he was painting my portrait and I wanted to wear my red jacket with gold buttons. Quig didn't want to paint them gold, but I insisted. They were important to me. "But, Quig, they're my buttons," I had said. But he never painted them gold!

He did, however, like to paint pictures of kids holding something that they liked. He painted Donny, my brother, with a baseball bat, and he painted Gerry, my sister, holding a dog on her lap, made of sheepskin, but the sheepskin dog never made it into the painting.

—Joan Cobleigh Gerbis, neighbor
from an interview on August 14, 2014

JOAN COBLEIGH GERBIS (1940s)
Oil on canvas, 27 x 23 in.
Private collection
Joan at ten

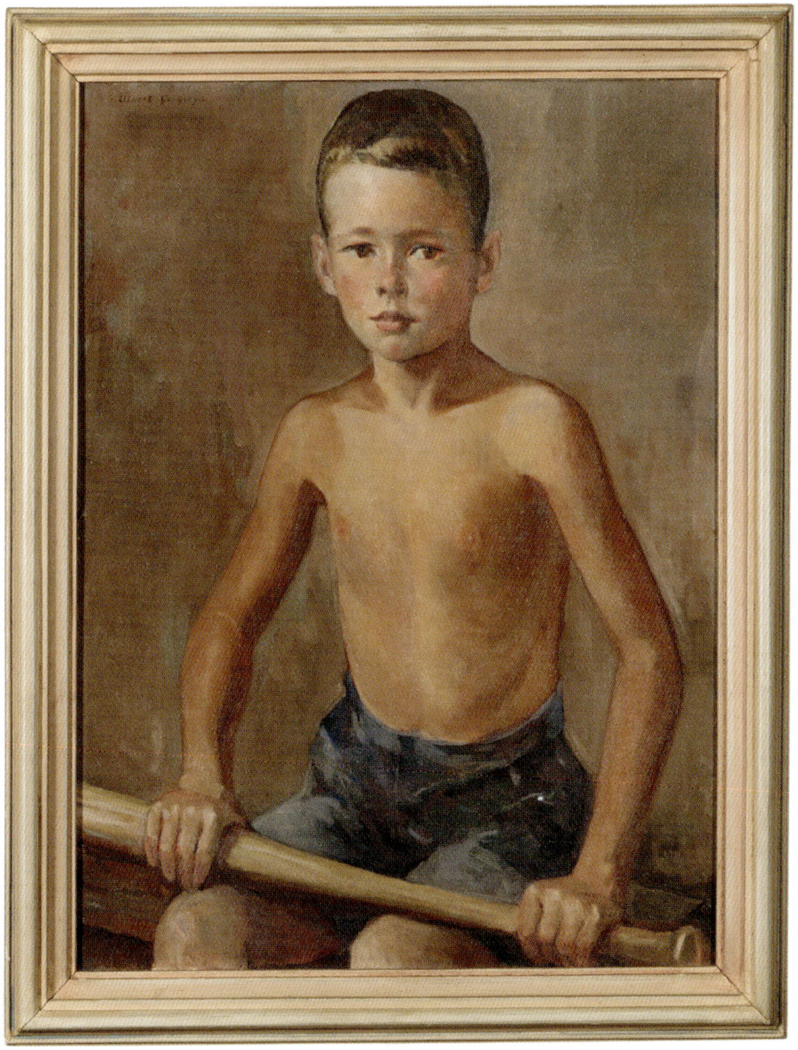

DONALD COBLEIGH
Oil on board, Quigley frame, 28 x 22 in.
Private collection

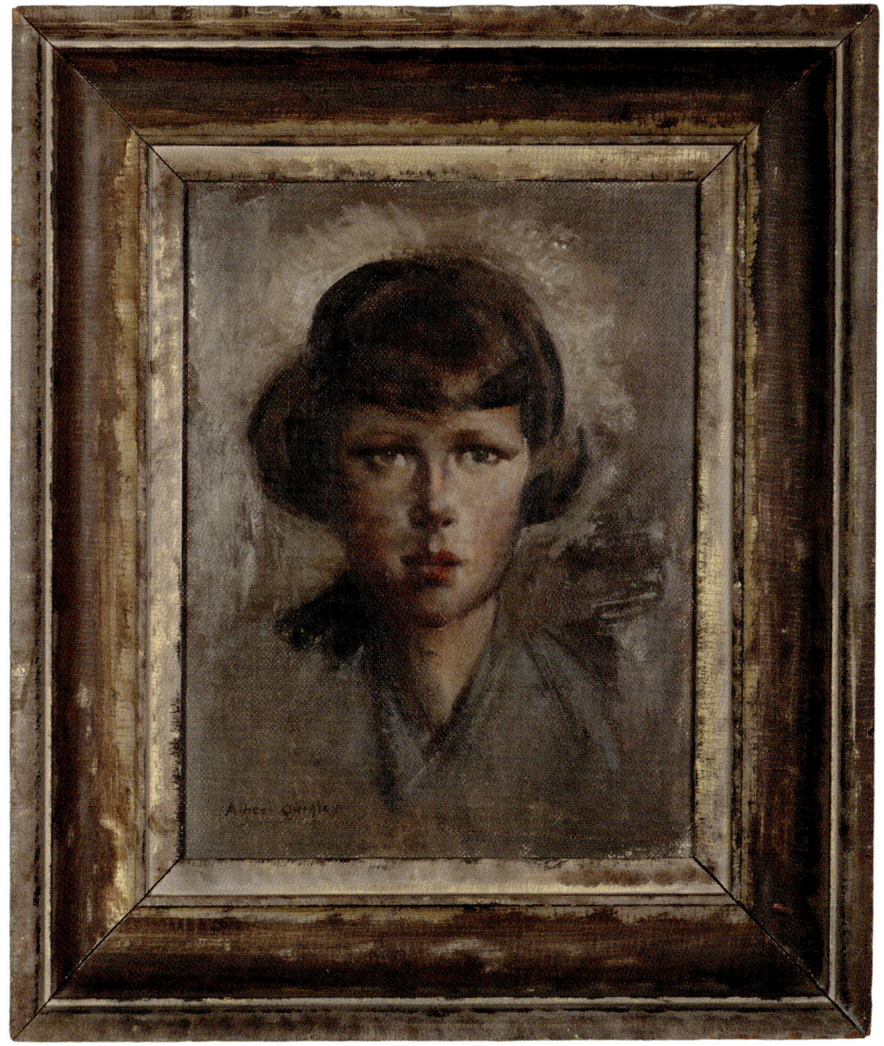

GERALYN COBLEIGH KELLEY (1948)
Oil on canvas, Quigley frame, 23 x 20 in.
Geralyn Cobleigh Kelley

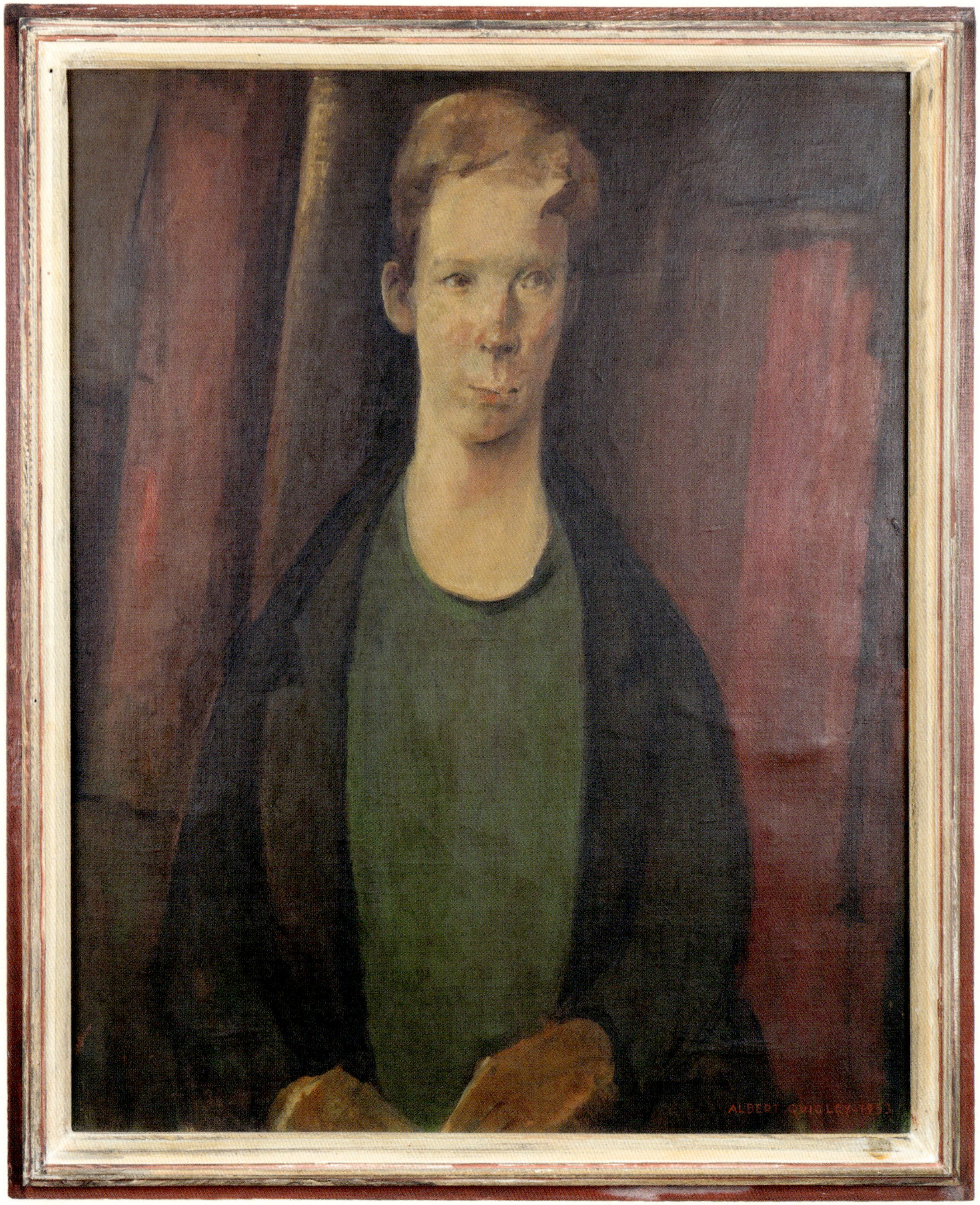

WARREN CURTIS
Oil on canvas
Quigley frame, 32 x 27 in.
Barney and Nancy Quigley
Arnold Adler, photographer

OPPOSITE CHECKERS GAME
PLAYED BY BARNEY QUIGLEY
AND PHIL STACK
Oil on panel
Quigley frame 30 x 36 in.
Barney and Nancy Quigley
Arnold Adler, photographer

A Gallery of Portraits

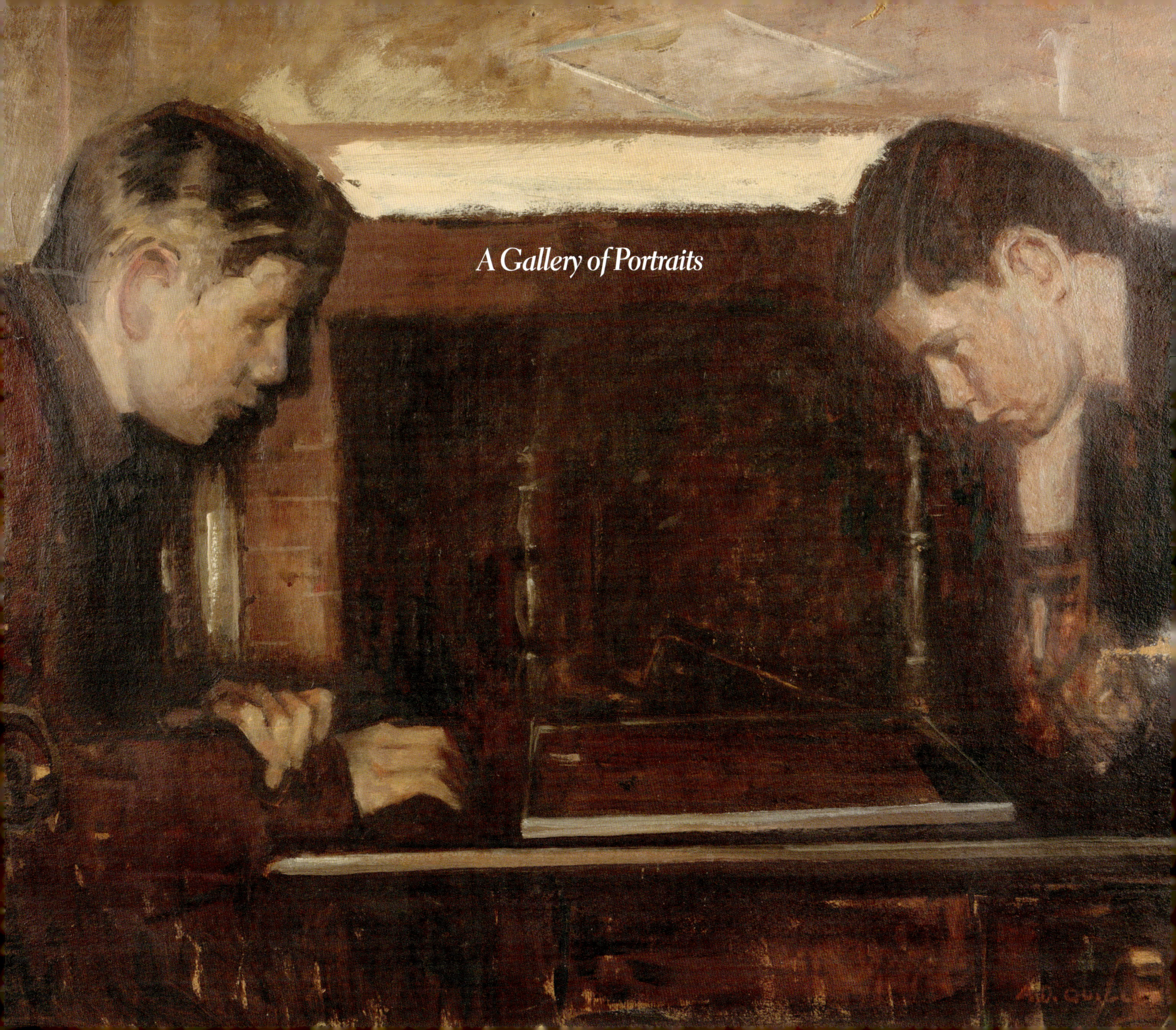

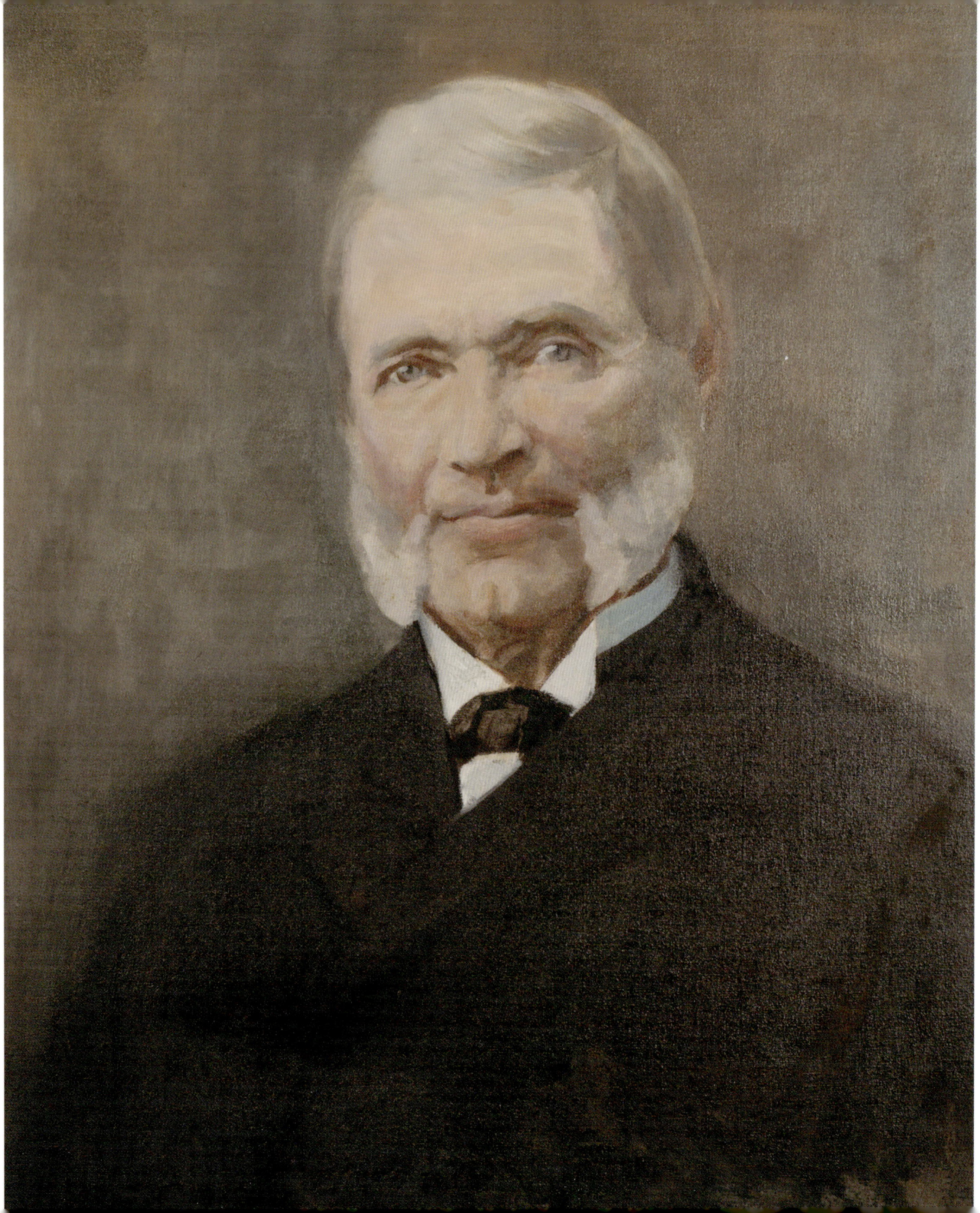

REV. WILLIAM MERRILL
Oil on canvas, 29 x 25 in.
Private collection

First minister (1891–1894) of the Methodist Episcopal Church in Munsonville, New Hampshire
WPA Federal Art Project

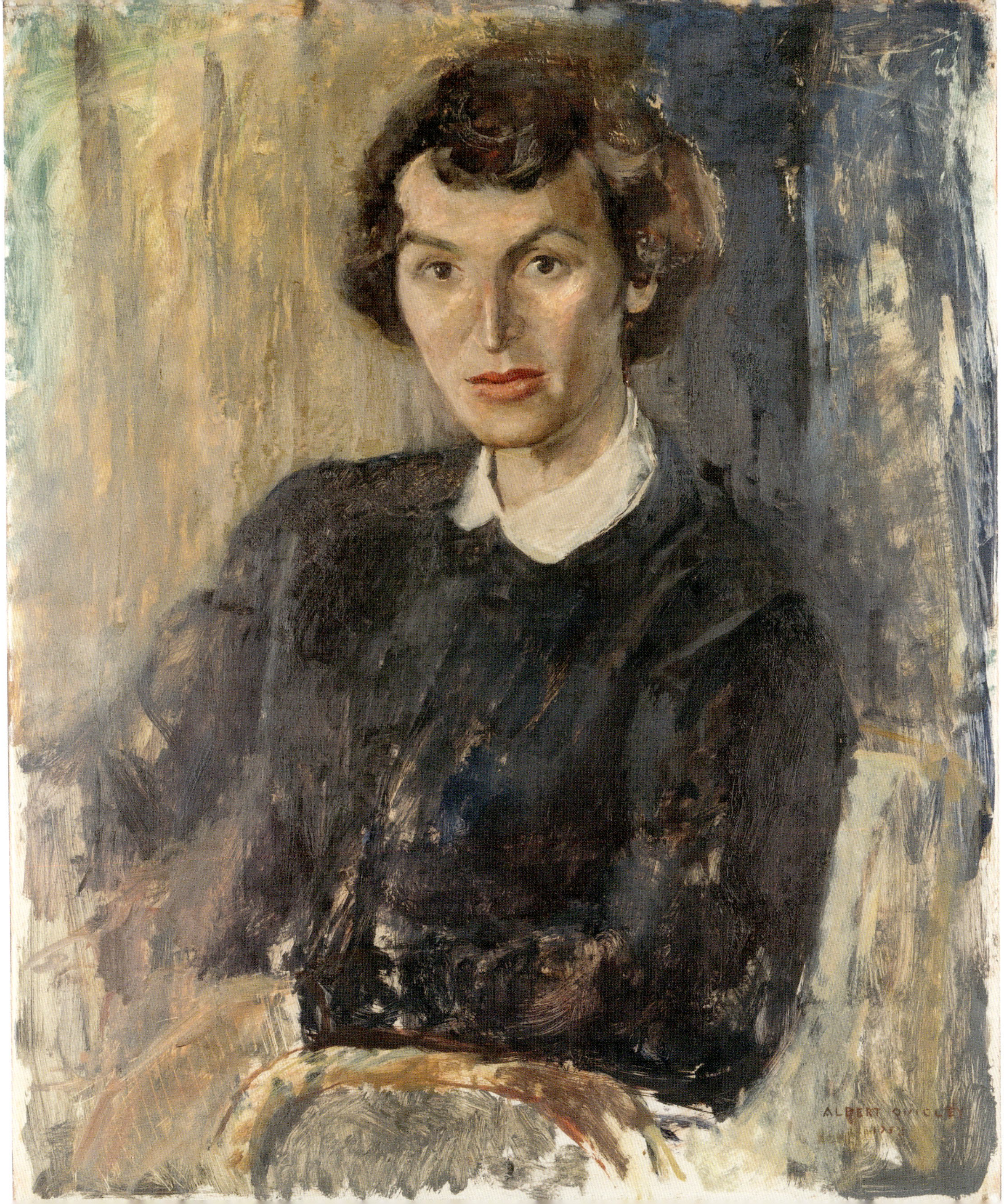

UNTITLED
Oil on board
Unframed
26 x 22 in.
Private collection

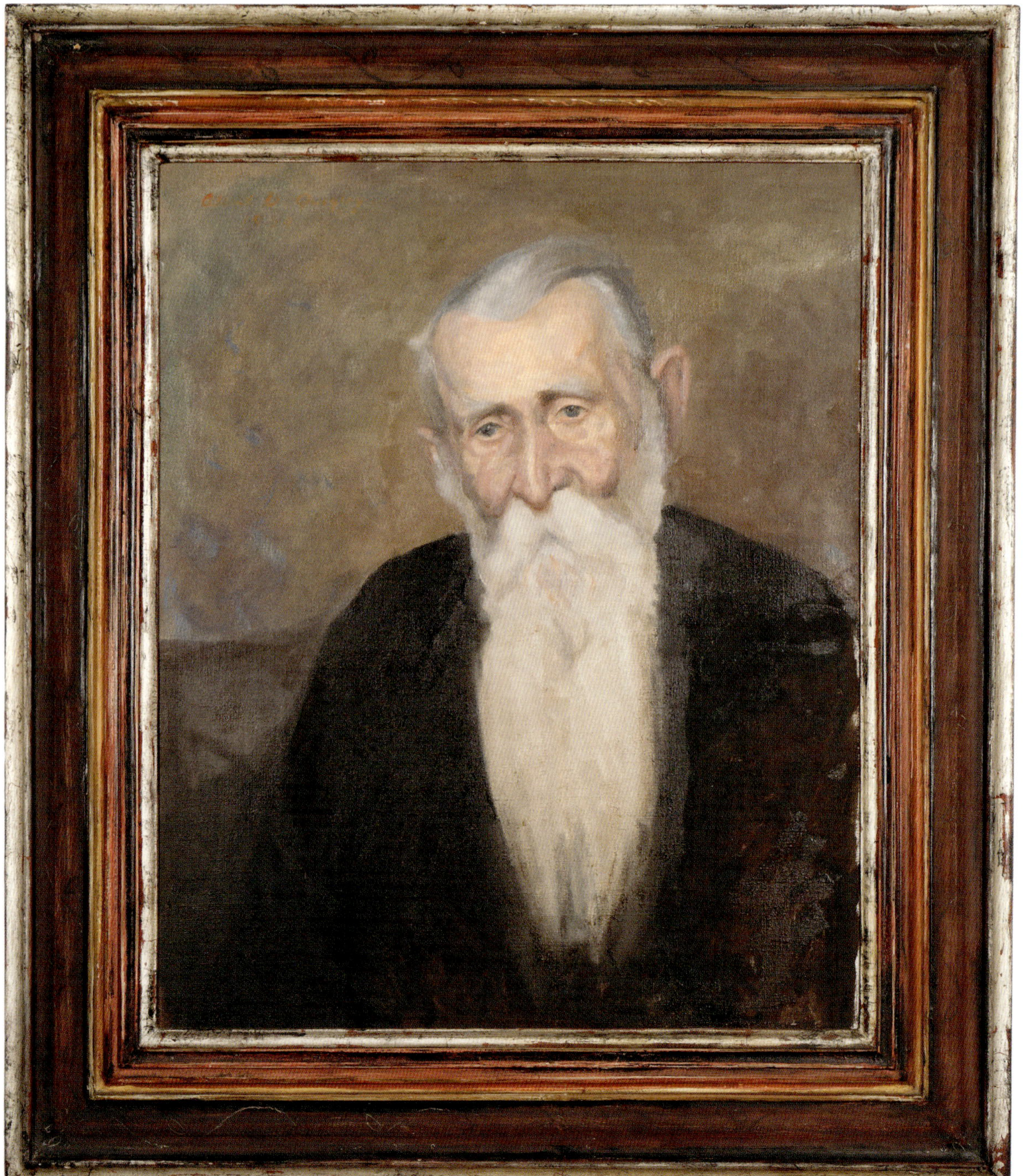

Rev. Millard Fillmore Hardy (1934)
Oil on canvas
Quigley frame, 32 x 28 in.
Nelson Congregational Church

Rev. Hardy (1850–1937) was a Nelson native and minister of the Nelson Church (1891–1893 and 1911–1930). According to Parke Hardy Struthers (editor of *A History of Nelson, New Hampshire: 1767–1967*), "Simple and sincere to the core, he speaks from a genuine spiritual experience." This painting was sponsored by the WPA Federal Art Project.

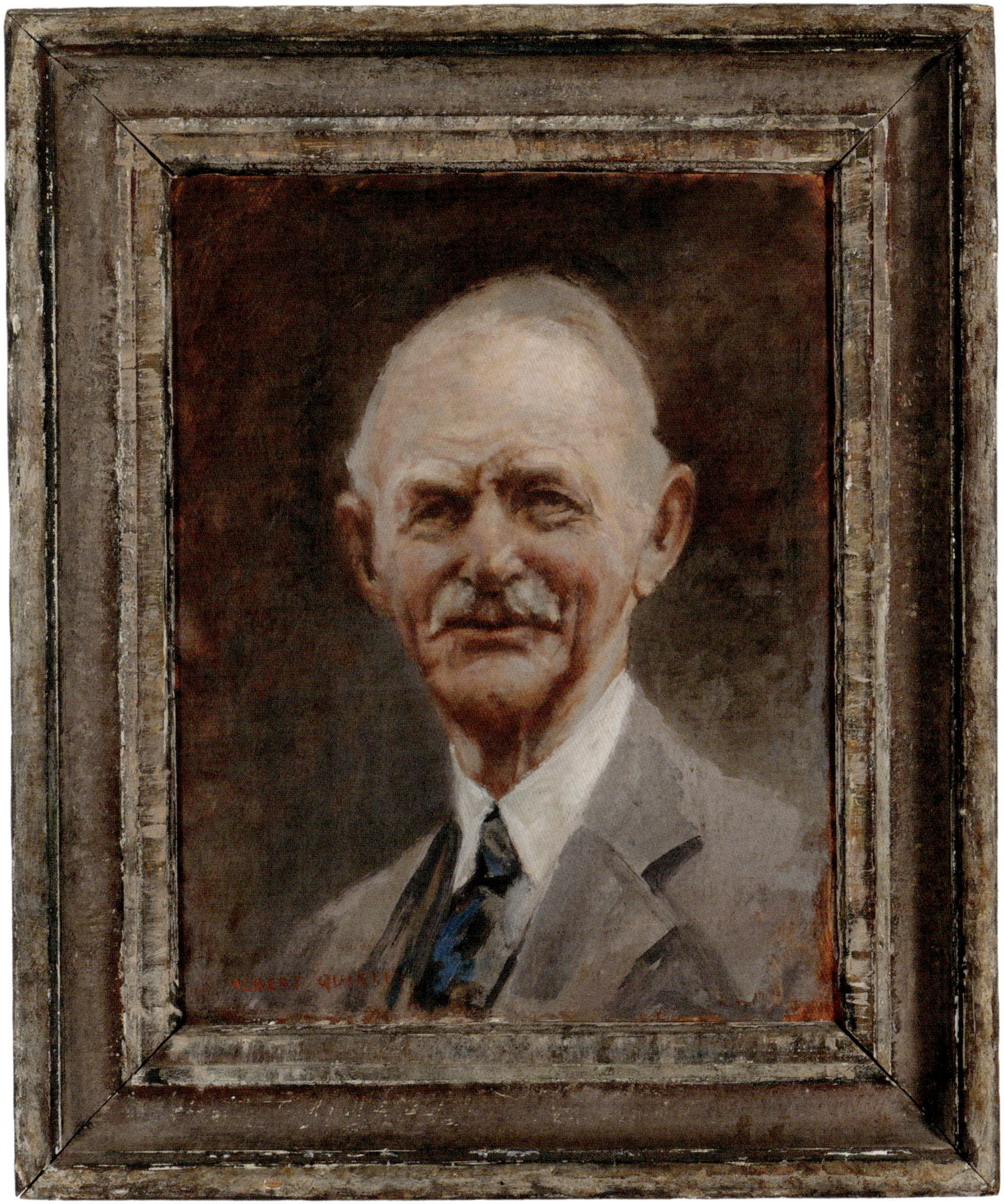

Wilmer Tolman (1870–1953)
Oil on board
Quigley frame
21 x 18 in.
Harvey and Frankie Tolman

Great-grandson of Ebenezer, grandson of Cyrus and son of Eben, Wilmer Tolman lived and died on the homestead in Nelson settled by his family in 1780. He followed his father as producer of lumber and shingles at their water-powered mill in Mosquitobush, an area in the southwest corner of Nelson (now part of Harrisville), developed a long-term lease plan for summer cabins on his property, served in the state legislature, and with his wife Etta, was a very active member of the community.

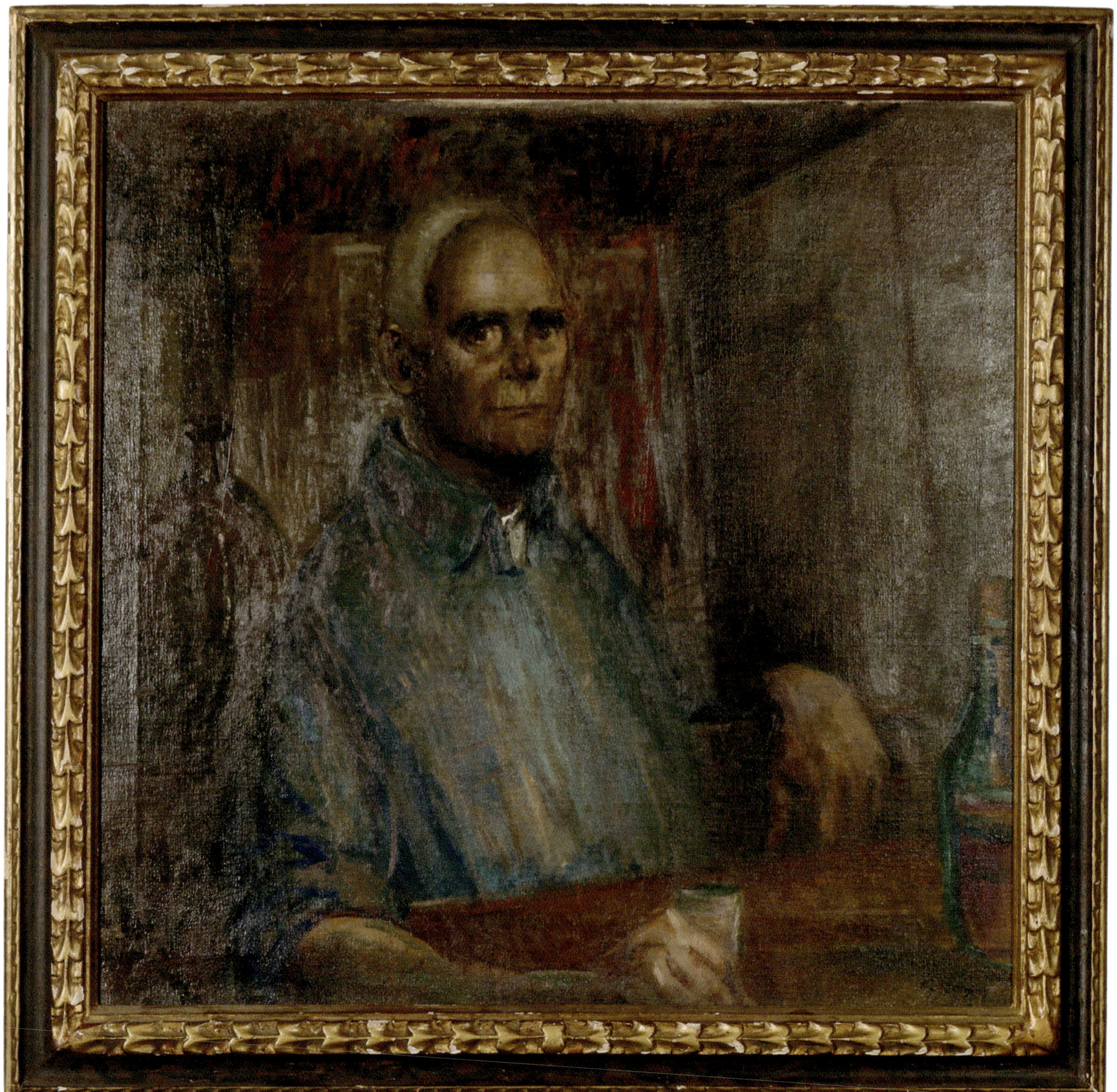

UNTITLED
Oil on canvas
26 x 27 in.
Mary Loftis and
Paul Tuller

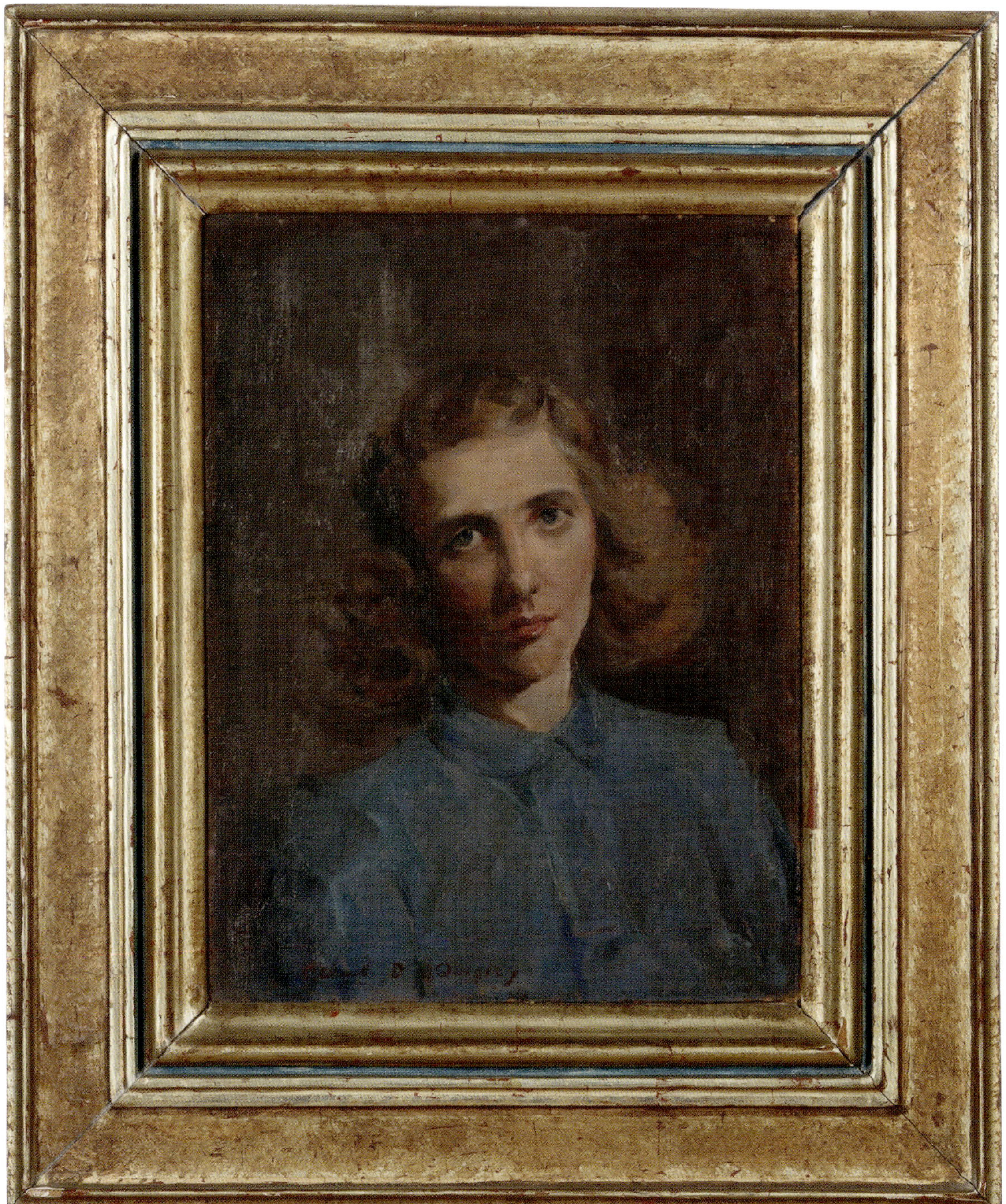

UNTITLED
Oil on board
Quigley frame
22 x 19 in.
Private collection

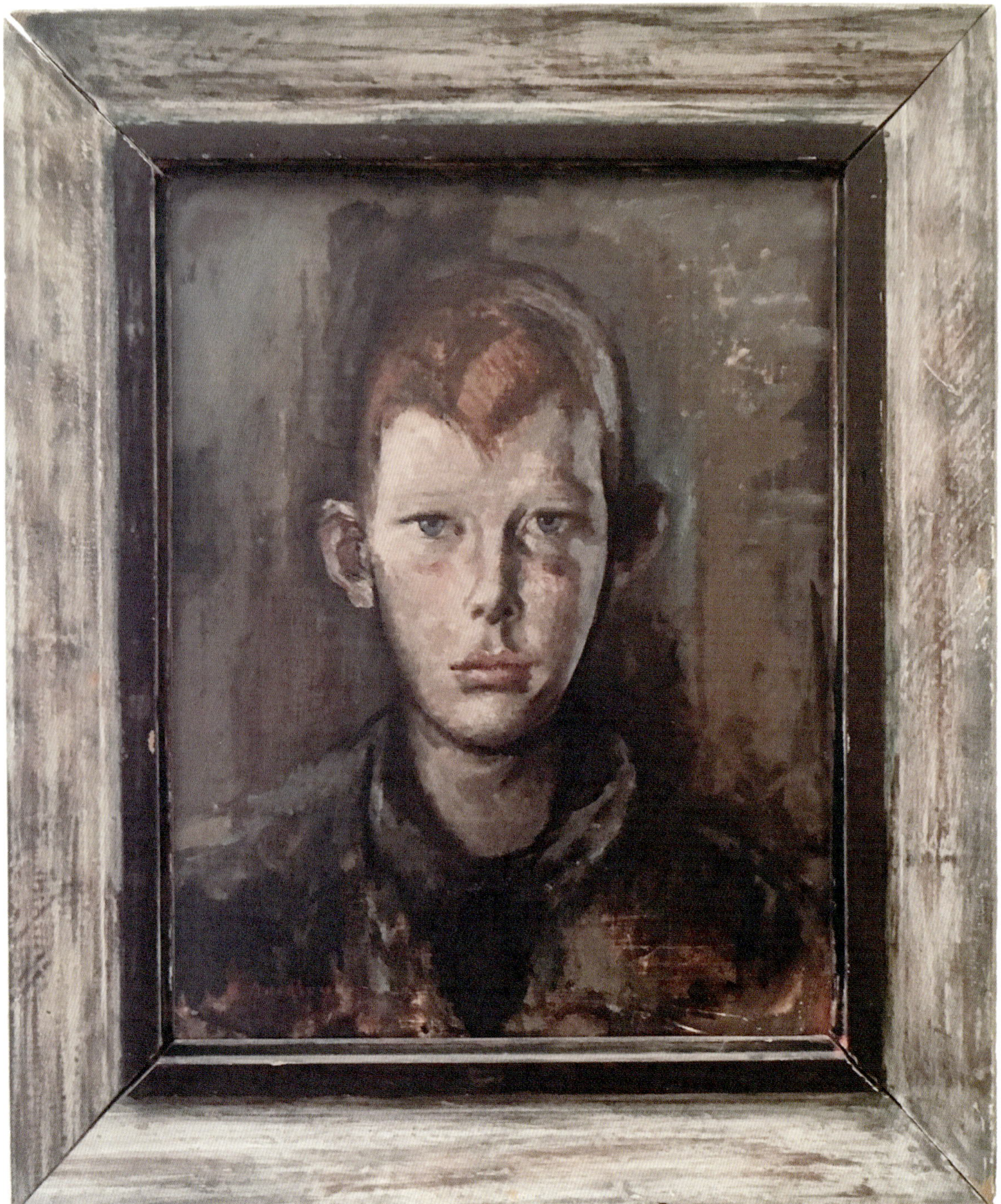

James Robinson (1960)
Oil on board
Quigley frame
24 x 18 in.
James Robinson
Courtesy photograph

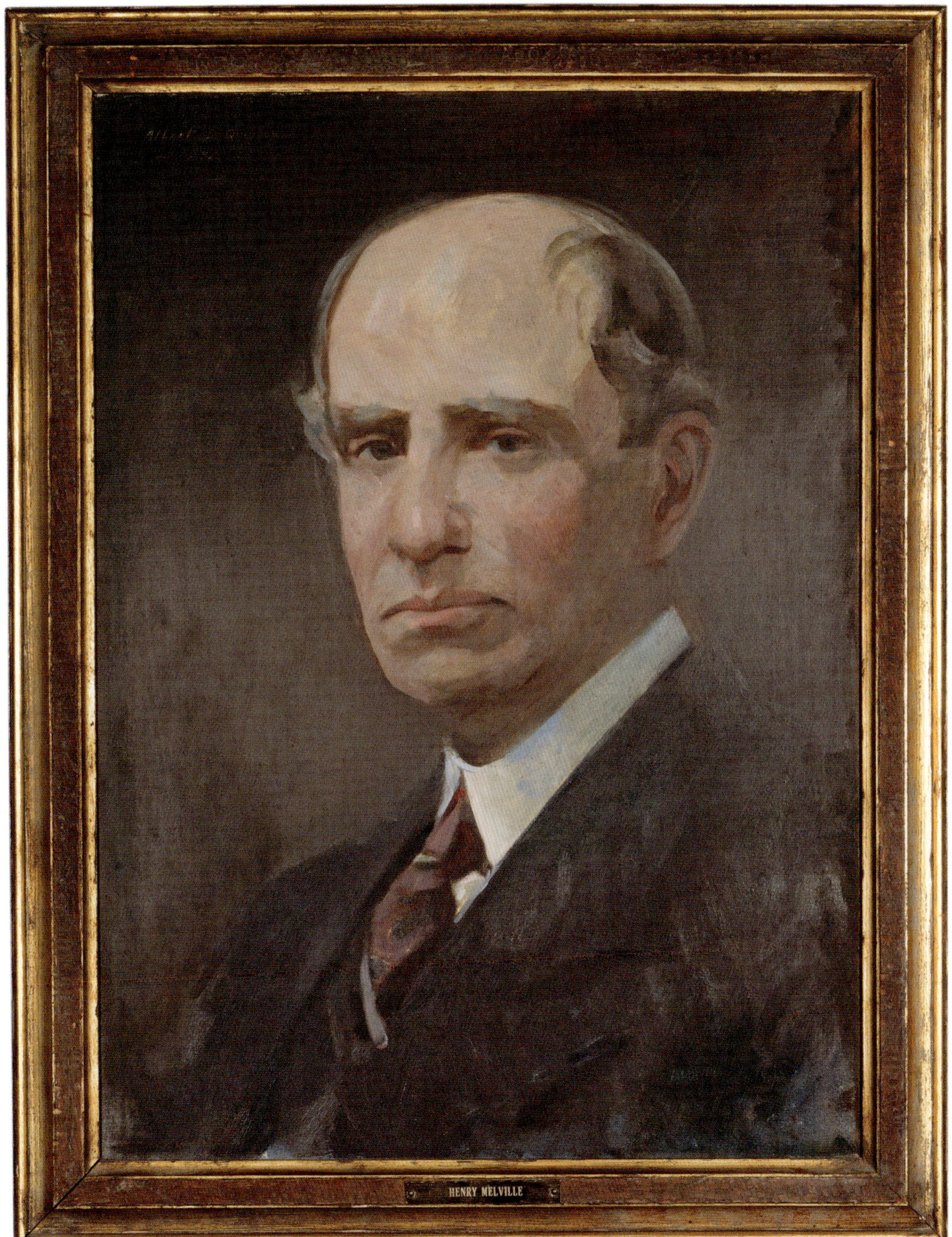

HENRY MELVILLE

Oil on canvas

Quigley frame

28 x 22 in.

Olivia Rodham
Memorial Library

Henry Melville (1858-1930) was born to a family that had settled in Nelson in 1790. After college and law school he became a prominent New York lawyer but maintained close ties to Nelson, frequently returning to the family homestead. He was a generous benefactor: in addition to donating the site for the original town library, he underwrote memorials to Nelson's Revolutionary and Civil War soldiers and sponsored numerous town improvement projects.

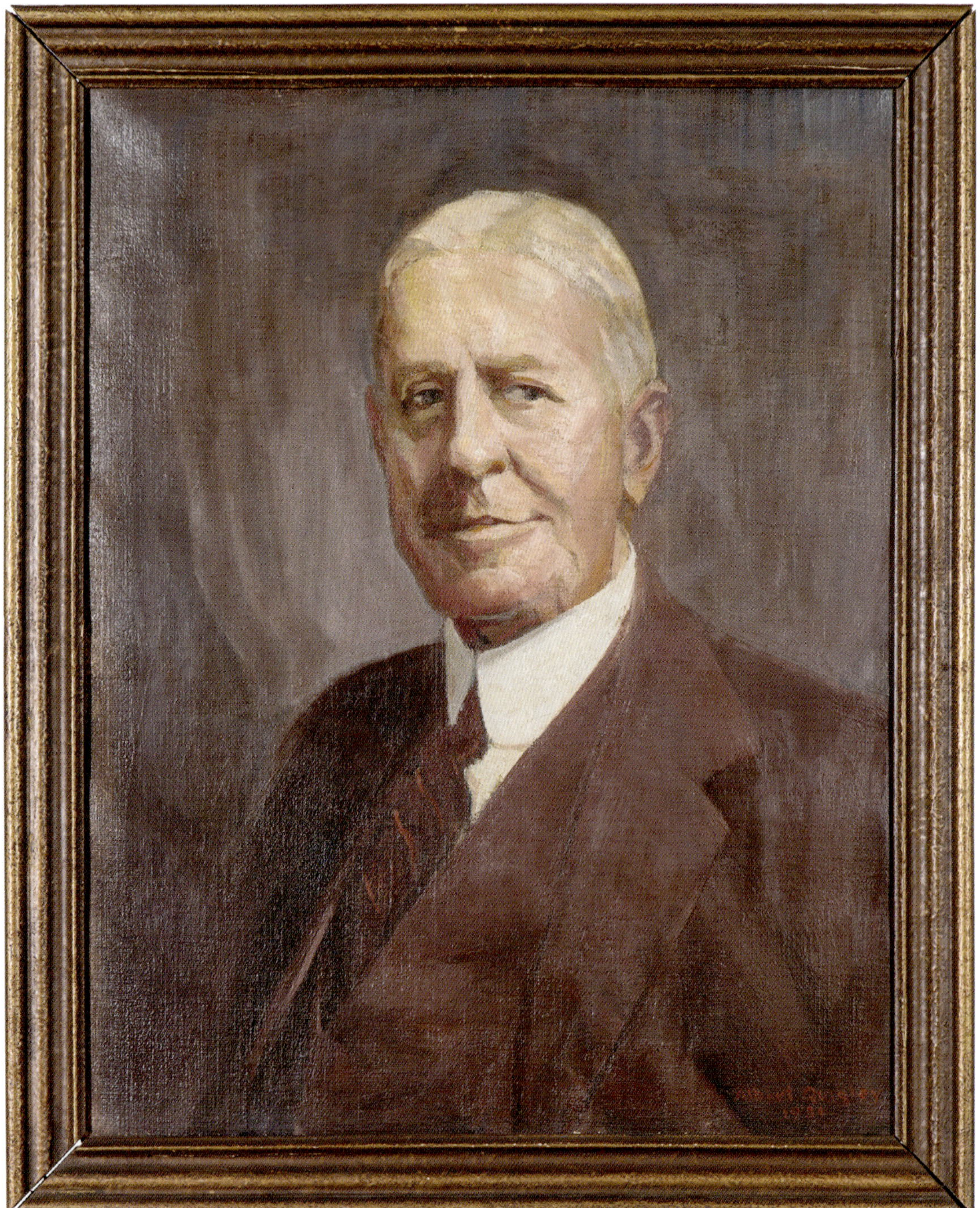

CHARLES GALE SHEDD (1931)
Oil on canvas
23 x 19 in.
Historical Society
of Cheshire County

The life of Charles Gale Shedd (1865-1930) centered on Keene. After high school, he became a pharmacist and remained with the same business for his entire career, eventually becoming a partner in The Bullard & Shedd Co. He was extraordinarily active in civic affairs, most prominently as president of the Keene City Council, mayor of Keene, member of both the New Hampshire House and the Senate. While in the Senate, he was responsible for legislation establishing the Keene Normal School, now Keene State College.

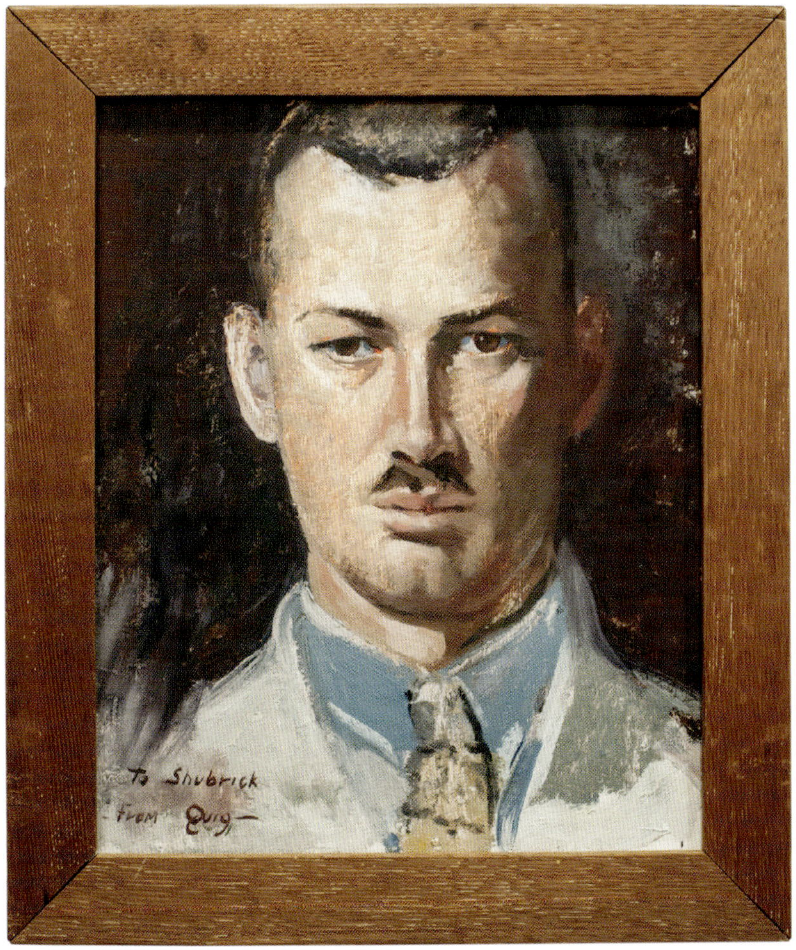

Shubrick Clymer
Oil on board
Private collection
Courtesy photograph

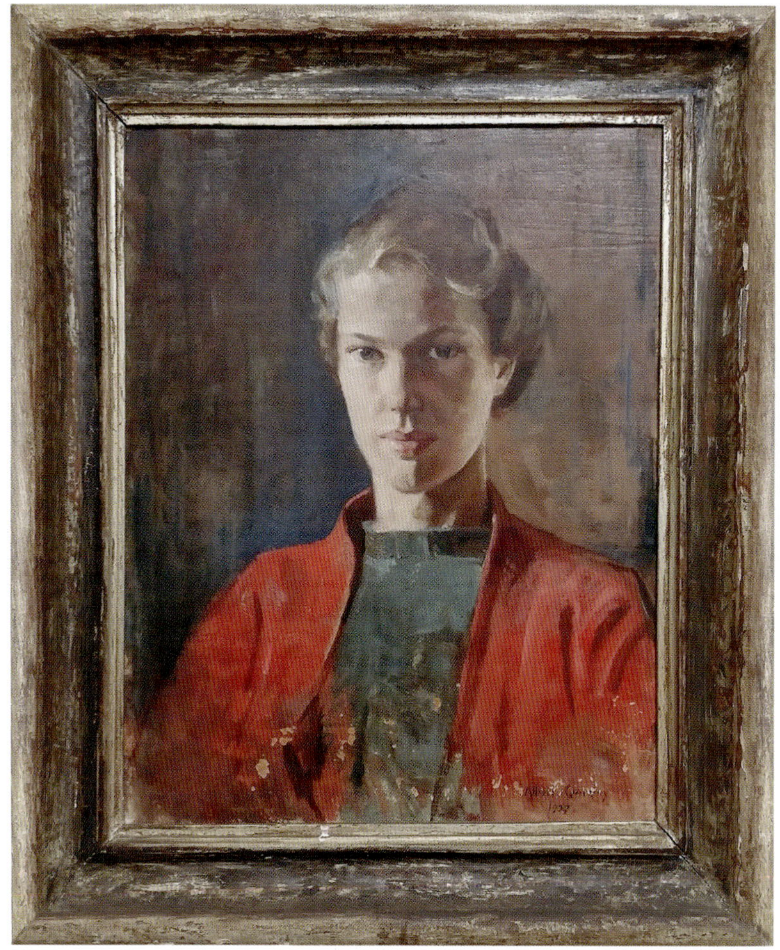

HENRIETTA FAULKNER (1927)
Oil on board
Quigley frame
26 x 22 in.
Private collection
Courtesy photograph

Sitting For Quig

That summer at Tolman Pond, I was nine years old. I recall swimming and catching frogs with my brother and other summer activities, but my most vivid memory is of climbing old stairs in a barn and sitting on a stool for several hours a day.

There I was, "sitting for Quig" as he painted my portrait. Raised as a Quaker, I did not find sitting still to be strange. I sat unmoving, but my eyes captured the shift of light through the barn windows from late morning to early afternoon, as I tried to be as helpful as possible, never disturbing his quiet, intensive process.

I was able to study his face as he studied mine. I memorized its gentle, kind lines, as he worked his brush.
We never spoke.

After one longer session, he stood back from the canvas and presented the finished work to my mother and me. We returned to pick up the portrait after the paint had dried, but that was not to be. In the brief interim, Quig had decided that he was not satisfied with the original and had begun painting another version of me over the original.

So, I climbed back up on the stool, and he began again.

What you see today is Quig's second, final portrait of me.

—Ellen R. Bowman, 2017

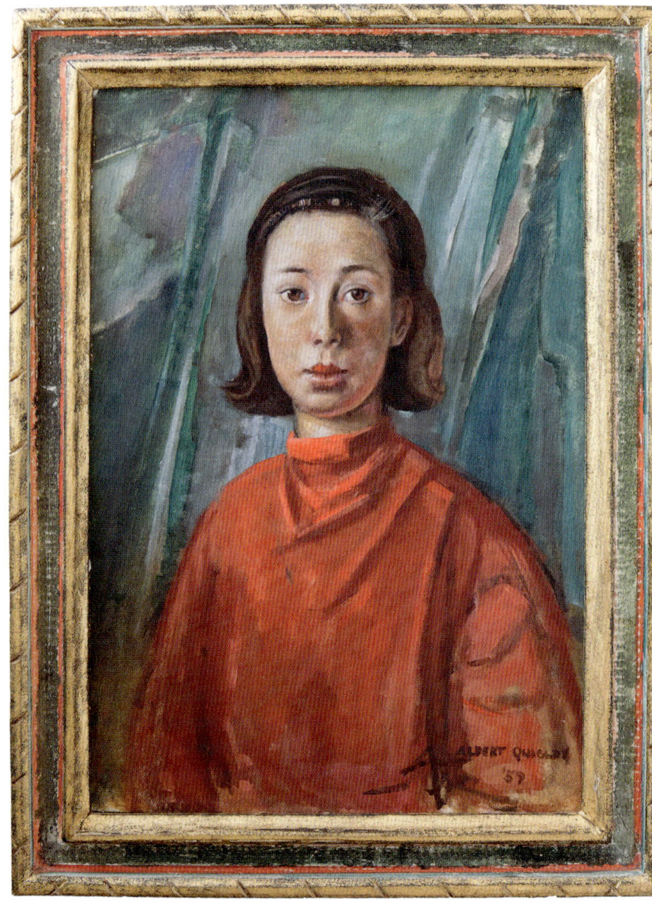

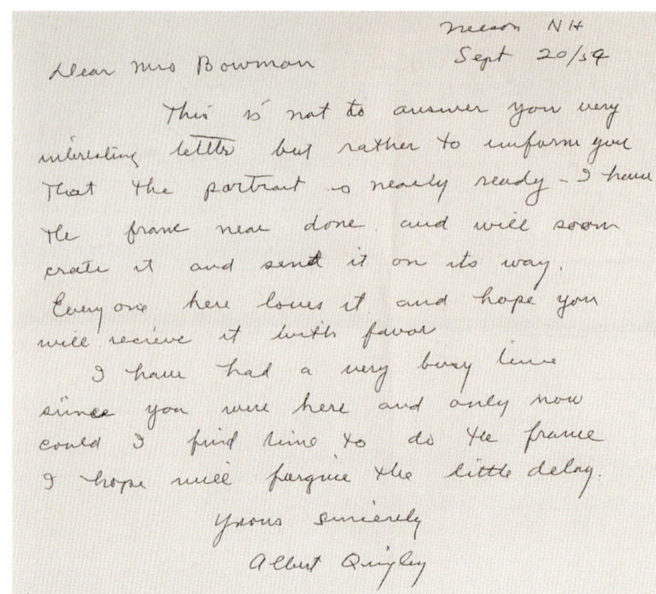

Nelson NH
Sept 20/54
Dear Mrs Bowman
This is not to answer your very interesting letter but rather to inform you that the portrait is nearly ready - I have the frame near done and will soon crate it and send it on its way.
Every one here loves it and hope you will receive it with favor
I have had a very busy time since you were here and only now could I find time to do the frame
I hope will forgive the little delay.
Yours sincerely
Albert Quigley

ABOVE RIGHT **ELLEN SITS FOR QUIG** (1954)
Oil on board, Quigley frame
29 x 22 in.
Ellen R. Bowman

RIGHT Letter to Mrs. Bowman,
originally attached to back of "Ellen Sits for Quig"

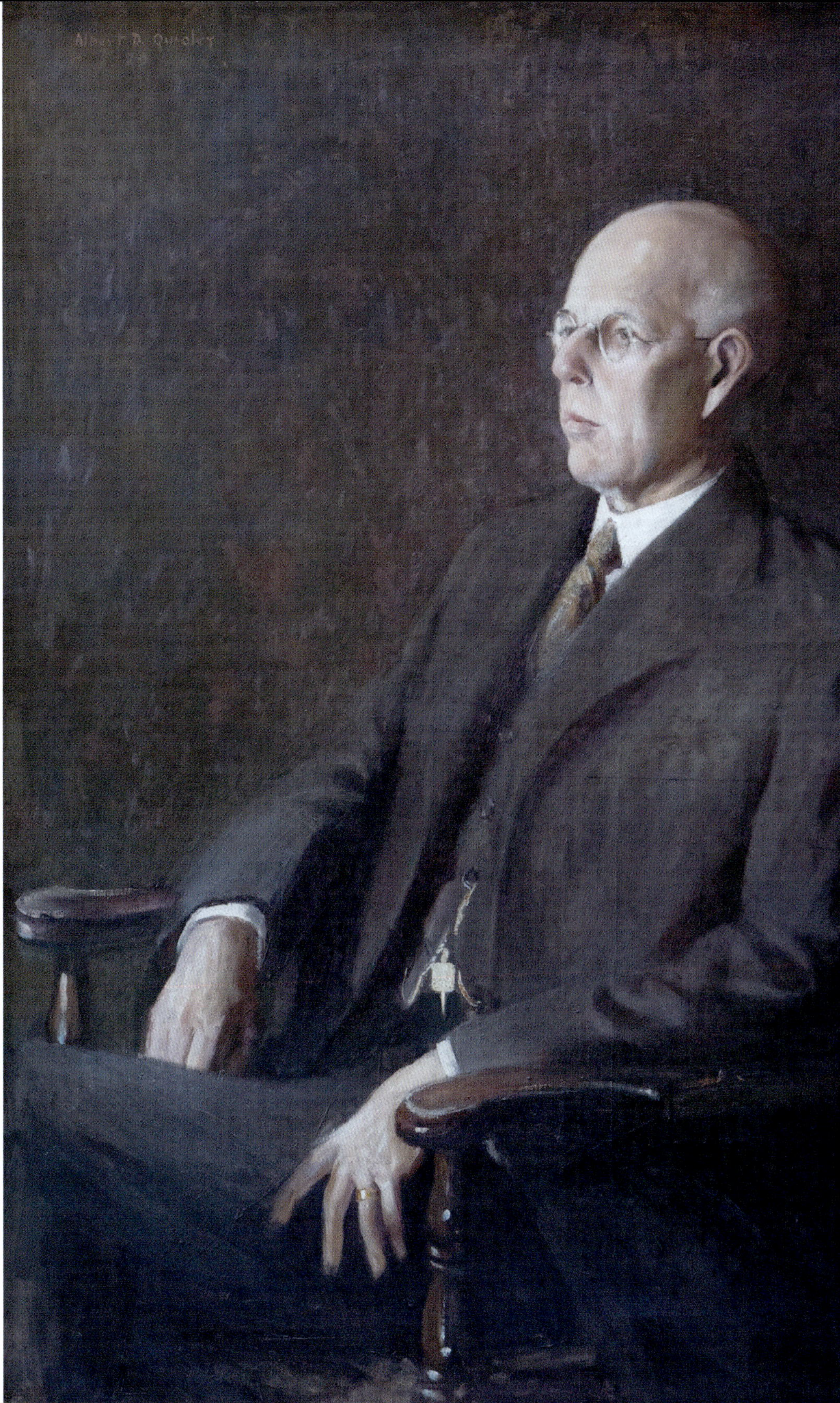

WALLACE E. MASON

Oil on canvas

49 x 39 in.

Thorne-Sagendorph Art Gallery
at Keene State College

Wallace E. Mason (1861-1944) was largely responsible for laying the foundation that enabled tiny Keene Normal School, founded solely to educate public school teachers, to become the diverse institution that is Keene State College today. A politically astute educator and lawyer, he served as the Normal School's second principal from 1911 to 1939, a time that sparked the rapid expansion of both the academic program and the buildings housing it. In recognition of his achievements, the Mason Library was named for him.

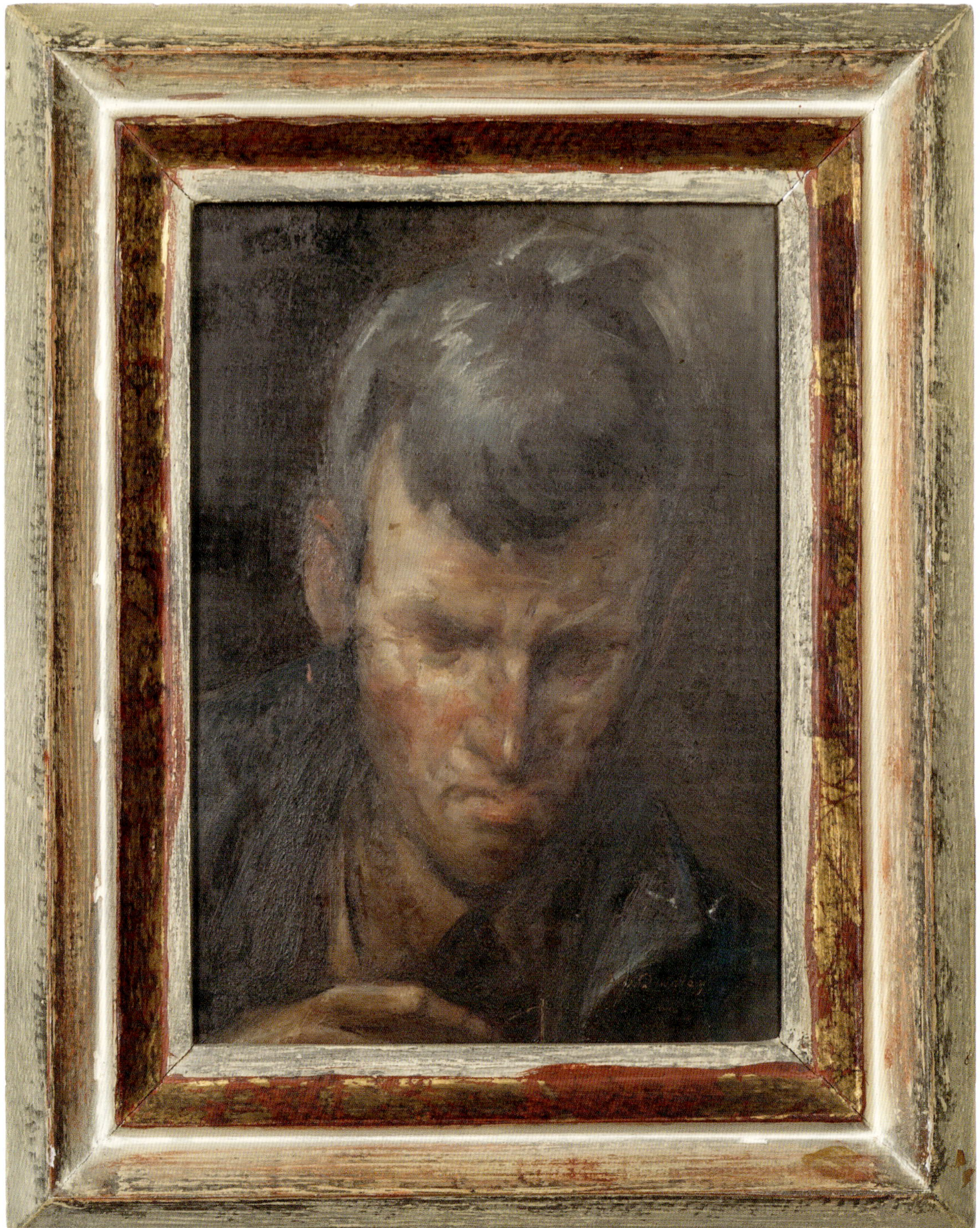

STUDY OF A HEAD
Oil on board
Quigley frame, 16 x 13 in.
Private collection
Board is part of an old pew door from the Munsonville church.

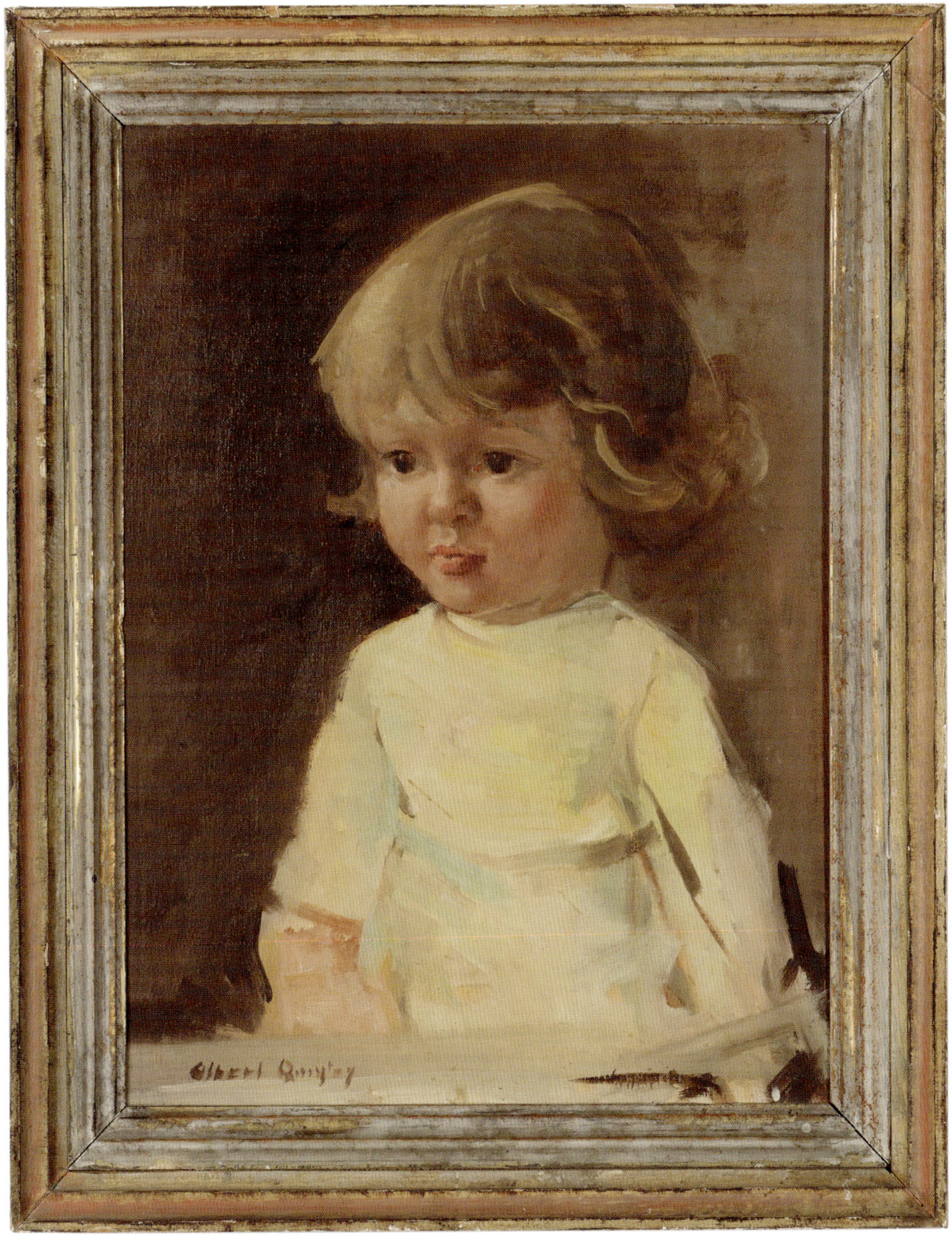

UNTITLED (1944)
Oil on board
Quigley frame
20 x 16 in.
Private collection

QUIGLEY'S REEL

"A current flows from bow to strings,
And the one-time tree happily sings."

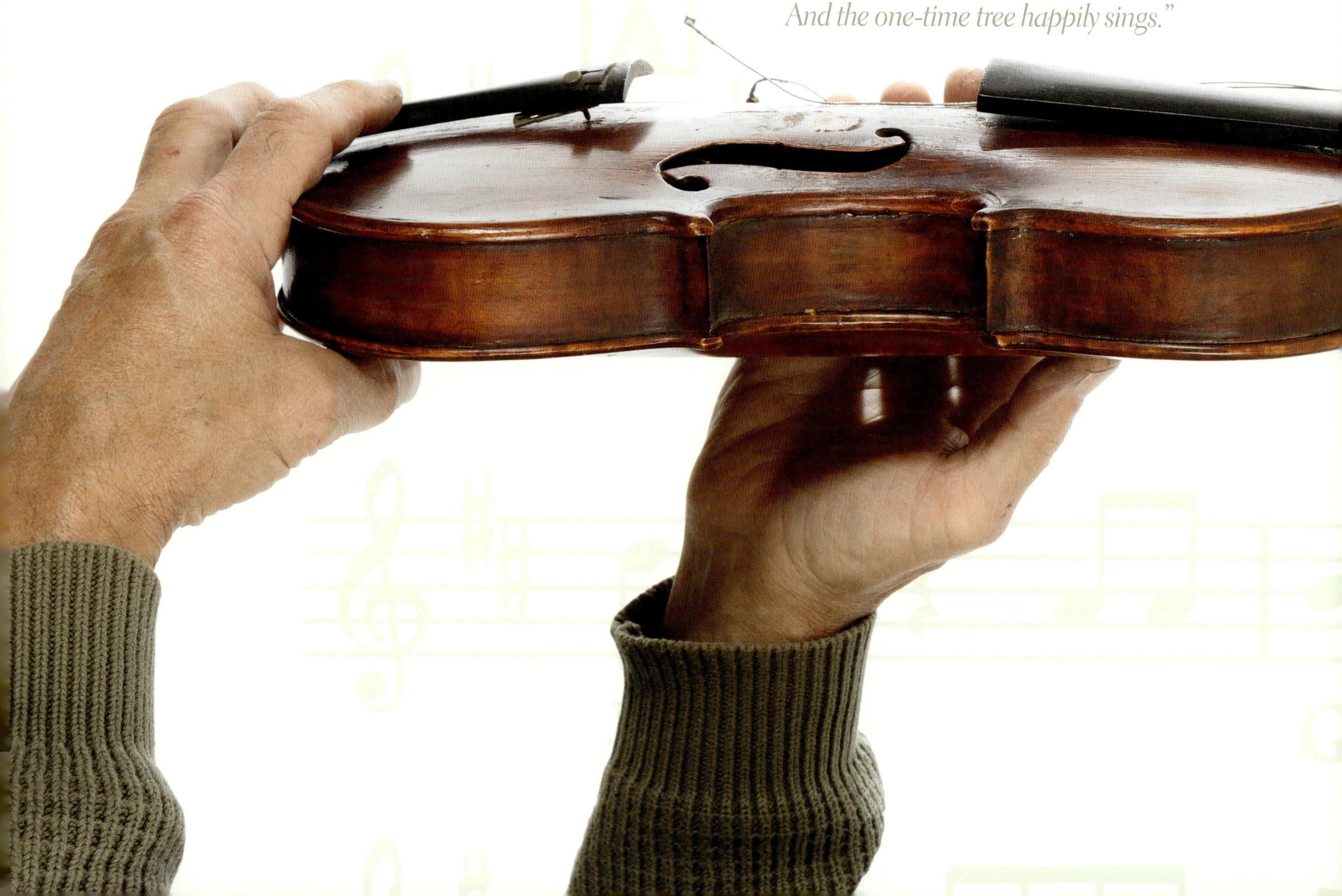

Music

From an interview with Renn Tolman, boatbuilder, musician, and author, March 23, 2014

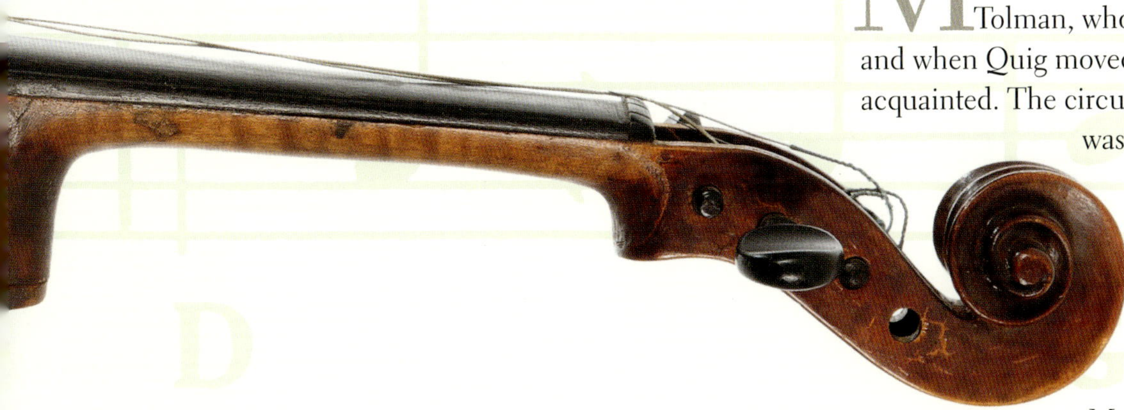

My name is Renn Tolman and I'm the son of Newt Tolman, who's a son of Nelson, New Hampshire, and when Quig moved to Nelson in the early '30s, they got acquainted. The circumstances are unclear—perhaps it was in some café in downtown Keene, or wherever. But there were only about sixty people in Nelson in those days, so there was a high probability of meeting one another.

Immediately upon meeting, it became apparent that Quig was from Maine and was a fiddler, and a very good fiddler. This delighted my father because there weren't many musicians to play with in those days. Newt played the flute at local square dances, but square dancing had mostly died out and he was absolutely thrilled to meet Quig, who was a musician of his own standing—which means that both of them had had what we might call classical training. They both had very good teachers who were cross-over players—that is that they would play both square dance music and a classical repertoire. In Quig's case, of course, it was Alvah Batchelder, and in my father's case, it was a cousin called Percy Folsom.

Albert Quigley's handmade violin
Brian and Jessie Quigley

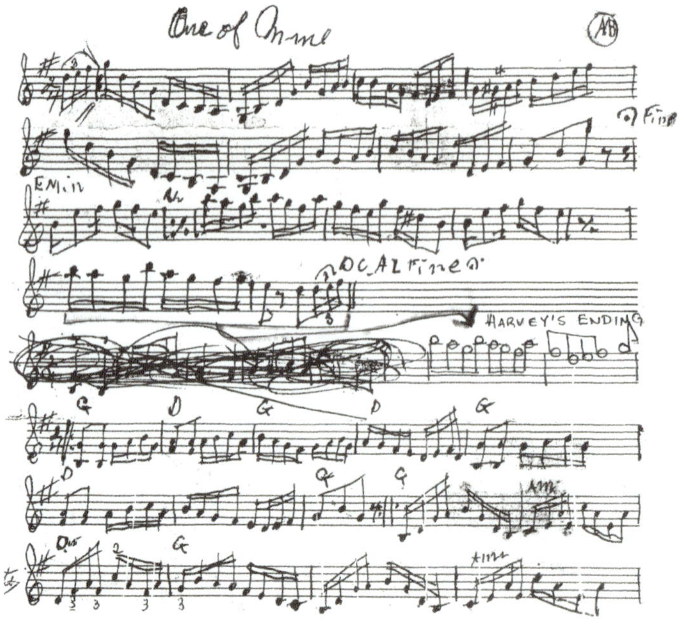

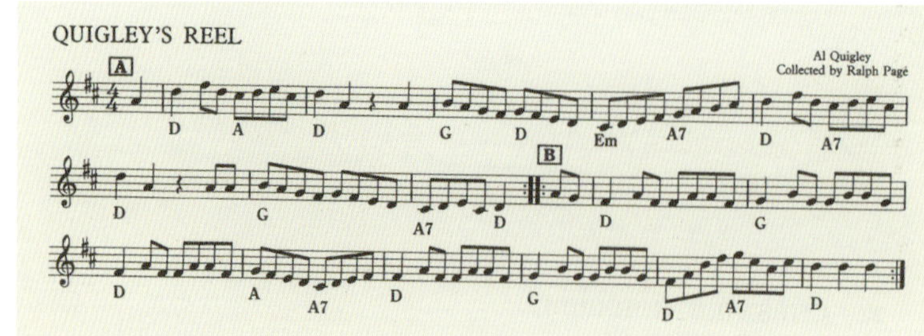

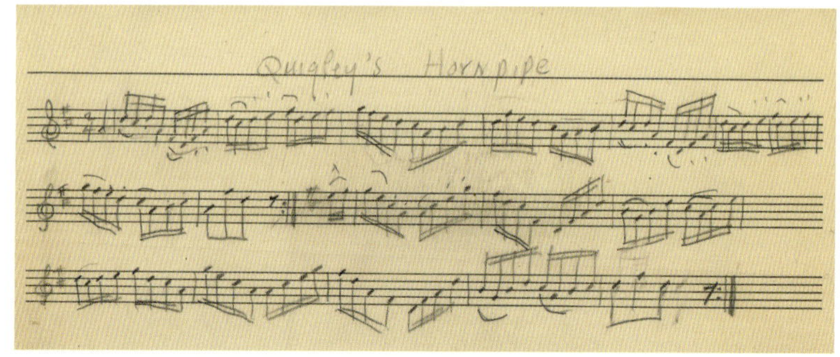

LEFT Albert Quigley's fiddle tune, "One of Mine," with Harvey Tolman ending Courtesy of Harvey Tolman

ABOVE RIGHT Fiddle tune, "Quigley's Reel," from The Ralph Page Book of Contras (English Folk Dance and Song Society, 1969)

BELOW RIGHT Fiddle tune, "Quigley's Hornpipe," in Albert Quigley's handwriting Courtesy of Harvey Tolman

Musically, they were kind of equals. So they had a great time playing together. Quig brought two tunes to Nelson that persist to this day—known far more widely throughout what's now known as the contra dance community. One is Ross's Reel. There are five Ross's Reels and we know that Alvah Batchelder knew them all and we know that Quig knew at least two of them, maybe more.

And with that Quig introduced a tune commonly called Batchelder's Hornpipe—not its original name, which was "Atlanta Hornpipe," but rather a version played by Batchelder—which was passed on to Quig.[1] Both of these tunes Quig made very popular and taught to my father. Everyone played them, and today they are still played, and are a mainstay of contra dance music with a strong Nelson association.

Another tune that Quig brought to Nelson from Alvah Batchelder, whose name is uncertain, but on the handwritten manuscript it just says One of Mine. The significance of this is that the terminology on the manuscript is in Italian which indicates that he had a musical education, and was anything but a country fiddler.

My father makes the point that when Quig first came from Maine, he was an extremely sharp fiddler, and they got a group together and played for a few years. This was the very first part of Ralph Page's career. Ralph Page was the most famous square dance caller of his generation, which lasted well into 1986. But in the early 1930s he was just getting started, so he and Quig and Newt, and Newt's brother Fran who played the piano, got together and played around. As things went along, Newt sort of dropped out and Ralph Page became famous and Quig

1. According to the Batchelder Violins website (www.batcheldervIolins.com), "The tune became so firmly associated with Quigley that it eventually gained the alternate title of 'Quigley's Reel.'"

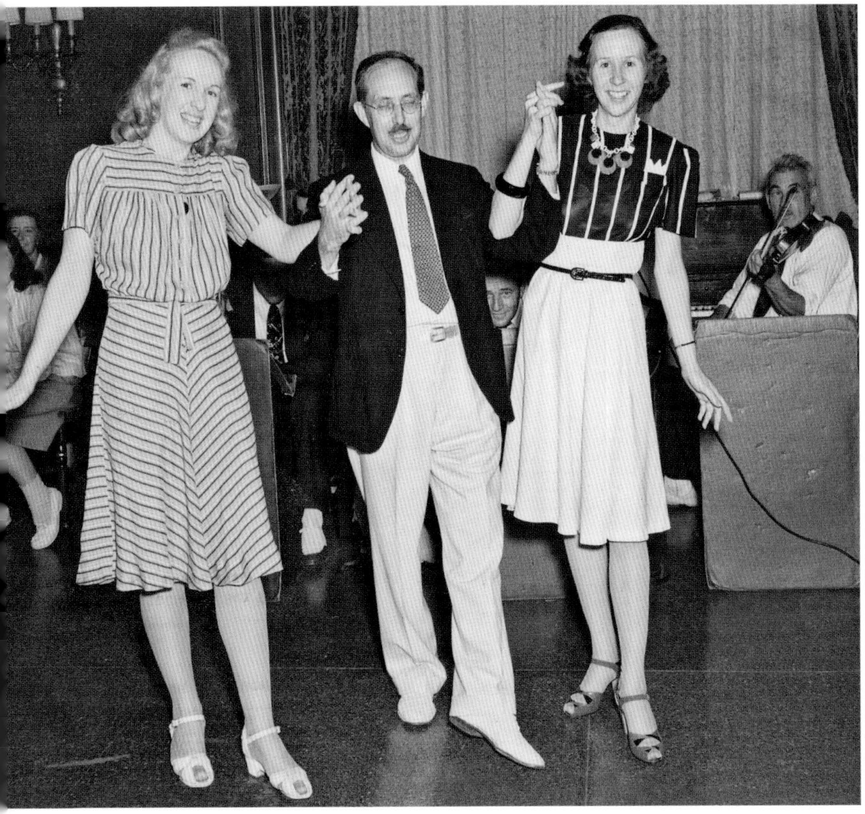

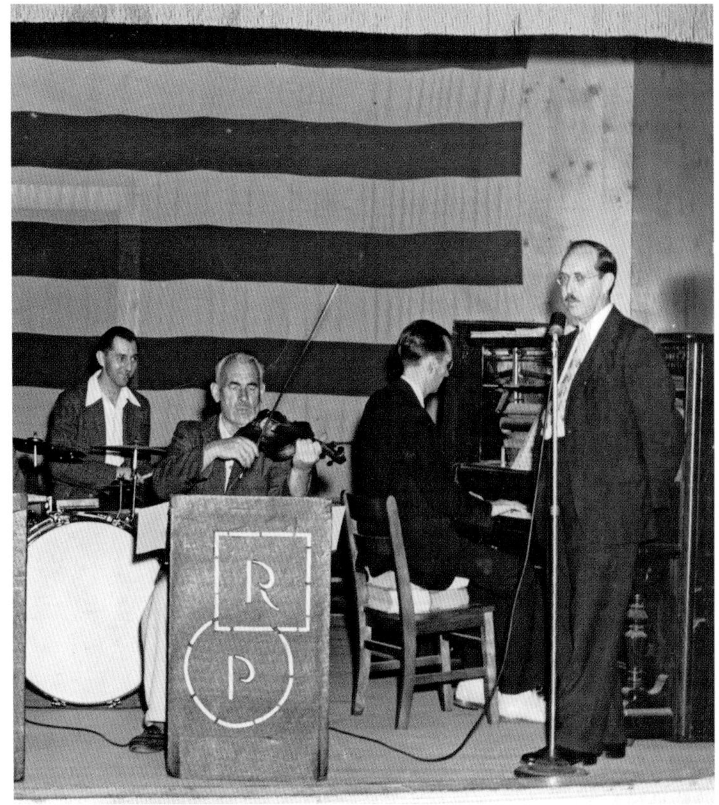

LEFT Albert Quigley plays and Ralph Page dances at a contra dance around 1950. Courtesy of Historical Society of Cheshire County

RIGHT Ralph Page Orchestra with Albert Quigley on fiddle Chesterfield Town Hall, August, 1943
Courtesy of Historical Society of Cheshire County

played for Ralph—sometimes seven nights a week.

Paradoxically, his fiddling declined. Although he was fiddling a lot, the caller's job was to specify what the band would play, and they increasingly became singing callers and wanted songs that they could sing with. They didn't want the old reels and jigs and hornpipes. They liked pop tunes and the same tunes had to be played over and over again, for every dance, so for a time, Quig never got the chance to play the tunes like Batchelder's Hornpipe or the Ross' Reels."

About 1943, when there were no longer any dances in Nelson, and after a dance in neighboring East Sullivan at Bushey's Hall—the local blacksmith who had a dance hall attached to the back of his house—where Newt had played in a pick-up orchestra, my folks thought there should be dances in Nelson again. There had been dances in Nelson in the past, but they had died out when World War II came along.

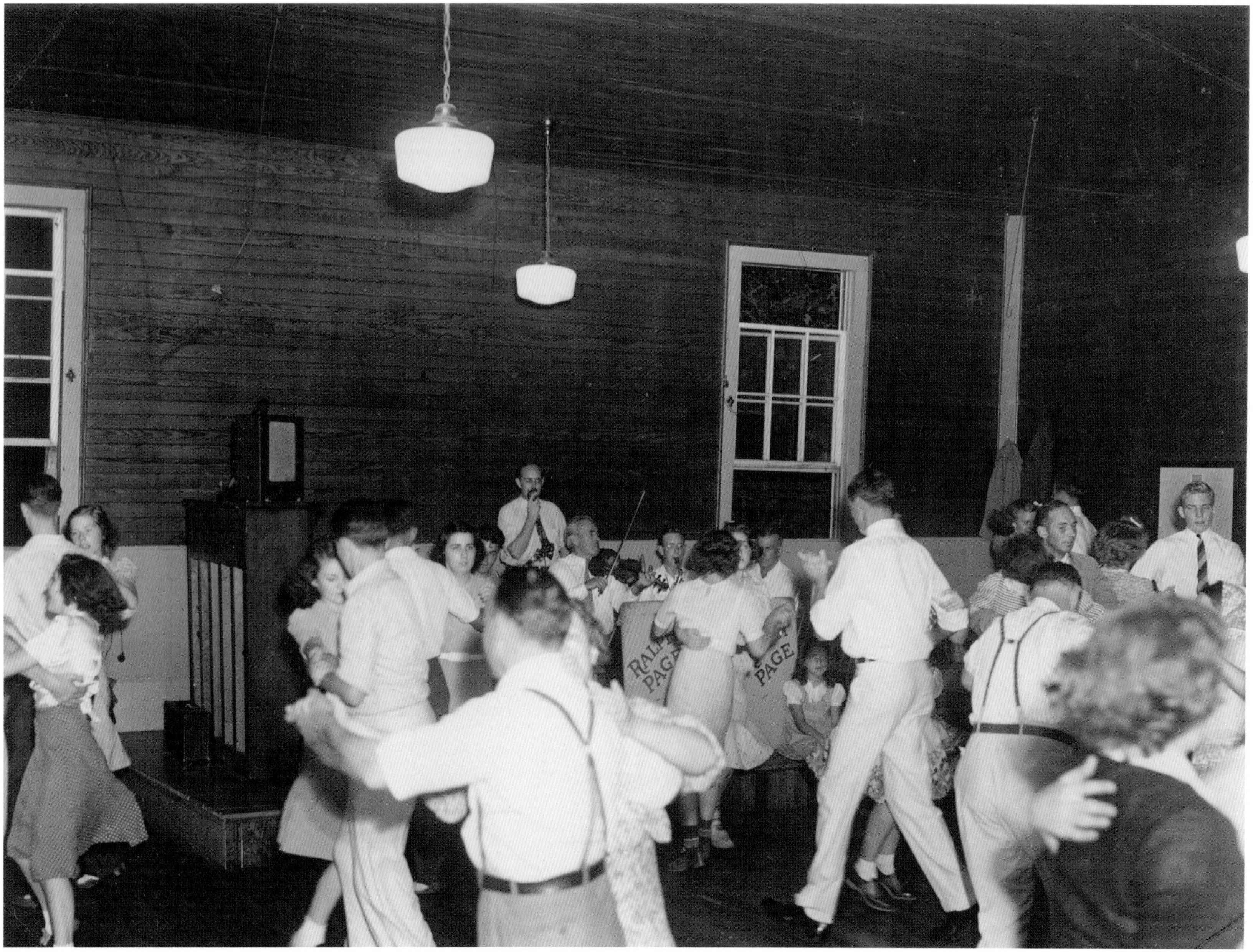

Dancing in the Nelson Town Hall, 1940s
Albert Quigley on fiddle and Ralph Page calling
Courtesy of Tolman Pond Archives

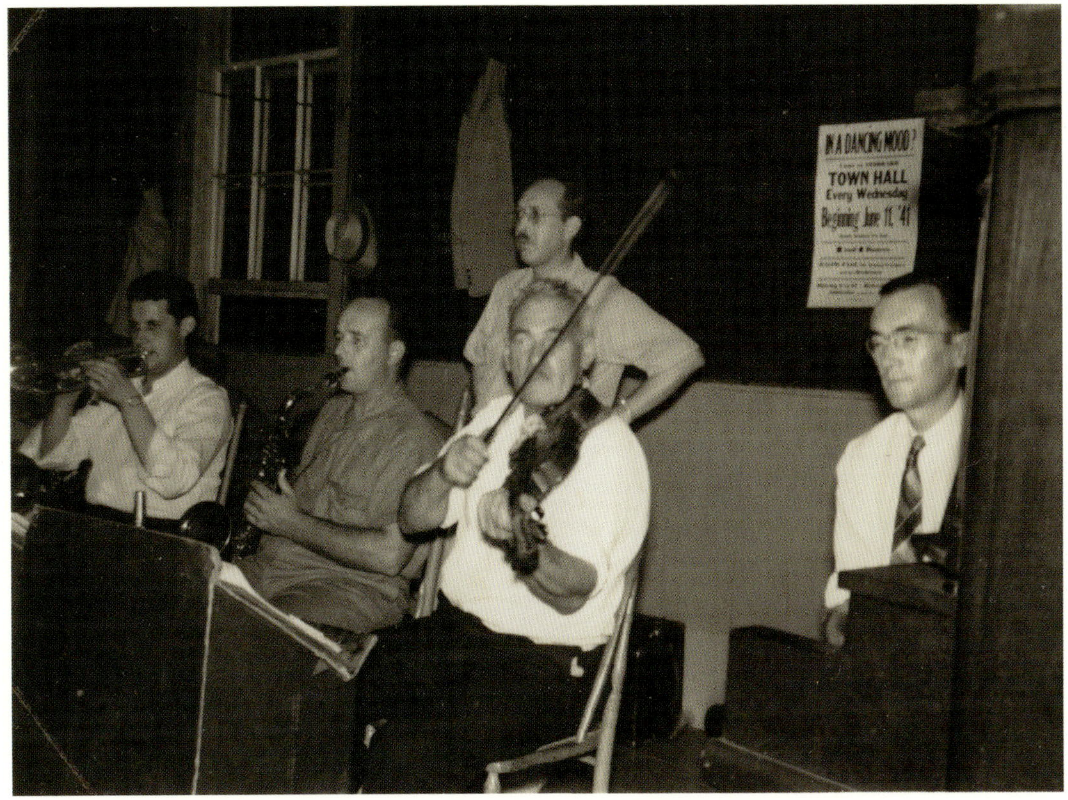

Albert Quigley on fiddle
Ralph Page standing
Courtesy of Tolman Pond Archives

My folks decided to run dances every Saturday night for one year in the Nelson Town Hall, which was a dubious proposition! Quig had been playing a lot for Ralph Page, but had recently cut way back and was available Saturday nights. He lived in the house next to the Town Hall, so it was very handy for him. He didn't even have to put his coat on. He could pick up his fiddle, walk out the door and around into the Town Hall.

I was a fourteen-year-old, just taking up the flute and trying to sit in with the band. What I remember about that era is that while we were setting up the hall, which involved lighting a fire in the woodstove in the winter, Quig would come over and go into an alcove at the back of the hall to practice. I remember him playing these wonderful tunes that he brought with him from Maine, but he never got a chance to play them for the dances because the caller told him what he had to play. Anyway, a lot of these tunes were so good and so intricate that they stuck in my head. And years later, when I got some more literature on the music, I ran into these tunes. I then learned them and play them today. However, the tragedy of it was that here were very good musicians who never really got a chance to show their stuff.

Rarely did they get to play these songs in public, but once in a while Newt and Quig got together to play them. But I remember one occasion they got invited to play for the Dublin Ladies' Club, which was a pretty upscale organization in nearby Dublin. It was quite an honor to get to play there, so Newt and Quig got together to have a little rehearsal beforehand. So when they got up on the stage, Quig turned to Newt and said, "You know I got thinking of a real neat tune that we didn't play the other night." And right away, he just started to play it. Newt was up to the occasion. He was very good at improvisation and harmony and that kind of thing. Newt hadn't ever heard of the tune, but he just played

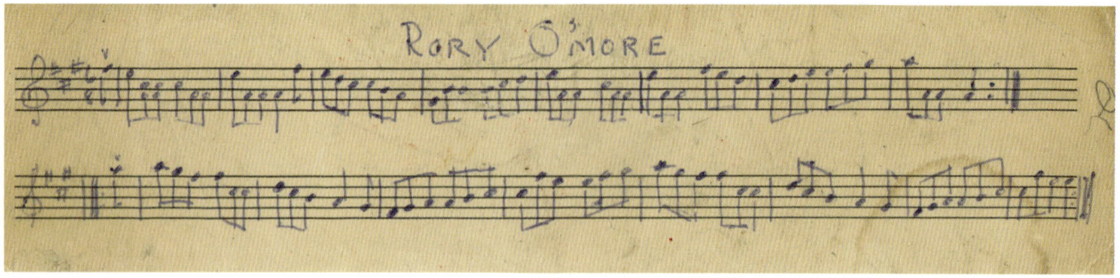

TRADITIONAL AND ETHNIC SQUARE DANCE MUSIC OF NEW ENGLAND 1955-1957

Side 1
The Nelson Square Dance Orchestra
Ross's Reel #4
Batchelder's Reel
Durang's Hornpipe
Speed the Plow

ABOVE LEFT Fiddle tune, "Rory O'More," in Albert Quigley's handwriting Courtesy of Harvey Tolman

ABOVE/BELOW RIGHT Cassette tape insert: Traditional and Ethnic Square Dance Music of New England, 1955–1957 Courtesy of Dudley Laufman

along. Then Quig said, "That reminds me of another one." And then he played another. And so it went. They never did get to play the tunes they rehearsed. Somehow they pulled it off very well at the Ladies' Club.

To get back to the dances in Nelson, I remember one night the caller was Larry Pickett from Keene—once the mayor of Keene who later went on to become a state-wide politician. As the caller, Larry was calling the shots, and at every dance, he'd call for a tune called "Rory O'More." Quig hated it and if you could see Quig's face—I can still see it to this day. But the protocol of the day was that you never complained to the caller!

This was about 1946 and it was a great thing in my life. I got to hear Quig play for a year and it was a great inspiration.

I was recently asked if Quig had ever been recorded. I understand that one time a guy did come to Quig's house and they had quite a lengthy recording session back in the days of reel-to-reel tape recording and the guy was apparently a very good recording artist. They recorded from around 8:00 in the evening and they were still going strong after midnight. Shortly thereafter his house burned down and all of his equipment and recordings with it.

THE NELSON SQUARE DANCE ORCHESTRA. Newton F. Tolman, flute, lives in Nelson, N.H. He is a writer, dog trainer, licensed guide, and musician. With Kay Gilbert he has published THE NELSON MUSIC COLLECTION, a book of square dance tunes, and a recording by the same title. His son Renn, flute, from Nelson when this recording was made, now lives in Alaska. Francis Tolman, piano, Newt's brother, lived in Nelson until his death. He was a guide and wood engraver and served in the state legislature. Albert Quigley lived beside the Nelson Town Hall until he died. He played fiddle for dances, worked in the mill at Harrisville, and was a landscape painter. Dudley Laufman, accordion, lived in Concord, N.H. at the time of these recordings. He now lives with Patty in Canterbury, N.H. where they play for dances.

But Quig also got recorded one time in the 1950s, here where we are today at the farmhouse at Tolman Pond (Nelson, New Hampshire). Dudley Laufman, musician and dance caller, somehow came by a reel-to-reel tape recorder and asked to record us. So we all showed up here at the farm and called ourselves the Nelson Square Dance Orchestra: my father, Newt Tolman, who played the flute; my uncle, Fran Tolman, who played the piano; Quig, who played the fiddle; Dudley Laufman, who played the accordion; and myself on the flute. It was a short session—ten or fifteen minutes long. Dudley later produced a cassette tape called *Traditional and Ethnic Square Dance Music of New England: 1955–1957*, and our band on the tape was the first of two.

• • •

During the three years . . . 1935–1938 as Editor of *Yankee Magazine* . . . I, along with the square dance caller Ralph Page, wrote a series of *Yankee* articles on country dancing, eventually published as *The Country Dance Book,* charmingly illustrated by Fran Tolman's line drawings. The books enjoyed five or six editions and served to make Ralph Page the most sought-after caller in New England.

Here, I should mention the weekly square dances we held in the Nelson Town Hall (Nelson, New Hampshire). For these, the Tolman orchestra (Newt on the flute, Fran on the piano, and Pop [Wayland] on the drums, with Albert Quigley (Quig) on the fiddle) furnished the music, while the caller was Ralph Page, protégé of Uncle Wally Dunn, who had been the chief caller of the region for years. It wasn't long after we began the weekly dances that the country dance mania swept New England.

—*Beth Barrell*
(Newt Tolman's first wife) from Family Notes

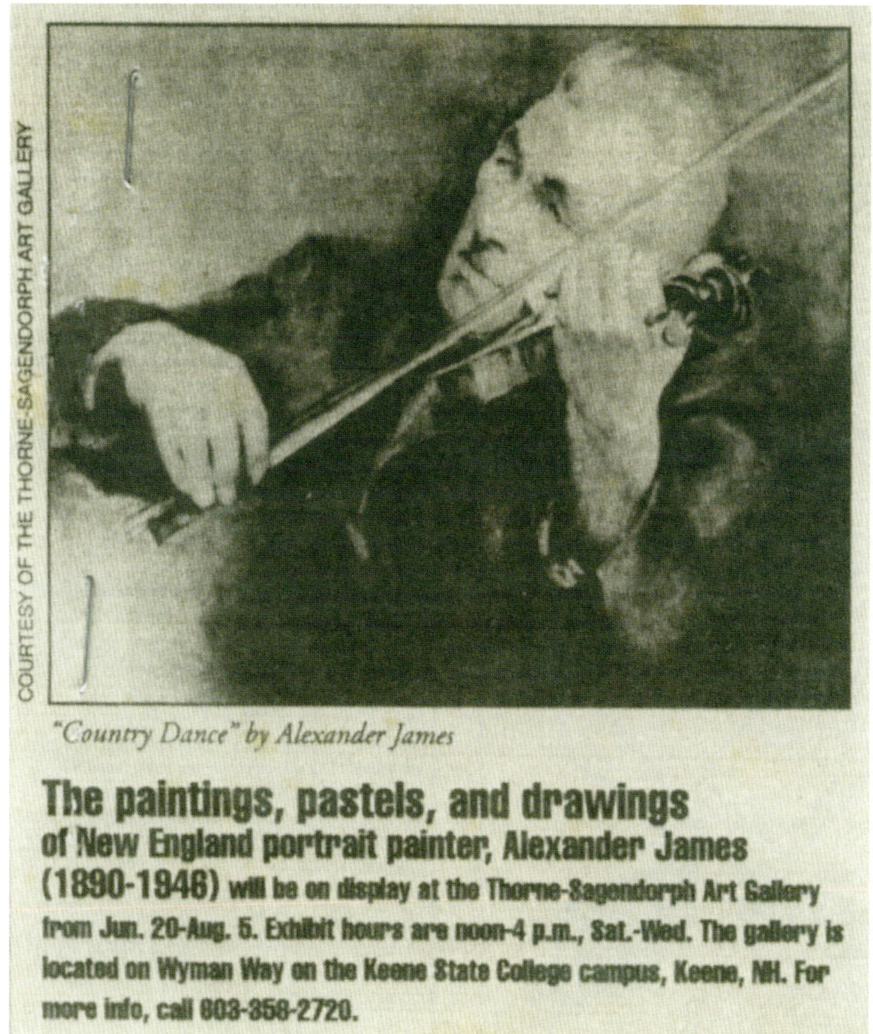
COURTESY OF THE THORNE-SAGENDORPH ART GALLERY

"Country Dance" by Alexander James

The paintings, pastels, and drawings of New England portrait painter, Alexander James (1890-1946) will be on display at the Thorne-Sagendorph Art Gallery from Jun. 20-Aug. 5. Exhibit hours are noon-4 p.m., Sat.-Wed. The gallery is located on Wyman Way on the Keene State College campus, Keene, NH. For more info, call 603-358-2720.

COUNTRY DANCE by Alexander James
Newspaper clipping advertising the exhibit by the Thorne-Sagendorph Art Gallery, 1980

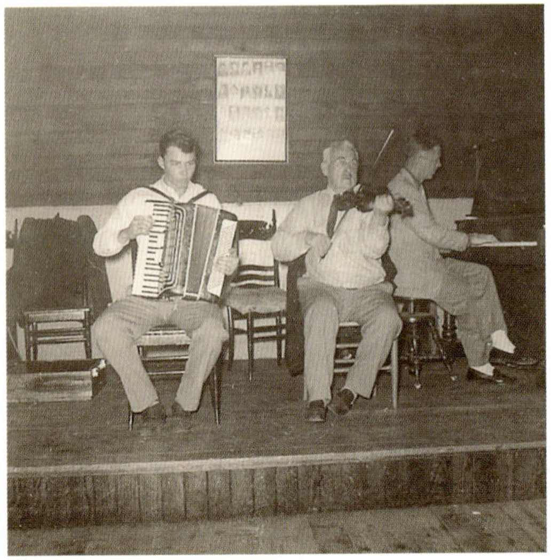

Dudley Laufman
Albert Quigley
Fran Tolman
Courtesy of
Dudley Laufman

Quig, Early 1950s

by Dudley Laufman

I took Greta Klinteberg, a lithesome Swedish girl from Melrose, Massachusetts, to a dance at the Fitchburg Quadrille Club in Fitchburg, Massachusetts. The dance had started when we got there. We could hear the Williams twins clicking away with the taps on their shoes as we climbed the stairs to the hall. Ralph Page was the caller. He had quite a line-up for musicians. In the front row were five fiddlers. Dick Richardson from Marlboro, Russ Allen from Keene, Al Quigley from Nelson, Llewelyn Powers from Brookline, and Will Ayers from Fitchburg. (Will was a former semi-pro baseball player.) They all had a head of white hair except Dick who had a fringe that was white. Llewelyn had long white hair. Their ages combined was 400 years. Junior Richardson was at string bass and Johnny Trombley was at keyboard. The five fiddlers were in a row, Quig in the middle leading the pack. What a sound.

It was April first and a Saturday night to boot. Ralph was having fun with the dancers. "Next dance is 'The Morning Star,' first, third, fifth, every other couple is active, do not cross over, right hand balance and swing." He did this four or five times, then stopped, said, "The top of the set is now at the other end of the hall, figure it out," and started the music right off, barely giving the dancers time to figure out who was active. After a while of this, he stopped, said "Top of the set over here on the right-hand side of the hall." And so on. Then "Next dance will be 'The Roberts.'" But the orchestra played "The Rye Waltz." Five fiddles playing "The Rye Waltz," with just enough New Hampshire roughness to it to tickle me. I couldn't dance it. I just had to go lean against the stage and take in all that wonderful rich music. I said to Greta, I said "Greta, I would love to dance this with you, but I just have to absorb this, if you want to go dance with Art Williams, I'm sure he will accommodate you." But Greta chose to lean with me against the stage and soak up that great music.

His strong right arm bows us a tune.
His fingers, to labor, not immune,
Apply pressure to a taut fiddle string,
That makes his violin resinously sing.
A current flows from bow to strings,
And the one-time tree happily sings.

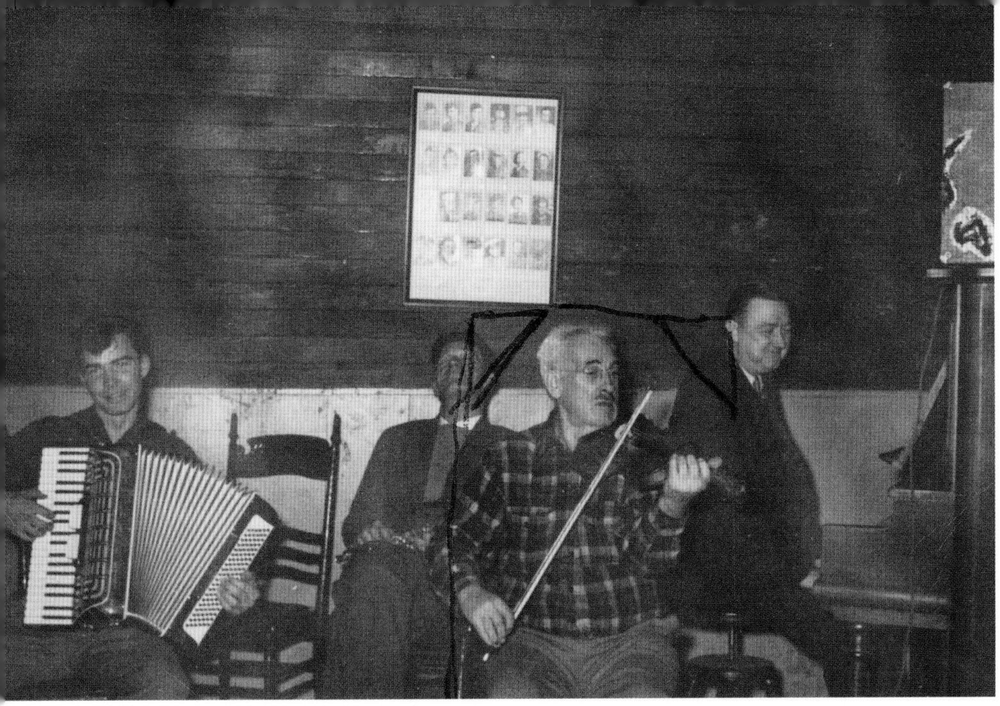

Dudley Laufman, Newt Tolman, Quigley on fiddle (noted by blue marker) and piano player Courtesy of Dudley Laufman

His quick-moving fingers cause bodies to dance;
O the skirl of his fiddle quickens romance.

These same fingers that flourish the bow,
Also hold brushes, patiently and slow.
He paints for us, pictures of the local lands,
And makes frames for them with his wood-loving hands.

If ancient sound waves could be snatched from air,
And his old tunes were still vibrating there,
We could capture his old reels, from memory, gone,
And bring back haunts of his country dance song.

He plays today in Vermont and Maine,
And in those green hills his gifts remain.
But in an old hall in New Hampshire's land,
His fiddle sings best, what the feet demand.

It was quite a place in the kitchen there. I remember I used to stop and visit with Quig and Mildred and they seemed always friendly and there were fiddles everywhere. Most of them were taken apart and one day Quig said, "Here, I want you to have this one." So I was happy to get it, of course, and he said, "Take it home and see what you can do with it." So I did take it home and I struggled with it for a while. And when I stopped in again, he'd say, "How's that fiddle coming?' And, I'd say, "Well, it's not really coming." So he'd get out a music book, usually Cole's 1000 Fiddle Tunes—the only book that was around in those days. And the big table in the kitchen was covered with fiddle parts, breakfast dishes and stuff. He'd just push it all aside so that he could put the book down and I'd struggle to try to read out of it. As I remember I didn't make too much headway at the time—this was probably in 1959—and it wasn't too long after that that Quig died.

—Harvey Tolman, fiddler
2007 New Hampshire Folk Heritage Award winner
from an interview on March 23, 2014

—Dudley Laufman, dance caller, musician, and writer
2009 NEA National Heritage Fellow
2007 Country Dance and Song Society
Lifetime Contribution, 2001 NH Governor's
Arts Award for Lifetime Achievement

In the early '30s a fine fiddler and artist from Maine named Albert Quigley moved to town. Quig knew a lot of the old square dance tunes, and he and Newt became friends. One day one or the other came up with a rare treat for those days, a bottle of liquor. So they invited some friends and had a music session. The venue was Quig's tumbledown cider mill by White's Brook. The bottle went 'round, the music picked up. Darkness came—there were no lights—and suddenly out of the gloom came square dance calls, loud, clear, in perfect time (no small accomplishment since the call must anticipate the music). It was Ralph Page, a young, local unemployed ne'er-do-well, as Newt characterized him. Until then no one had ever heard Ralph call. But there was a connection: Ralph was the nephew of Wallace Dunn, the last of the old-time square dance "prompters," as callers were then called. Wallace had died a half dozen years before and square dancing in Nelson had for the most part died with him. But the calls survived in Ralph's memory.

A band was formed . . . . The band (it had no name) not only played in Nelson, but was popular enough to play in other dance halls all over southwestern New Hampshire and even some nearby in Vermont and Massachusetts.

—*Renn Tolman,* Newt Tolman and the Haynes Flute, 2013

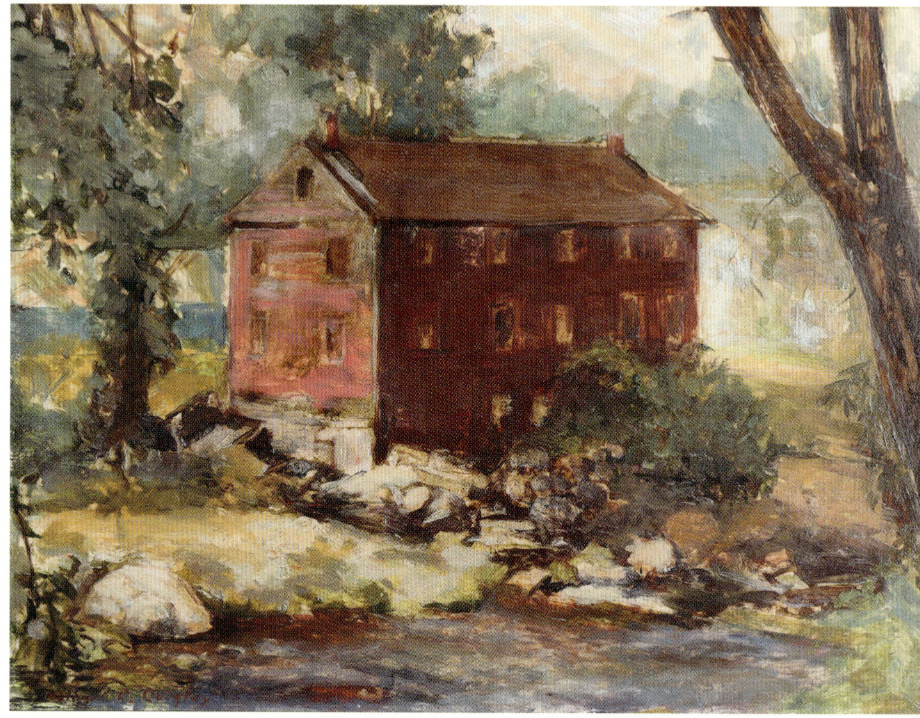

ABOVE **CIDER MILL**

Oil on board, 16 x 20 in., Peter and Martha Wright

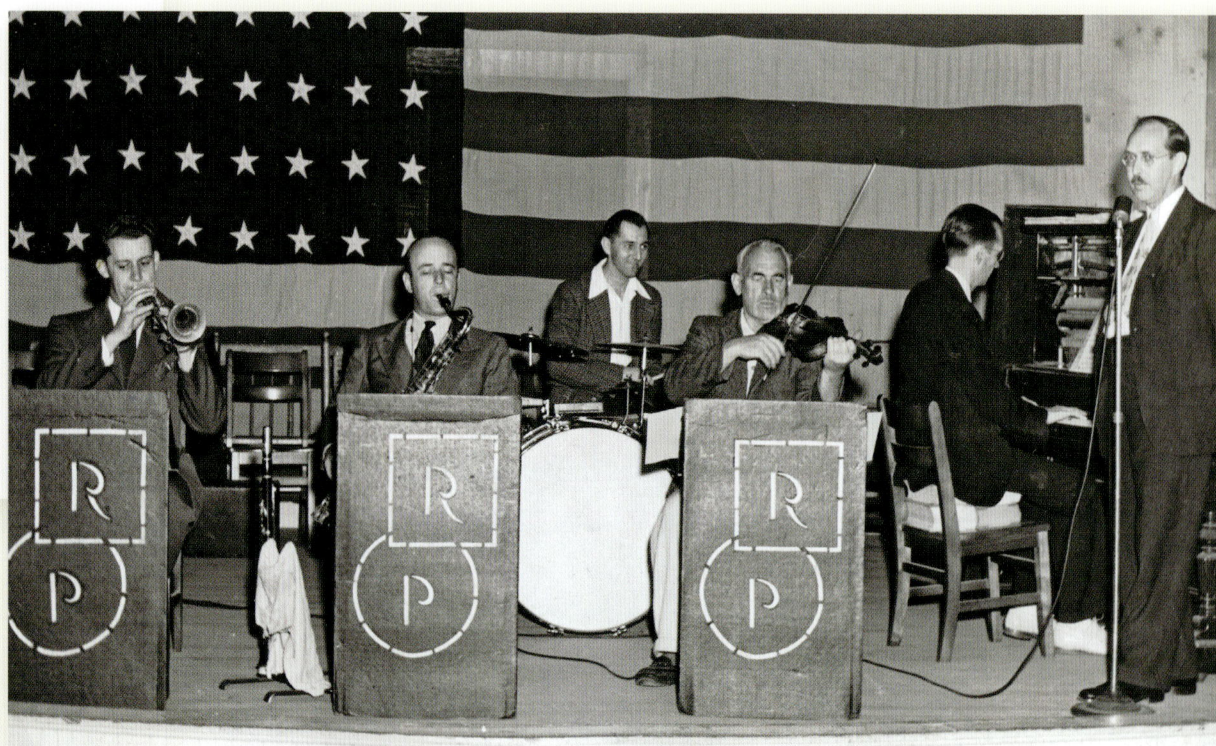

RIGHT Ralph Page Orchestra with Albert Quigley on fiddle, Chesterfield, 1943

Courtesy of Historical Society of Cheshire County

Albert Quigley of Nelson, New Hampshire . . . has played for dances since he was a barefoot boy. His father had a local orchestra (in Maine), and Quig says he "can't remember when Saturday didn't mean hog-wrestle night to me." With the exception of Arthur Maynard of Keene, New Hampshire, we believe no one in Cheshire County can approach Quig's ability at jigging and reeling. Quig is another true fiddler, able and willing to extemporize on a tune. He also is an excellent example of the versatility of many of our musicians . . . . As knitting work he will turn out a fine fiddle, but more important, he is rapidly becoming recognized as a remarkable landscape painter, and his hand-carved picture frames are the envy and despair of imitators. He also can tell a story about as palatably as anyone we've ever heard.

—*Beth Tolman and Ralph Page*, The Country Dance Book: The Best of the Square and Contra Dances and All About Them

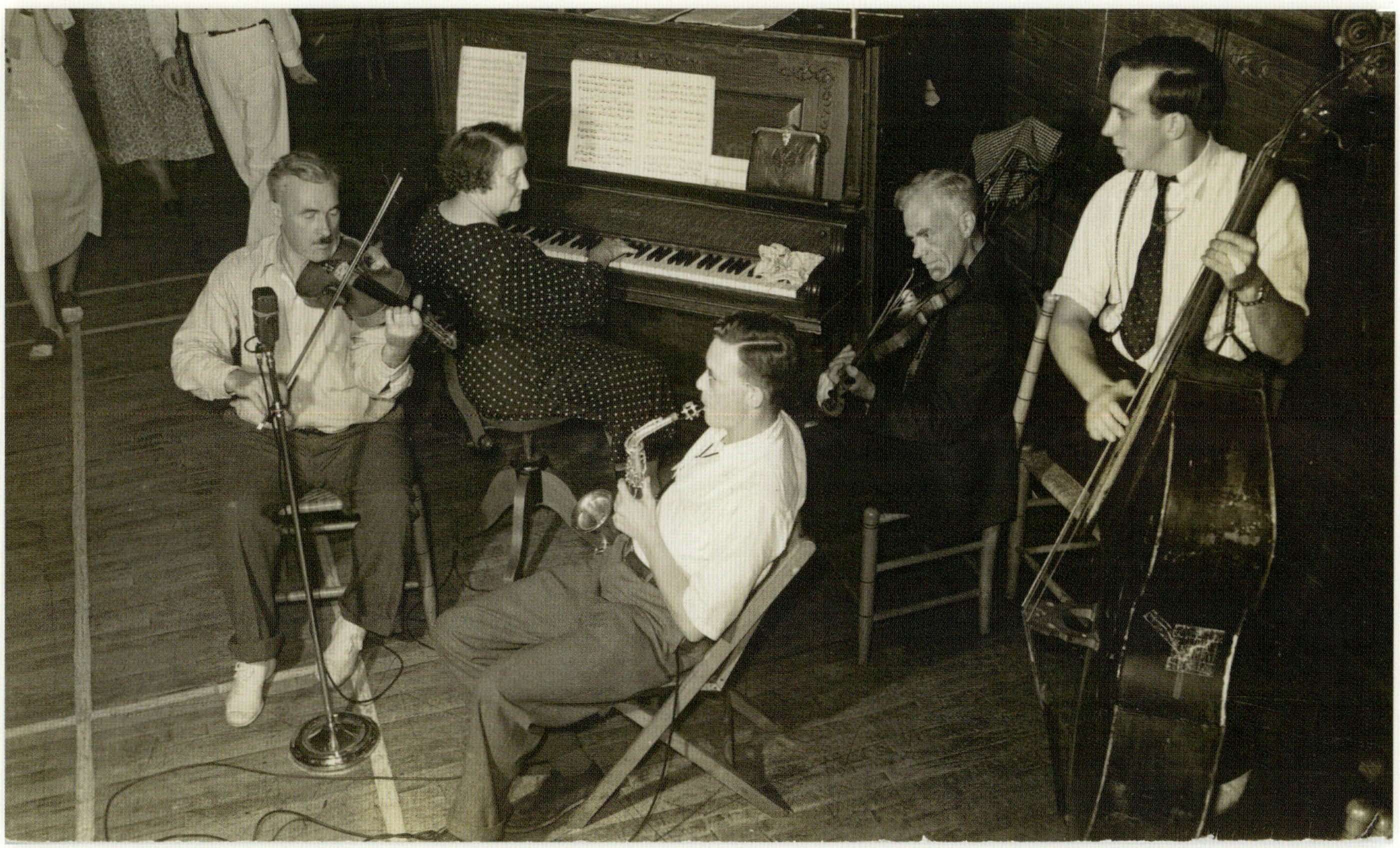

Albert Quigley on fiddle, playing in New York
William Terzian, photographer
Courtesy of Tolman Pond Archives

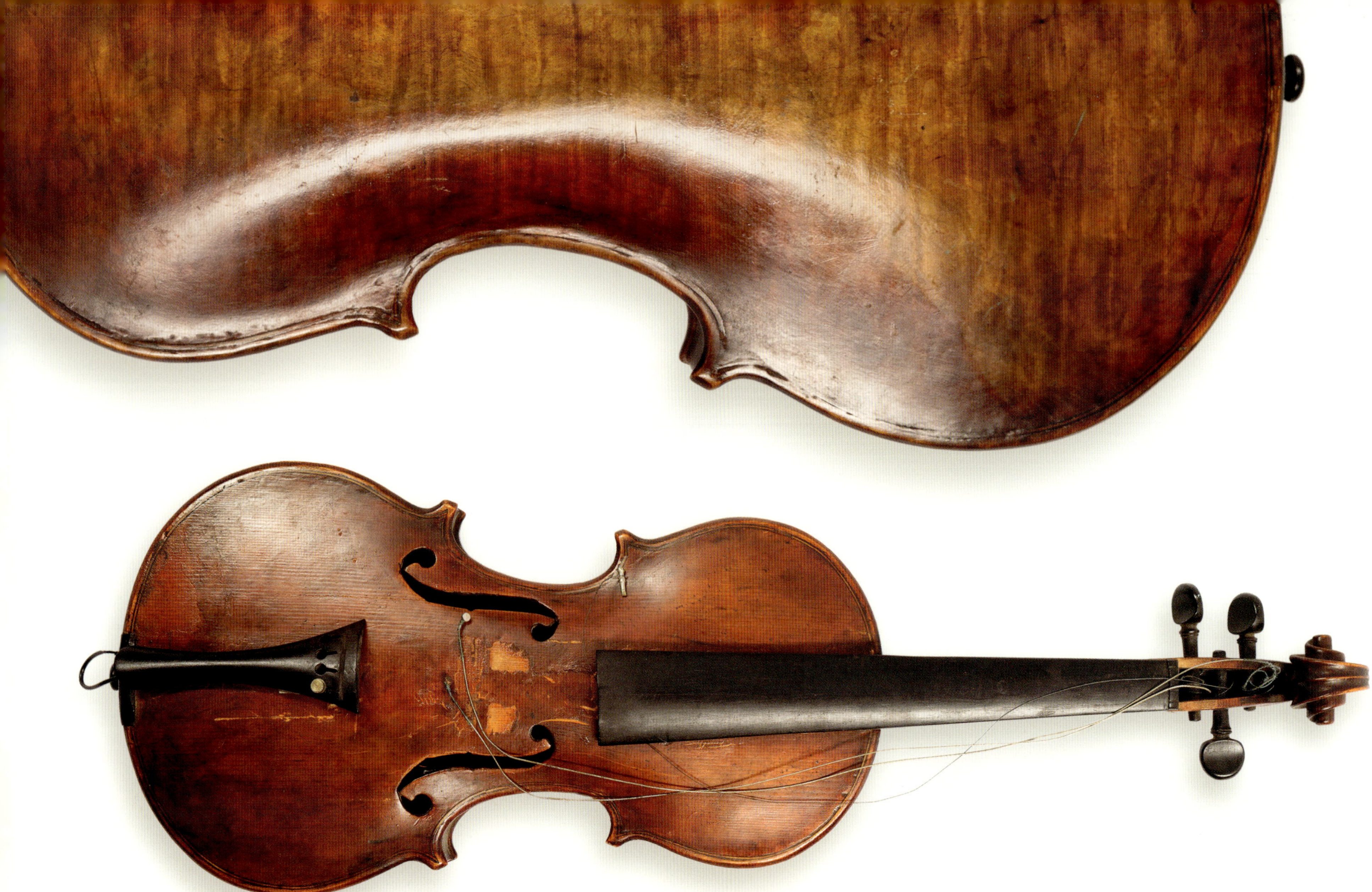

ABOVE Back and face of Albert Quigley's handmade violin
Brian and Jessie Quigley
OPPOSITE ABOVE Photograph of Alvah Batchelder, fiddlemaker, 1958
Courtesy of the Quigley family

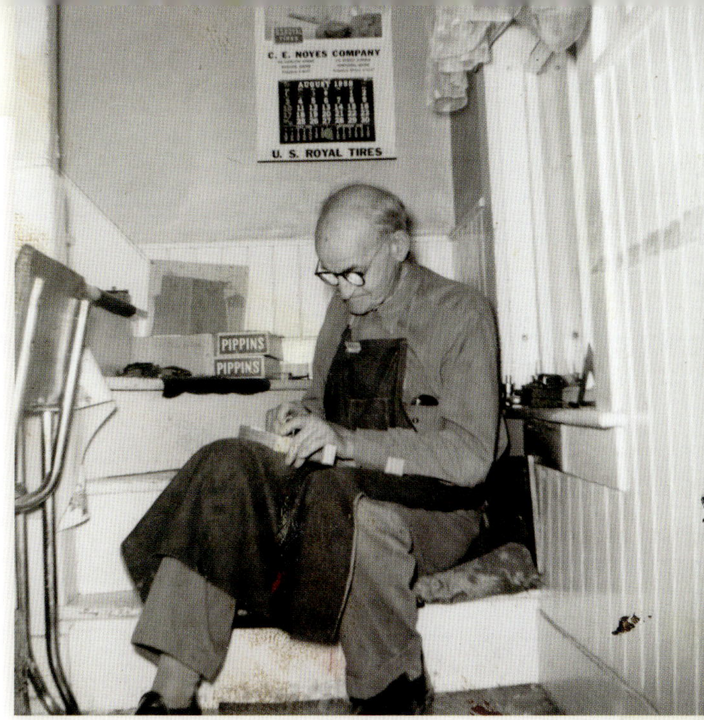

Quig continued to work some at the woolen mill in Harrisville, New Hampshire, until he retired and then he spent most of his time painting and conversing with his old friend, Alvah Batchelder, in Maine, who had become a violin, viola, and cello maker, and I believe he made one bass violin.

We'd go to Maine and visit, because Quig still had family there, and we'd go over and see Al Batchelder. He and Quig would have a great time. Quig said, "Well, I've been repairing fiddles for a long time and I've always called on you for help when I needed some information and," he continued, "now I'm going to make a violin."

Al Batchelder scurried around and brought him out a bunch of tools that he'd made by hand for measuring thicknesses and for finding out where the sound post should be set and other pieces, and not only that but how to finish the wood down so that it was perfectly graduated because you'd never get the right tone out of the instrument if you didn't follow these graduations very accurately.

Al had made by hand all these sets of calipers that you could measure what you were supposed to. And he was telling Quig all about this and what he should do. And Quig was very enthusiastic because he wanted to make this violin. Al then went out into the back room and came out with a brand new fiddle. I believe it was his seventy-eighth violin, which he then gave to Quig and I inherited it after Quig died. I've still got it.

When Quig got home from Maine, he crated up one of his paintings and sent it to Al as a thank-you gift.

Quig did make one violin and after he passed away my mother gave it to my brother. It is now in the hands of my nephew.

But I do remember some of the instructions that Al Batchelder gave my father. He said that there's only one way to finish the inside or the outside of a violin. He said that once you've taken it down and your measurements are pretty close, you want to go out and break some window glass until you get a piece with a curve that's in the right shape. The final finish has to be done with that glass because if you try to get the wood down close and sand it, it destroys the ends of the wood fiber and then the violin will always have a fuzzy sound. But if you cut it off with the window glass it will give you a good clear tone.

—Barney Quigley
from an interview on March 23, 2014

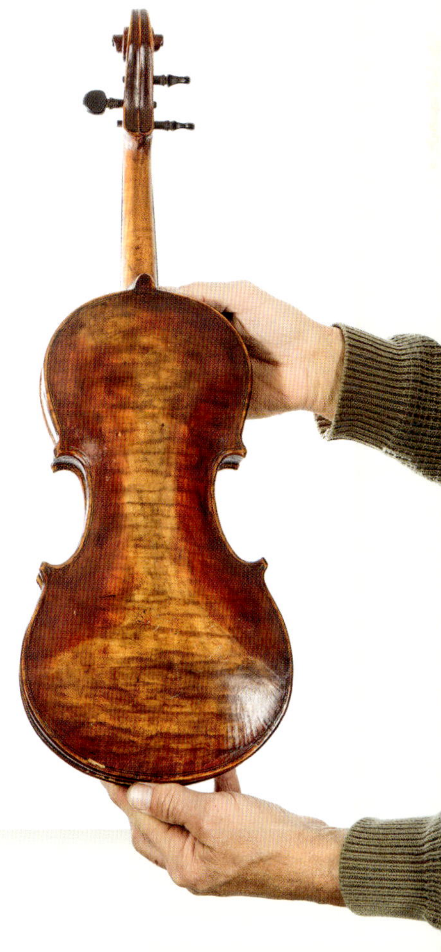

Square Dancing Had Ups and Downs, Say Fiddlers

"I can't remember a time when there was not square dancing," Mr. Quigley told a *Sentinel* reporter Wednesday. "But just to show you how it's varied in popularity across New England, I can remember playing for dances with my father in Maine in 1910. The foxtrot was popular and you could hardly get people onto the floor for a square dance. Three years later, in Hardwick, Vt., they had police on the floor to keep people from doing the foxtrot."

. . .

Mr. Quigley came here from Maine and while talking with a *Sentinel* reporter Wednesday was sanding down a sound post for a violin. In addition to playing fiddles he builds them. He made his last complete fiddle in 1915 but since that time has been repairing them, rebuilding them and refinishing them. Interested in tonal quality he said that the Italians were unequalled in the making of violins.

"They combined a vast knowledge of the tonal quality of wood and beautiful craftsmanship with an art of varnishing that seems to be lost. The Italians knew the value of time, of waiting between every process of the building of a violin."

. . .

He lives directly beside the town hall in Nelson where Ralph Page's orchestra began playing for dances back when "Red Sails in the Sunset" and "Roll Along Covered Wagon" were part of their repertoire. Mr. Quigley is the subject of "Choose Your Partner," one of the paintings in the Alexander James exhibit now hanging at the Currier Gallery in Manchester. An intimate friend of James, he learned painting from him and began, with him, to be interested in the making of picture frames. Now he is considered an expert in the complicated craft.

—The Keene Sentinel,
Keene, New Hampshire, August 8, 1947

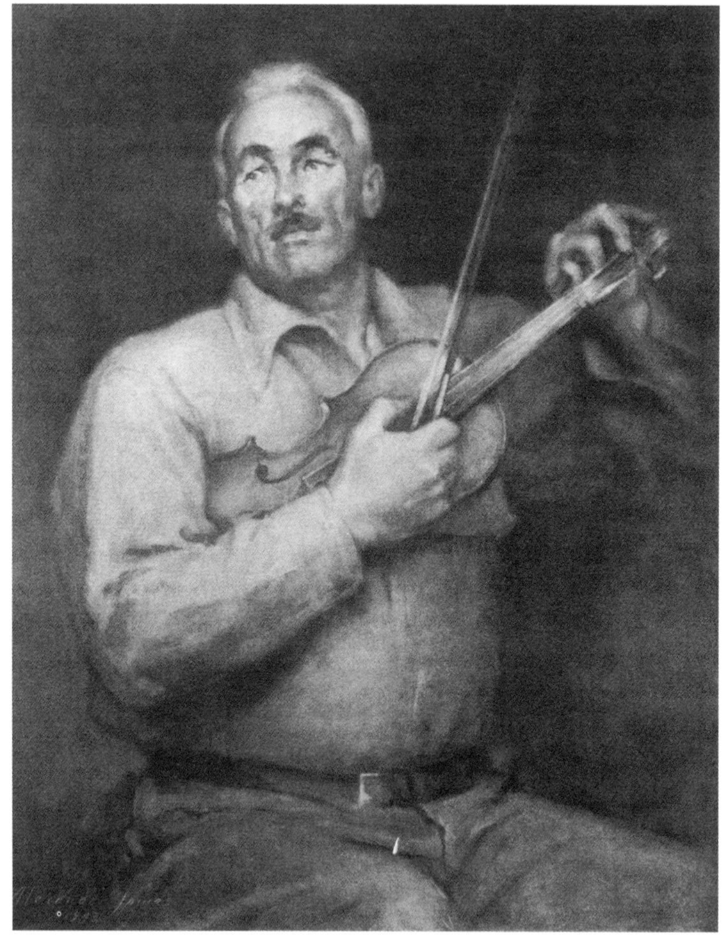

ABOVE **CHOOSE YOUR PARTNER** (1943) by Alexander James
Oil on panel, 30 x 25 in.
Reproduced from the catalogue of the 1947 Memorial Exhibition of James' work at the Currier Gallery of Art, Manchester, New Hampshire

Mount Monadnock

"If a mountain
could be a town . . ."

Prologue

If a mountain could be
a town,
Mt. Monadnock would be ours,
our center,
our meeting place,
the rising point
that greets our days,
the long black body that
spreads across the starry sky
and guards
our nights.

If that mountain
were a town,
in that town
would live
painters and writers,
farmers and hikers,
dancers and fiddlers,
and
lovers,
their stories
written on the walls.

Great gray granite
blade,
sharpened on sun
and ice.
Enduring presence
On a warring planet,
you were here
long
before us.
You will be here
long
after us.
Mother of lore,
your stories
are told now.

We listen.

—*Edie Clark, from* Monadnock Tales

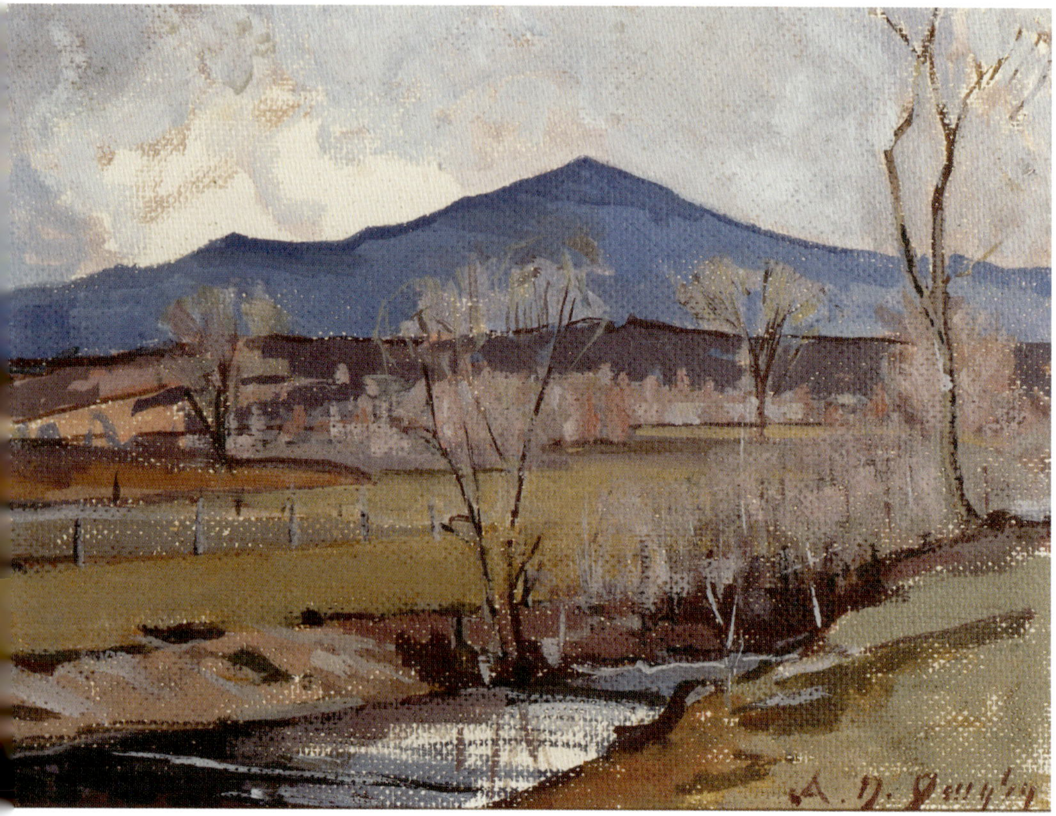

MOUNT MONADNOCK
Back of Masonite board, 11 x 14 in.
Private collection

Monadnock Uplands Painters

by William L. Bauhan

Albert Quigley, 1891–1961, (Quig to his many friends) carved out a special place of his own among a group of highly gifted painters who adopted (and were adopted by) the Monadnock uplands: Thayer, Brush, Phelps, Meryman, Alexander James. He can be seen as part of a distinguished tradition.

The difference was that Quigley was self-taught—almost entirely. He had to rely more on that "inner fire;" he had a harder row to hoe—financially and in achieving proficiency—than his better-known colleagues, who had the advantages of concentrated academic study and soon gained national recognition for their work.

He did manage to get in two quite brief interludes of academic training: in Paris after the first World War and at the Boston Museum School in the early 1930s. But essentially he remained a loner, reliant on his own acute observations and a steady application of his native talent.

The breakthrough for Quigley came through his meeting in the 1920s with Alexander James (son of William, the psychologist, and nephew of Henry, the novelist), who became his fast friend, co-worker, colleague and mentor. Mentor, although James (1890–1946) and Quig were almost exact contemporaries. From

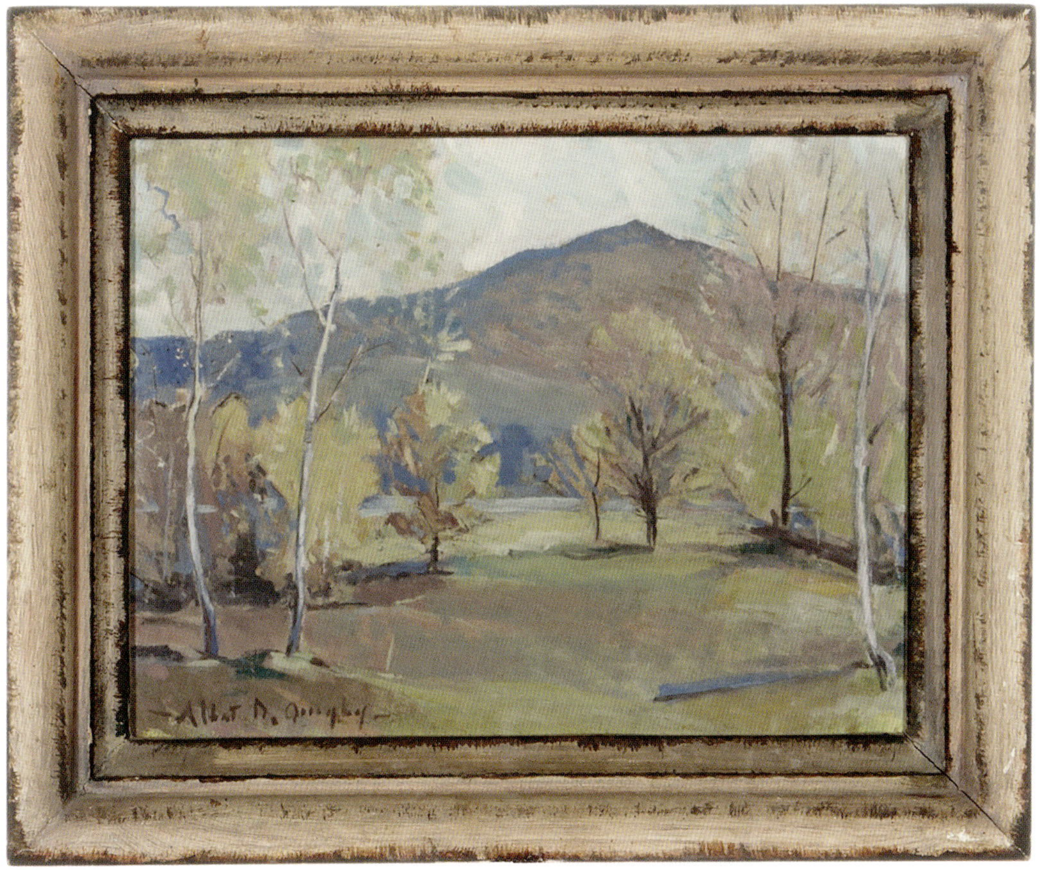

MOUNT MONADNOCK
Oil on board, Quigley frame, 12 x 15 in.
Private collection

the beginning James fostered Quigley's career as an artist and his gifts as a painter and craftsman, though as time went on, they interacted more on each other.

It was through James, too, that Quigley developed his skills as a framemaker. Quigley frames, notable for their beautiful workmanship and originality, are prized possessions of major American museums, where some day it is safe to say his paintings will be equally admired and recognized.

Reviewing a Quigley exhibit in 1946 at the Rodman Gallery in Fitzwilliam, New Hampshire, the noted art critic Dorothy Adlow wrote in *The Christian Science Monitor*: "It is surprising to find such grace and facility in the brush of an unschooled painter from a little village in Cheshire County, New Hampshire. . . . He seems to find his stride in genre and portraiture. . . . There is nothing pedestrian or conventional about his portraits."[1]

Quigley lived to see his work exhibited at major museums in New York, Boston, Washington and at the Currier Gallery in Manchester, New Hampshire.

—William L. Bauhan, historian and publisher
Dublin, New Hampshire, written for The Paintings of Albert Quigley: The Nelson Years, 1934–1961
a 1995 exhibit at the Nelson Town Hall

1 "Paintings by Albert Quigley on Exhibition at Fitzwilliam," by Dorothy Adlow, *The Christian Science Monitor*, August 1, 1946.

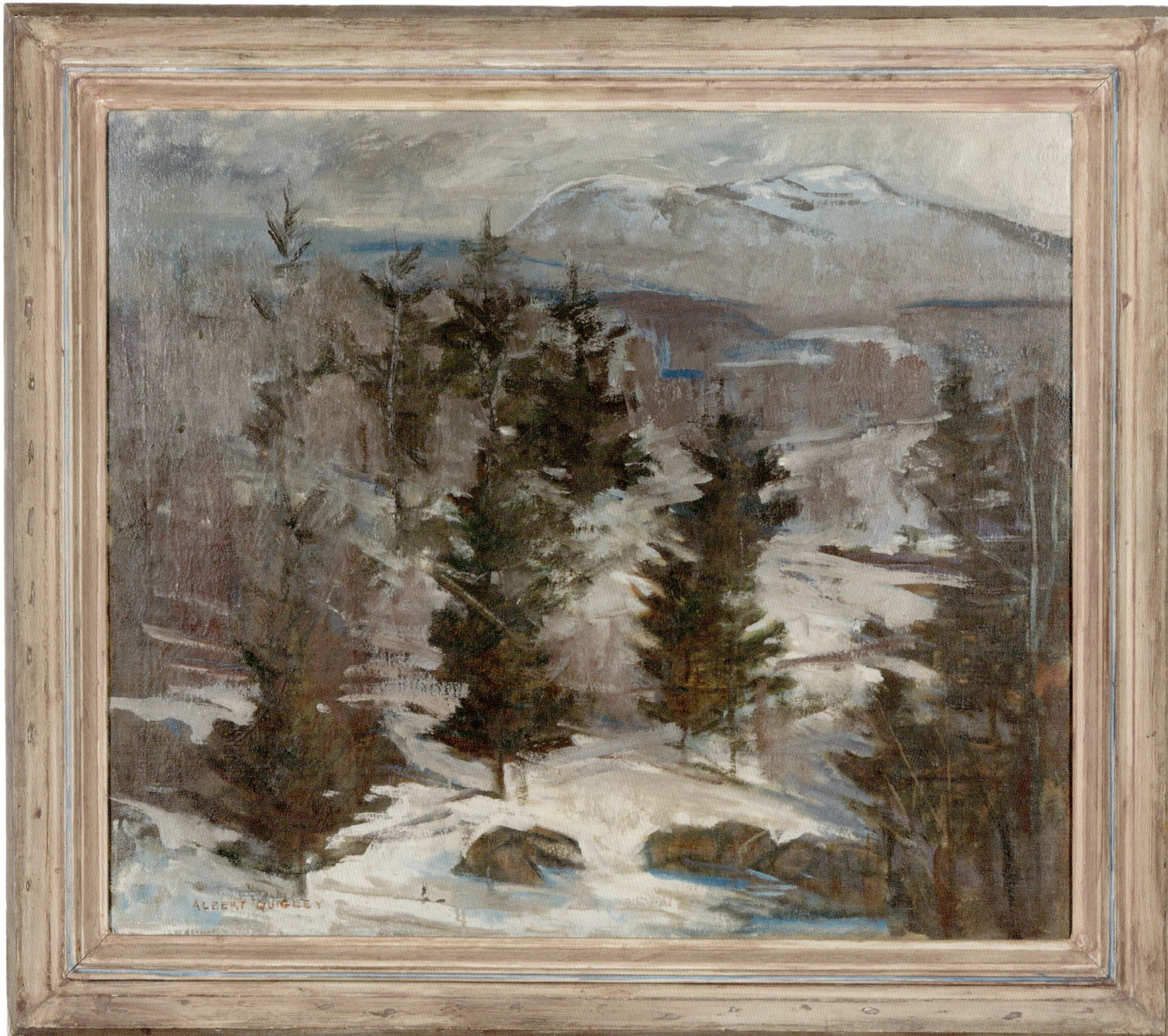

MOUNT MONADNOCK

Oil on canvas, Quigley frame, 30 x 35 in.

Private collection

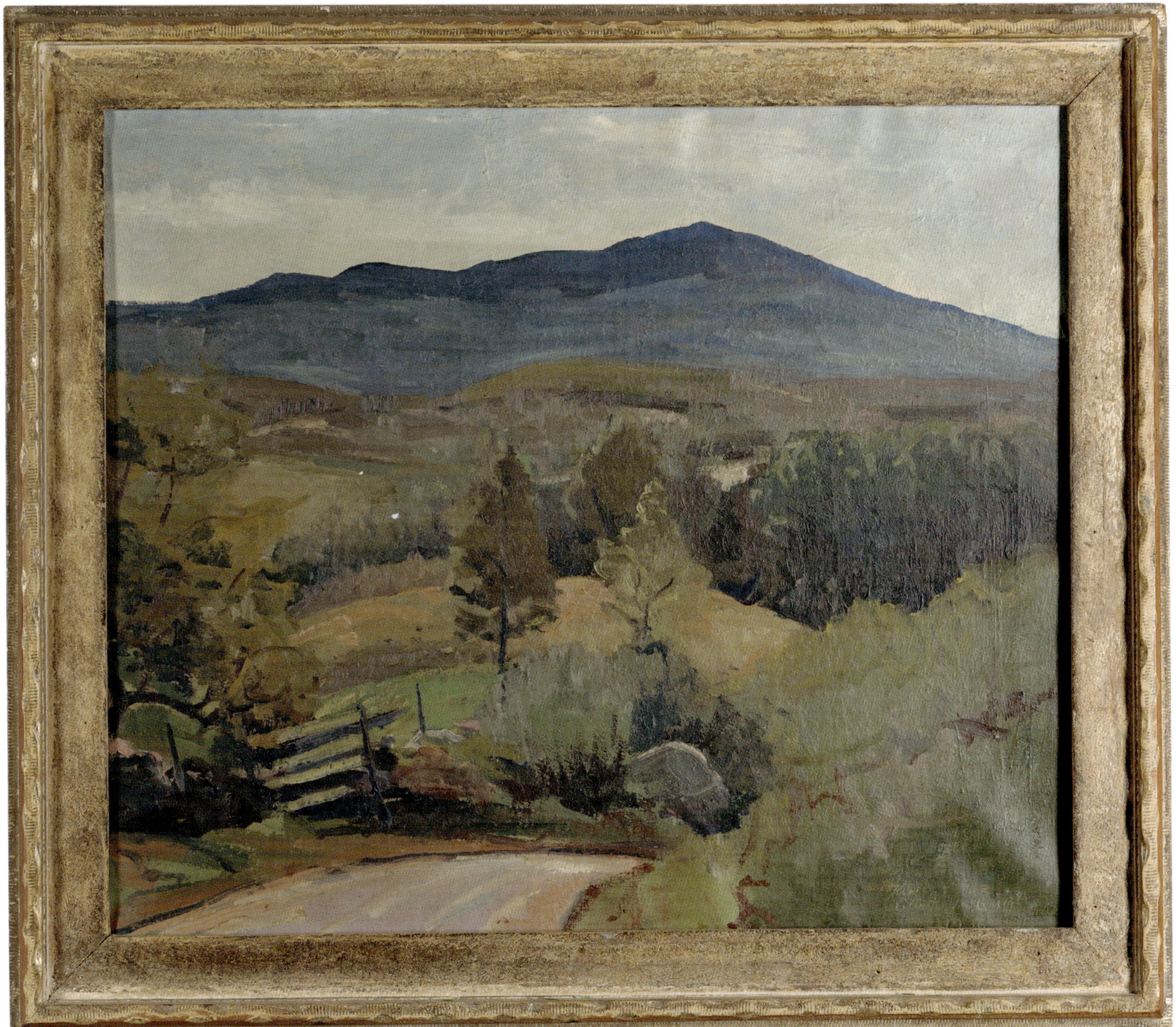

MOUNT MONADNOCK (1936)
Oil on canvas, Quigley frame, 24 x 28 in.
Private collection

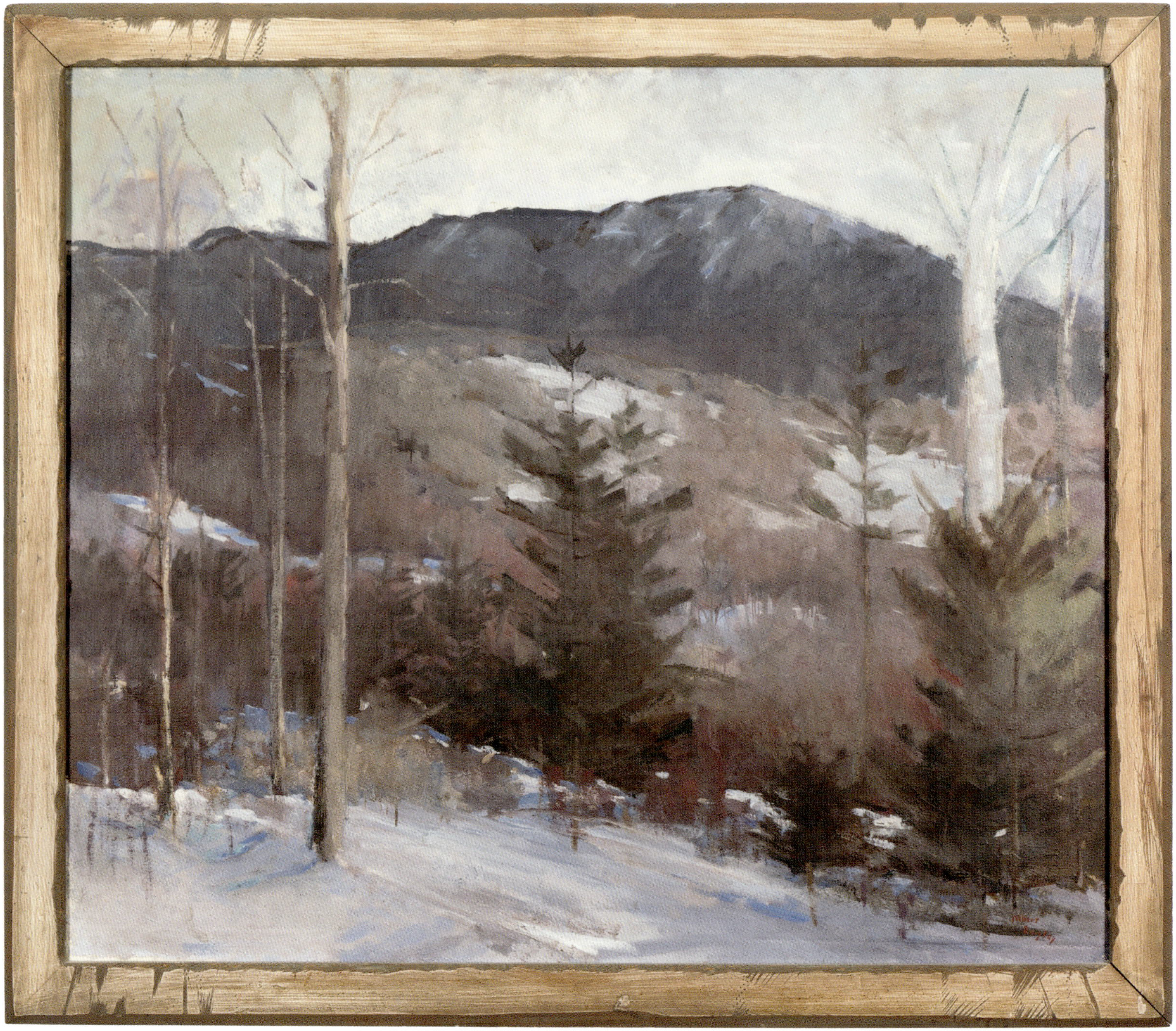

MOUNT MONADNOCK

Oil on board, Quigley frame, 14 x 20 in.

Private collection

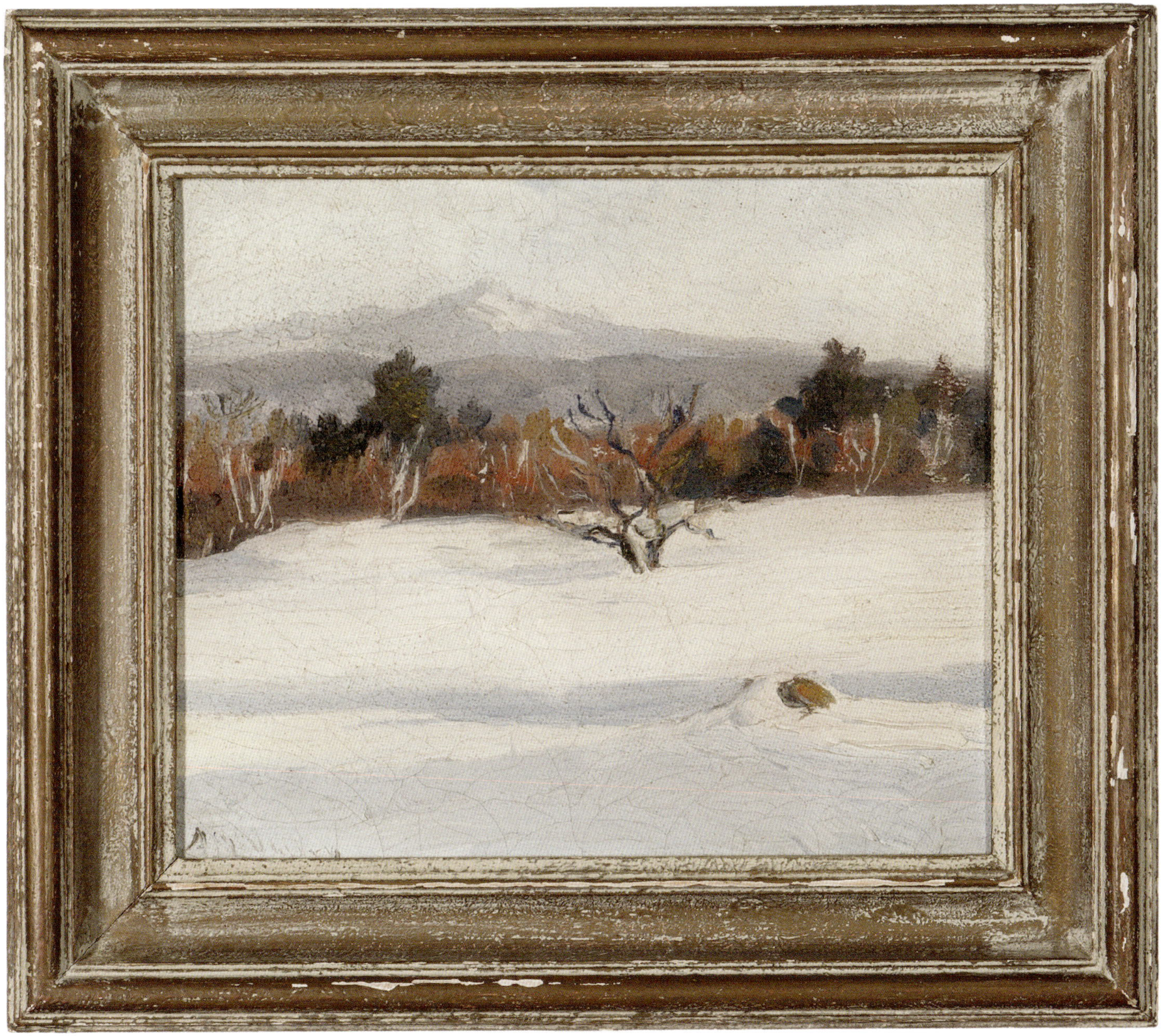

MOUNT MONADNOCK (1925)
Oil on board, 12 x 14 in., Alston W. Barrett
Inscribed on back: "To L. G. Barrett, February 1925 by A. D. Quigley."

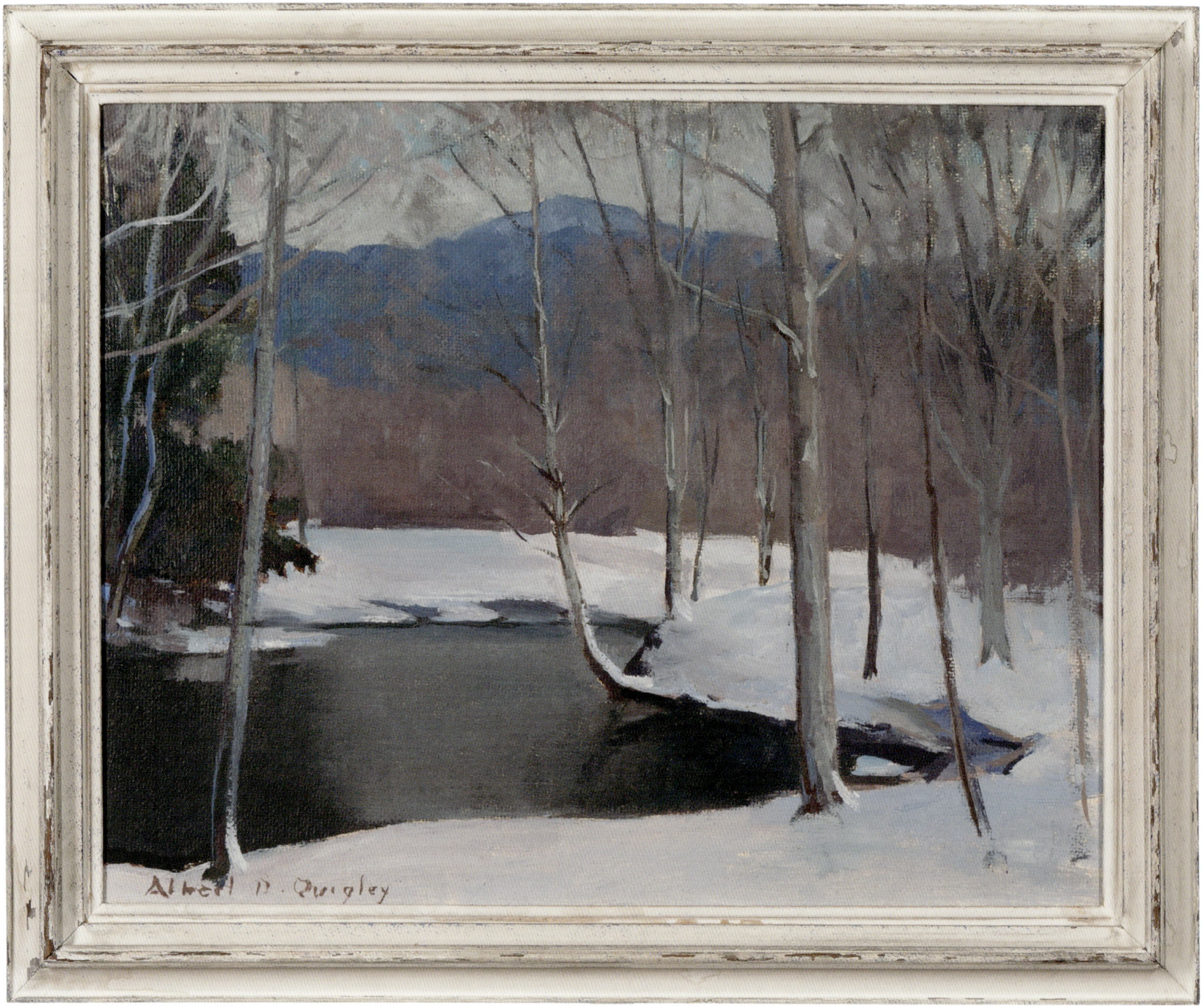

Untitled

Oil on canvas, Quigley frame, 17 x 21 in.

Private collection

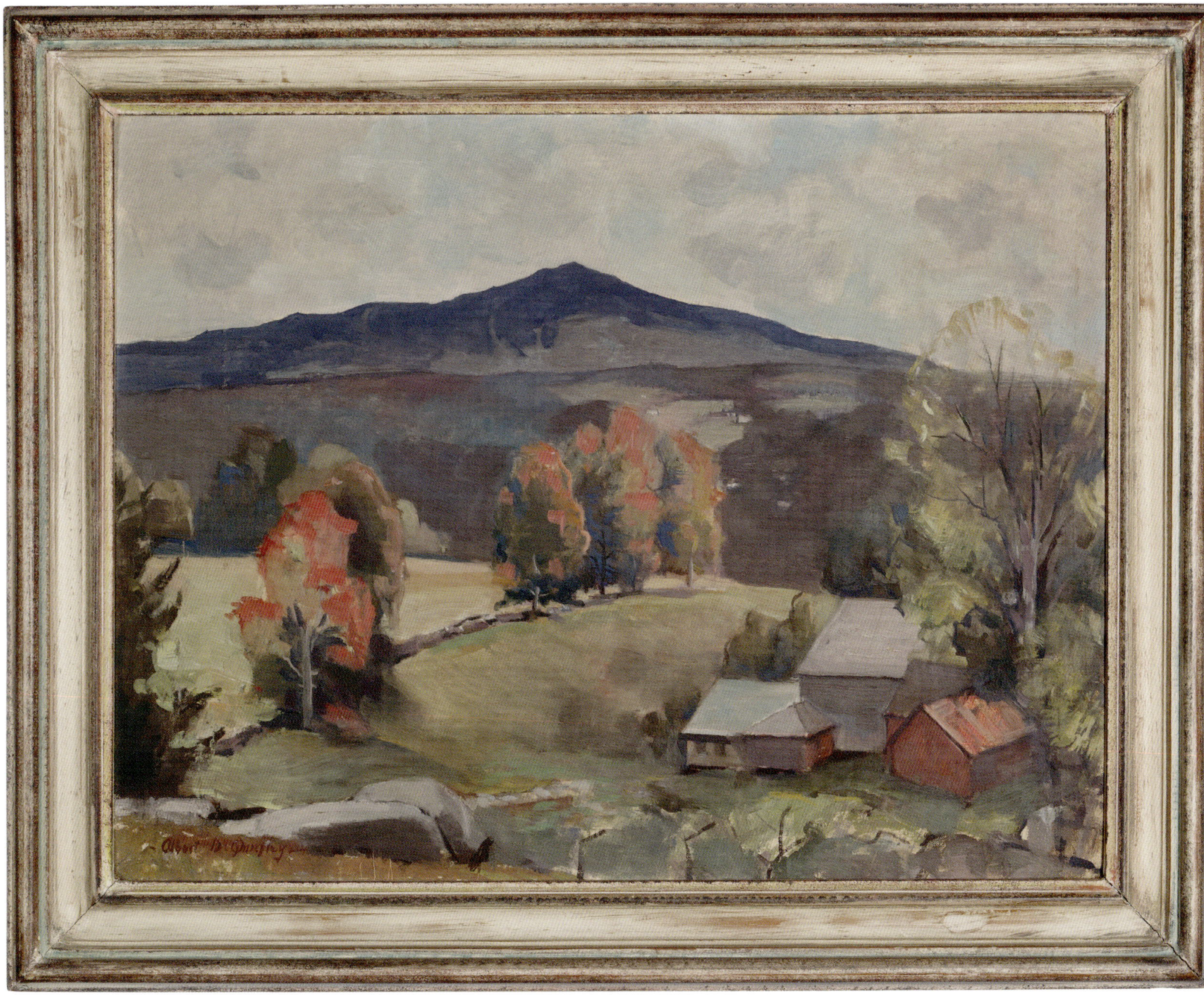

MOUNT MONADNOCK (1940)

Oil on board, Quigley frame, 23 x 29 in., Henry M. Frechette, Jr.

A view from the Hutchins place on Beech Hill, with glimpses of the housetops of Marlborough, New Hampshire, in the distance

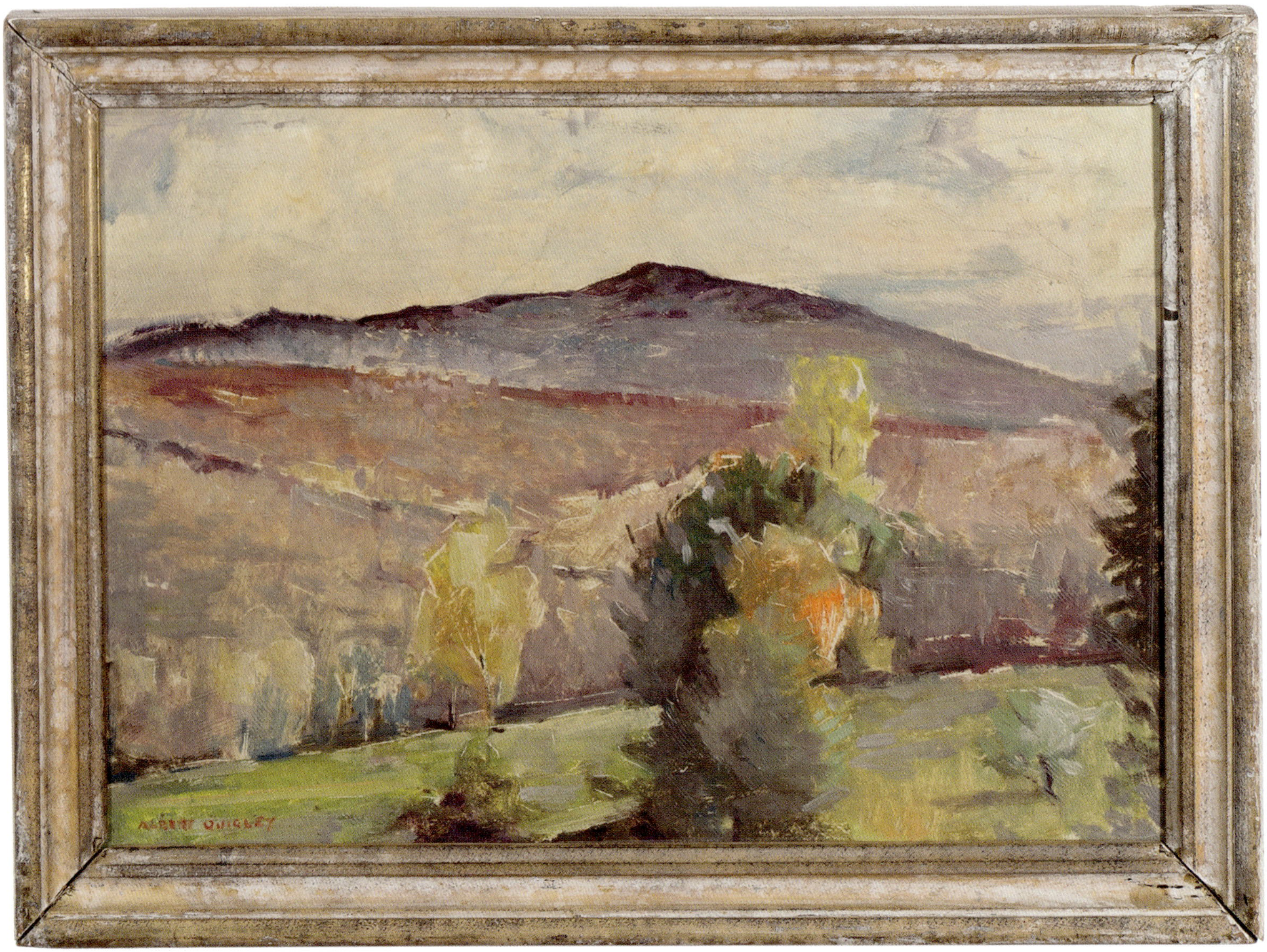

MOUNT MONADNOCK

Oil on board, Quigley frame, 14 x 20 in.

Private collection

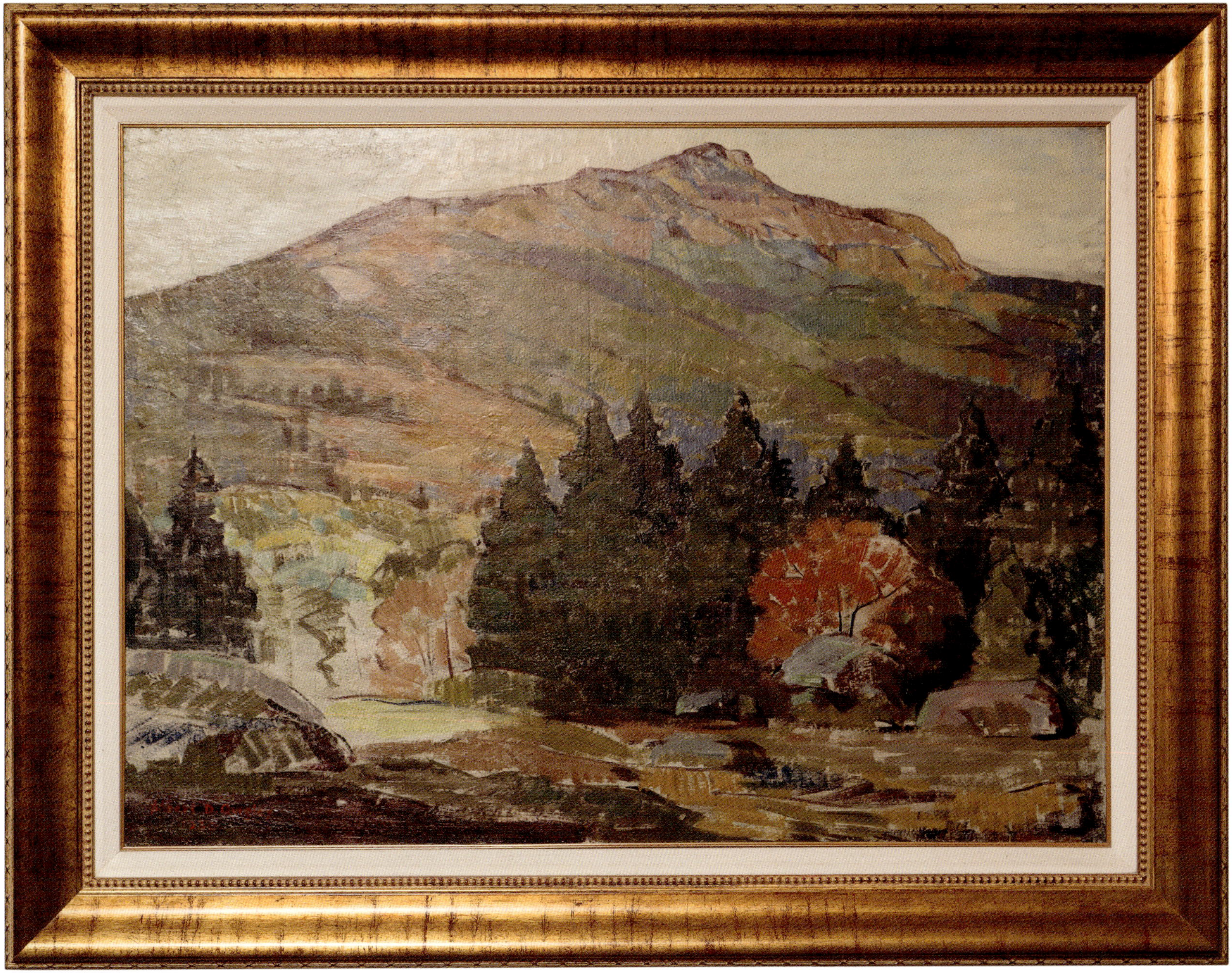

MOUNT MONADNOCK (1930)
Oil on board, 38 x 50 in.
Cheshire Medical Center/Dartmouth Hitchcock, Keene, New Hampshire

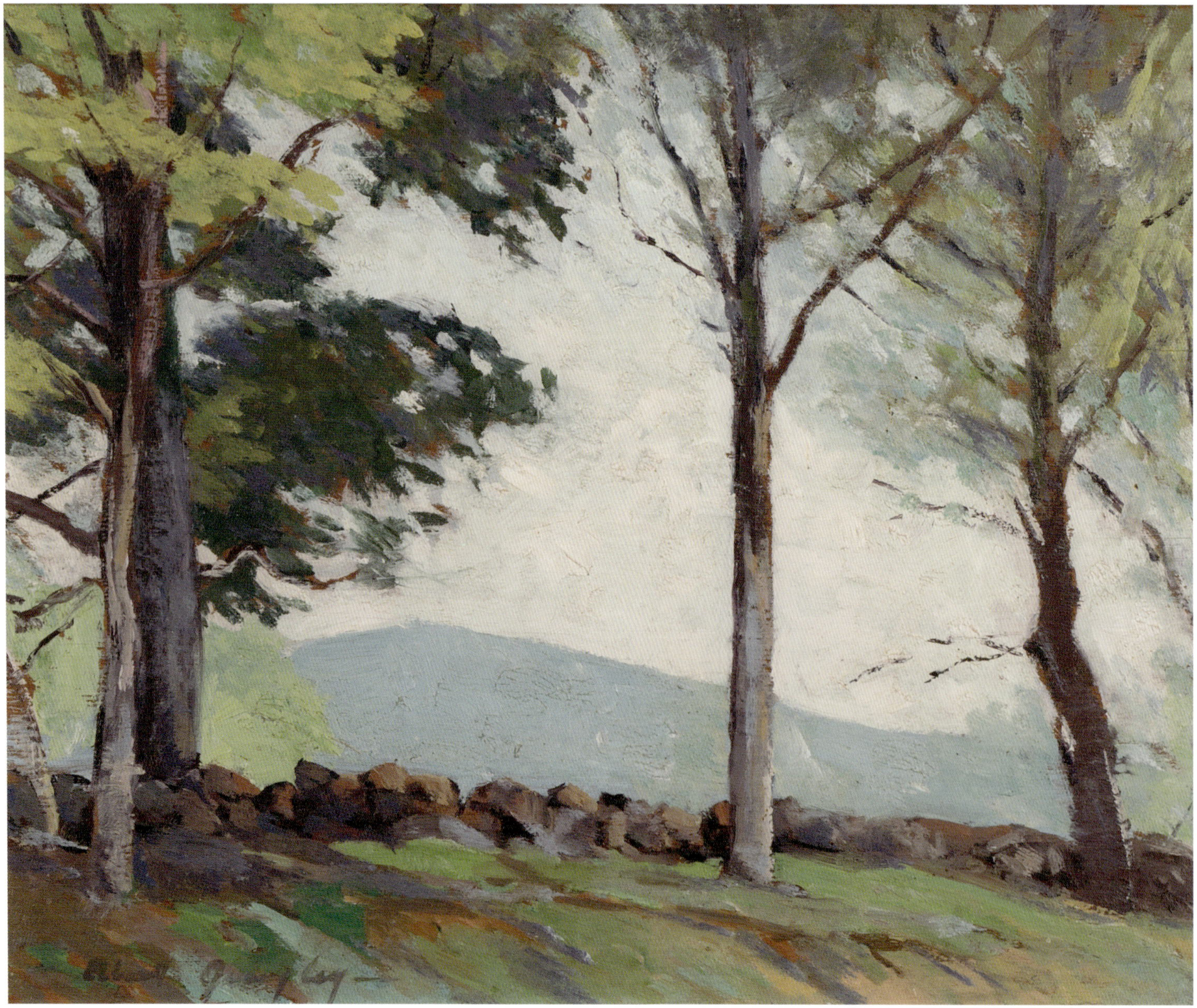

MOUNT MONADNOCK

Oil on board, 16 x 19 in.

Private collection

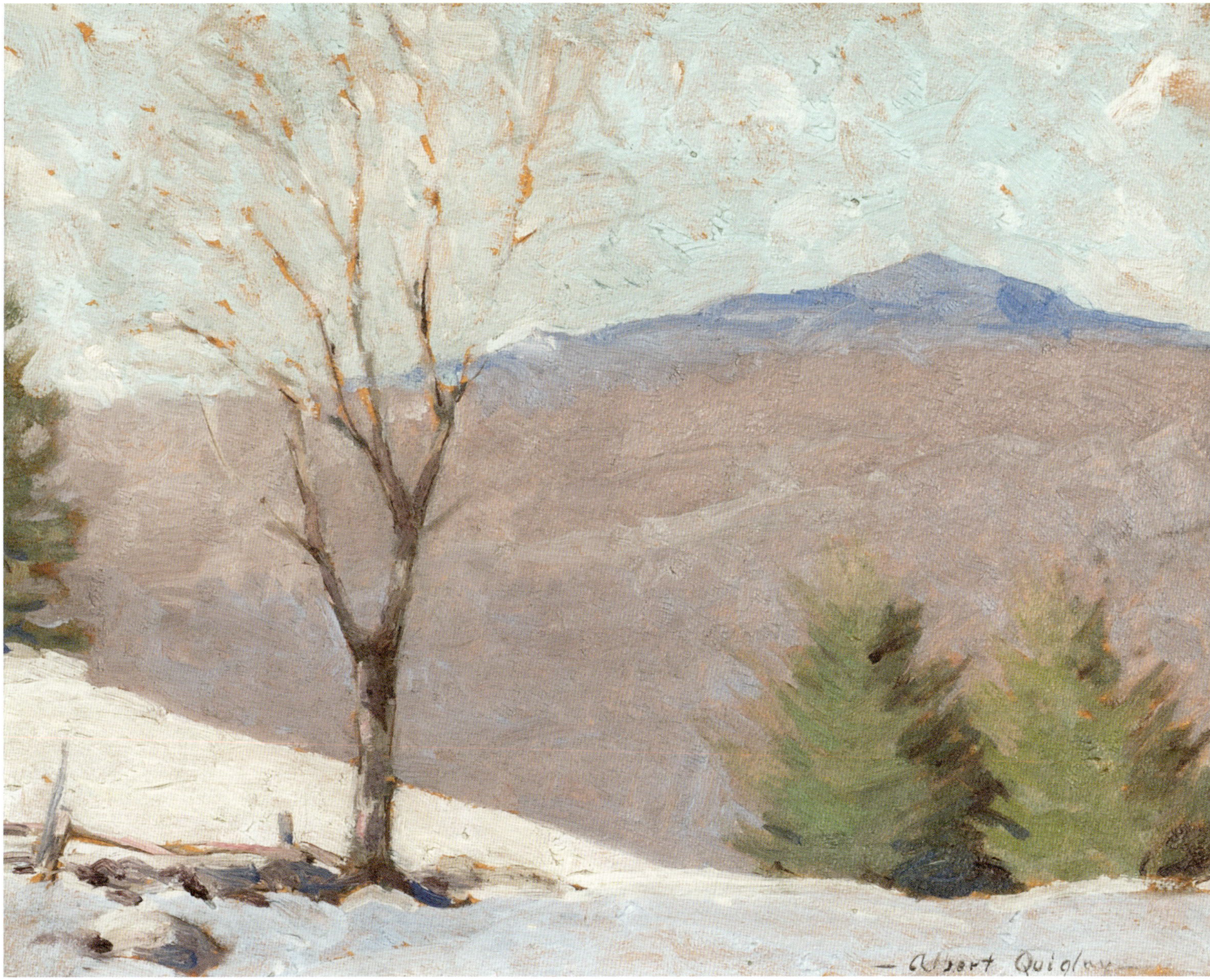

MOUNT MONADNOCK
Oil on board, 13 x 16 in.
Earle H. Staples

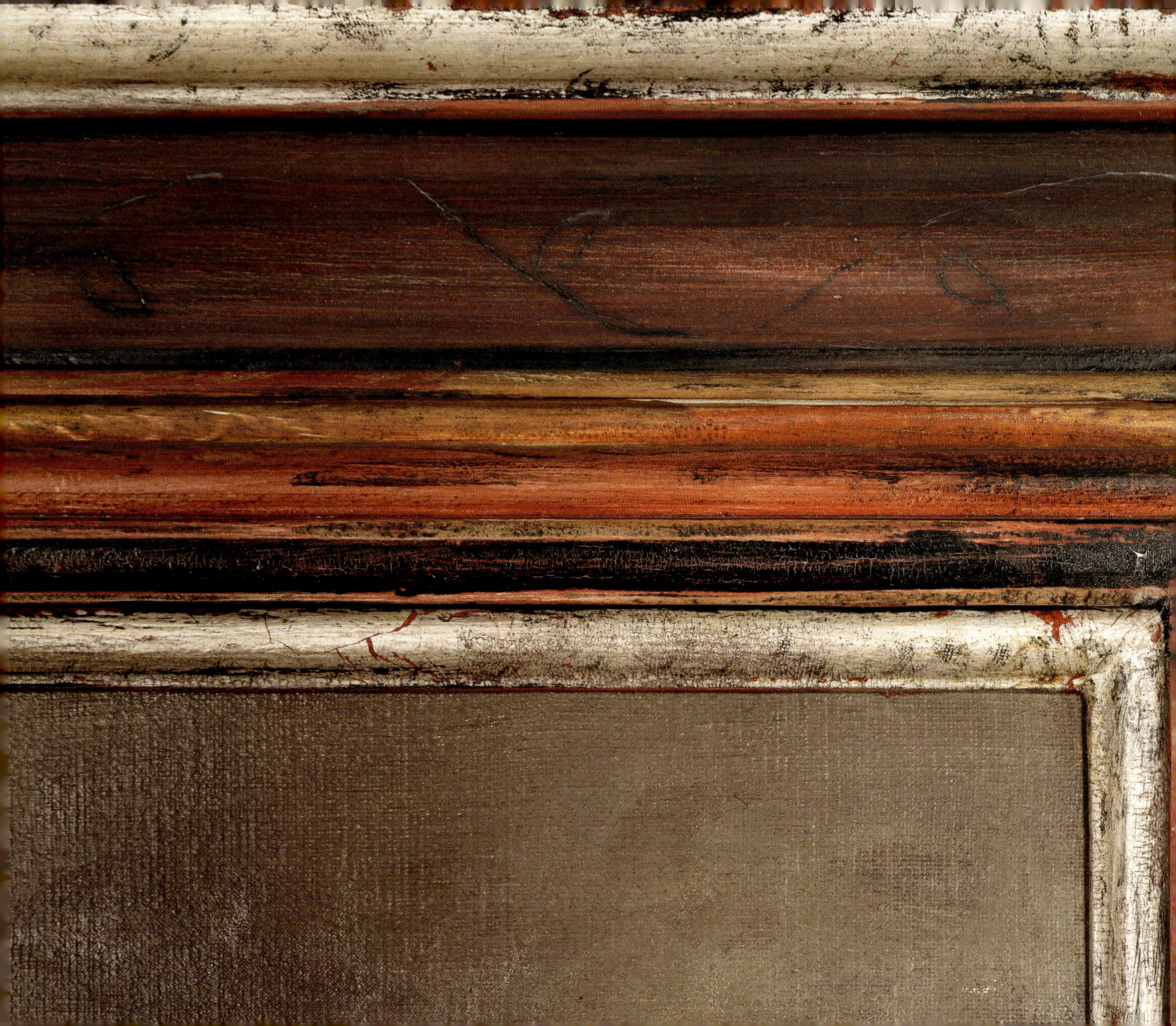

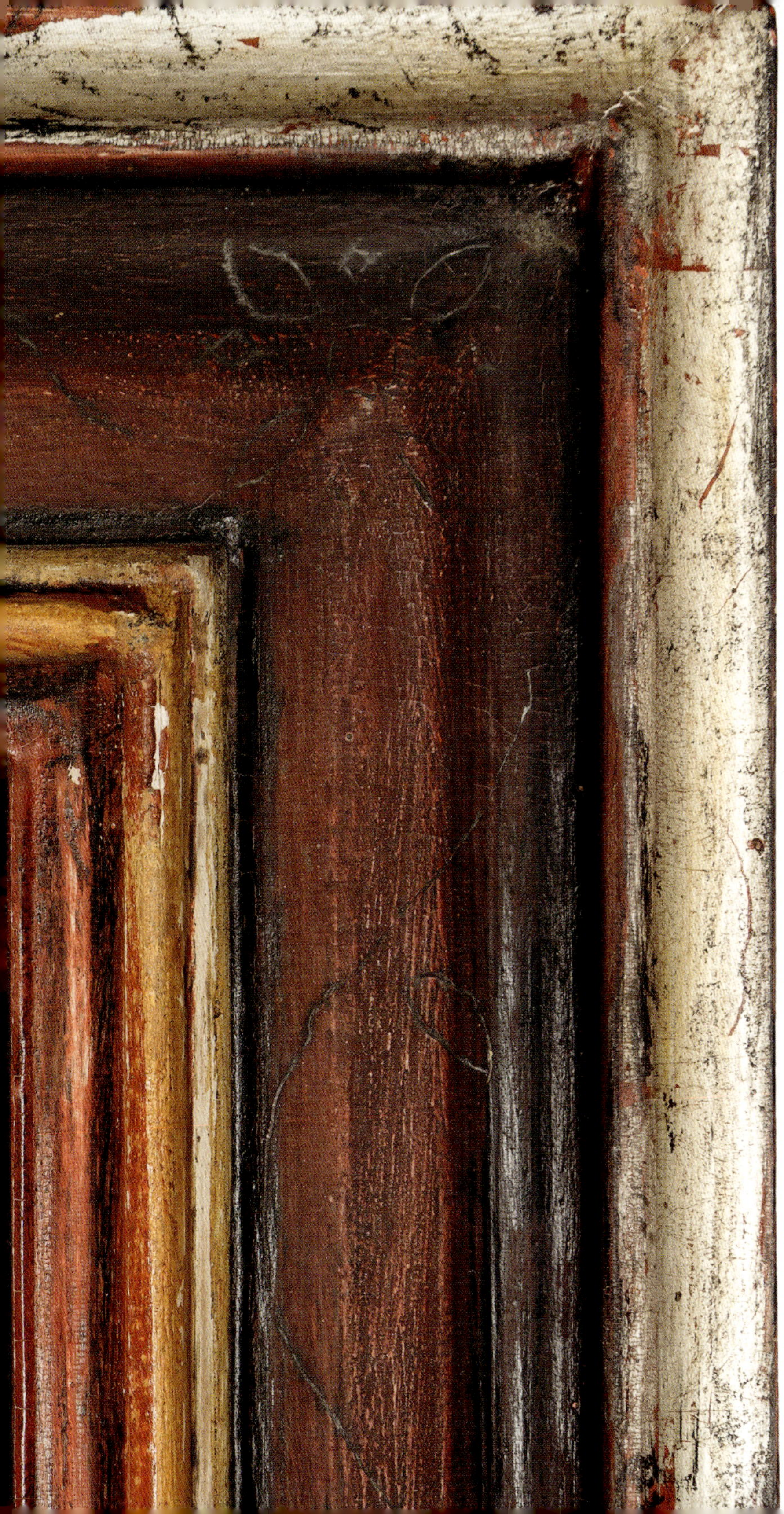

Frames

ALEXANDER JAMES used Quigley exclusively as a framer for his paintings and recommended him to his friends. Many of Quig's frames were hand-carved, some painted or gold-leafed and they were often tinted to in some way match or complement the painting. They were thought to be the very finest frames available at that time. Mildred, who was also very deft with her hands, helped him with this aspect of his work and was known to be quite good at it. They often gold-leafed frames together, which they apparently did in their living room as often as they played cribbage together.

—Edie Clark, author
written for the 1991 Quigley art exhibit sponsored by the Community Church of Harrisville and Chesham, New Hampshire

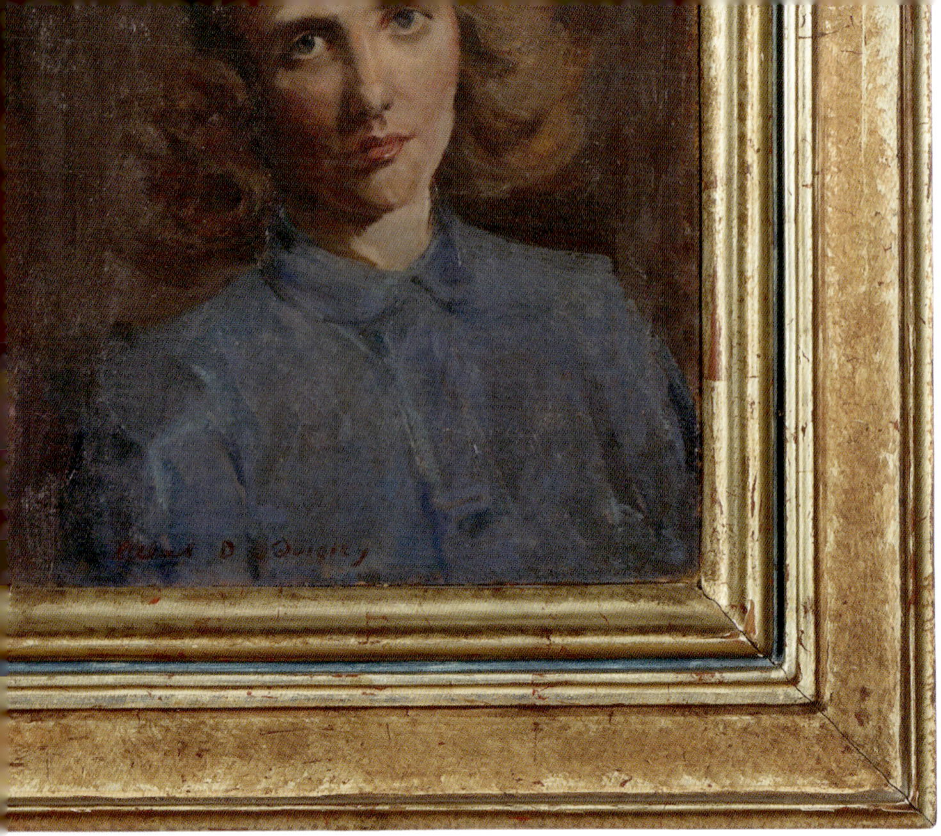

Quig had a paintbrush, and he'd lay out the gold leaf, which is something like a millionth of an inch thick and you can't touch it with your fingers because you'd just pull it apart and you'd never get to use it. So he had this brush which he'd brush through his hair and the oil on his hair was just enough, and with the static electricity he'd put the brush down and pick up the gold leaf and place it on the frame where it would then stick down. When he lost his hair, he'd call on one or the other of us kids to come over so that he could run the brush through our hair.

—Barney Quigley
from an interview on March 24, 2014

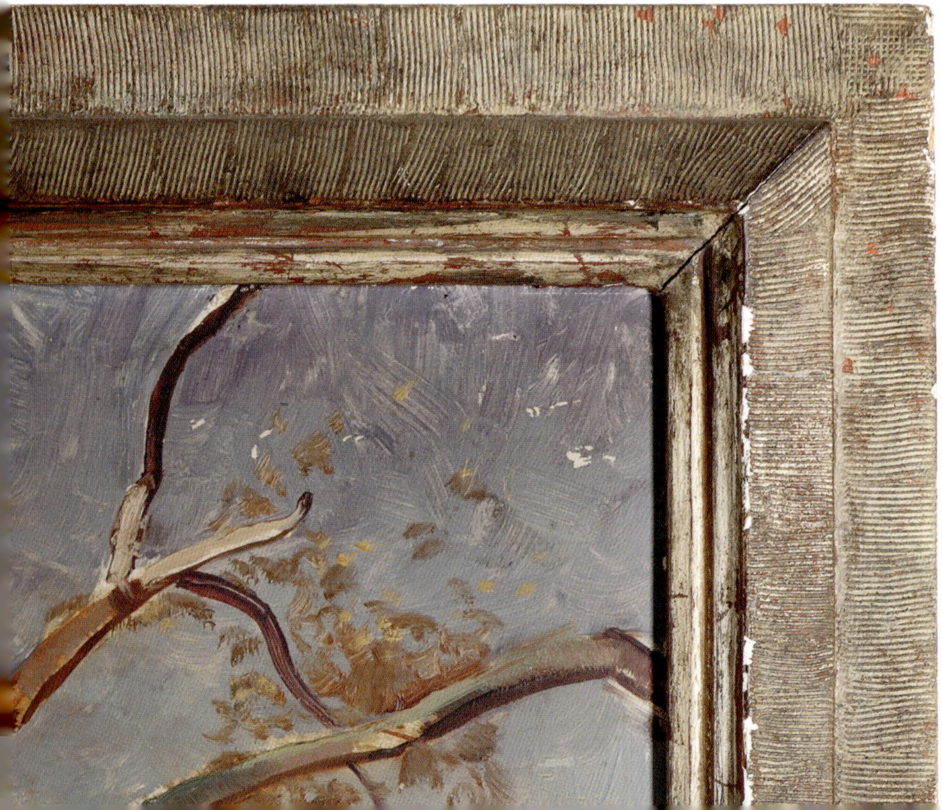

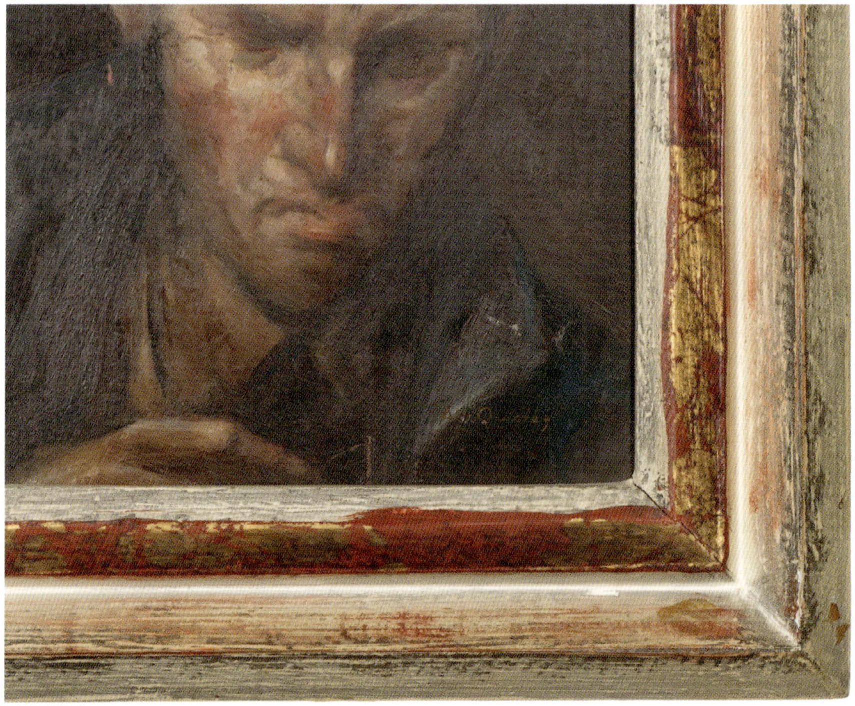

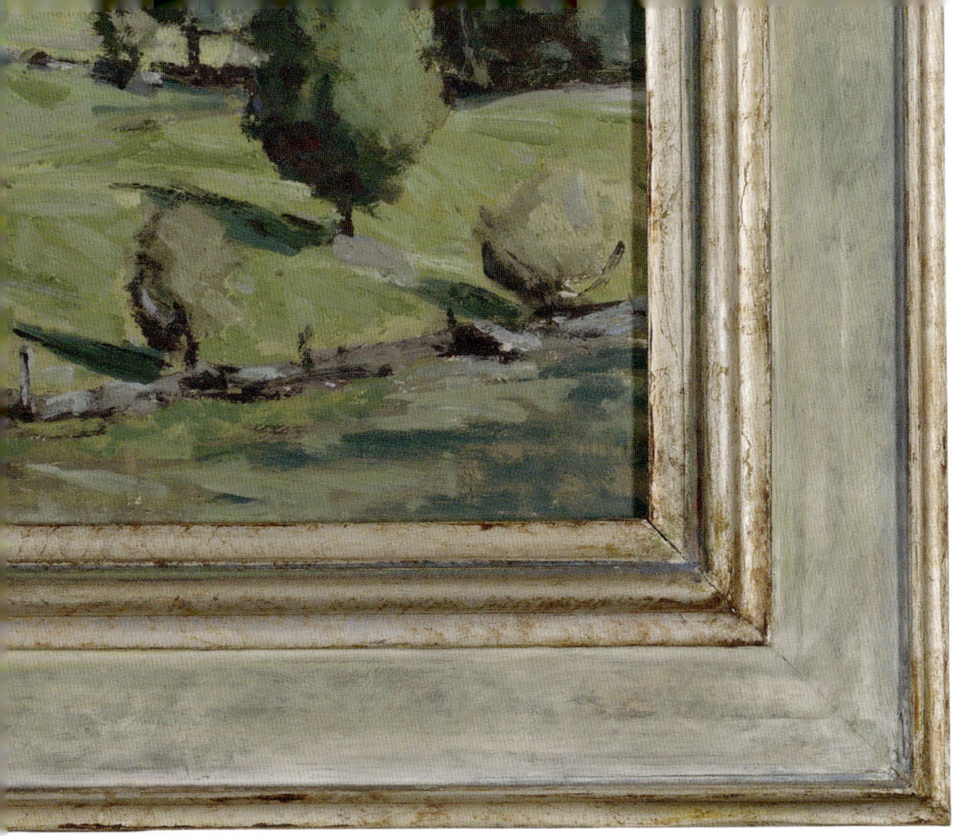
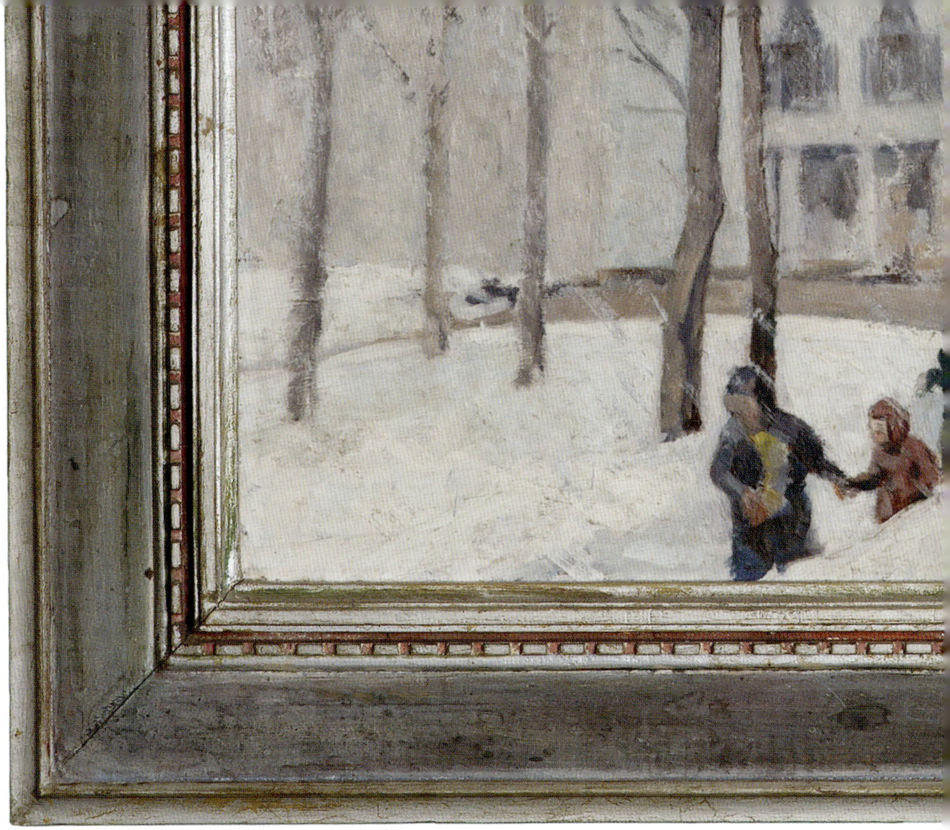
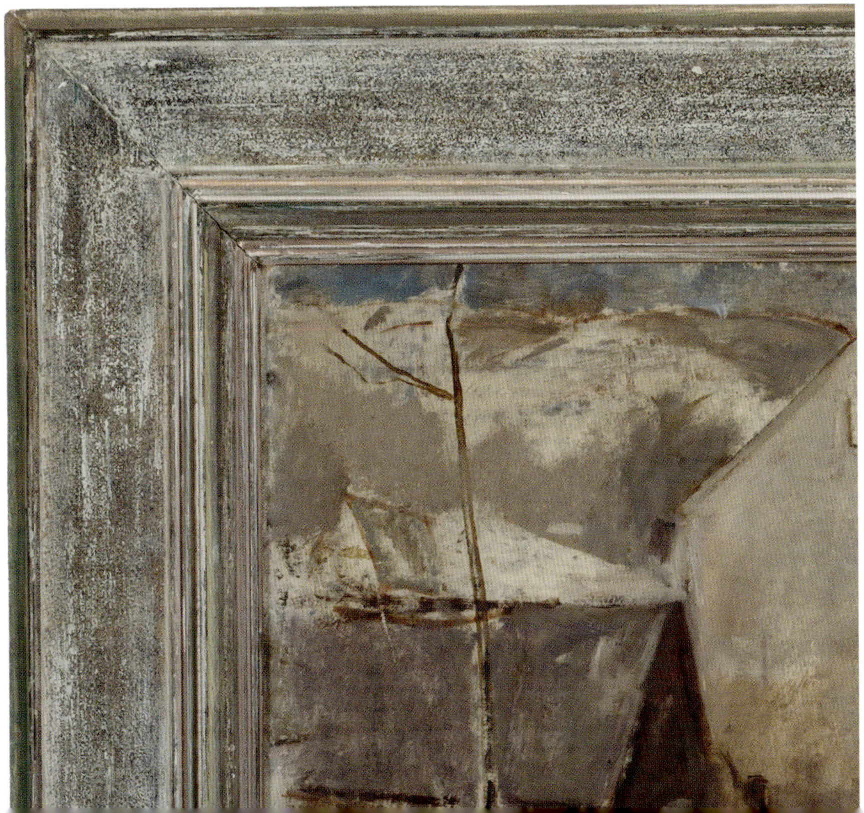
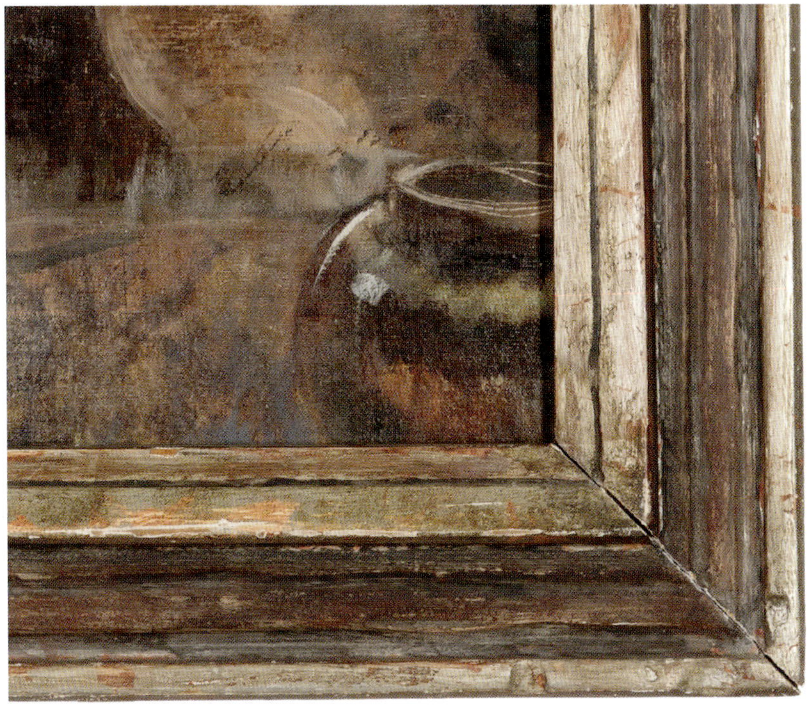

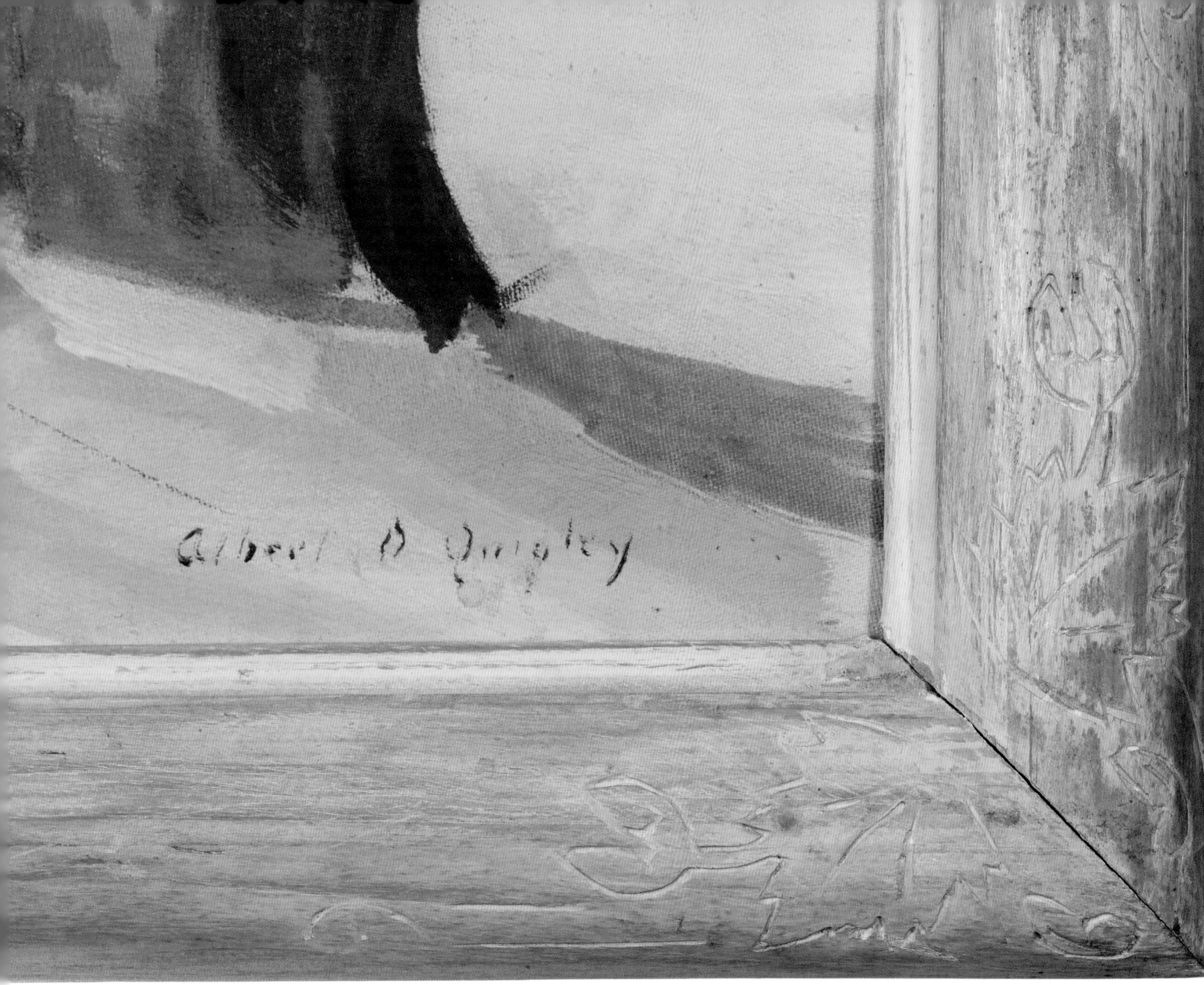
Albert D Quigley

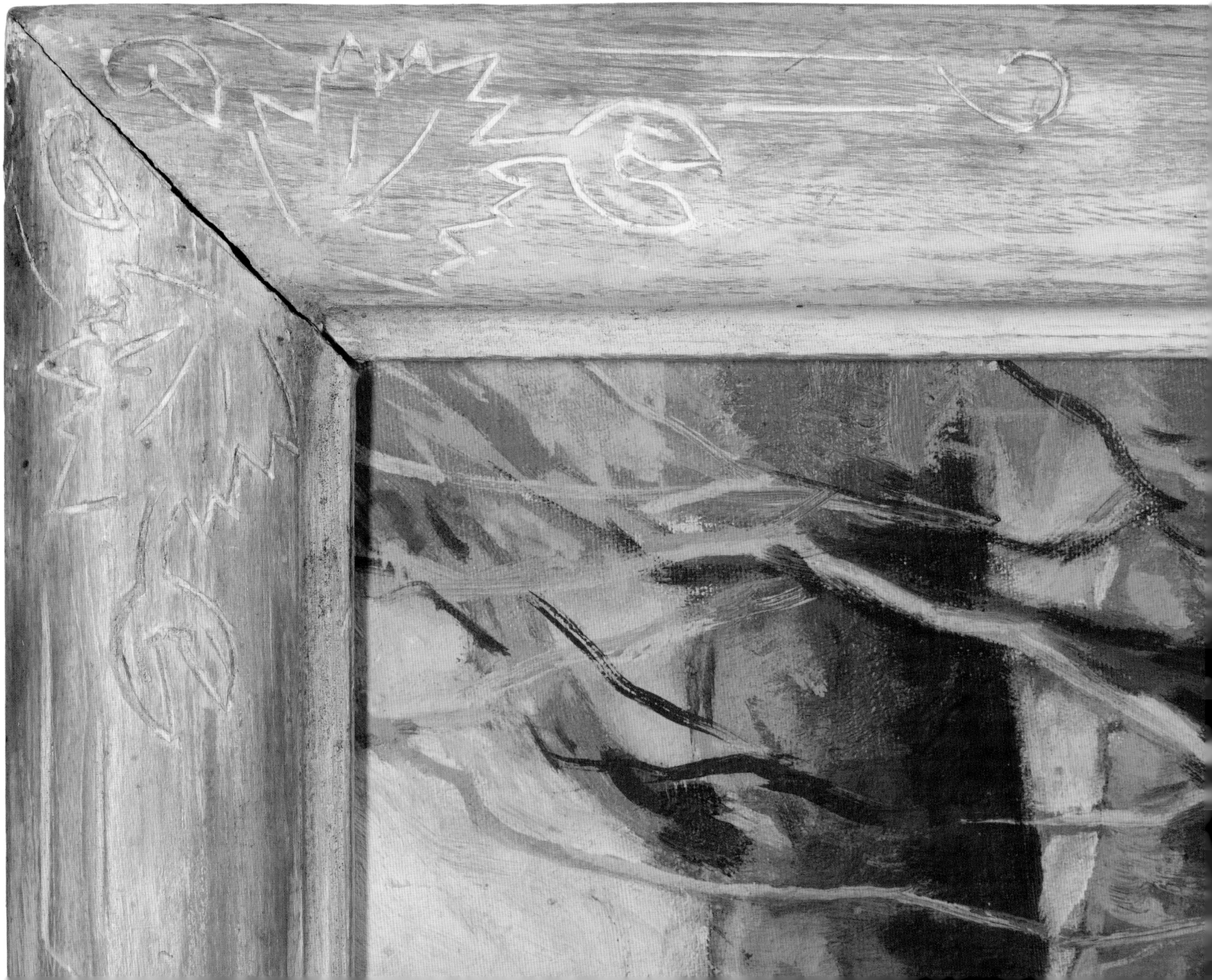

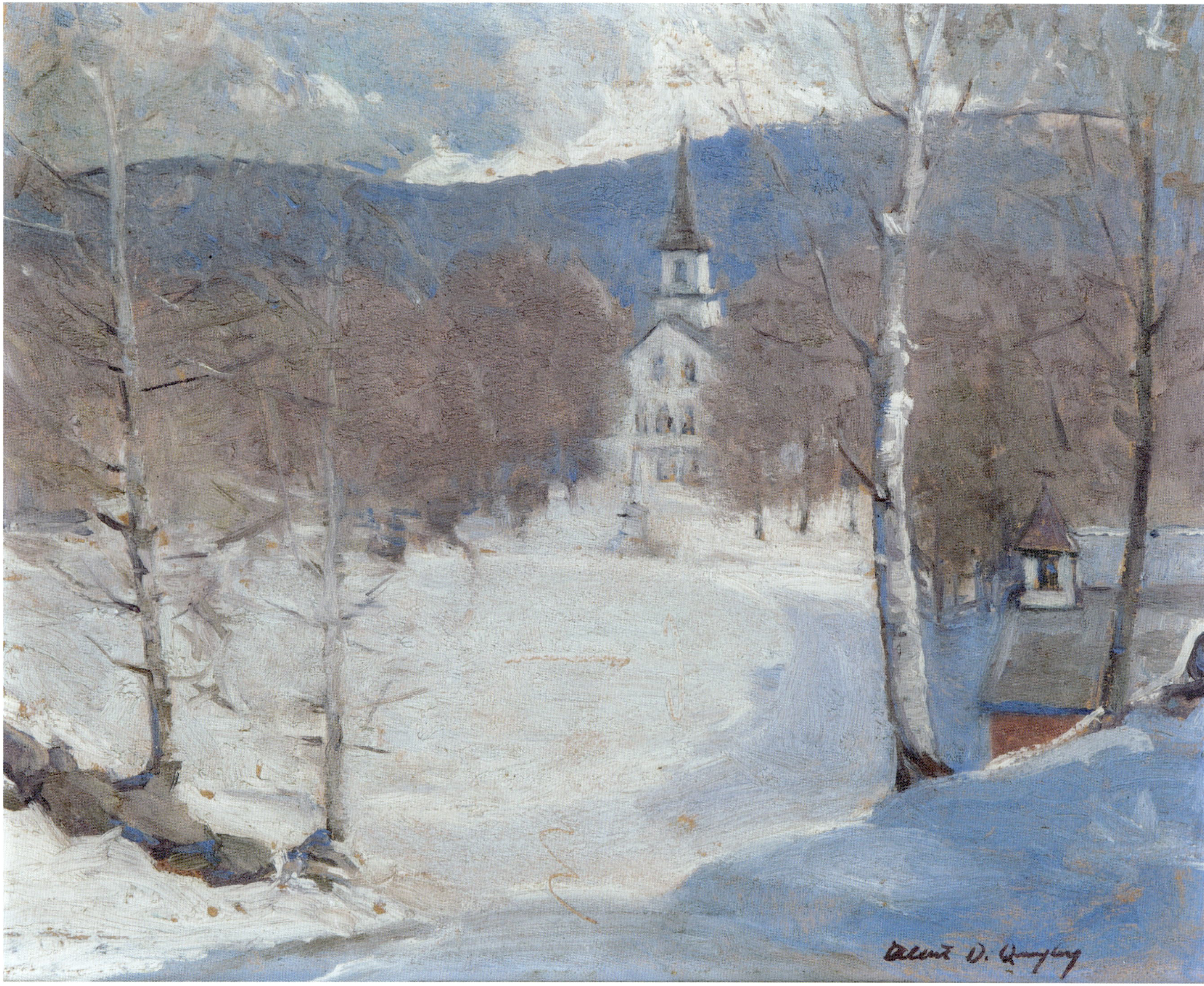

The Nelson Congregational Church

THE NELSON CONGREGATIONAL Church was one of Quig's favorite subjects, or at least one that he painted with great frequency. He could see the church from his house and it made a good study on a winter day when the weather was too harsh for outside work. And he could watch the light change on the steeple, waiting in comfort at the window for the right moment. Quig was endlessly entranced by the natural world that surrounded him and was often, in the words of May Sarton, "silenced by a fit of looking."

—Edie Clark, author
written for the 1991 Quigley art exhibit
sponsored by the Community Church of
Harrisville and Chesham, New Hampshire

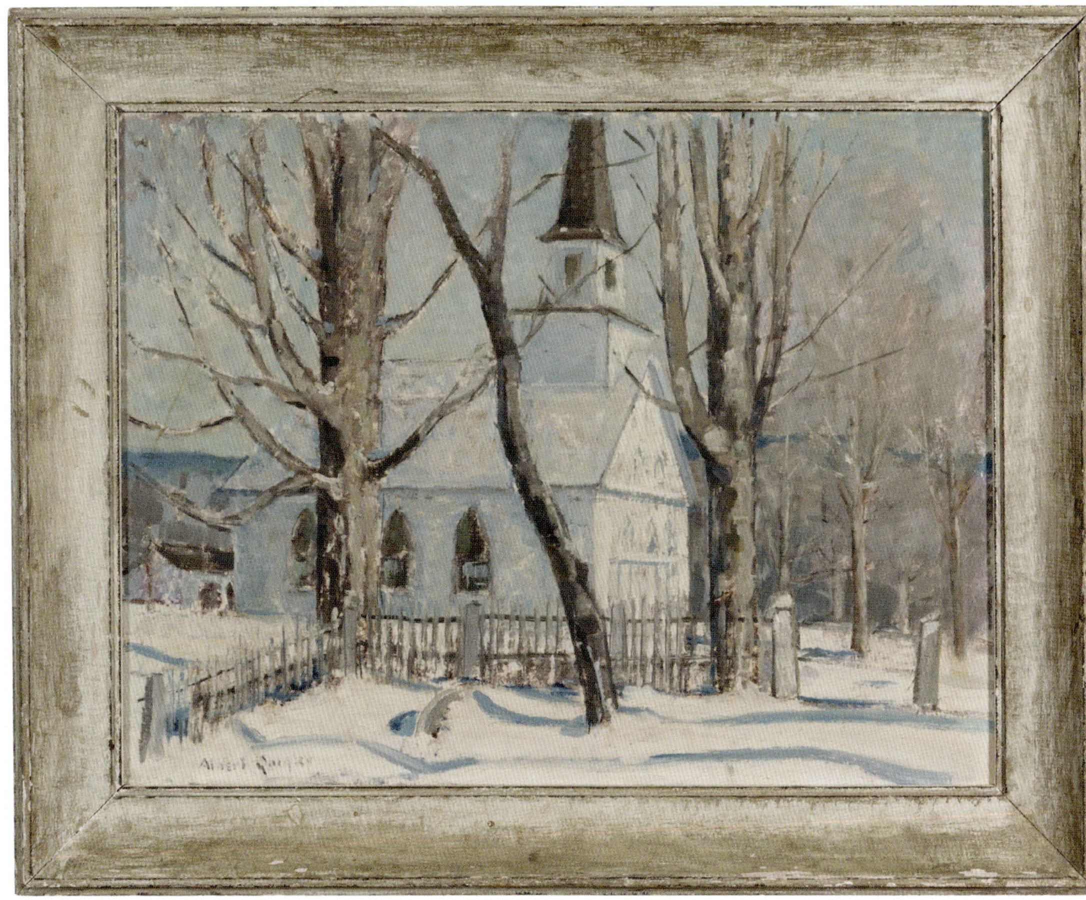

NELSON CHURCH
Oil on board, Quigley frame
23 x 29 in.
Estate of Bonnie Riley

OPPOSITE NELSON VILLAGE WITH CHURCH
Oil on Renaissance Panel, 27 x 31 in.
David P. Johnson collection
View from knoll on Lead Mine Road

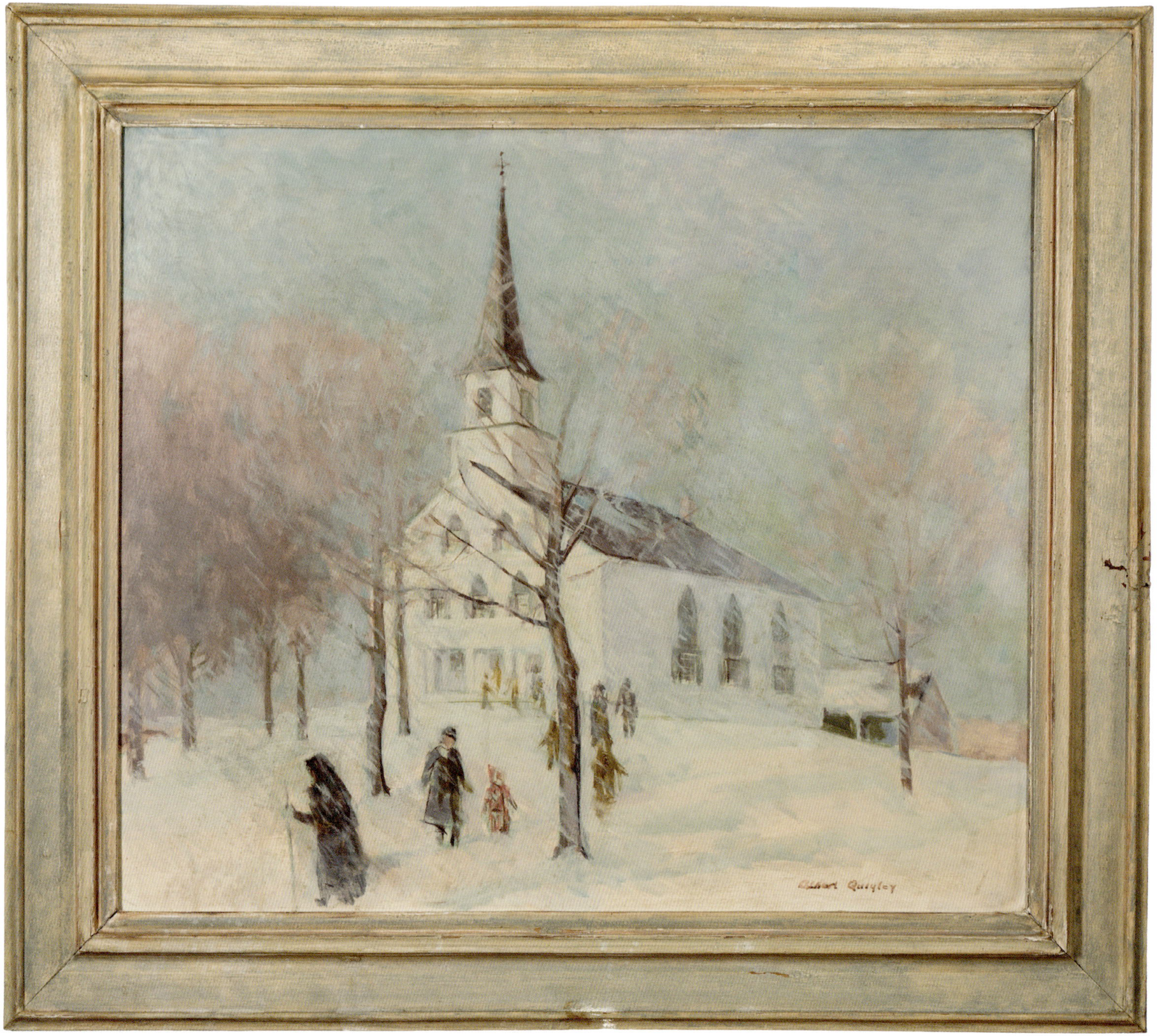

NELSON CHURCH

Oil on board, Quigley frame, 23 x 29 in.

Private collection

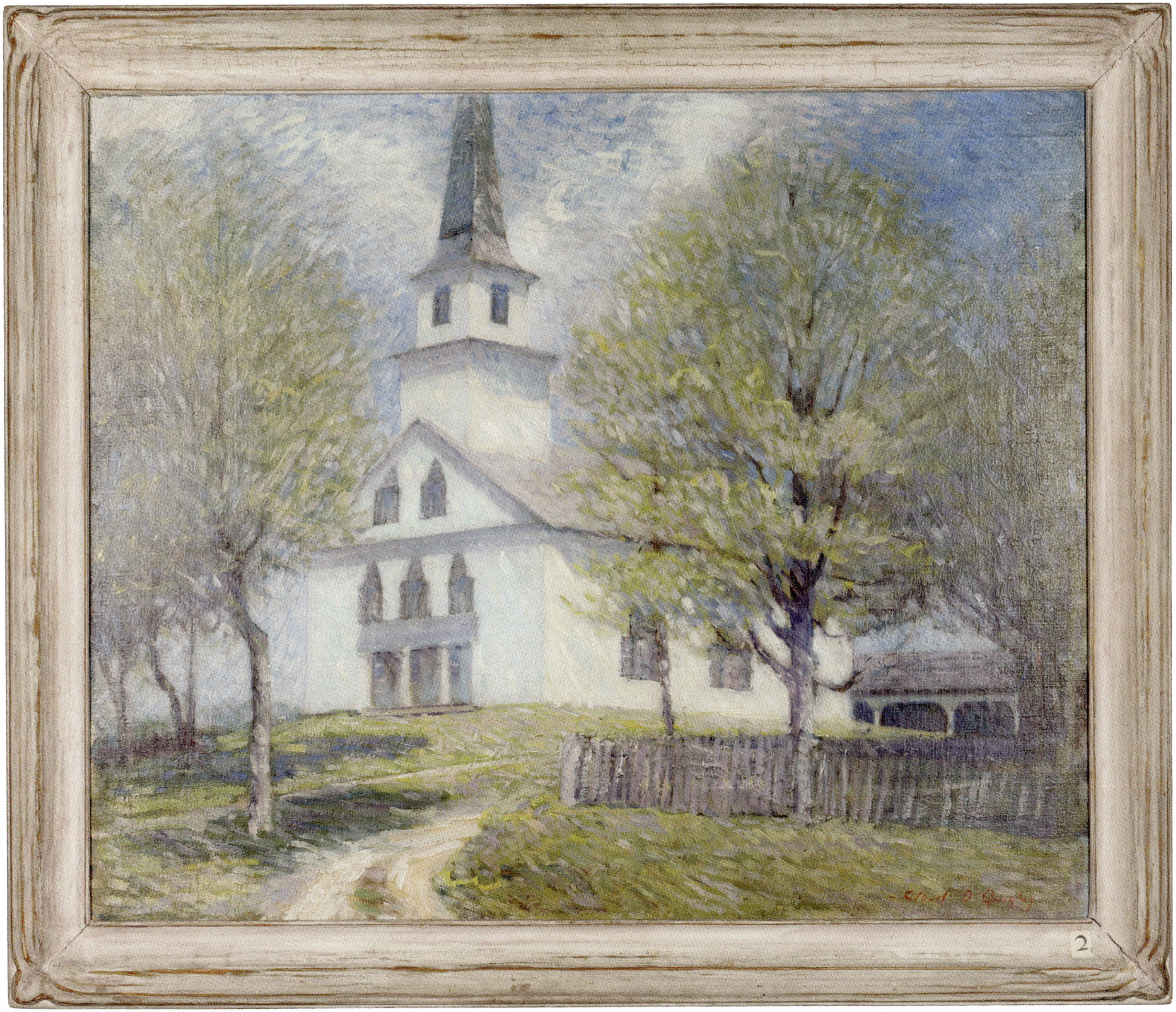

NELSON CHURCH

Oil on board, Quigley frame, 29 x 35 in., private collection

Early painting of the church on an Alexander James board

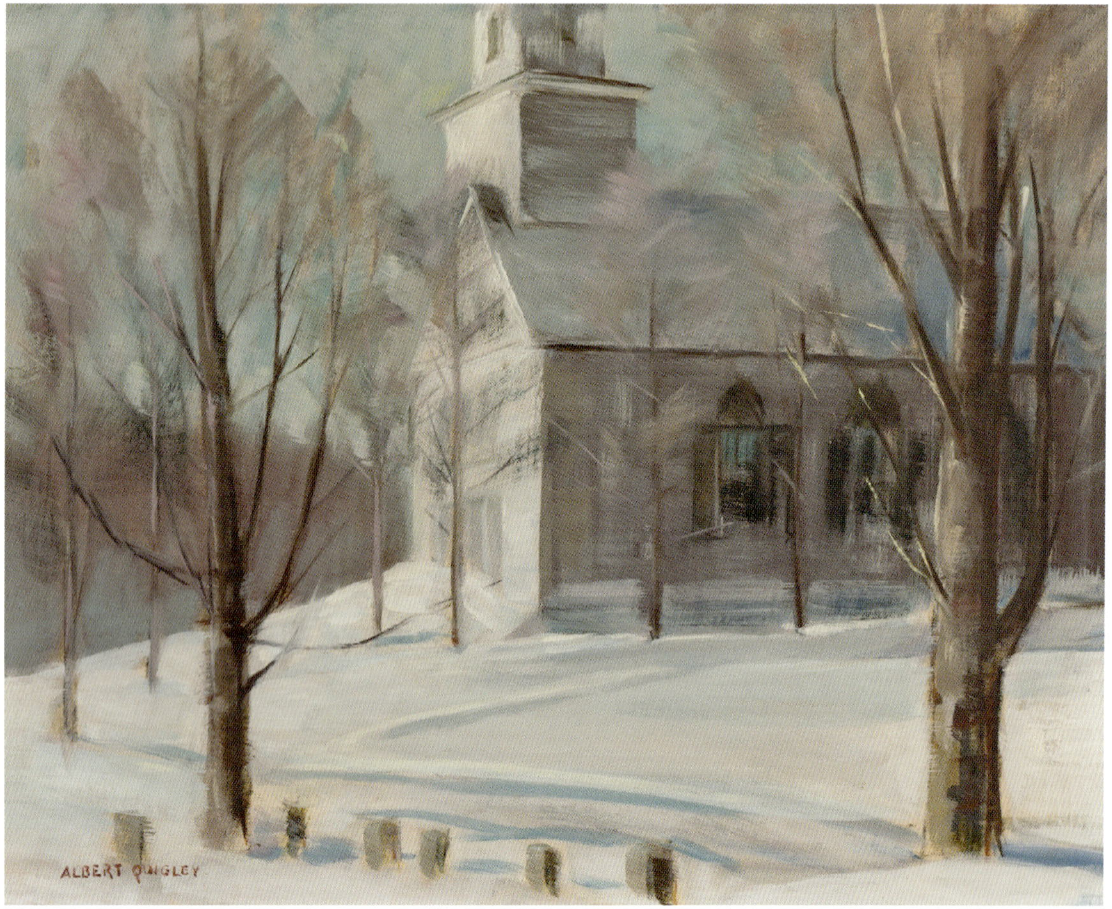

NELSON CHURCH
Oil on board
Quigley frame
21 x 24 in.
Harvey and Frankie Tolman

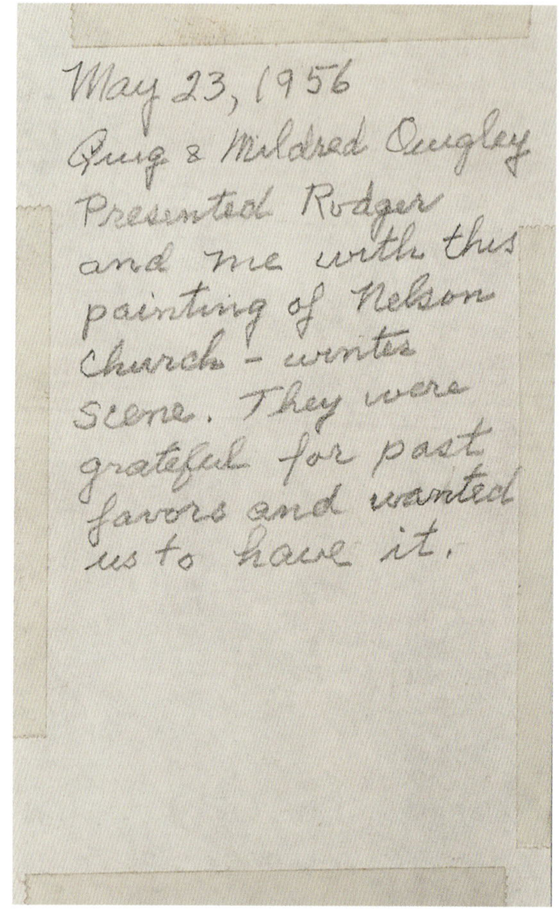
May 23, 1956
Quig & Mildred Quigley
Presented Rodger
and me with this
painting of Nelson
Church - winter
scene. They were
grateful for past
favors and wanted
us to have it.

Note by Frances Tolman attached to
back of painting to the left

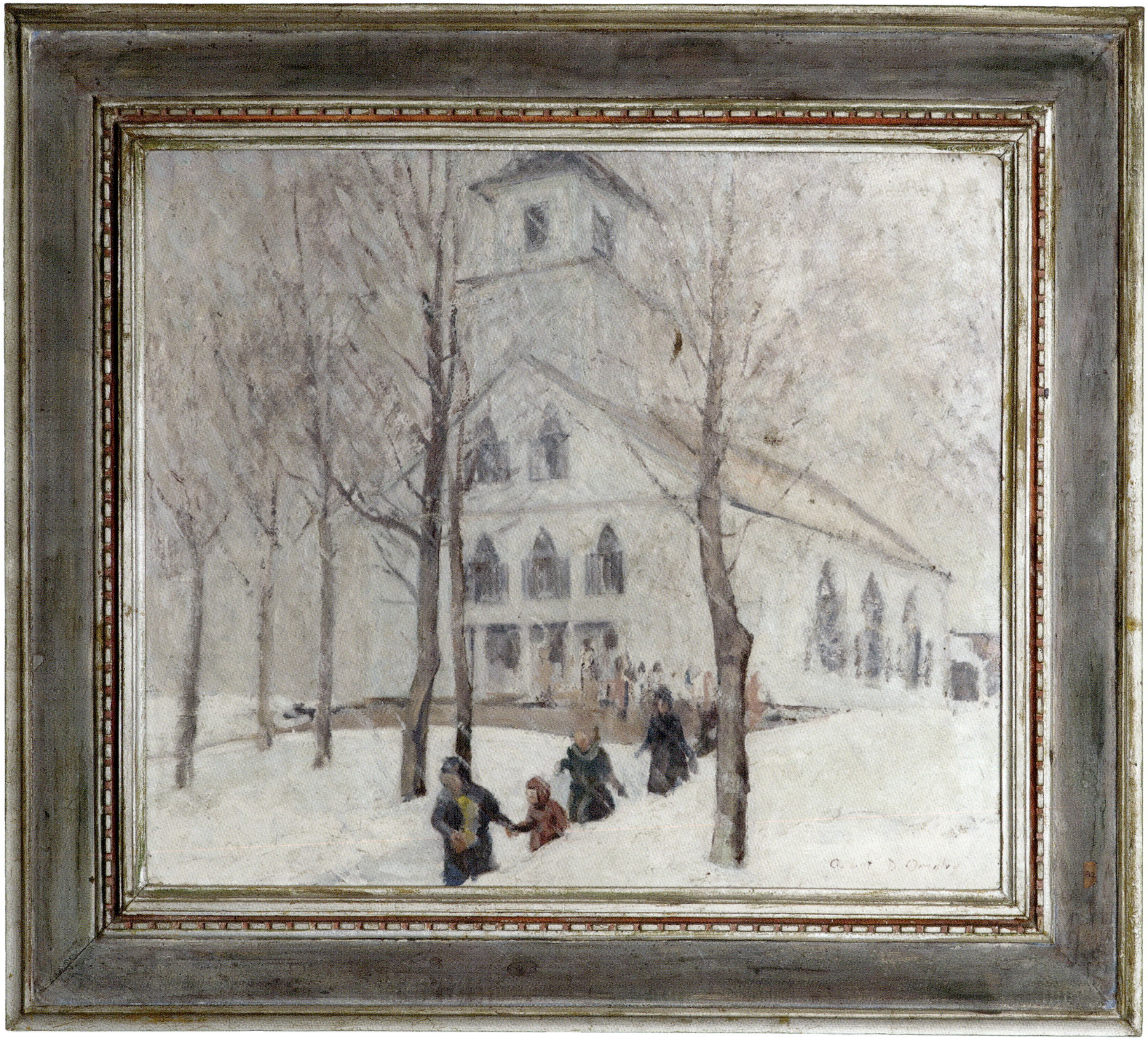

NELSON CHURCH

Oil on board, Quigley frame, 28 x 32 in.

Private collection

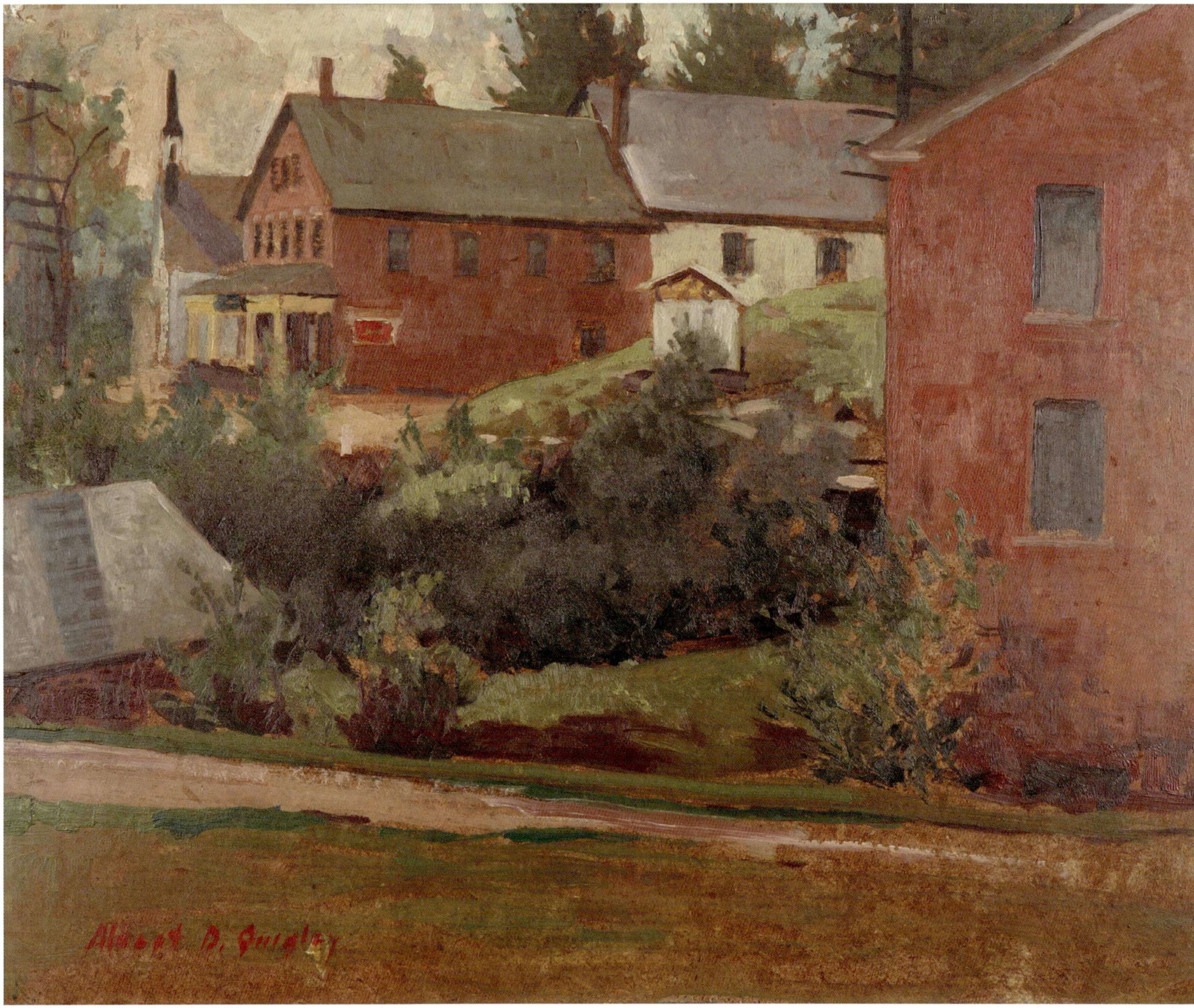

HARRISVILLE, NEW HAMPSHIRE

Oil on board, 16 x 20 in. without frame

Private collection

Buildings and Settings of the Countryside

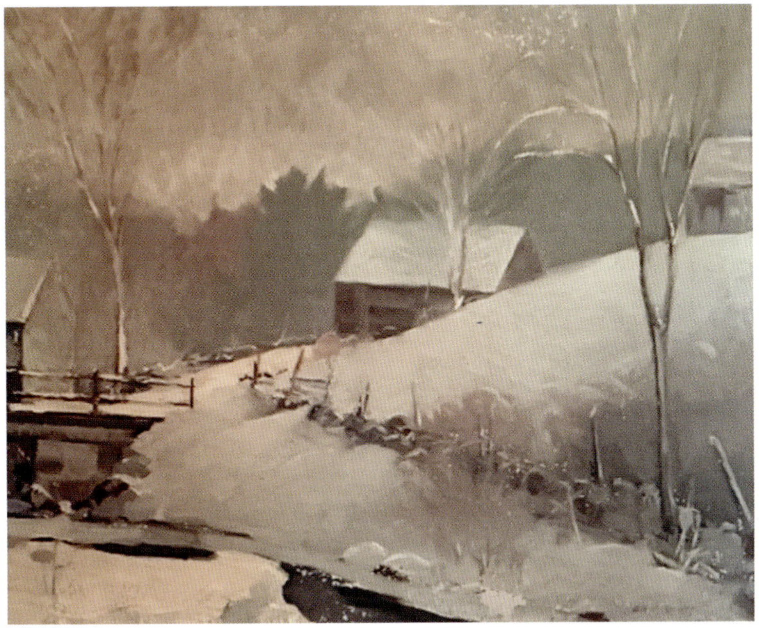

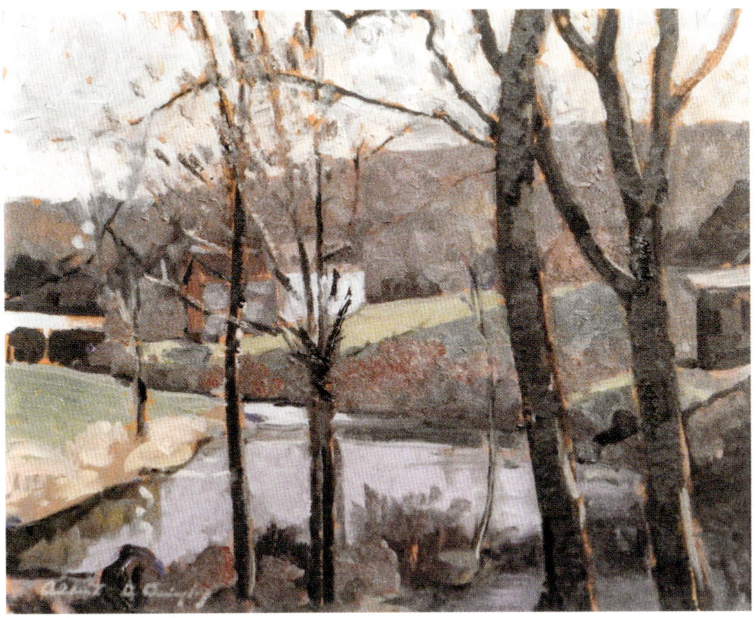

ABOVE UNTITLED Quigley frame, private collection, courtesy photograph

BELOW UNTITLED Quigley frame, private collection, courtesy photograph

What Quig left us is a record of a village and a countryside not in a historian's words but in a painter's vision; people, old and young; the buildings and settings of the village and how insistently they remind us of its capacities and dexterity and interests past and present; farther afield, another church in Alstead, an old house in East Sullivan looking across to Apple Hill Road, and our dominant landmark, Mount Monadnock.

—Bonnie Riley, educator
co-curator of The Paintings of Albert Quigley: The Nelson Years, 1934–1961, *a 1995 exhibit at the Nelson Town Hall*

He received little formal recognition of his painting during his lifetime even though his career spanned almost forty years. During that time he captured and preserved the Monadnock region, its color and moods, its seasons, shapes and forms.

. . . Many of Quigley's paintings achieve a wonderful synthesis of solid, tightly balanced compositions contrasted with spontaneous brush strokes and fresh, true colors. . . . [To] see a bulk of Quigley's work is to recognize a unity, sensitivity and strength.

Quigley was a man who painted for himself, and his paintings reflect this awareness, love and clear vision of the area.

—Schuyler Bemis (now Schuyler Gerstenzang)
curator of Albert Quigley, 1891-1961, *an exhibit at the Thorne-Sagendorph Art Gallery, Keene State College Keene, New Hampshire, August 31–September 28, 1980*

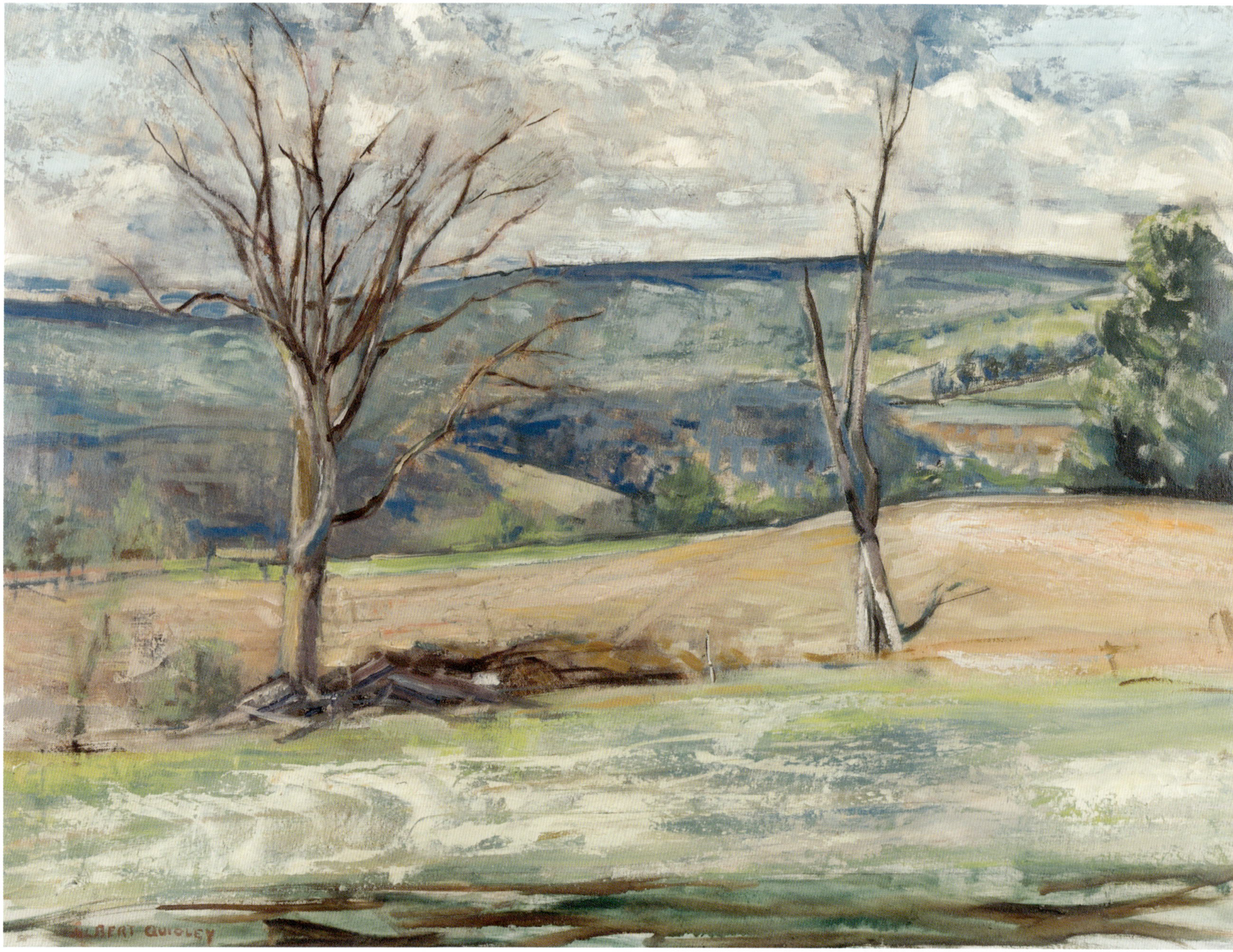

UNTITLED

Oil on canvas, 28 x 36 in.

Private collection

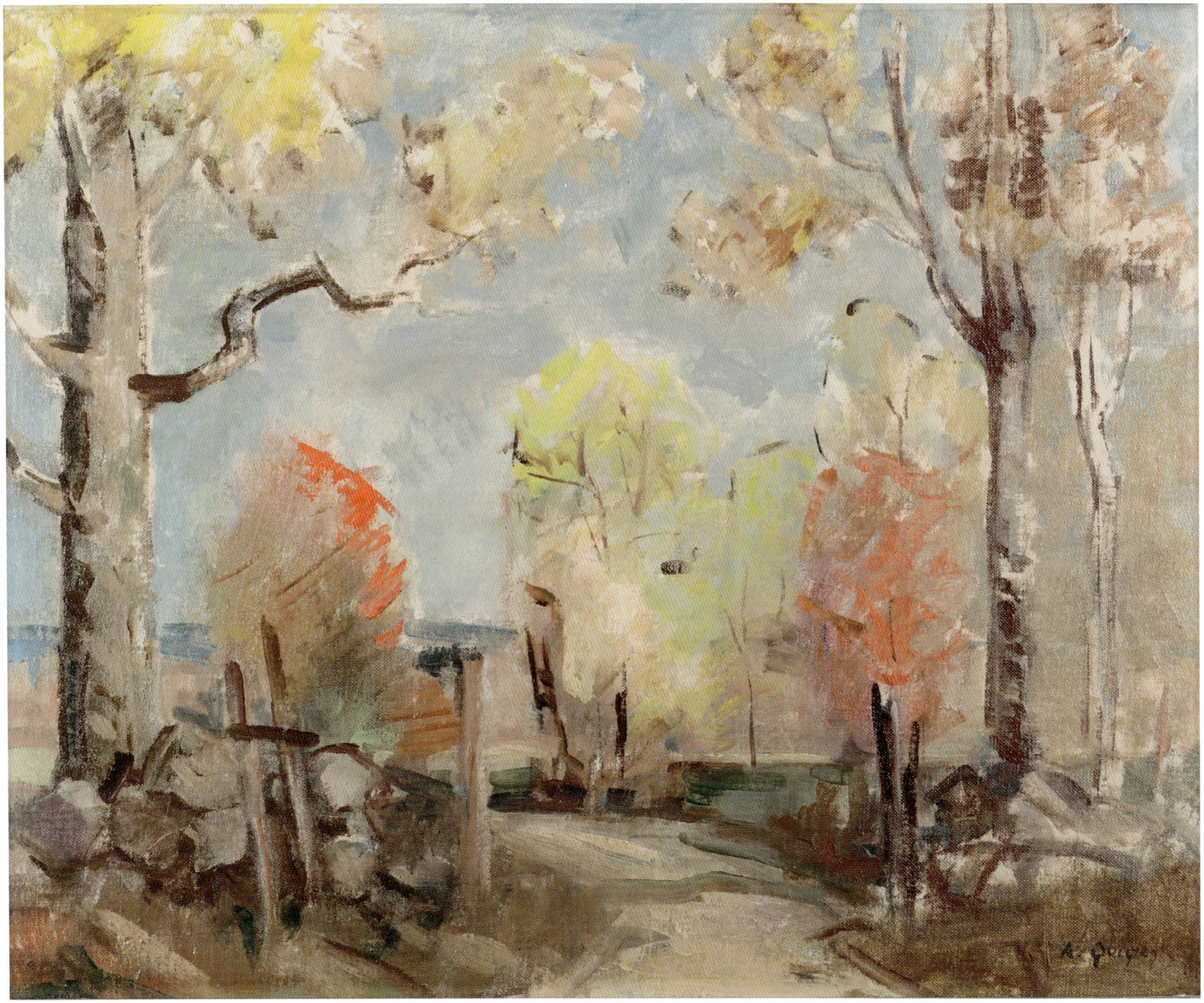

AUTUMN ROAD

Oil on board, 21 x 25 in.

Peter and Martha Wright

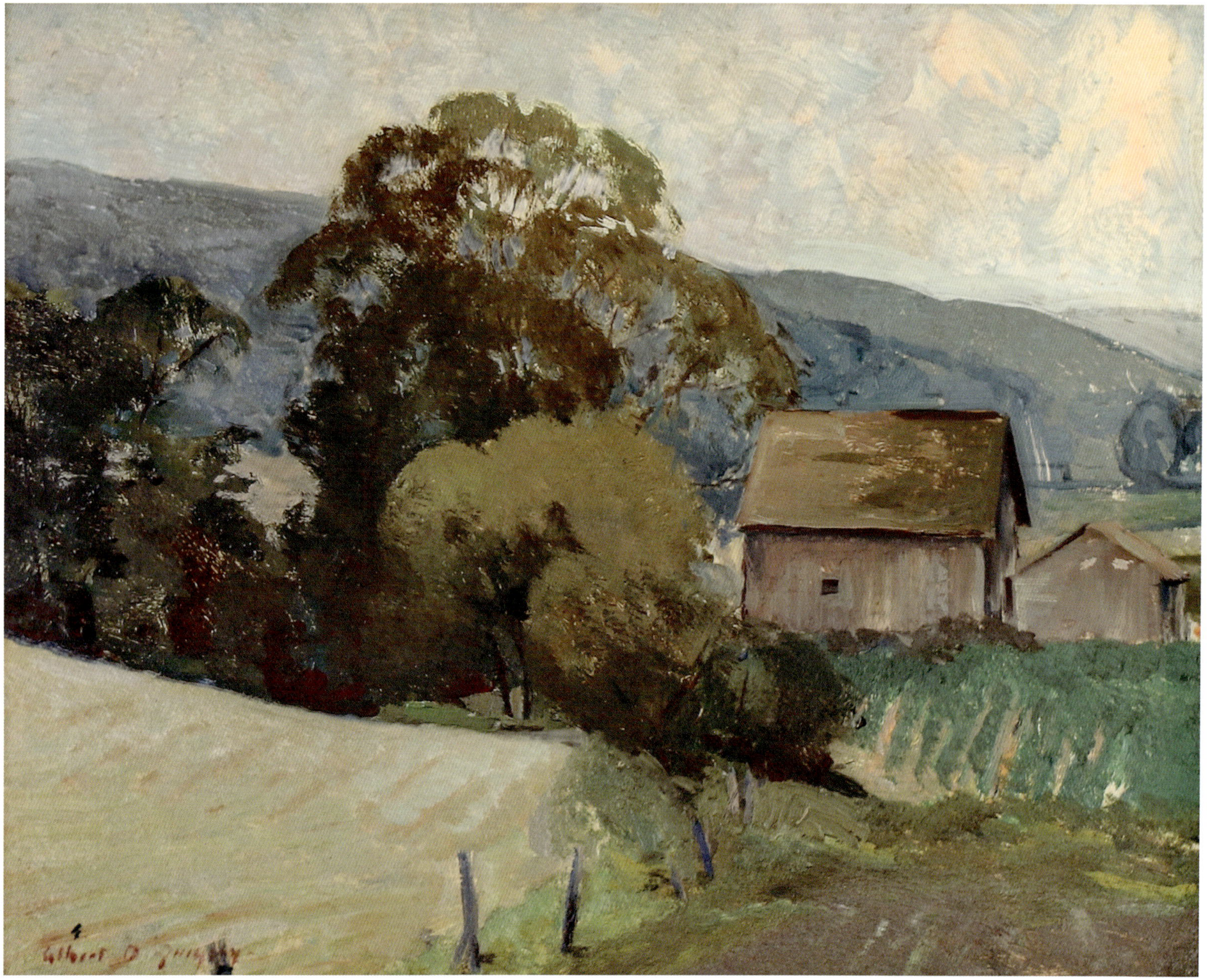

UNTITLED

Oil on canvas, 19 x 23 in.

Private collection

Jane Benson Ackerman, photographer

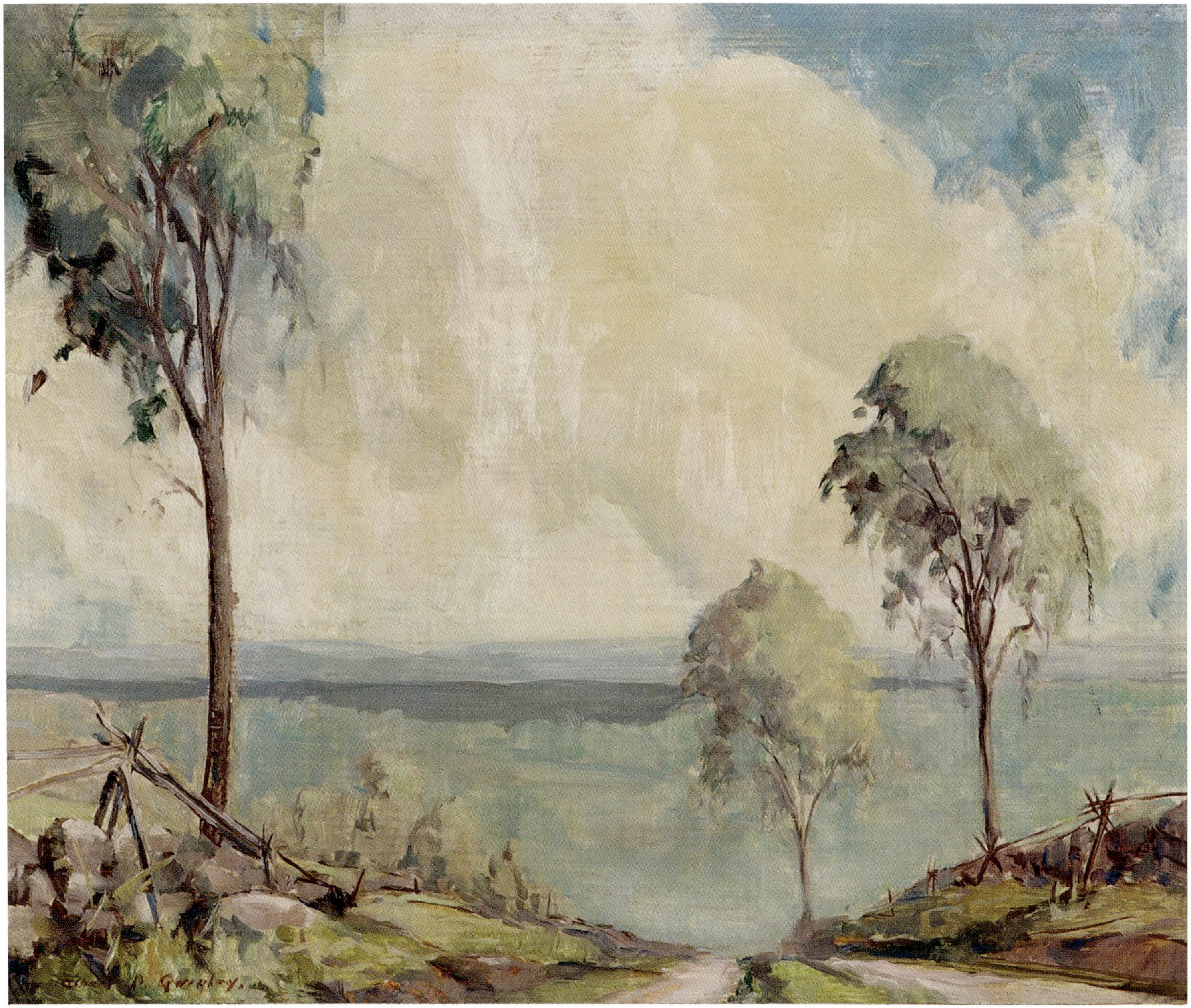

UNTITLED
Oil on board, 18 x 21 in.
Private collection

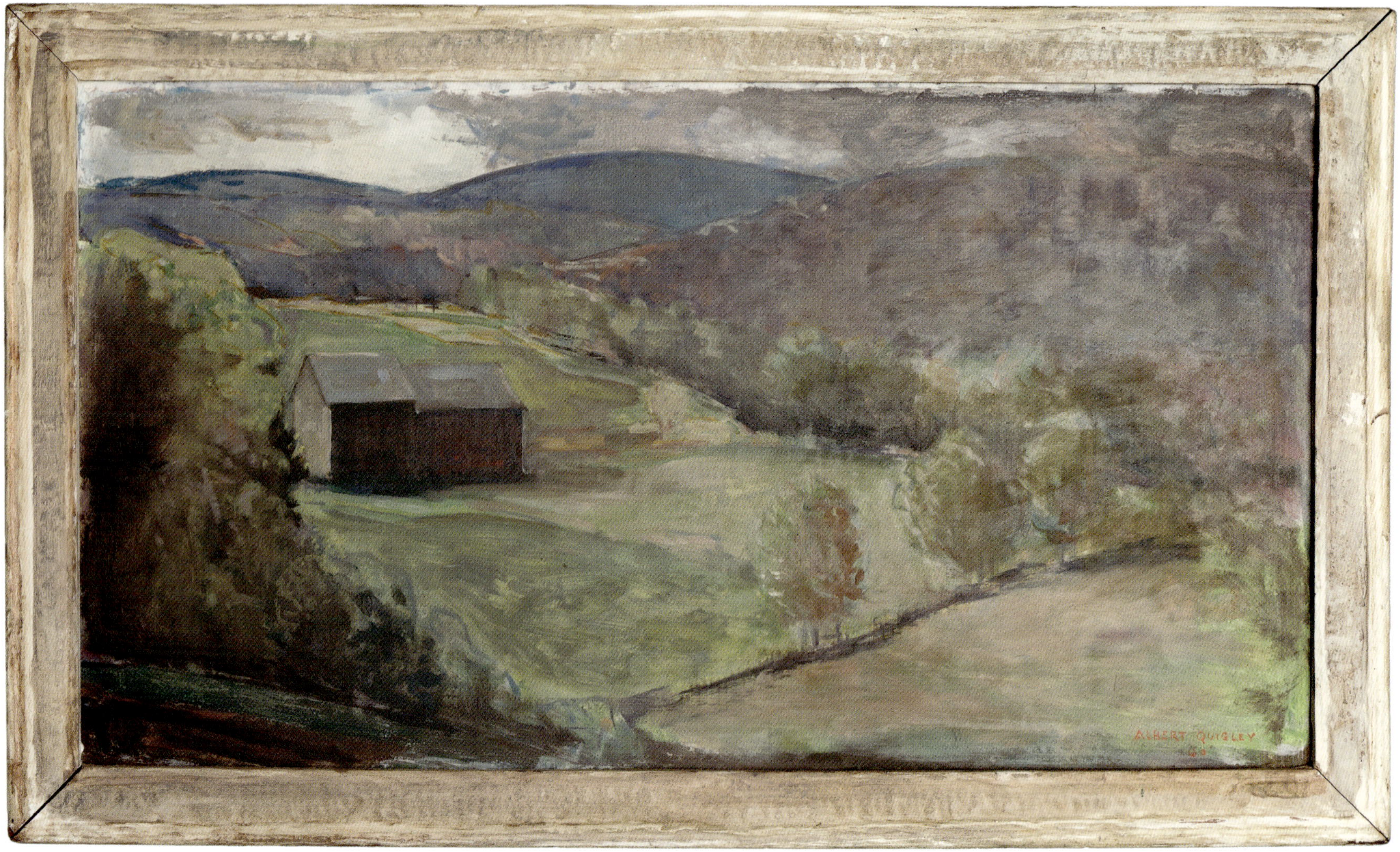

UNTITLED
Oil on board, Quigley frame
16 x 28 in.
Private collection

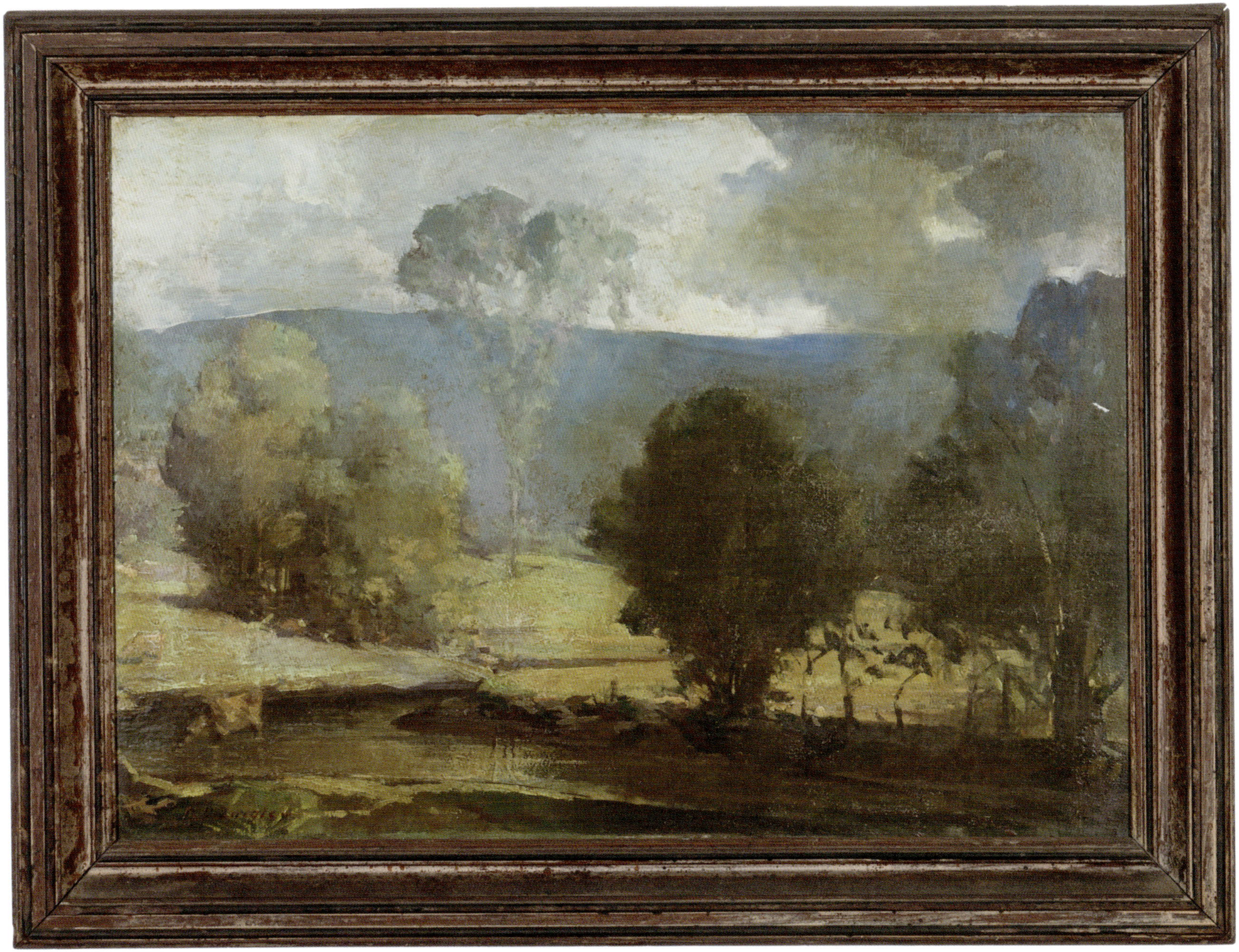

UNTITLED

Oil on board, Quigley frame, 21 x 28 in.

Private collection

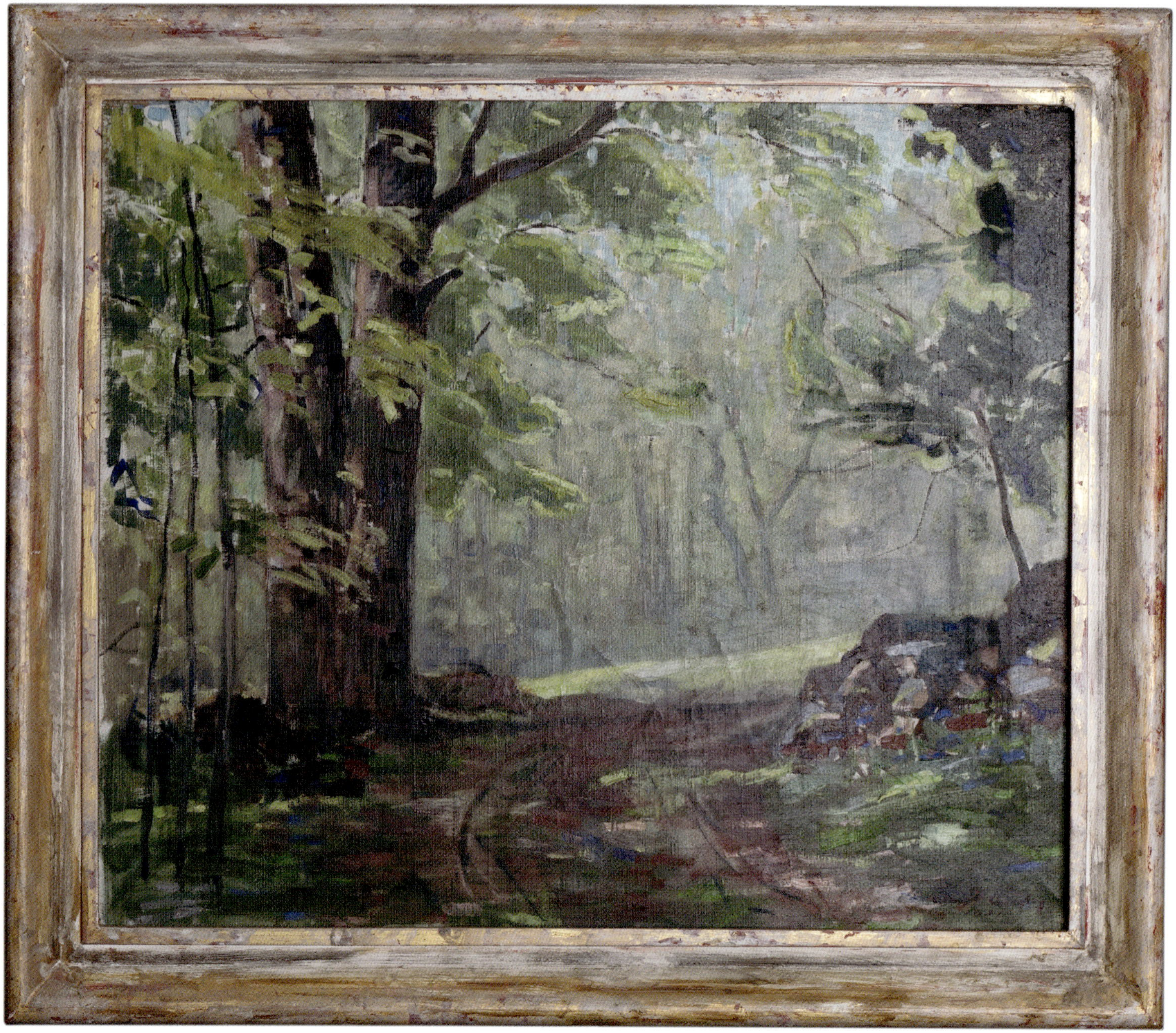

UNTITLED

Oil on canvas, Quigley frame, 24 x 28 in.

Private collection

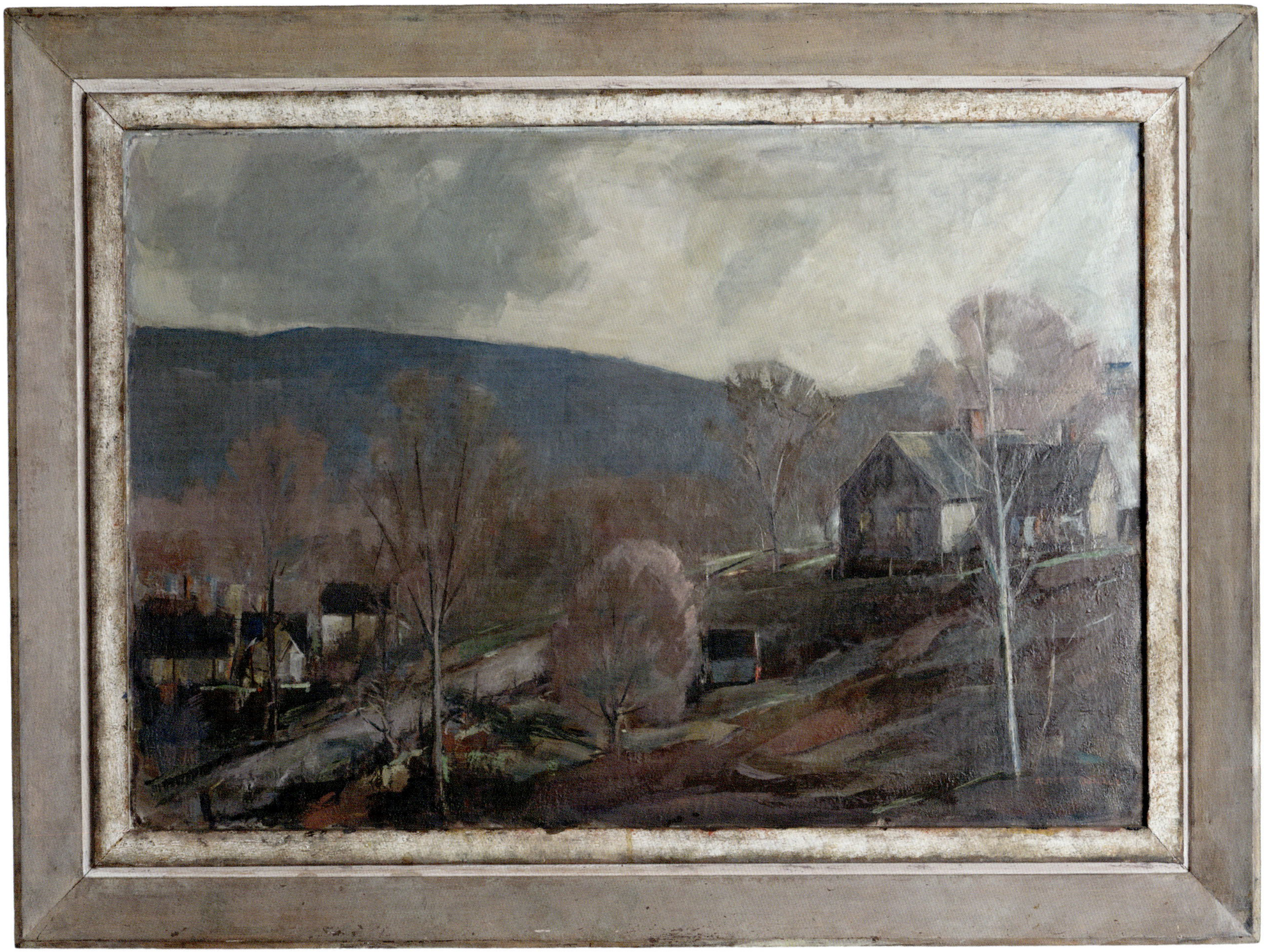

UNTITLED
Oil on canvas, Quigley frame
26 x 36 in.
Private collection

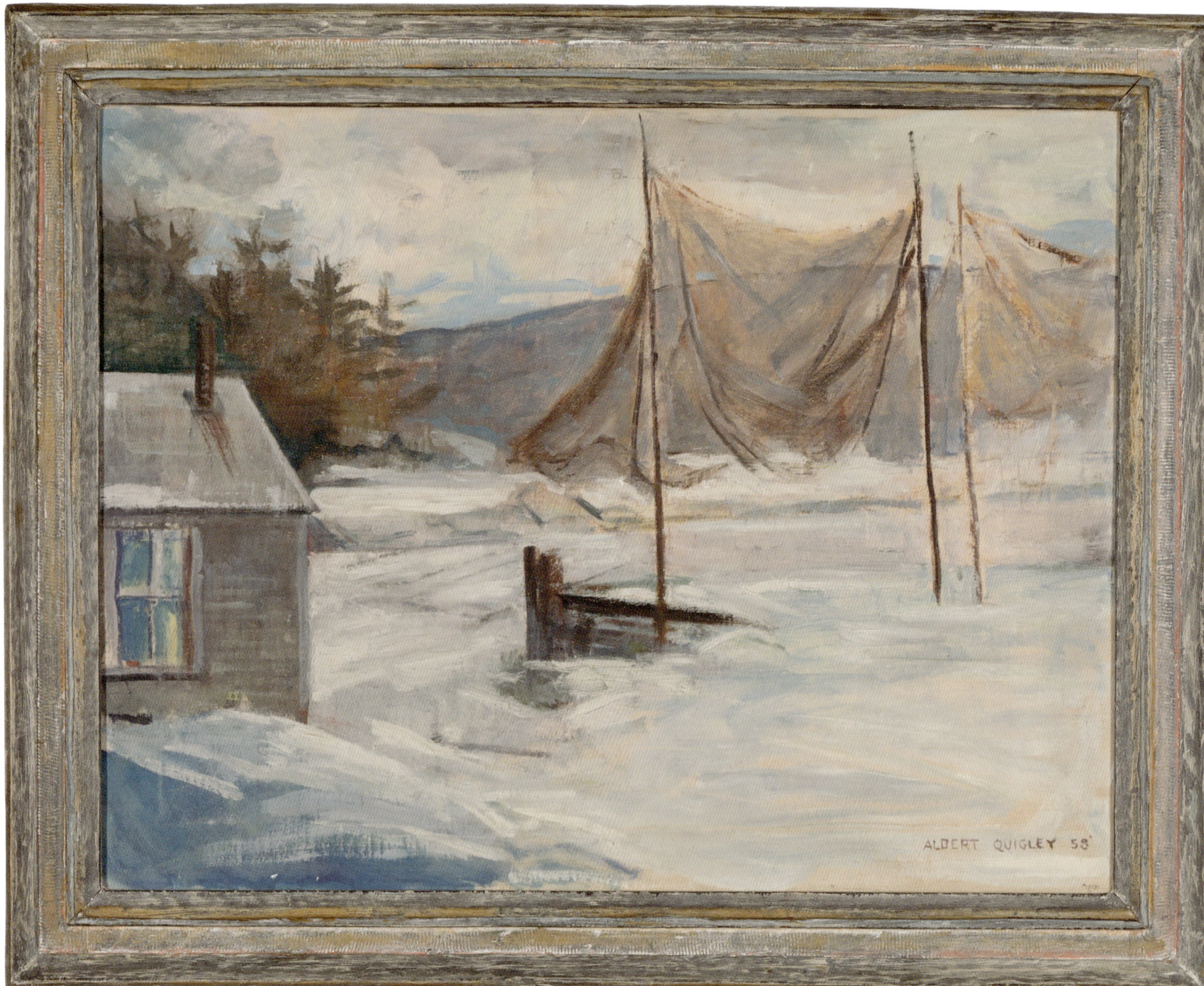

DRYING SMELT NETS (1958)
Oil on canvas, Quigley frame, 22 x 28 in.
Private collection

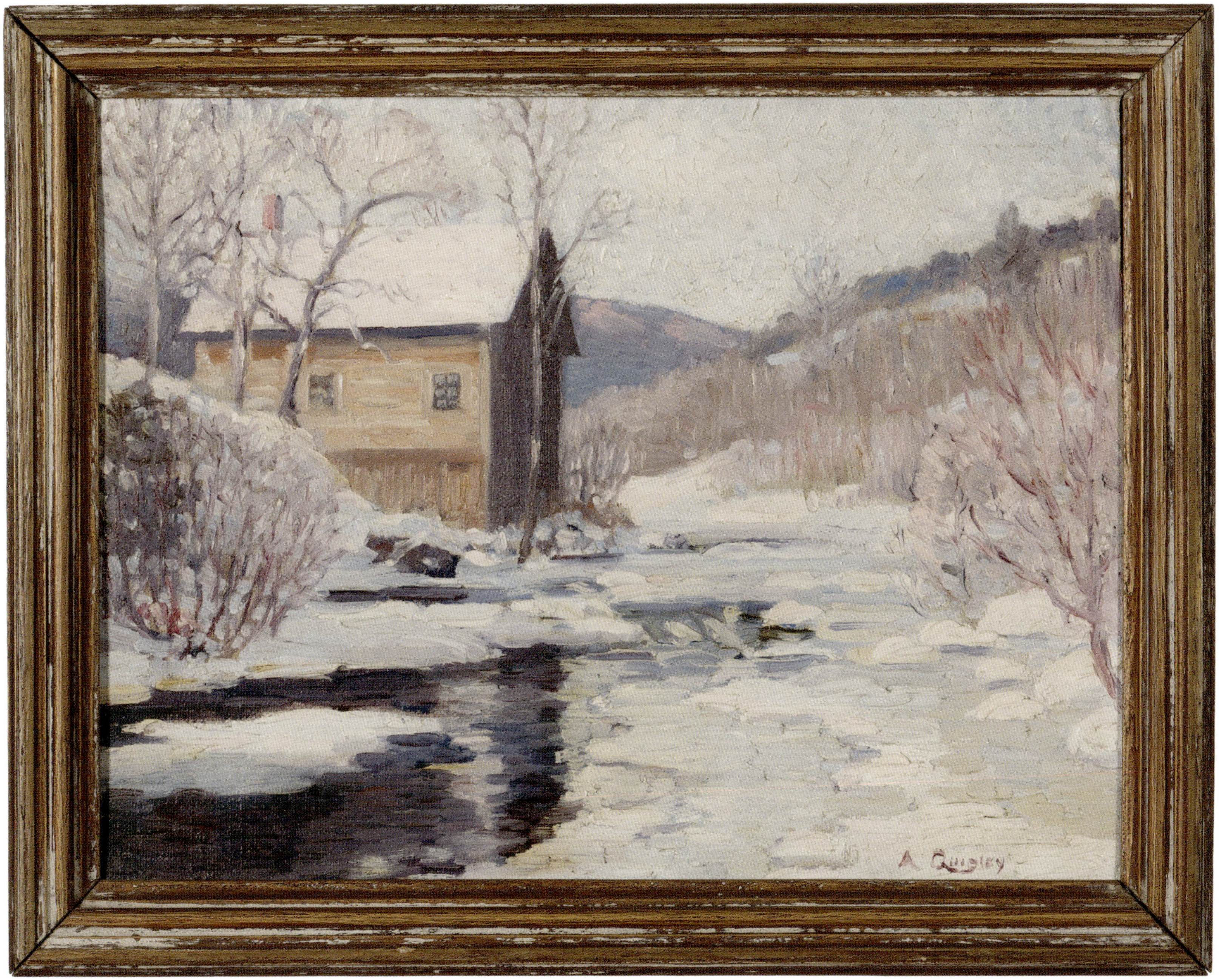

UNTITLED

Oil on board, 15 x 19 in.

Alston W. Barrett

Looking south on the Ashuelot River from the Marlow/Gilsum town line toward mill building, woods, and distant hills

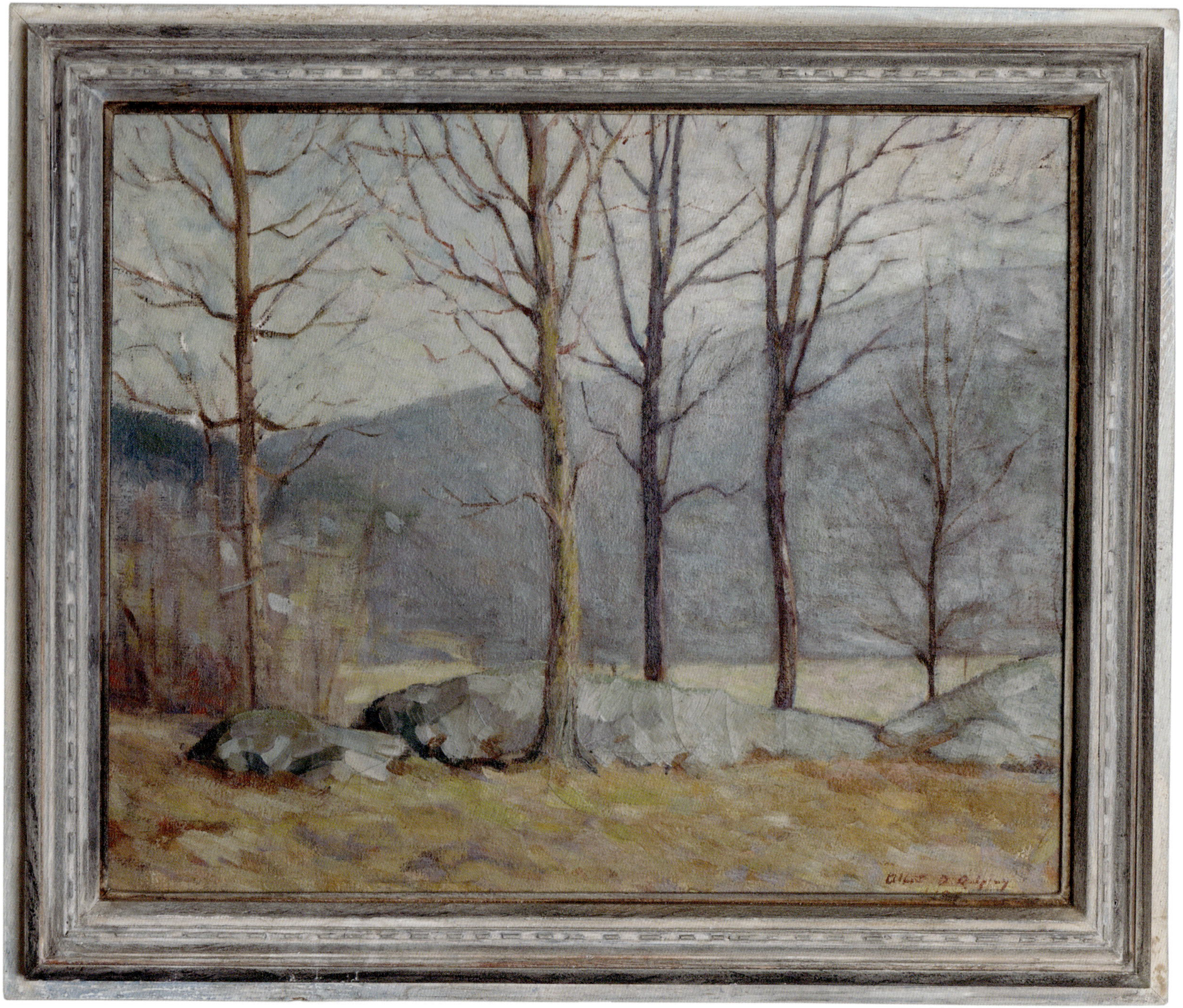

UNTITLED

Oil on canvas, Quigley frame, 20 x 24 in.

Private collection

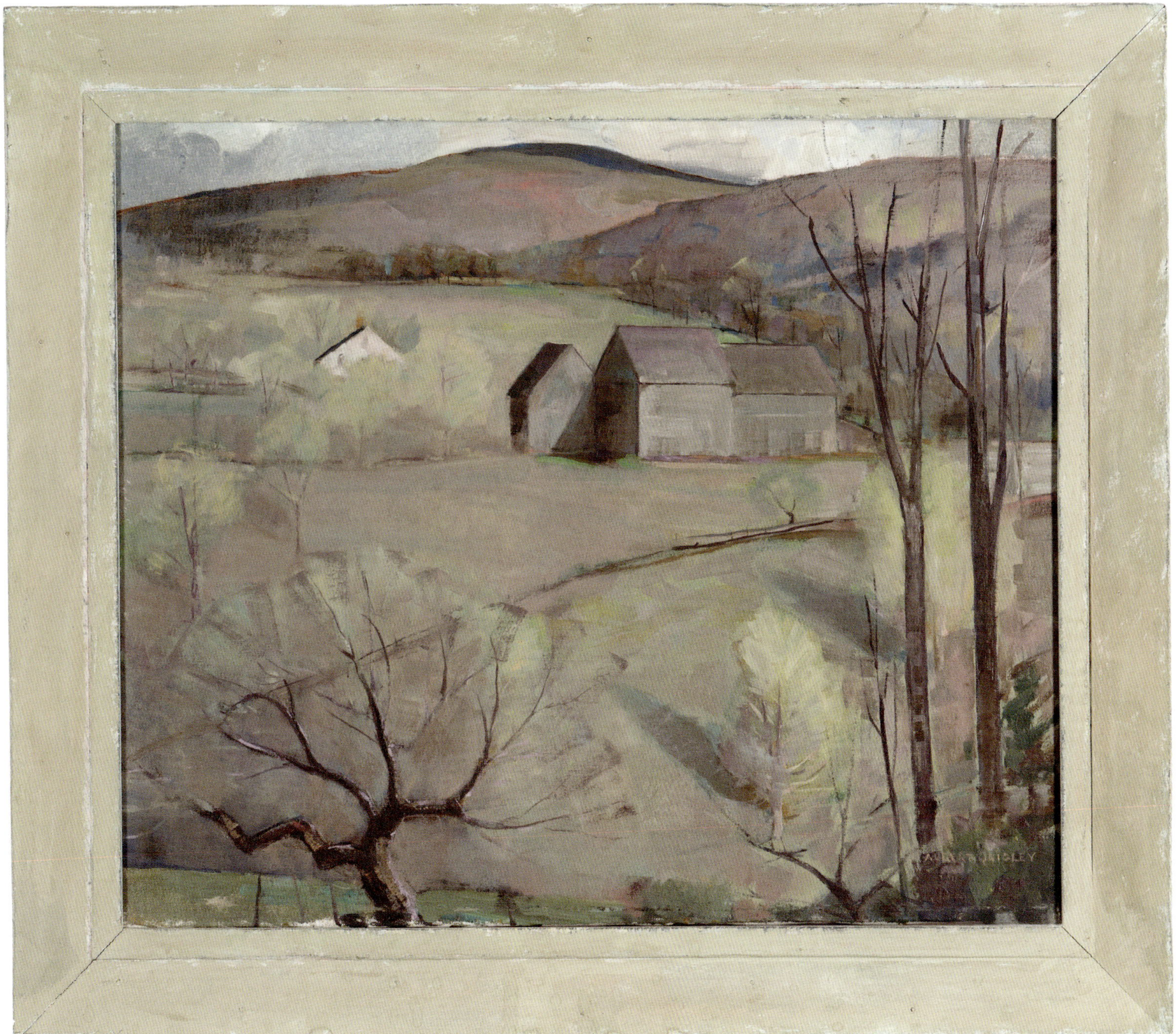

SULLIVAN, NEW HAMPSHIRE

Oil on canvas, Quigley frame, 25 x 29 in.

Private collection

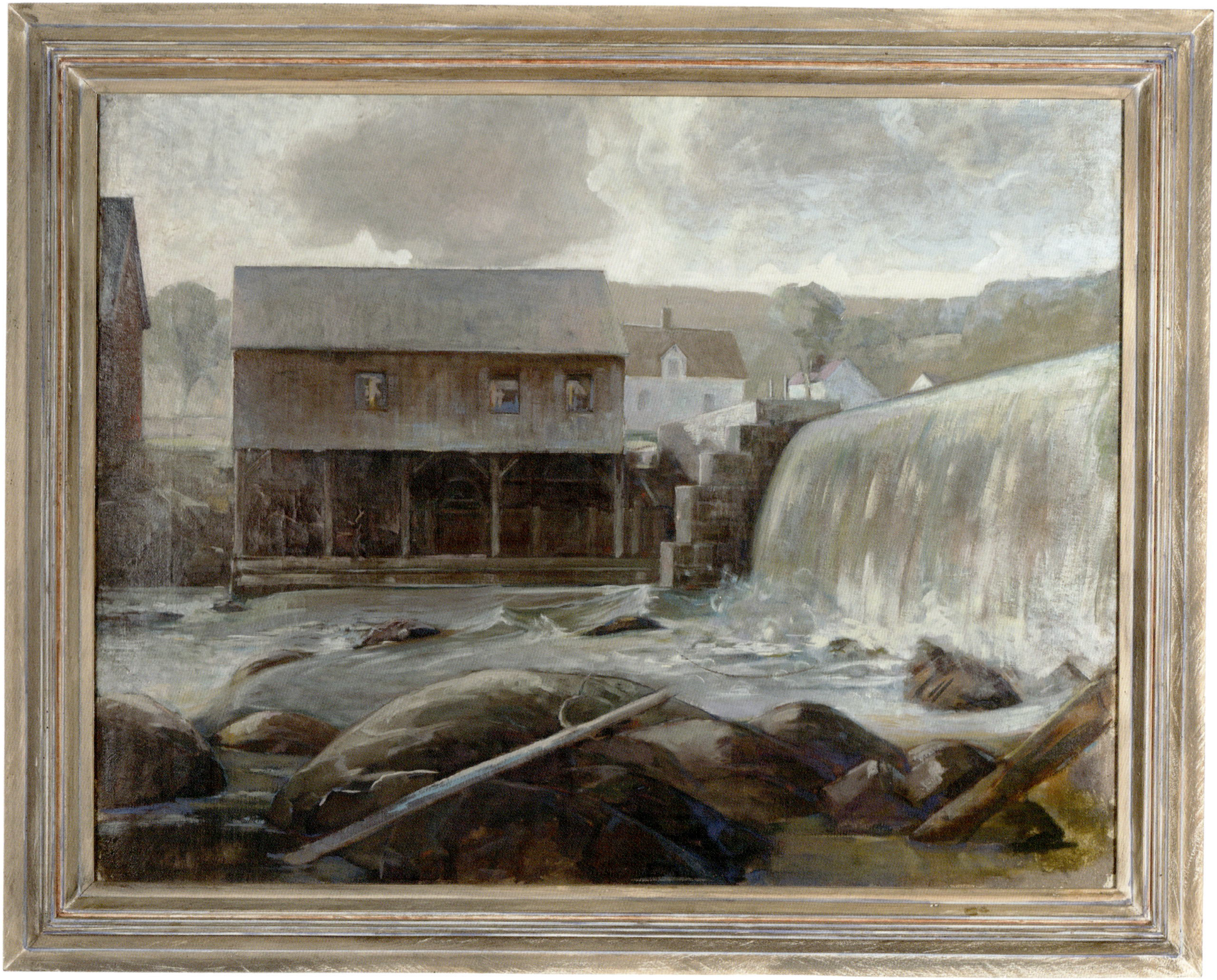

MILL SCENE, FRANKFORT, MAINE

Oil on canvas, Quigley frame, 36 x 47 in., private collection

Quigley painted this scene from memory in his later years

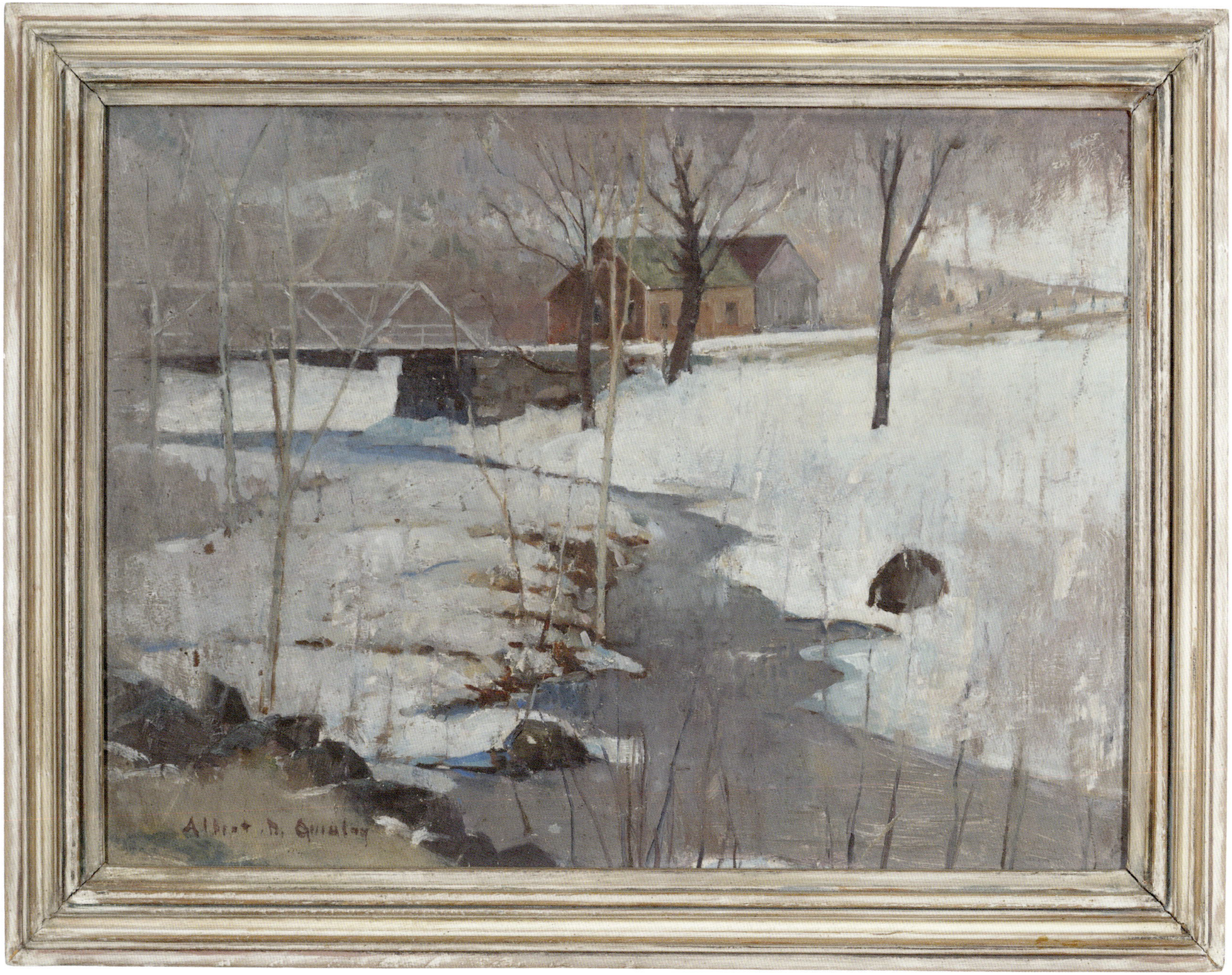

UNTITLED

Oil on board, Quigley frame, 19 x 24 in.

Camp Glen Brook

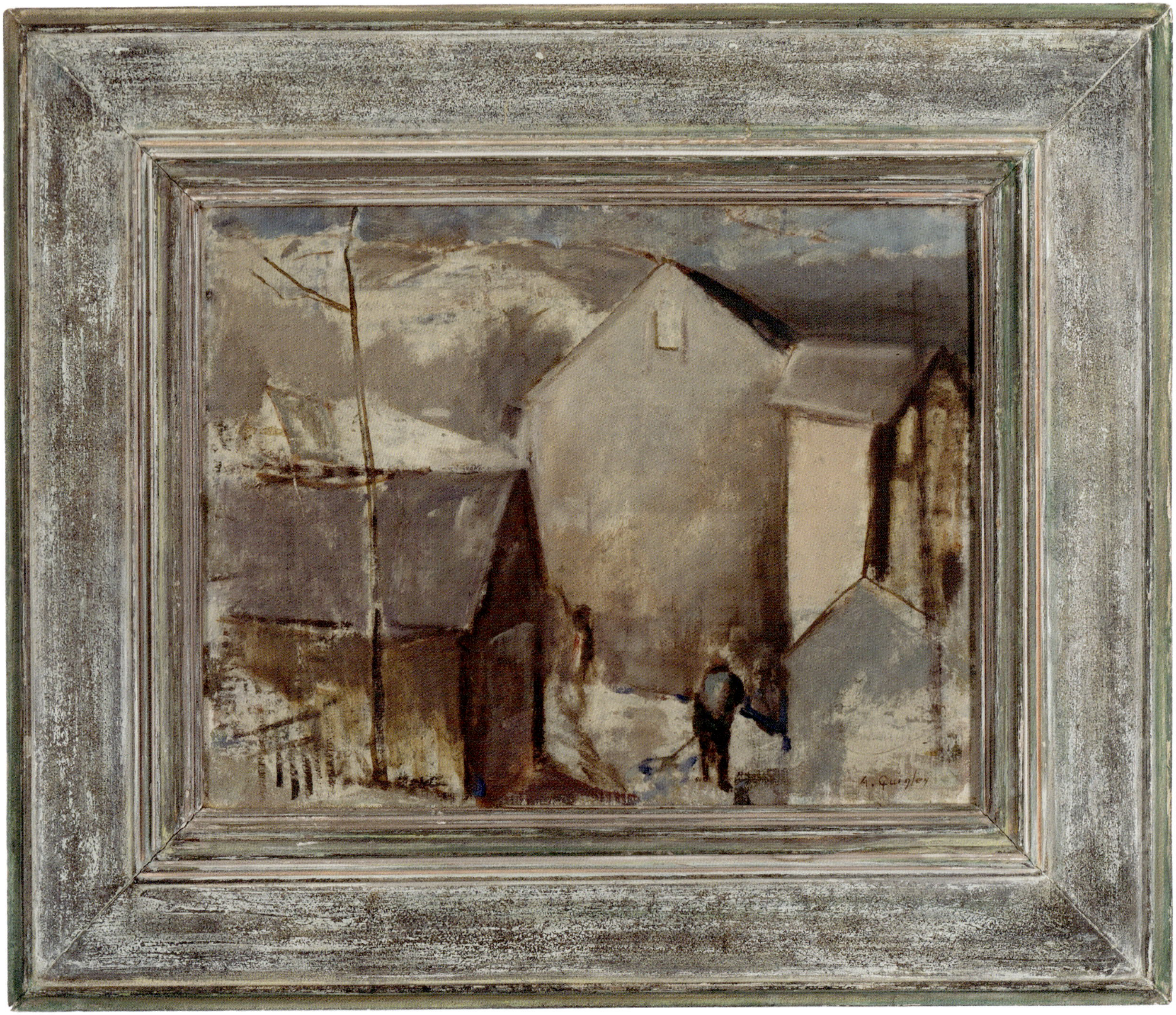

DRYING FISH IN MAINE

Oil on board, Quigley frame, 20 x 24 in.

Private collection

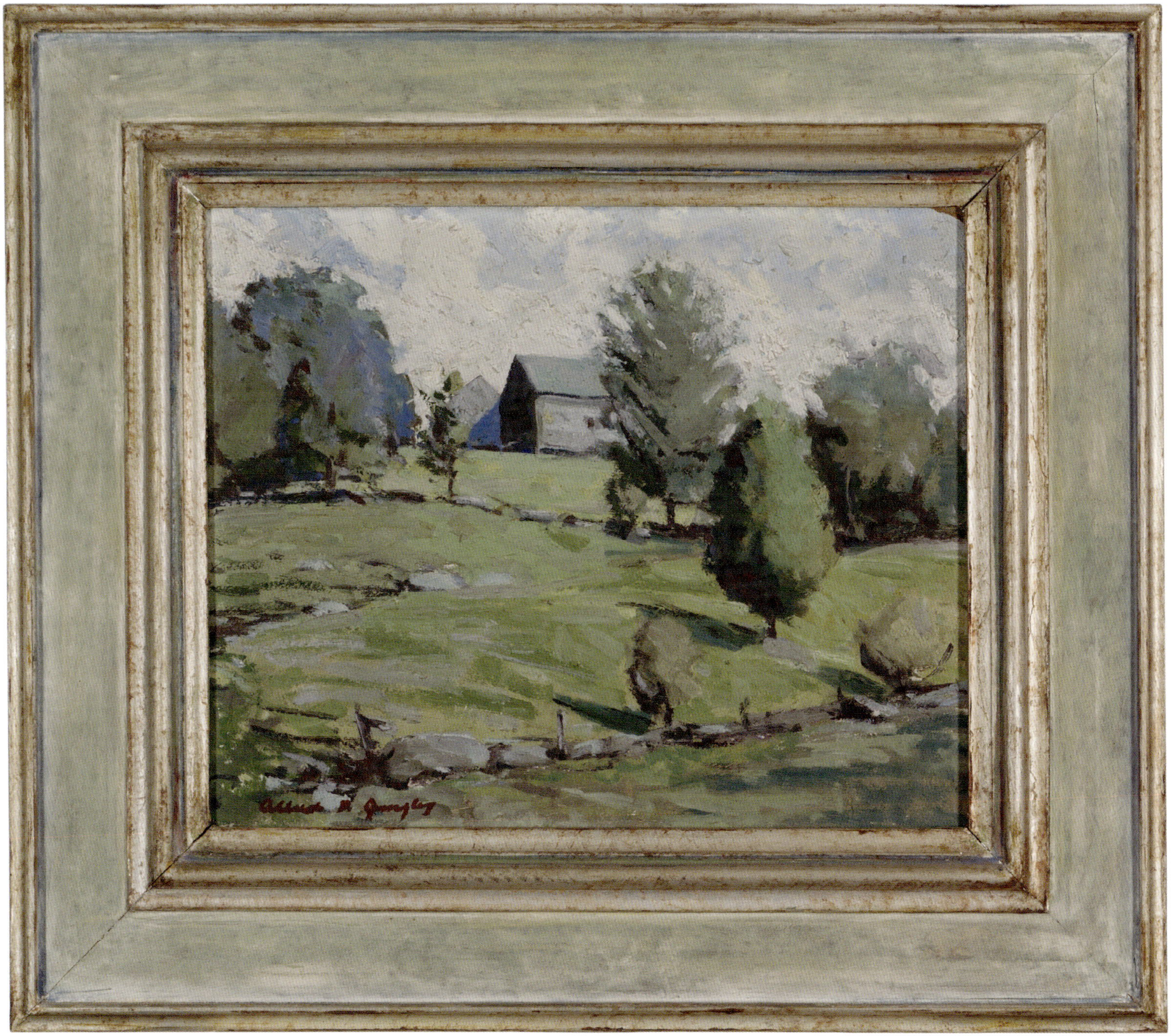

RENNEY DAVIS FARM

Oil on board, Quigley frame, 21 x 24 in.

Private collection

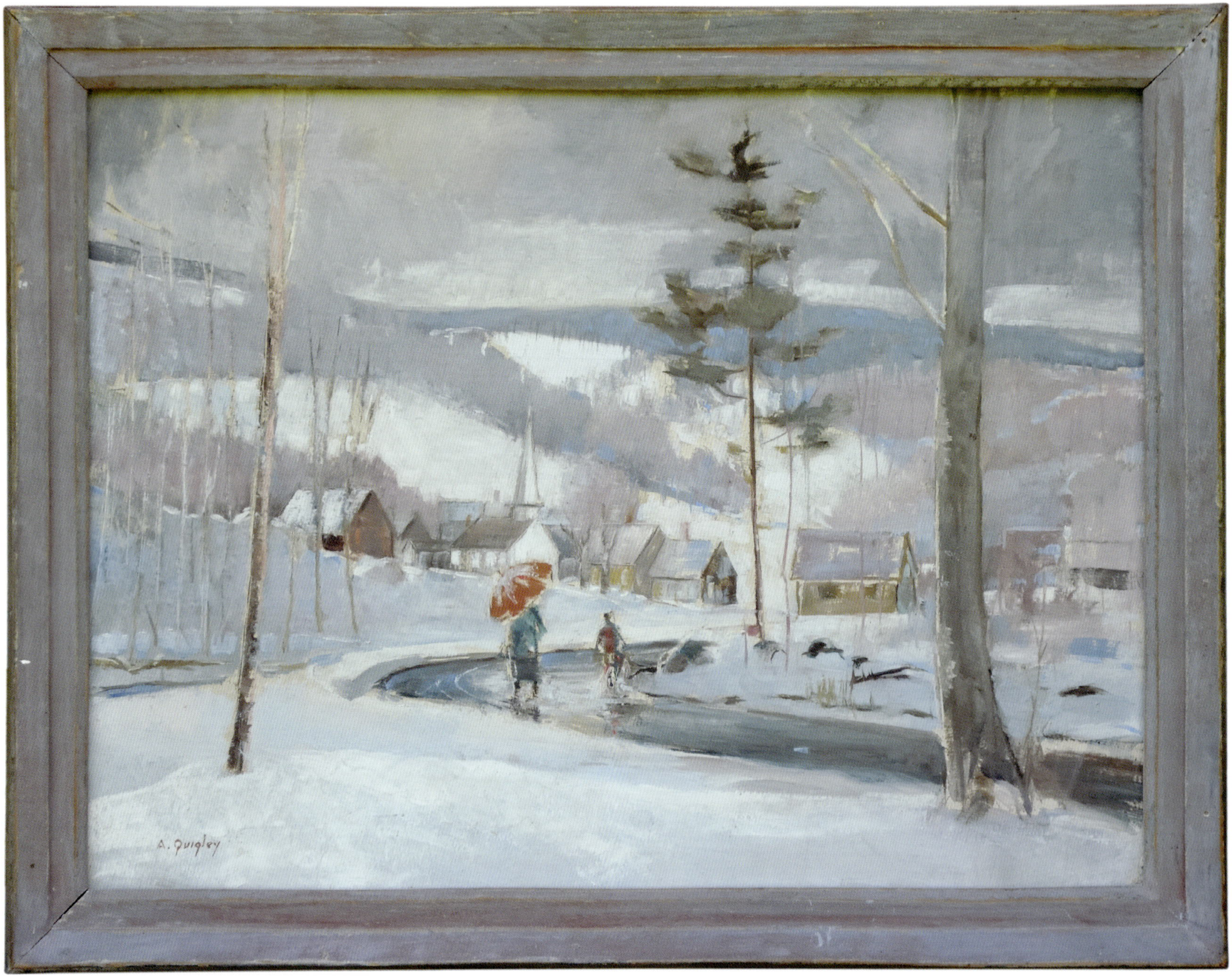

UNTITLED

Quigley frame, 21 x 27 in.

Mark Quigley

Lisa Quigley Valliere, photographer

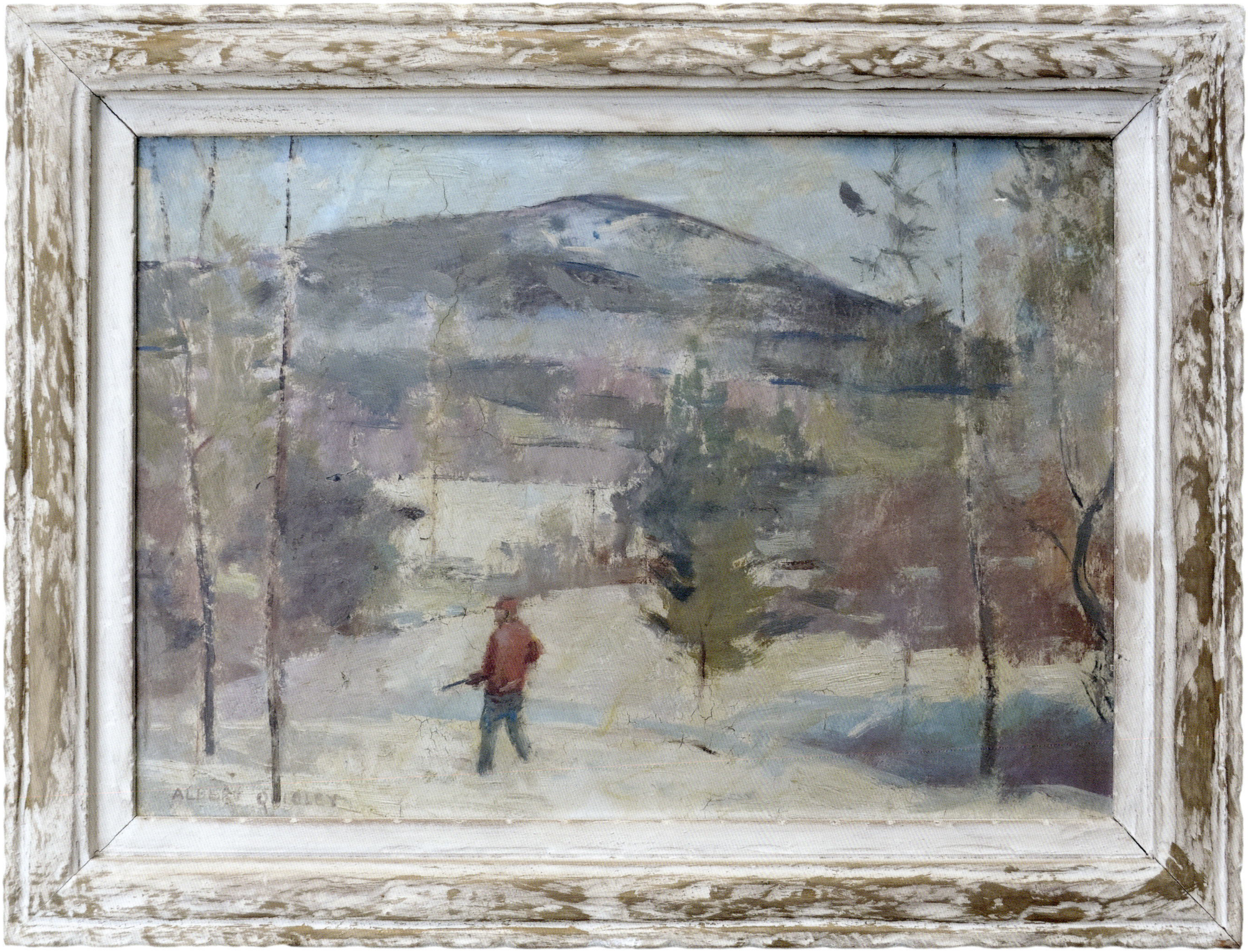

MOUNT MONADNOCK WITH HUNTER

Oil on canvas, Quigley frame, 15 x 21 in.

Mark Quigley

Lisa Quigley Valliere, photographer

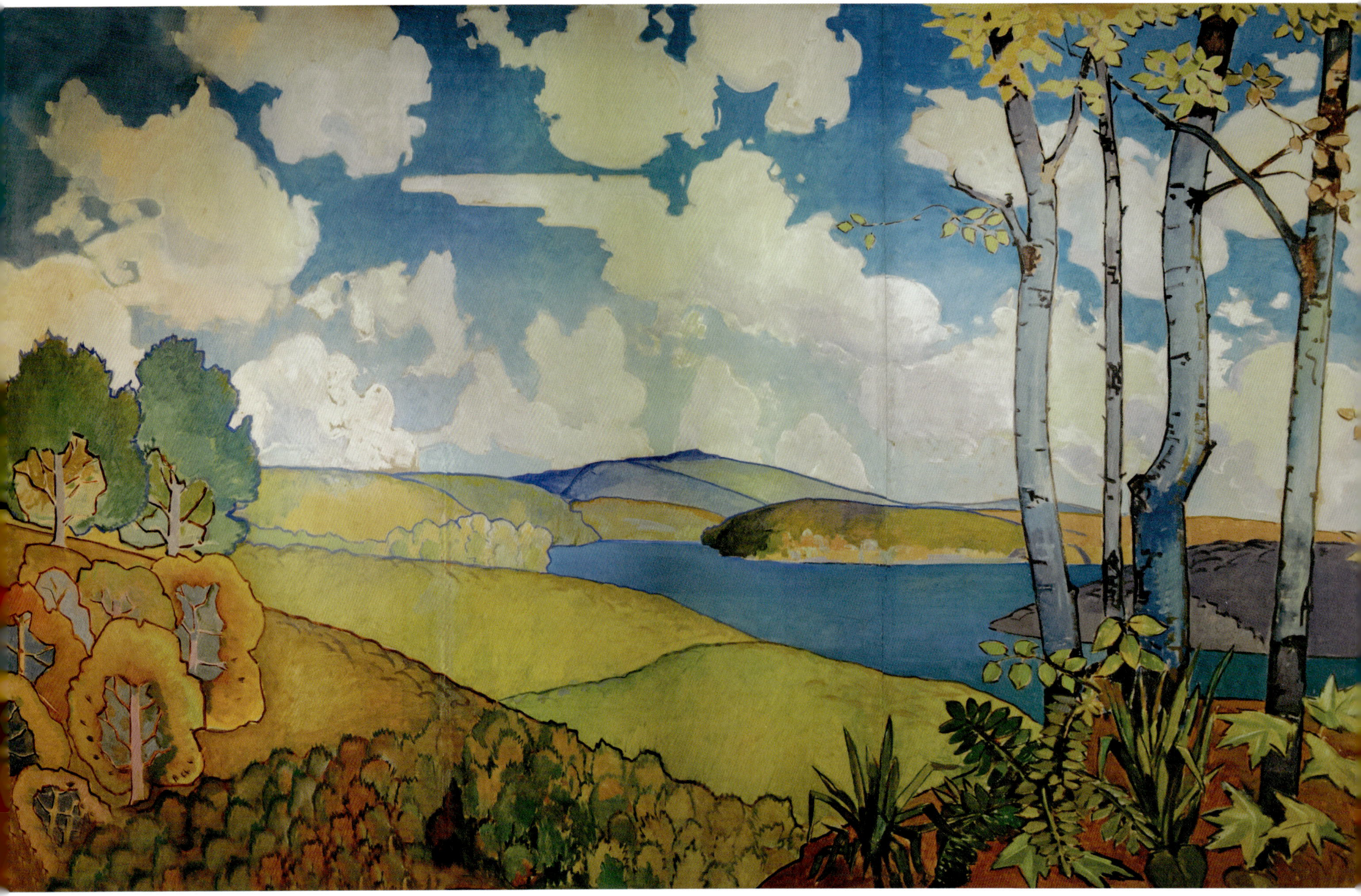

SPOFFORD LAKE MURALS

A composite of photographs of the mural painted in 1936 in the upstairs hallway of a cottage on Spofford Lake, Chesterfield, New Hampshire

Harriet Wise, photographer

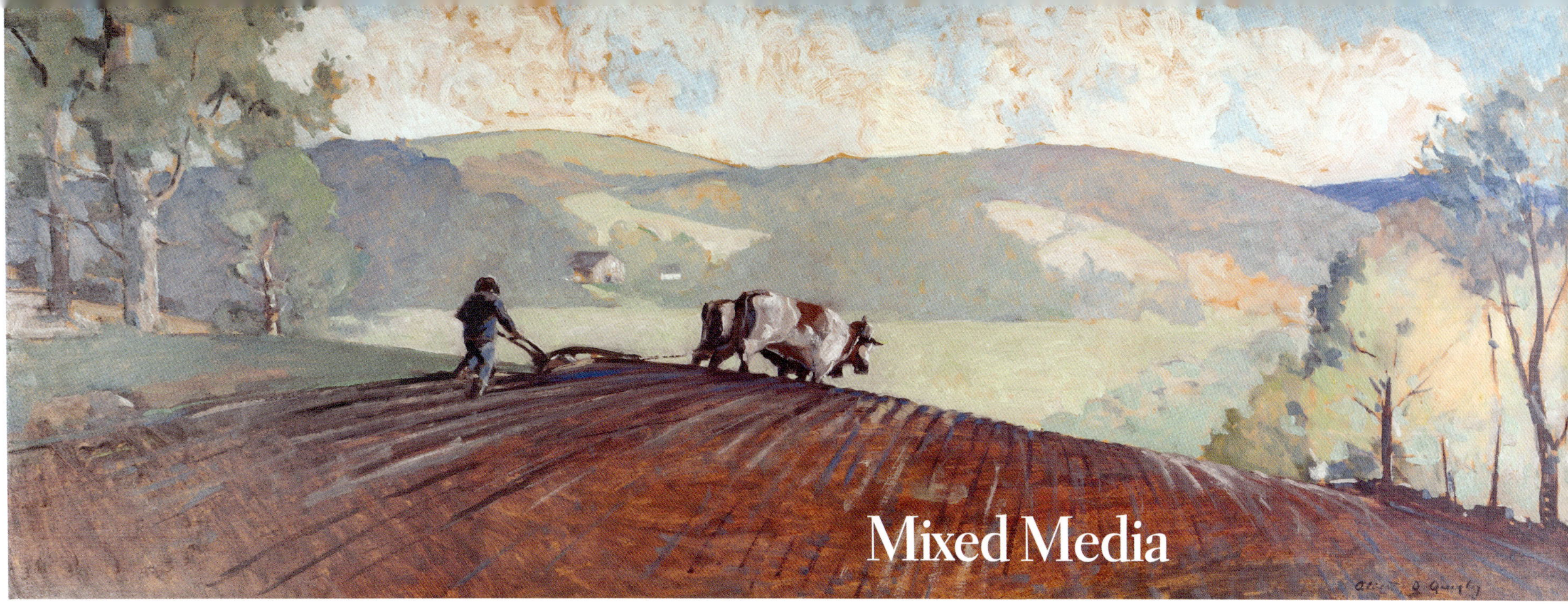

Mixed Media

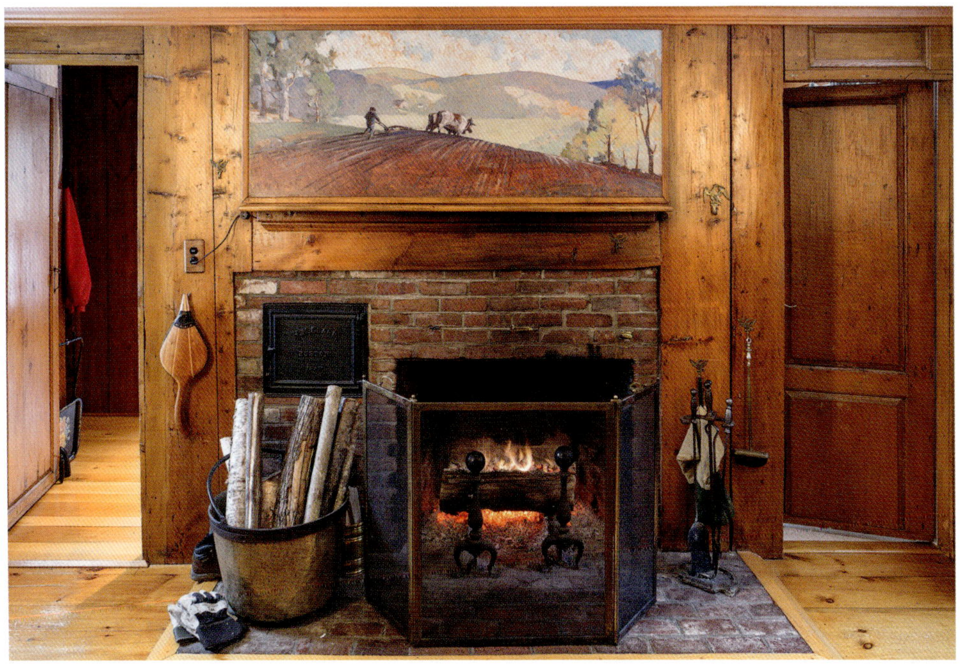

ABOVE **TEAM OF OXEN IN FIELD**
Oil on board, 27 x 69 in., private collection
Mural set in pine frame, mounted
into the wall over fireplace

BELOW Photograph of living room
showing mural over fireplace

Murals: Trading Goods for Services and the WPA Program

DURING THE DEPRESSION, there was this program supported by the Government [the Works Progress Administration, or WPA], and my father, Quig, was hired to paint murals. One of the jobs that he got was painting murals in the Munsonville Church of the local scene around Granite Lake. Those murals were there for years, but apparently the moisture and humidity eventually caused problems with the walls. Some of the walls deteriorated and others were covered up. Recently a local artist, Sienna Giffin, has been able to peek behind the replacement walls, and she thinks that some of the murals still exist.

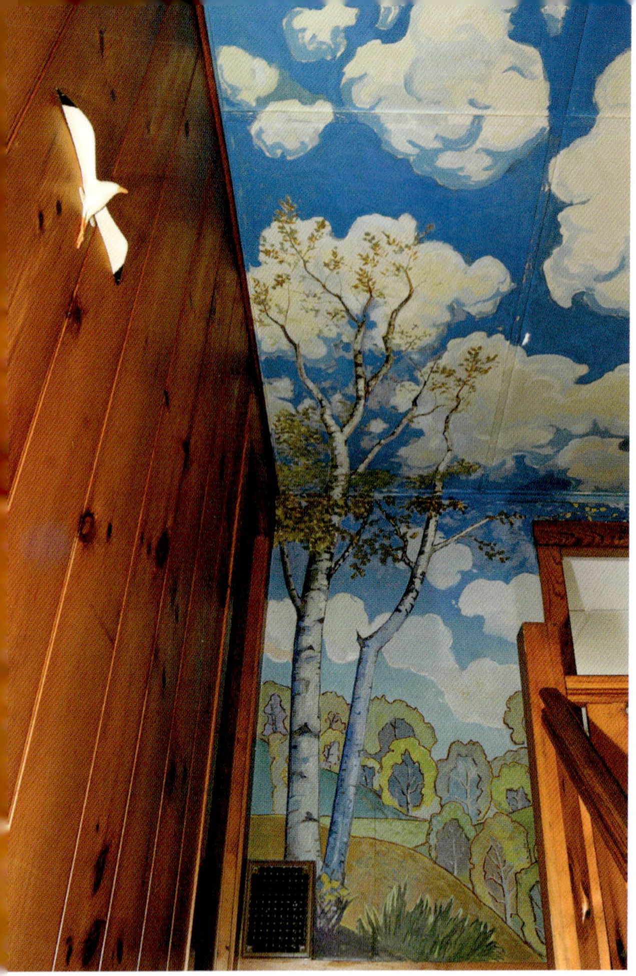

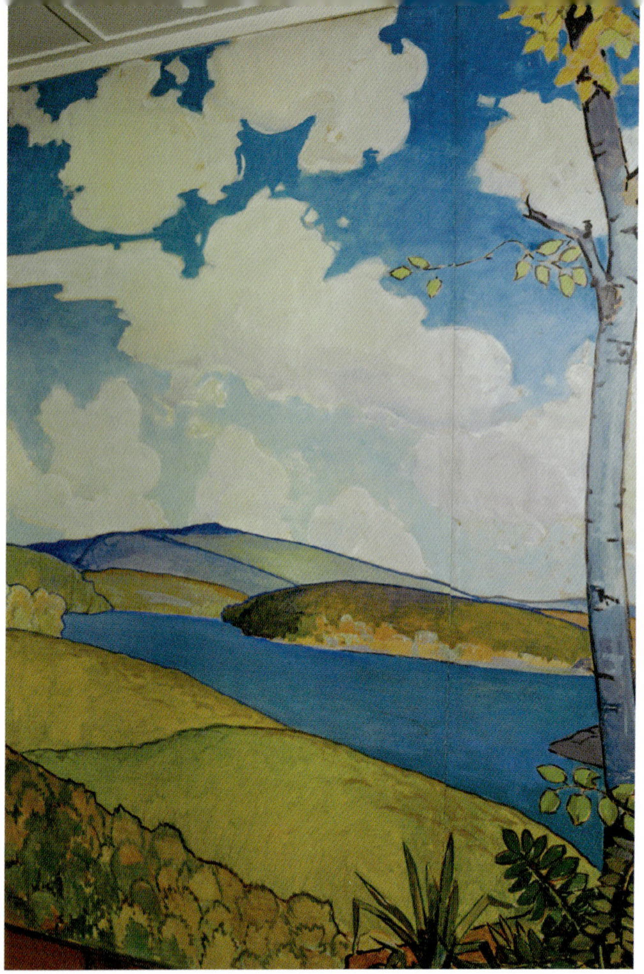

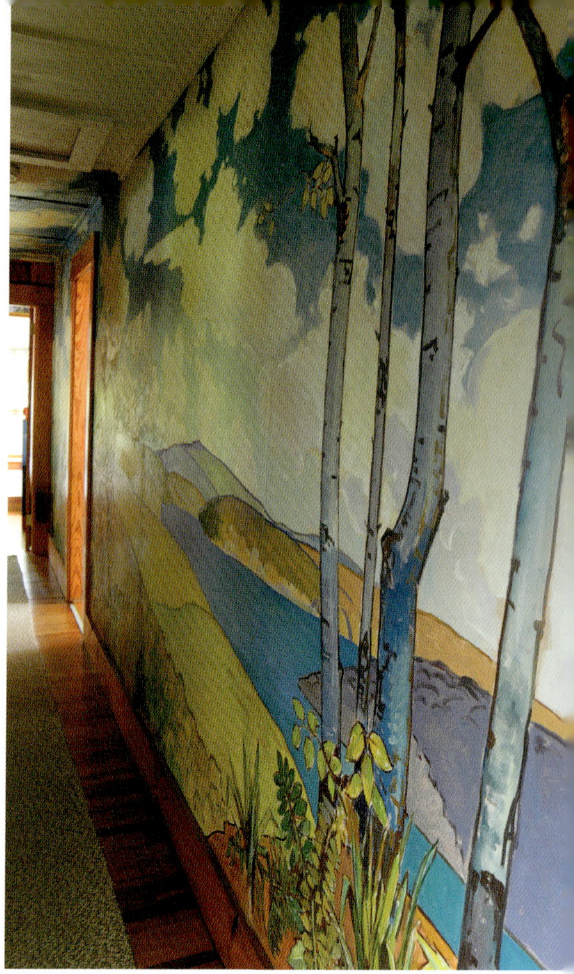

SPOFFORD LAKE MURALS
Harriet Wise, photographer

Quig didn't have a lot of ready cash flow, and during the '30s, when the three of us children were born, Quig had become friends with several of the doctors in Keene, and had actually played golf with a lot of them, and we were sort of products of a barter system. The Elliot Community Hospital, in Keene, got paid with murals in the children's ward. The doctors got paintings and the doctor who delivered me got murals in his summer cottage on Spofford Lake [in Chesterfield, New Hampshire], which I hadn't really known about until just a few years ago. I was contacted by the people who are the descendants of the doctor, and who still own the cottage, and they invited me to see them. I invited a friend of ours, Harriet Wise, who is a professional photographer, to come along to photograph the murals. These murals go all the way up the stairs throughout the upstairs rooms and look like they were painted last week. The murals are all dated 1936—and that was payment for me.

—*Barney Quigley*
from an interview on March 23, 2014

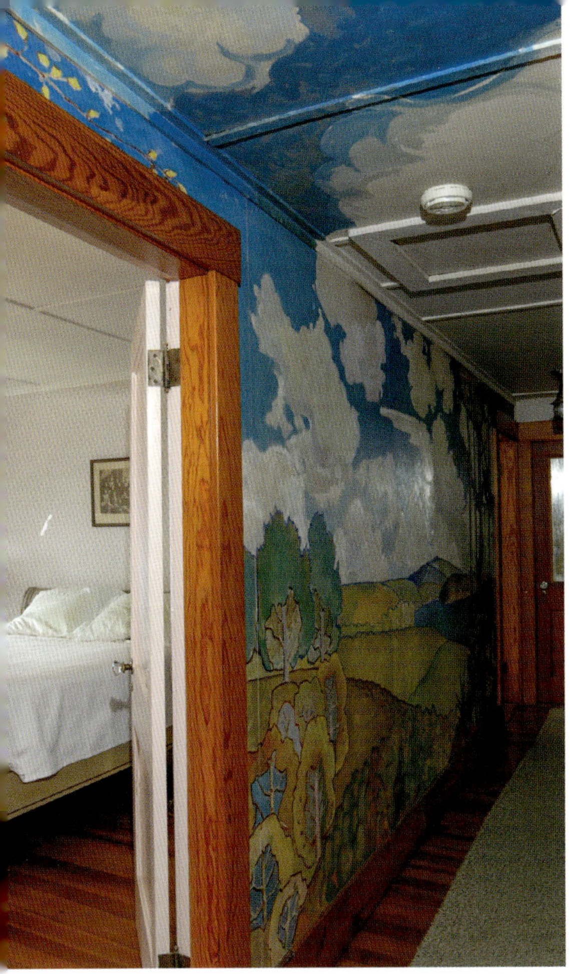

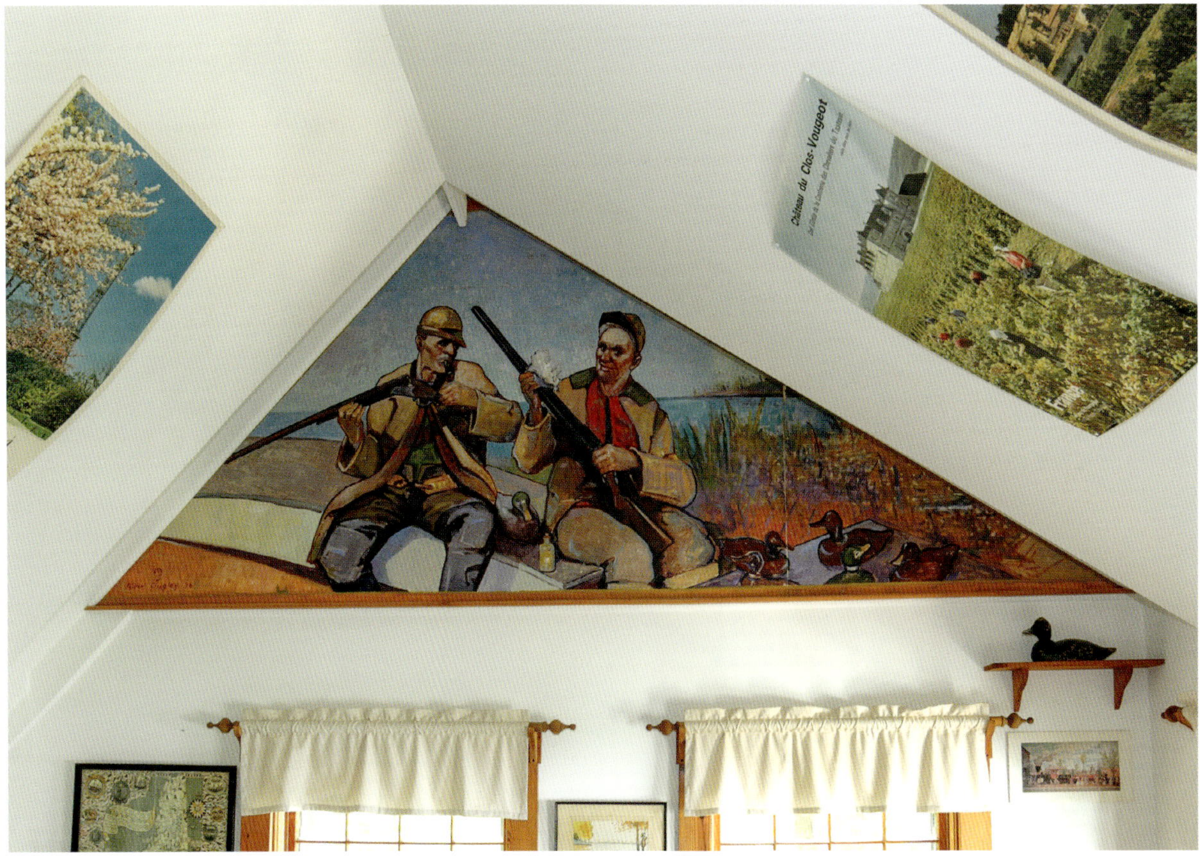

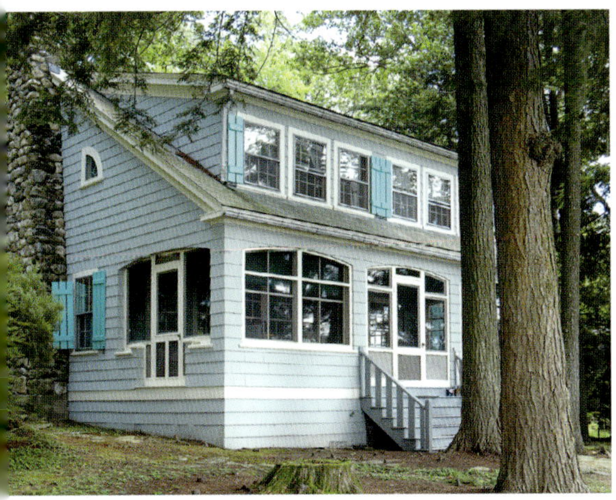

SPOFFORD LAKE COTTAGE
Harriet Wise, photographer

Renn Tolman: I can add one more thing about the murals. When I was a kid, Dr. King, who was a dentist in Keene, had a children's room where you got your teeth cleaned, and the whole of the walls of the children's room were murals by Quig.

Barney Quigley: That was probably a dental bill for when Quig had his teeth out and got false teeth. There's still a drawing that Quig did of Dr. King's German Shepherd.

—exchange between Renn Tolman and Barney Quigley
March 23, 2014

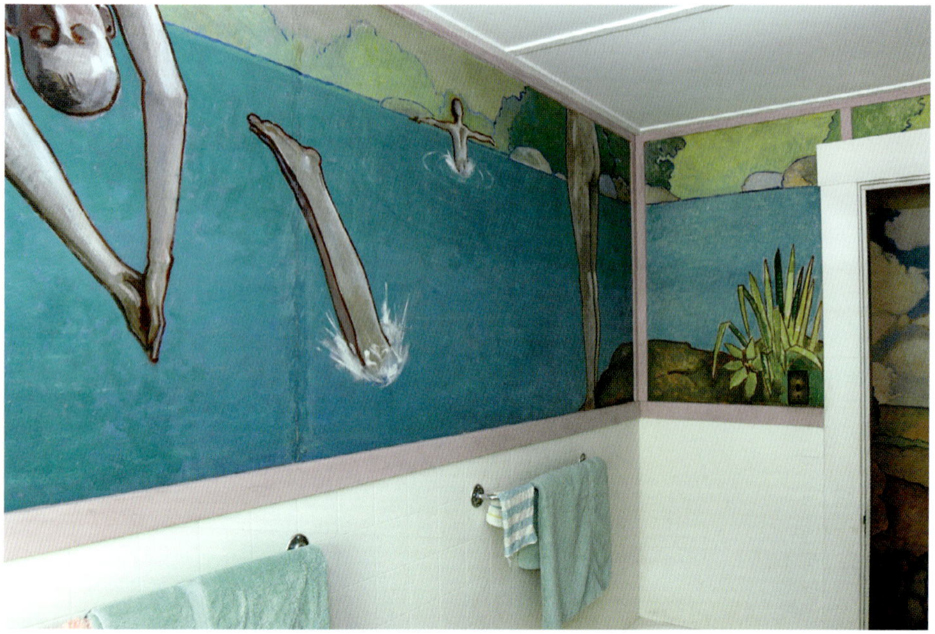
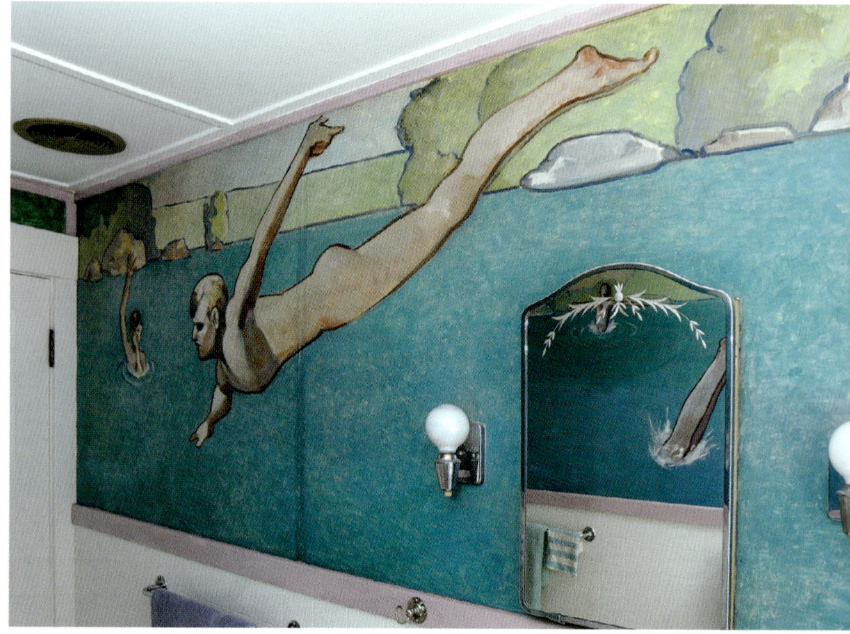
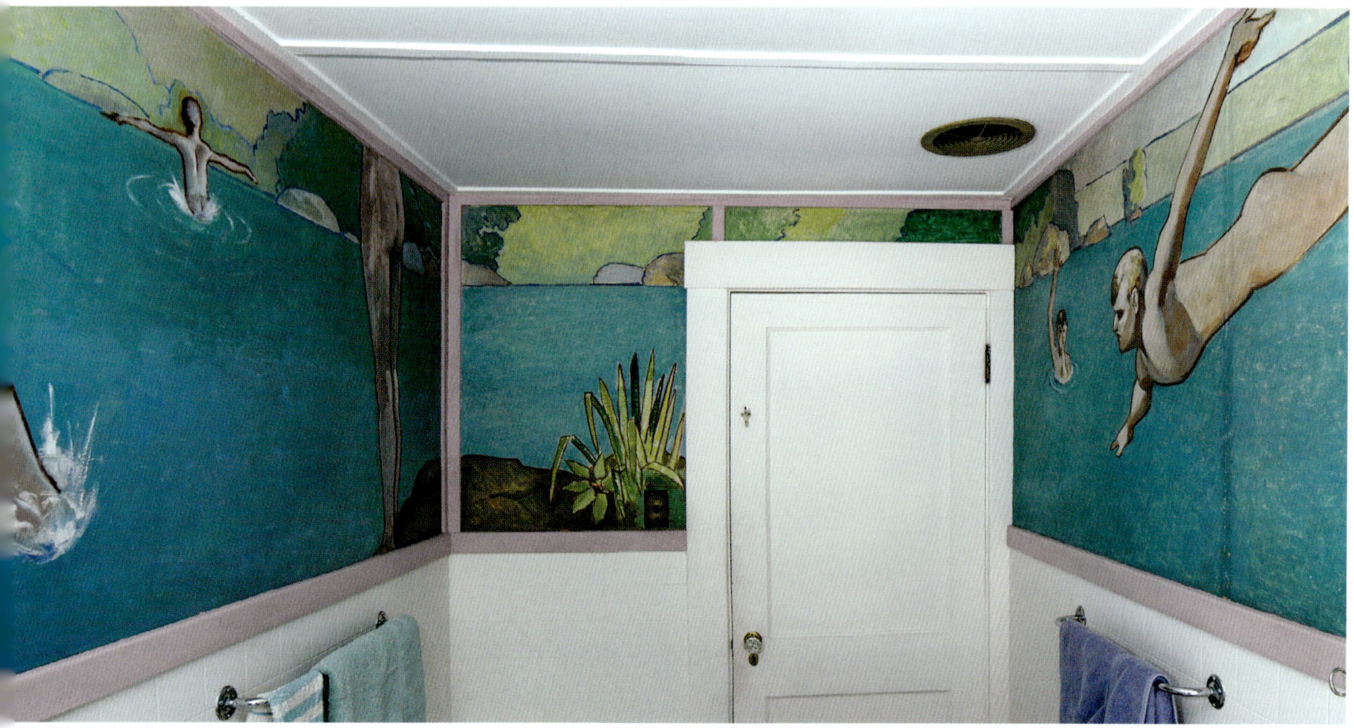
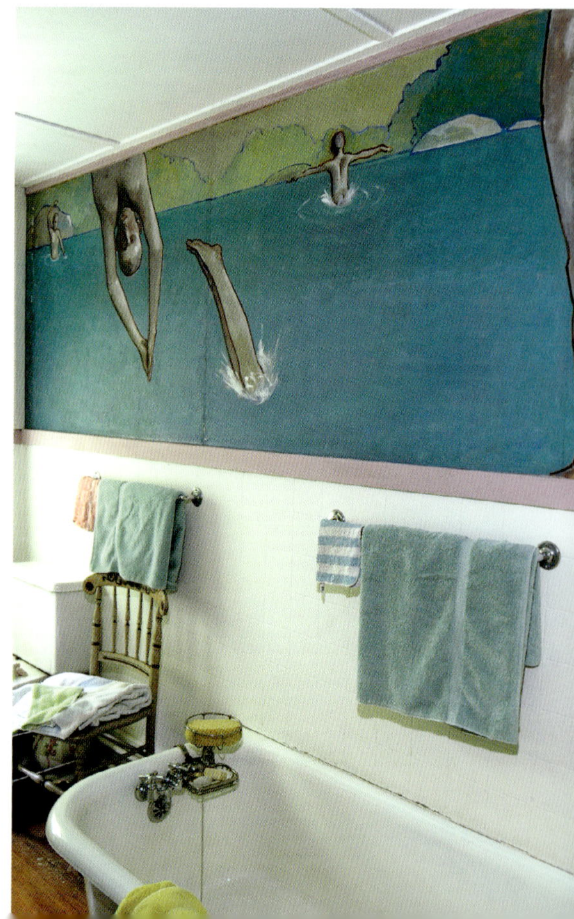

SPOFFORD LAKE MURALS
Harriet Wise, photographer

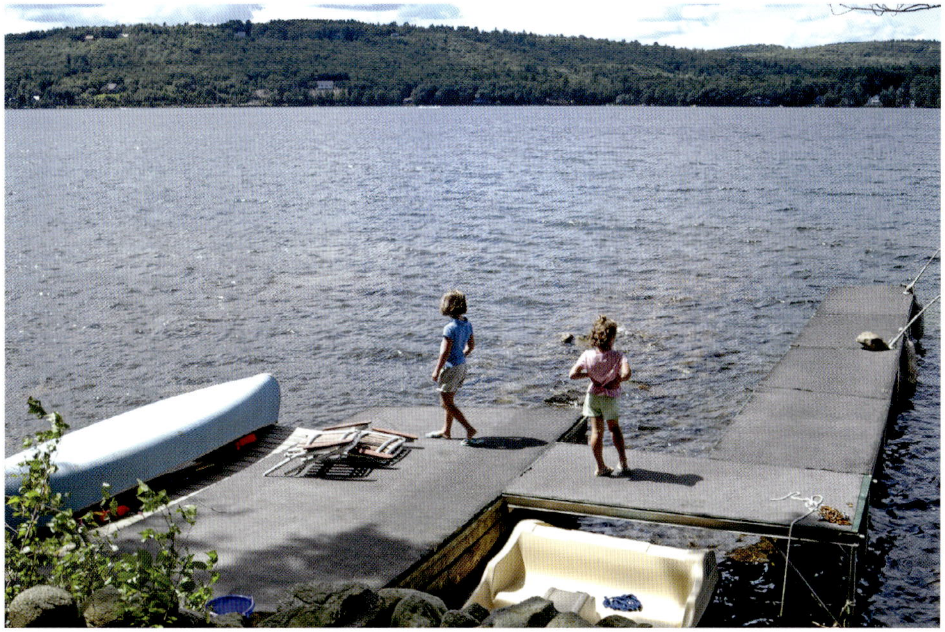

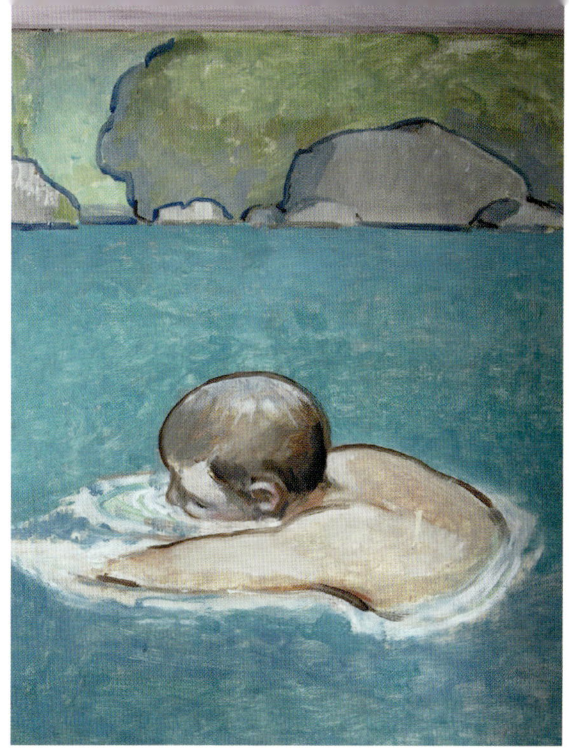

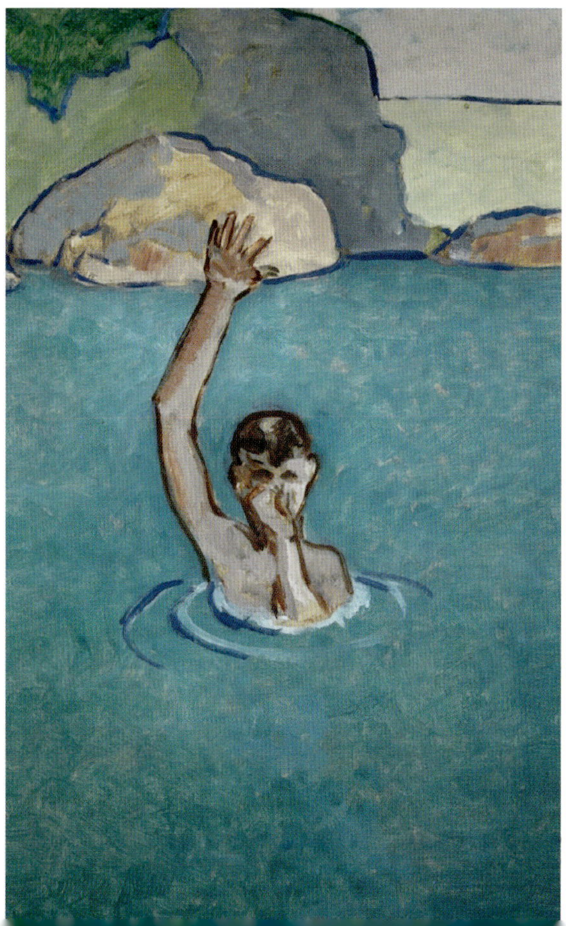

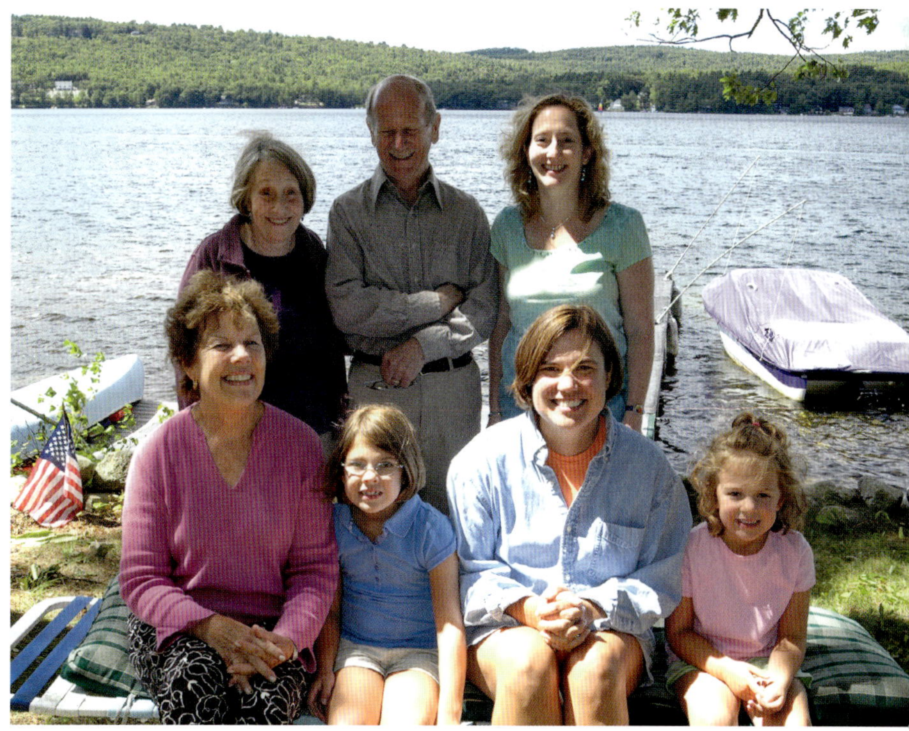

ABOVE LEFT View of Spofford Lake from cottage

BELOW FAR RIGHT At Spofford Lake
Front row: co-owner and family
Back row: Nancy, Barney, and Darcy Quigley
Harriet Wise, photographer

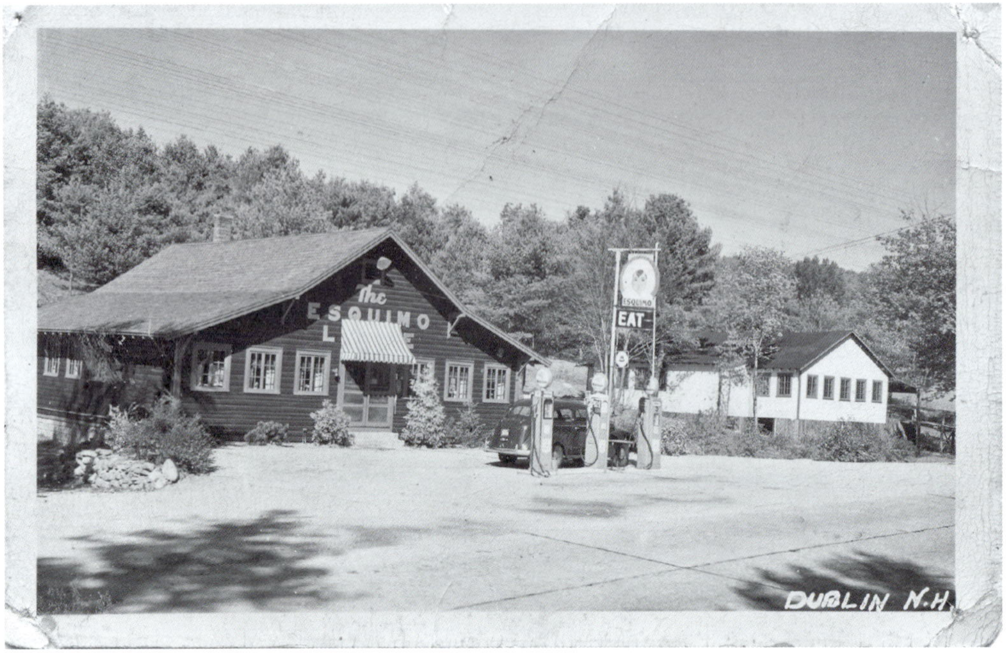

The Esquimo Lodge

We don't know for certain if this sign painted by Albert Quigley was a Works Progress Administration (WPA) project or painted earlier, but we do know that he painted murals in public places as a WPA employee, as mentioned elsewhere in this catalogue.

We're pretty certain, however, that he frequented the dance hall, to the right in the accompanying photograph of the Esquimo Lodge, to play at the many square dances held there during this time.

This location had known a number of incarnations during the 1900s. It started out as the Esquimo Lodge in the 1920s, owned and operated by Gordon Bemis and later by his son Norman and his daughter-in-law, Eleanor. It was a popular family restaurant and lodge with rustic cabins and an outdoor dance floor where for many years patrons listened to live music and danced the night away under the stars and the whispering pines.

The dancing came to an end after World War II, as did the rustic cabins, but the Esquimo hung on as a popular local eatery until well into the 1960s.

—*Tom Hyman*
Village on a Hill: A History of Dublin, New Hampshire, 1752–2000

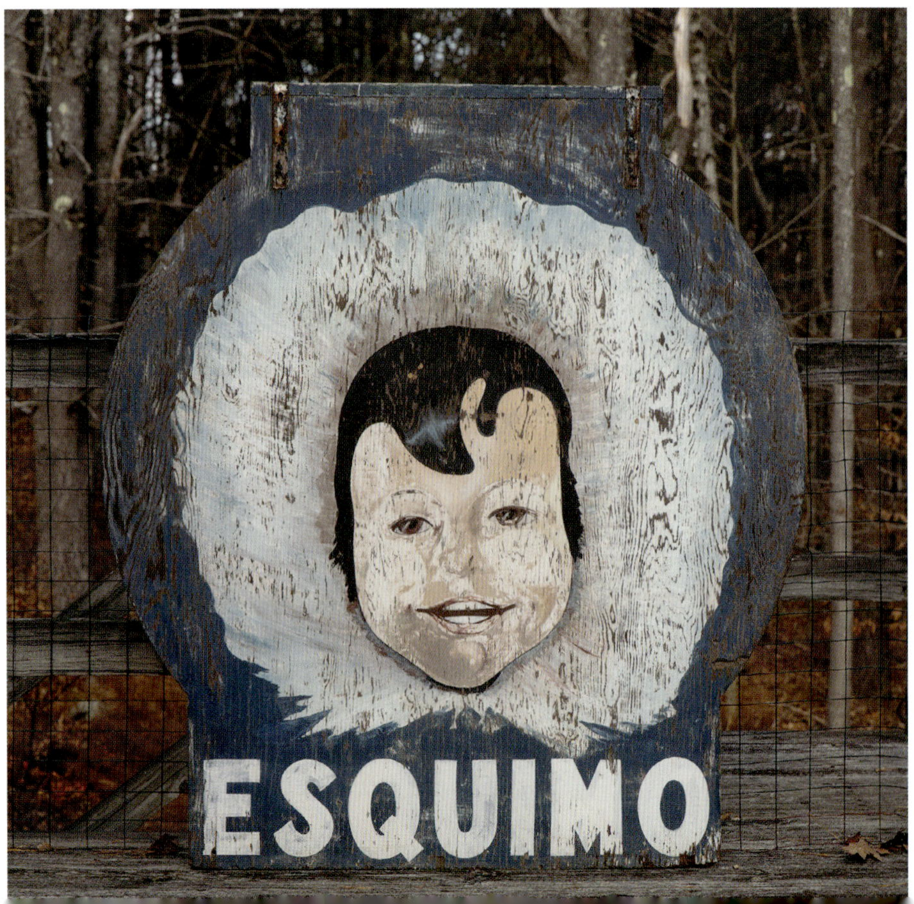

ABOVE The Esquimo Lodge in the 1940s
Dance hall on right
Courtesy of the Dublin Historical Society

BELOW Outdoor sign that marked the location of the Esquimo Lodge

Watercolor Sketches for Greeting Cards

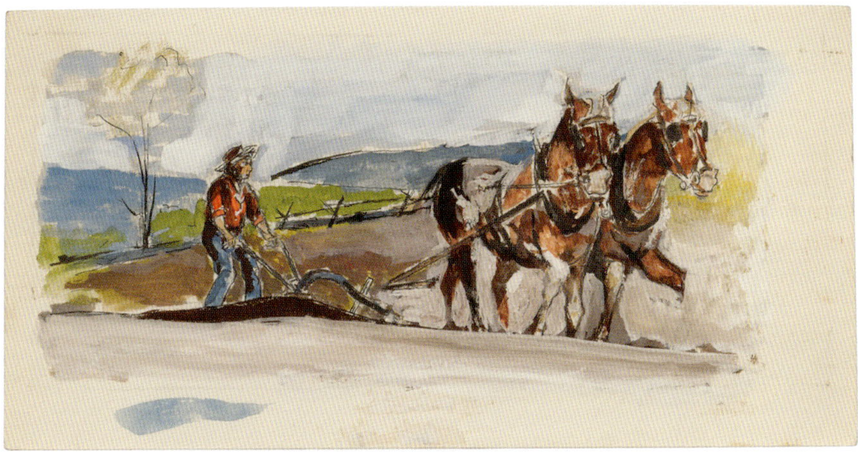

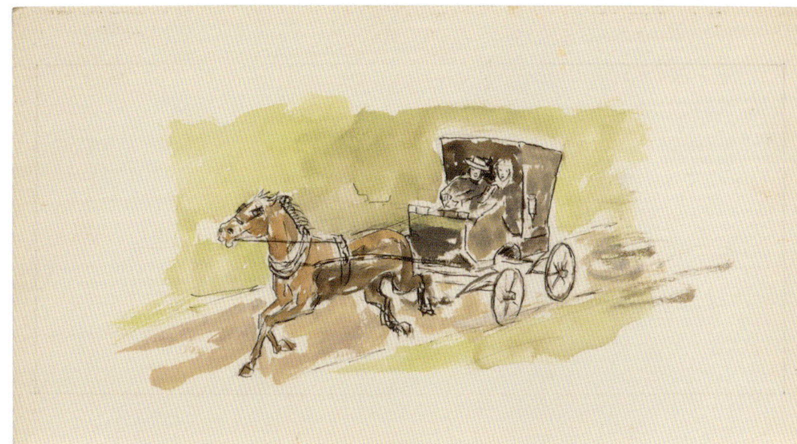

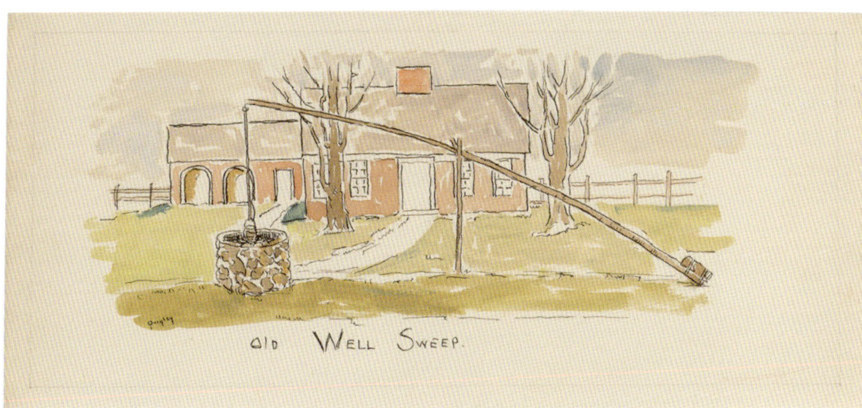

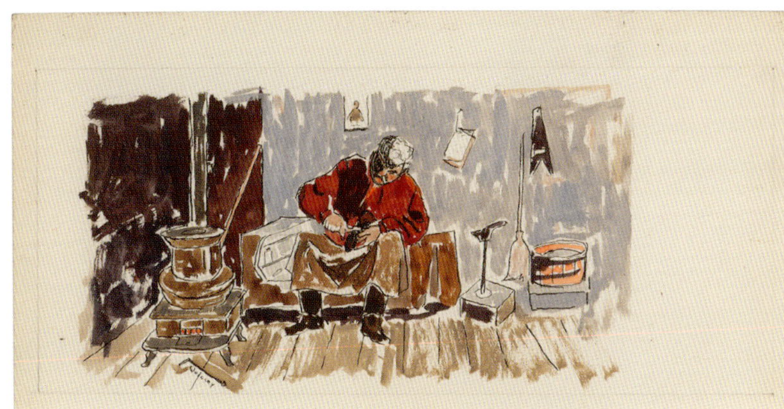

ABOVE **PLOWING TEAM**
Unfinished watercolor on matboard, unframed
6 x 14 in., Barney and Nancy Quigley

BELOW **THE OLD WELLSWEEP**
Watercolor on matboard, unframed
6 x 14 in., private collection

ABOVE **HORSE AND BUGGY**
Watercolor on matboard, unframed
6 x 14 in., private collection

BELOW **THE COBBLER**
Watercolor on matboard, unframed
6 x 14 in., private collection

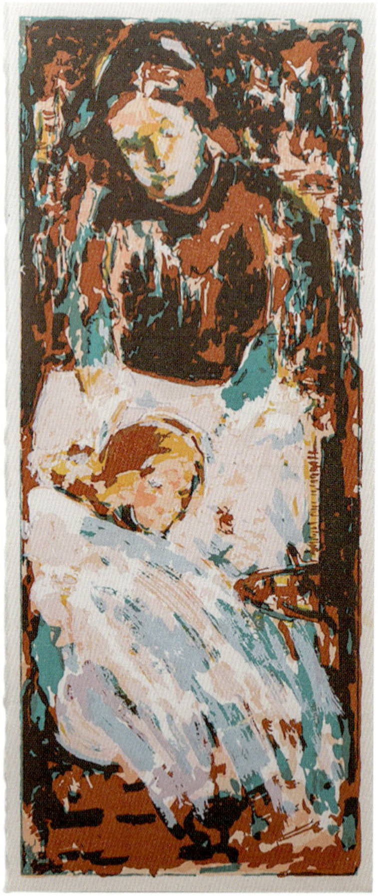

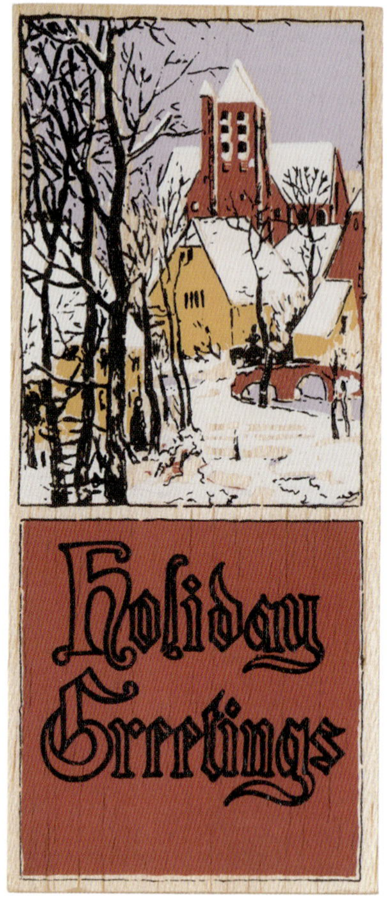

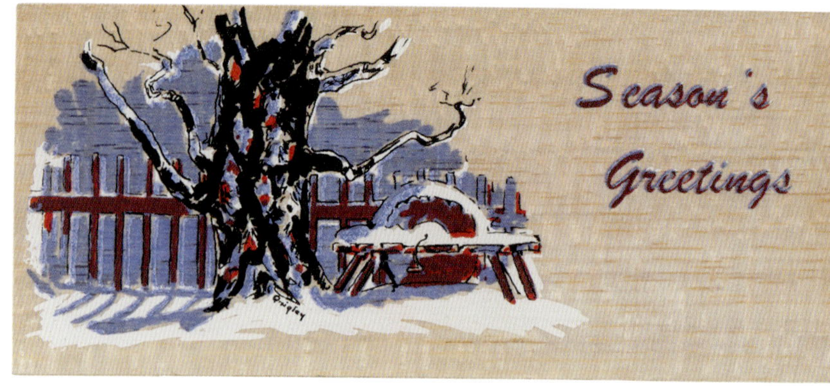

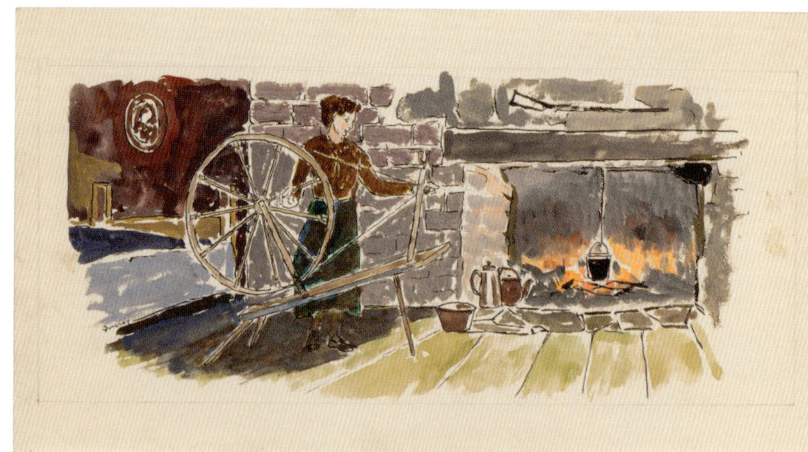

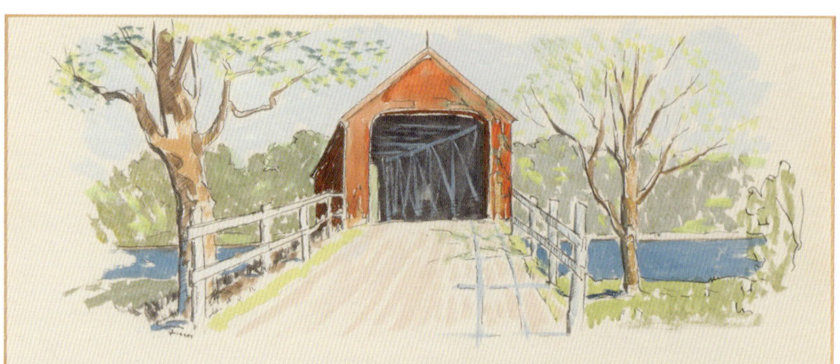

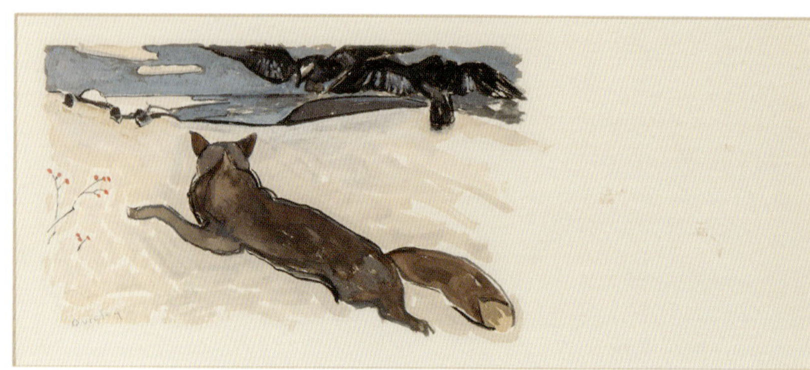

Greeting cards on balsa wood and watercolor sketches on matboard, various sizes
Private collections

A Few Drawings

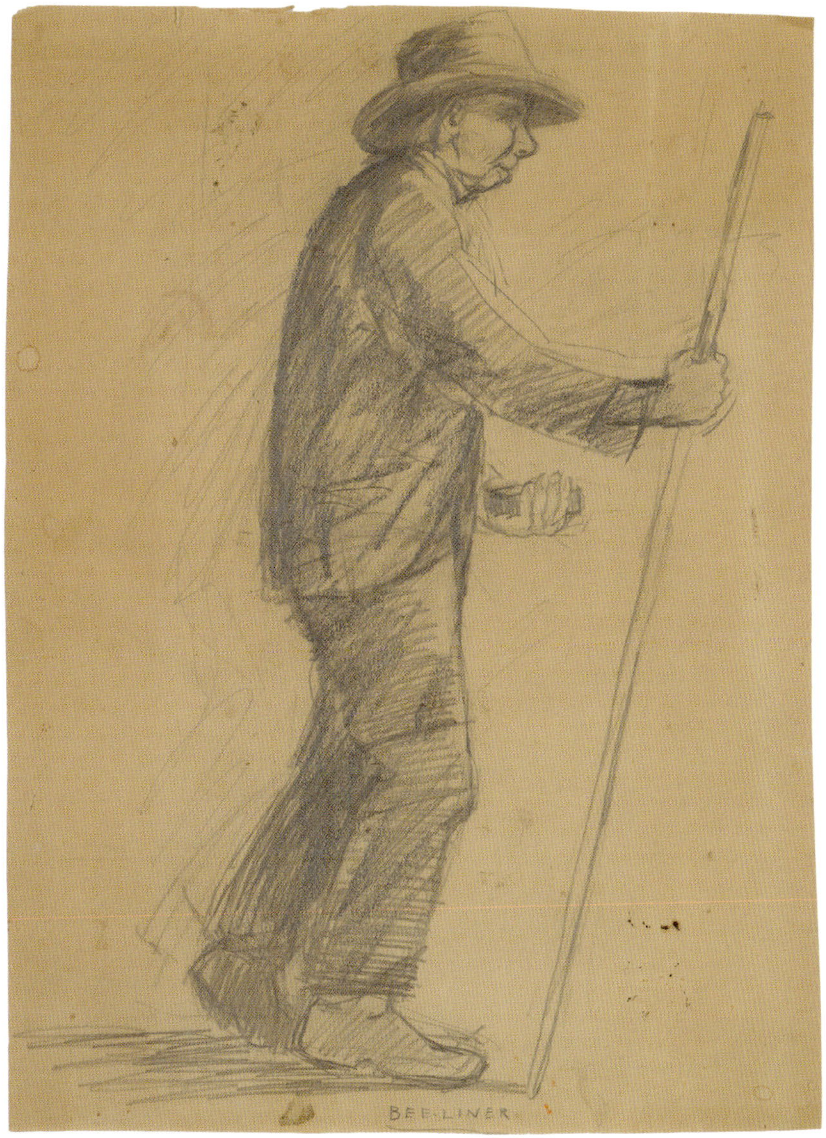

BEELINER

Pencil drawing, unframed, 16 x 12 in.

Private collection

An old-time way to find the hives of wild bees

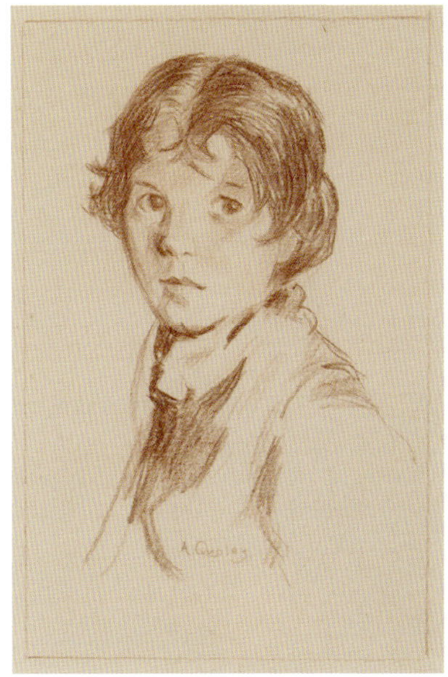

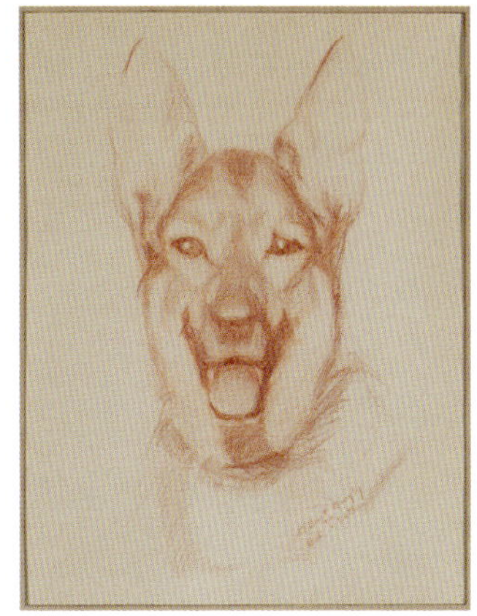

ABOVE Sketch of German Shepherd

Conte crayon, unframed, private collection

LEFT Pencil drawing

Private collection

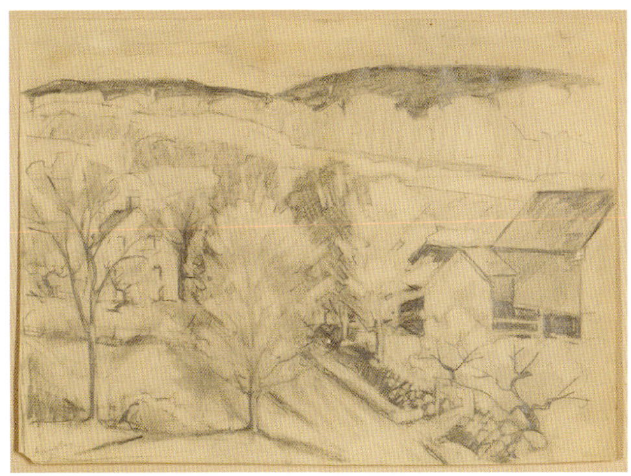

LANDSCAPE

Pencil sketch on paper, unframed

9 x 12 in., private collection

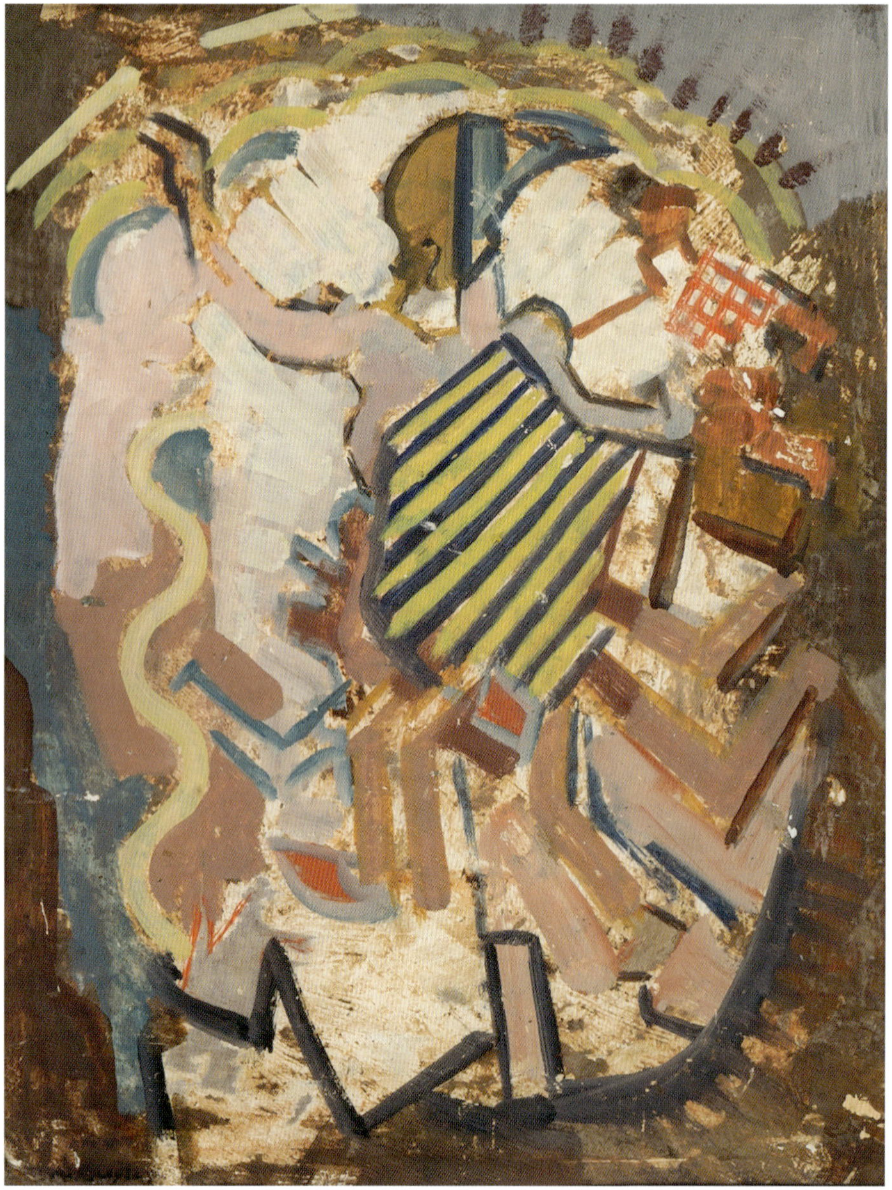

Taking a Turn at Abstract Painting

Quig took a turn at doing something that we now might consider abstract modernistic painting. I've got a picture hanging on the wall in our bedroom of this guy that looks sort of like a demon with this violin that has a bright light shooting out of it around the bridge where the music would come from, and with this abstract background. Quig called it "The Devil's Dream," named after a square dance tune.

—Barney Quigley
from an interview on March 24, 2014

LEFT **UNTITLED**
Oil on board, 18 x 14 in.
Private collection

RIGHT **THE DEVIL'S DREAM**
Oil on panel, Quigley frame, 31 x 40 in.
Barney and Nancy Quigley
Arnold Adler, photographer

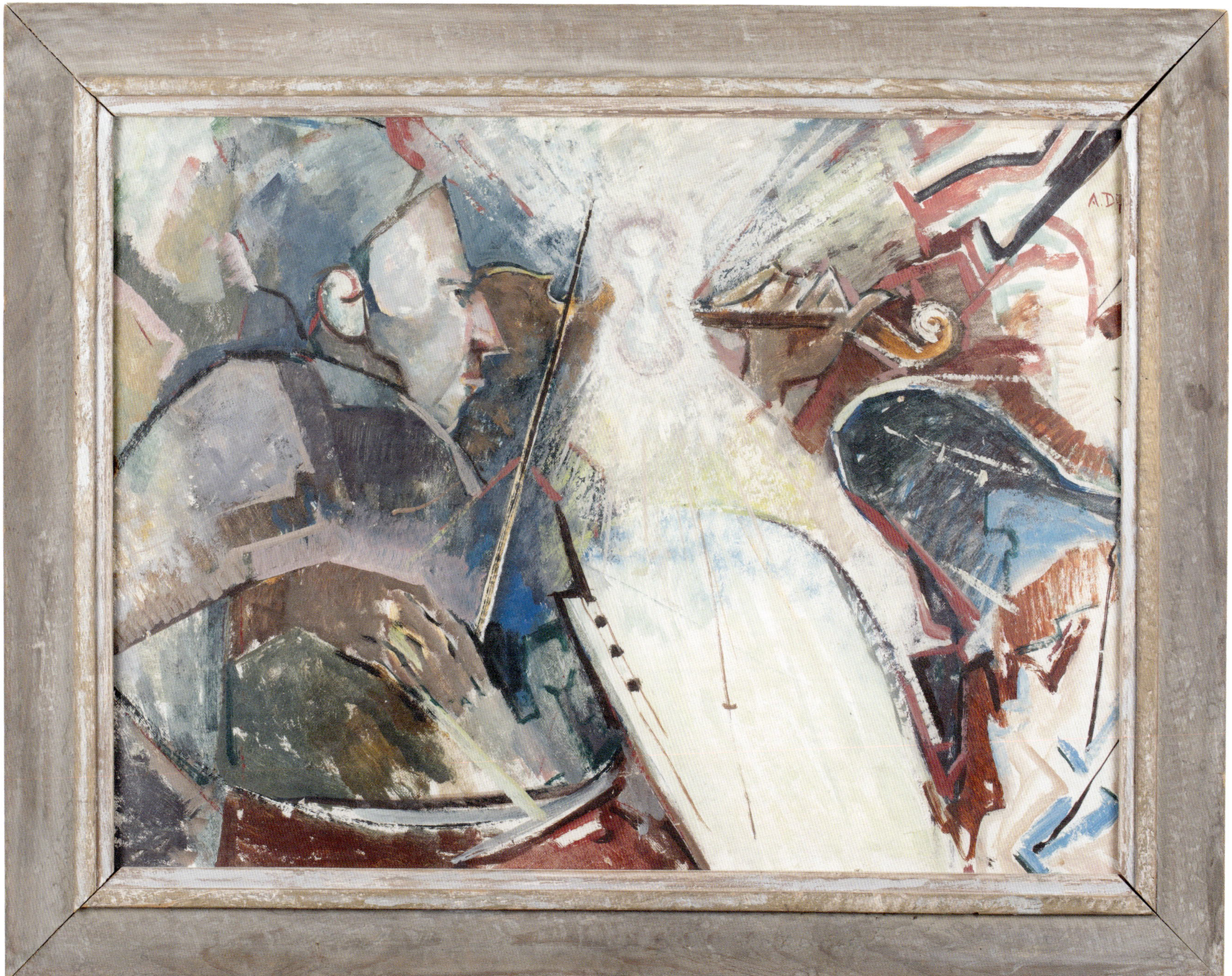

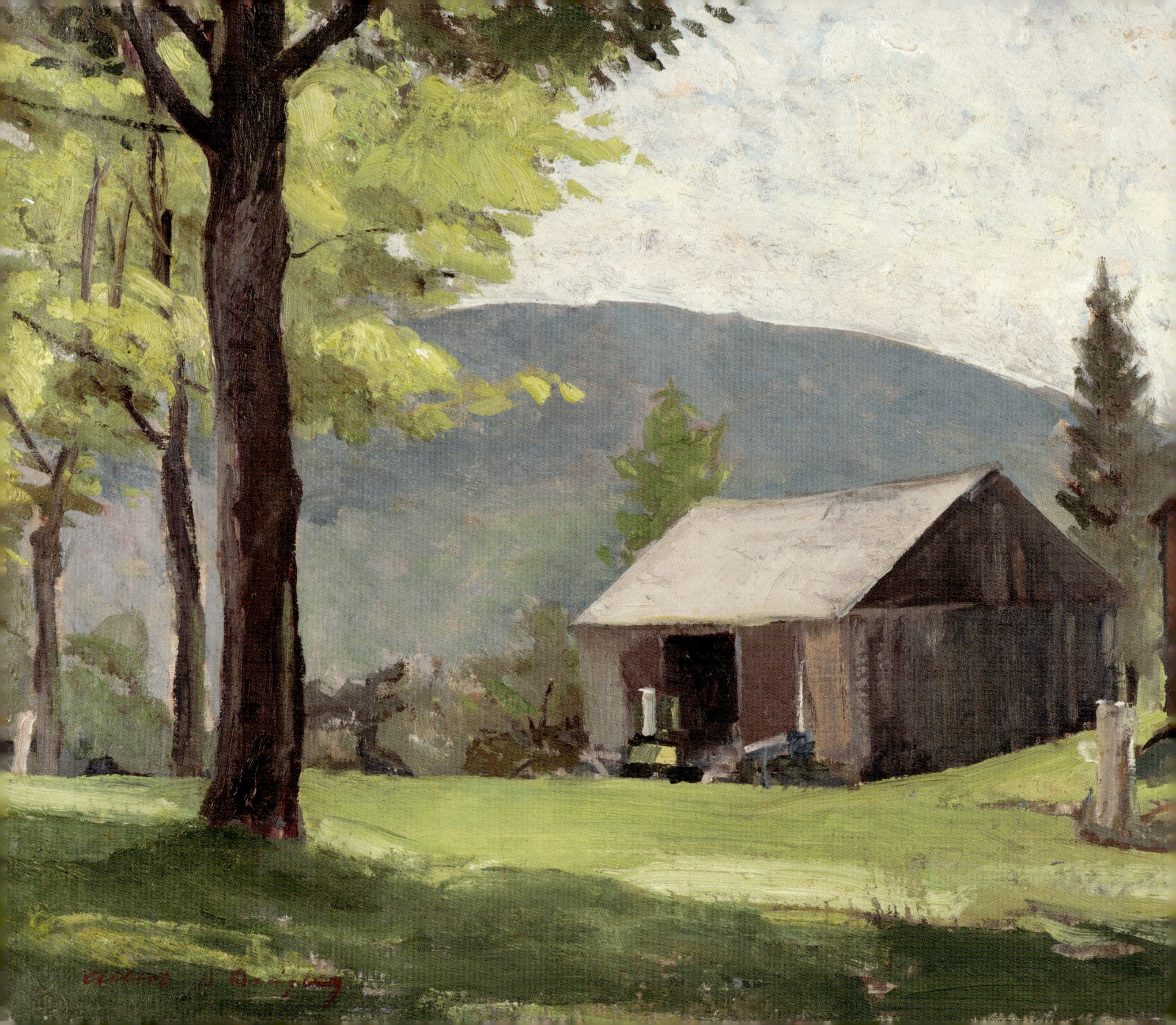

Farms and Homesteads

Quig, as he was always known, was a good-natured man. I think it was hard for him wanting to take time to paint portraits and landscapes. He had gone to art school after serving his country and before coming to Nelson.

When he moved up here in 1949 we first met Quig when we registered our Jeep. We found out he was working at the nearby Harrisville Mill on the same shift as John, my husband, and was looking for a ride to work. So from then on John took him to work and through these trips John became interested in his art. John never wanted to become an artist—just to have fun with paints.

Quig was also a great fiddler and very often would sit outside his little red house, where our library now stands, and play for passersby and some of us would sit around and listen as he practiced for the next square dance.

Quig's living room was his workshop and covered with easels and half-finished art work, palettes daubed with splotches of colored paint. He was an avid cigarette smoker, and full ashtrays were everywhere. It was also his wife Mildred's Town Clerk's office so residents would come and go and visit too.

As Quig grew older, the mill scaled back operations so Quig spent more time with his painting—beautiful paintings of farms and homesteads. He also did a lot of portraits.

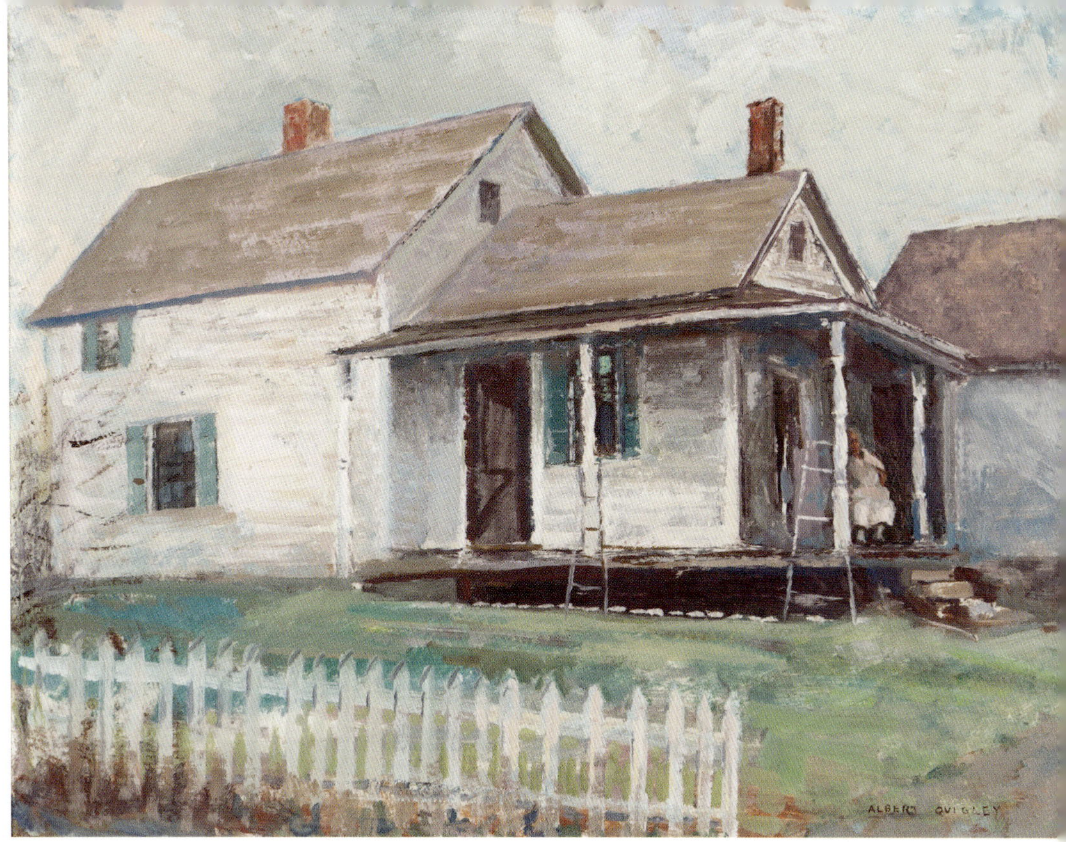

The one thing he expressed to John was that you can't learn to be an artist. You have to feel it, and your eyes and hands do the rest—you paint for your own satisfaction.

When Quig became ill, John drove him back and forth to doctors' appointments. Mildred, Quig's wife, never drove. I was with Mildred at the hospital when he passed away.

I wouldn't have missed my times with Quig. Although he was raised in Maine, his coming to Nelson has been a wonderful part of the town's heritage. He touched so many area folks with his humor, his painting and his fiddle! I am really glad to have been a friend to the Quigley family.

—Priscilla Walter, friend

UNTITLED
Oil on board, 17 x 22 in.
Private collection

OPPOSITE UNTITLED (1938)
Oil on canvas, stock frame enhanced by Quigley (not shown), 19 x 23 in.
Alston W. Barrett
Homestead barn set against mountain background in summertime

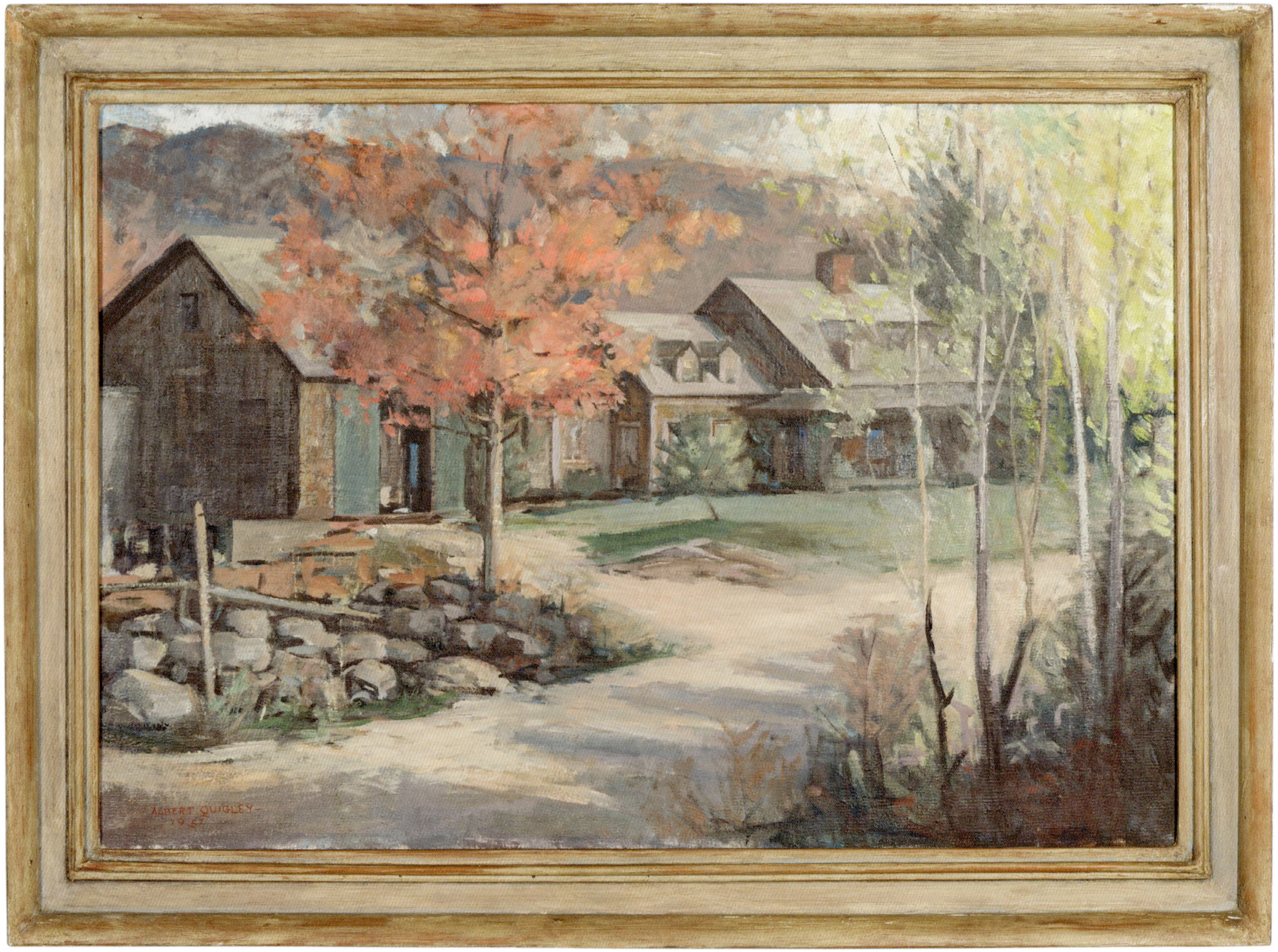

TOLMAN POND FARMHOUSE

Oil on canvas, Quigley frame, 25 x 34 in.

Gretchen and Michael Ezell

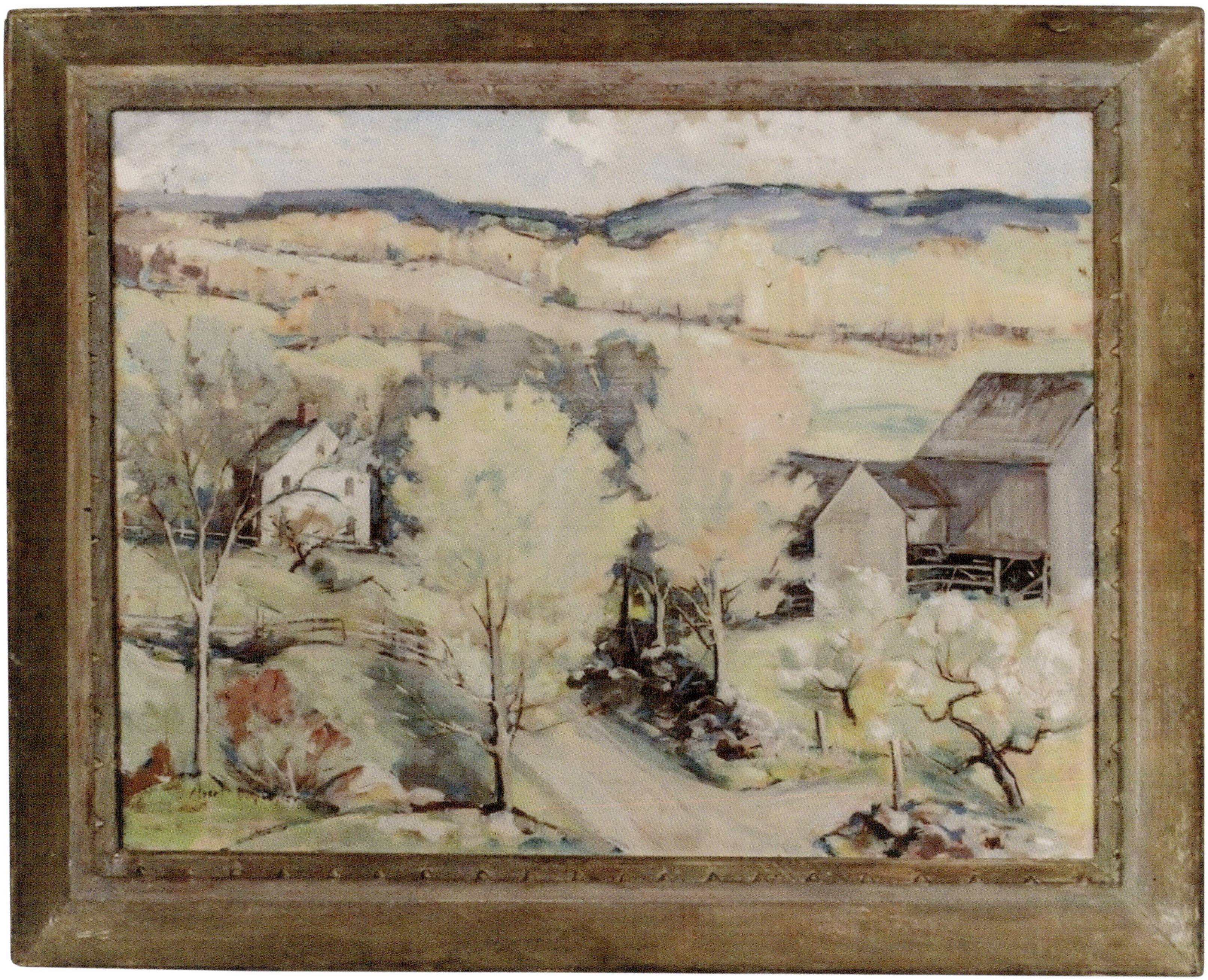

UNTITLED
Oil on canvas, Quigley frame, 22 x 28 in.
Private collection
Courtesy photograph

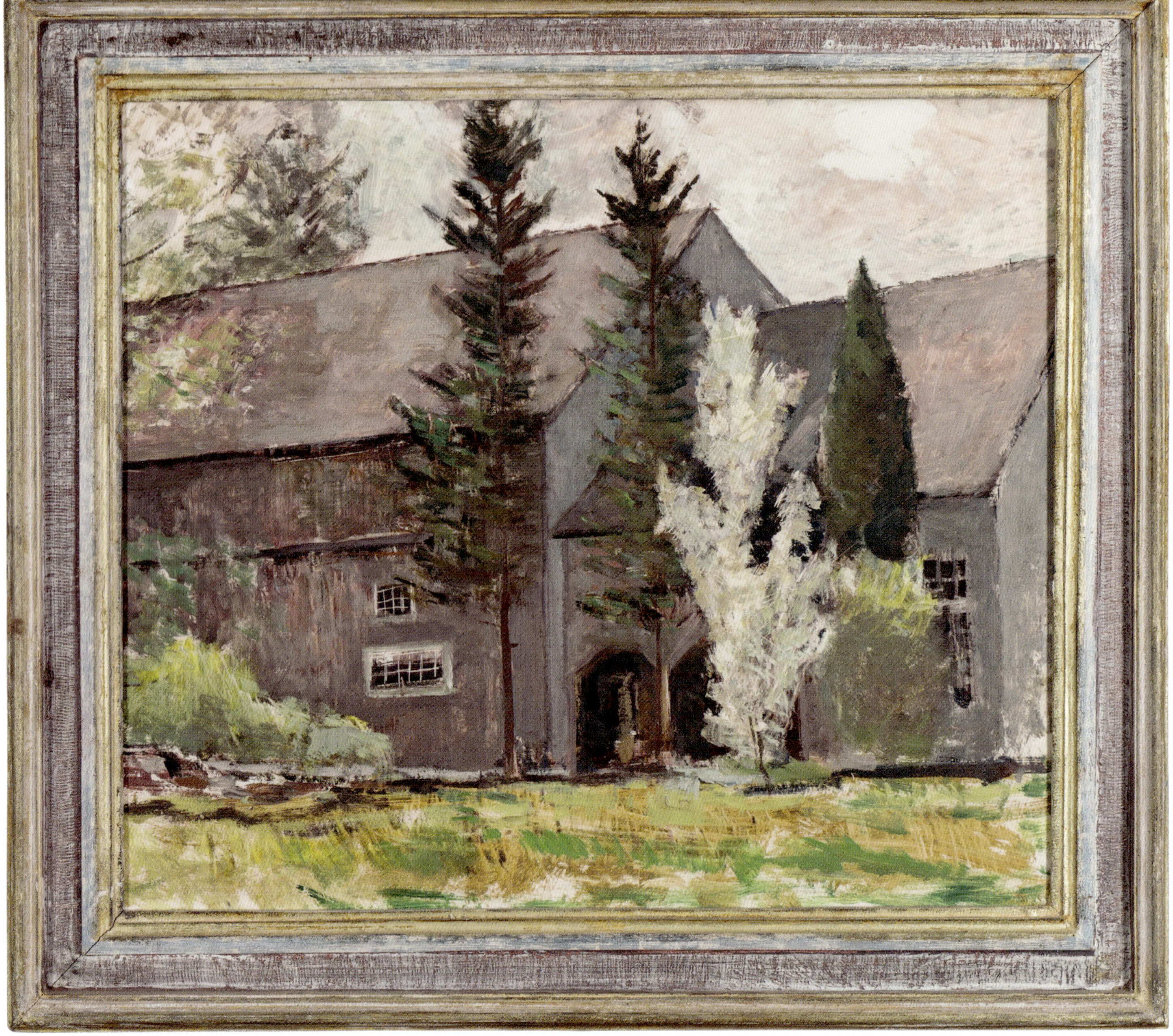

UNTITLED (1943)
Oil on board, Quigley frame, 25 x 29 in.
Colin Tolman

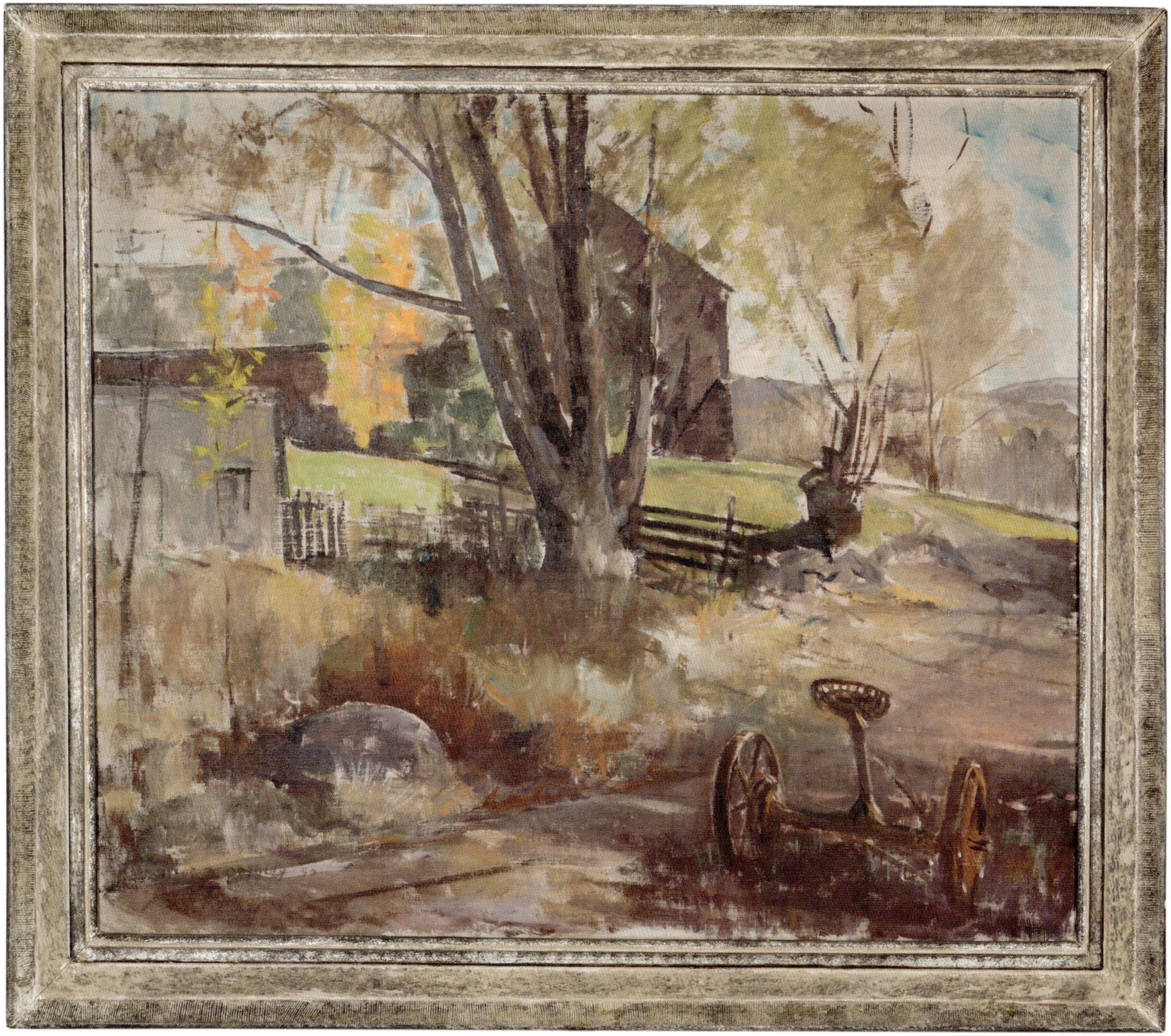

WILDER FARM, SULLIVAN, NEW HAMPSHIRE

Oil on canvas, Quigley frame, 29 x 34 in.

Private collection

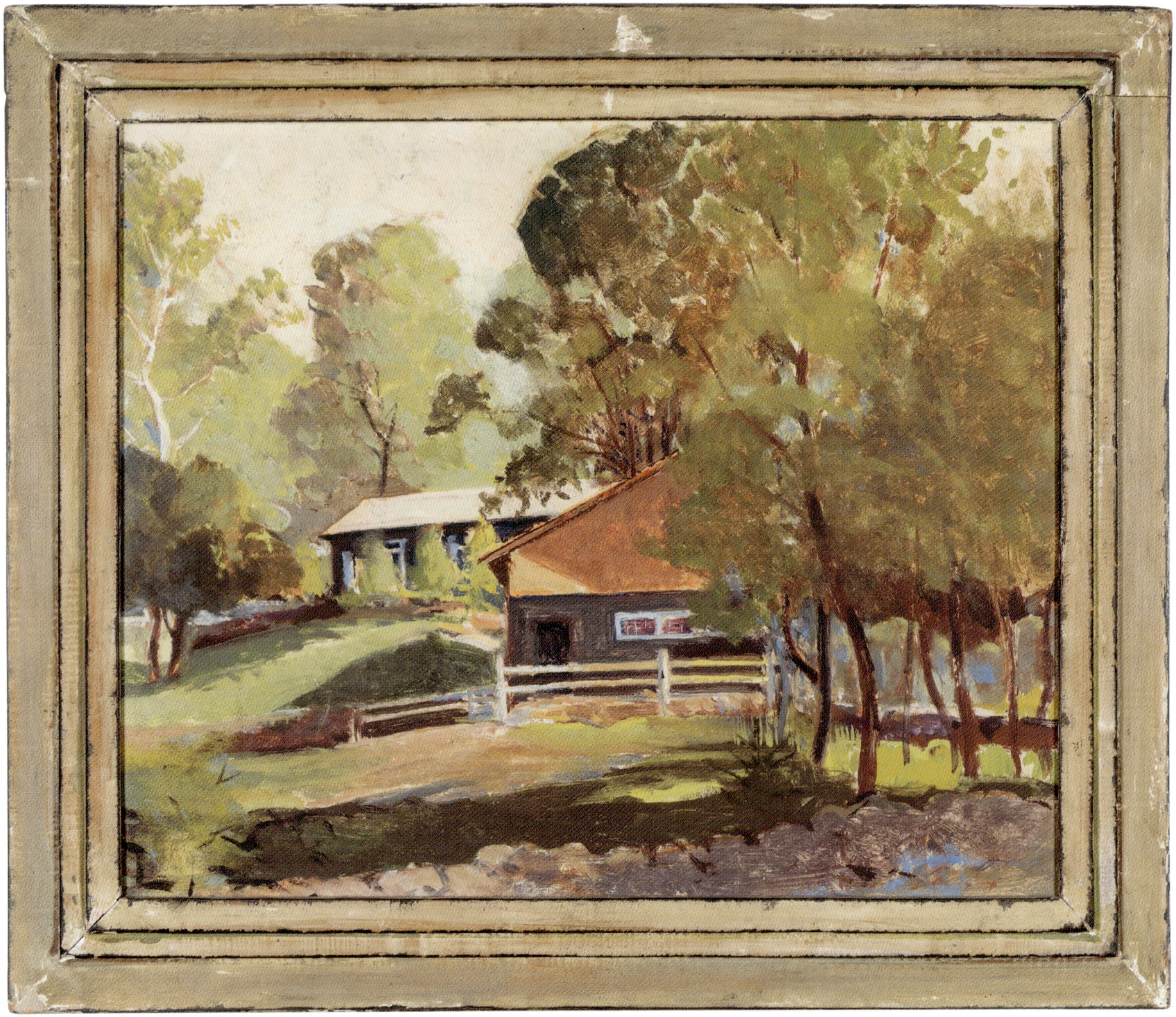

THE STABLE AT TOLMAN POND

Oil on board, Quigley frame, 21 x 25 in.

Private collection

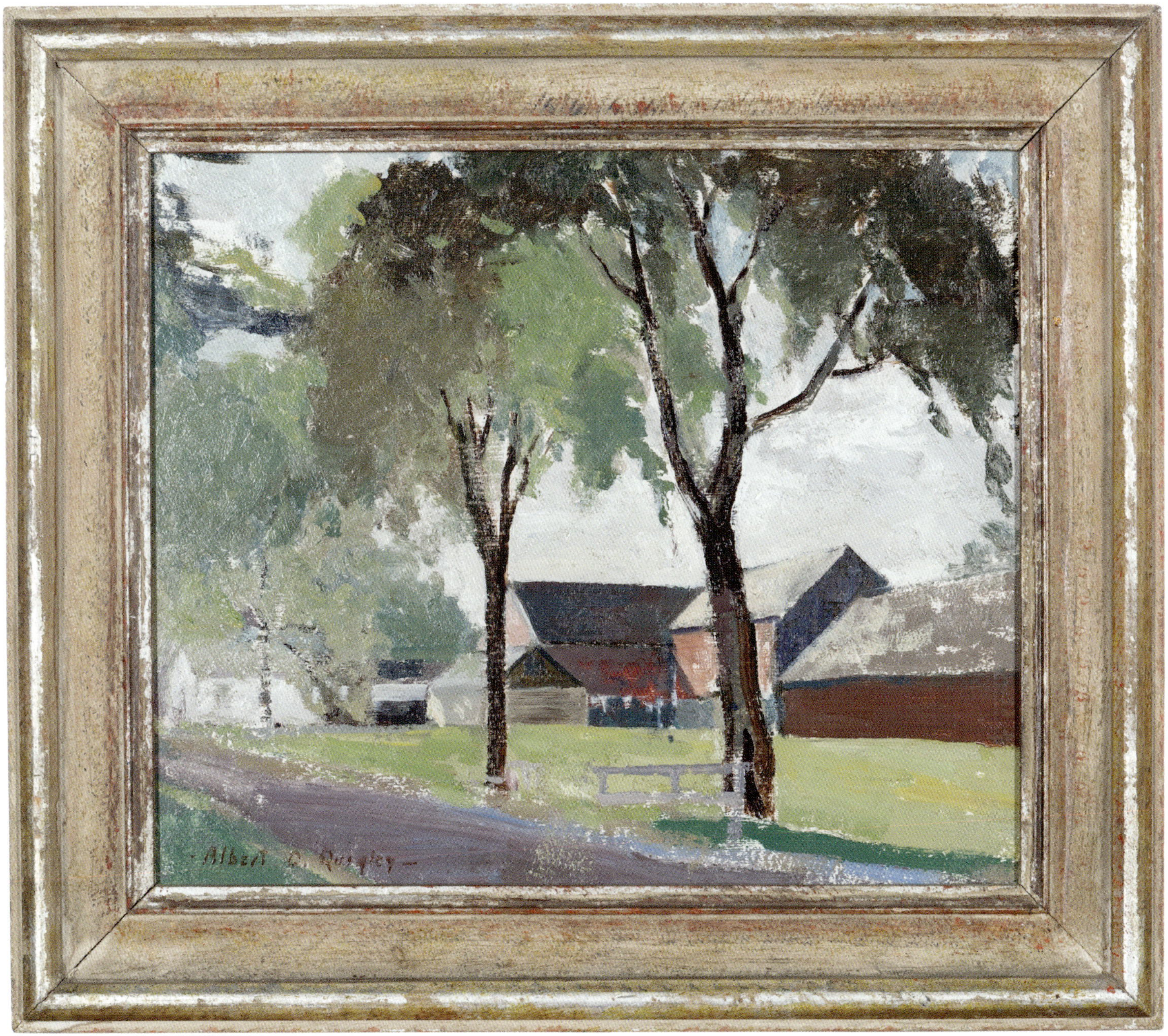

UNTITLED

Oil on board, Quigley frame, 14 x 16 in.

Private collection

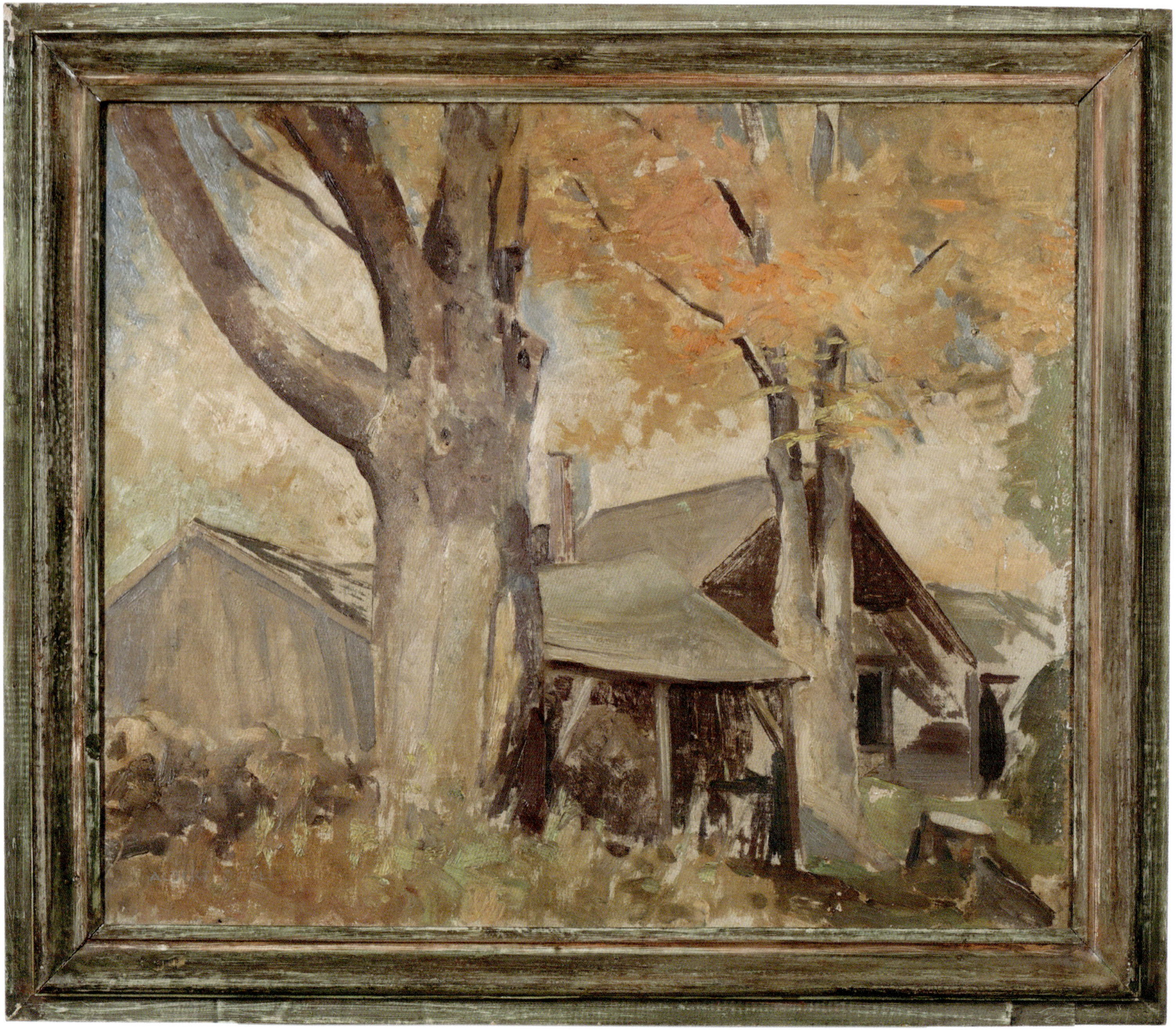

OLD SECTION OF ALEXANDER JAMES SUMMER HOME IN RICHMOND, NEW HAMPSHIRE

Oil on canvas, Quigley frame, 21 x 25 in.

Darcy Quigley

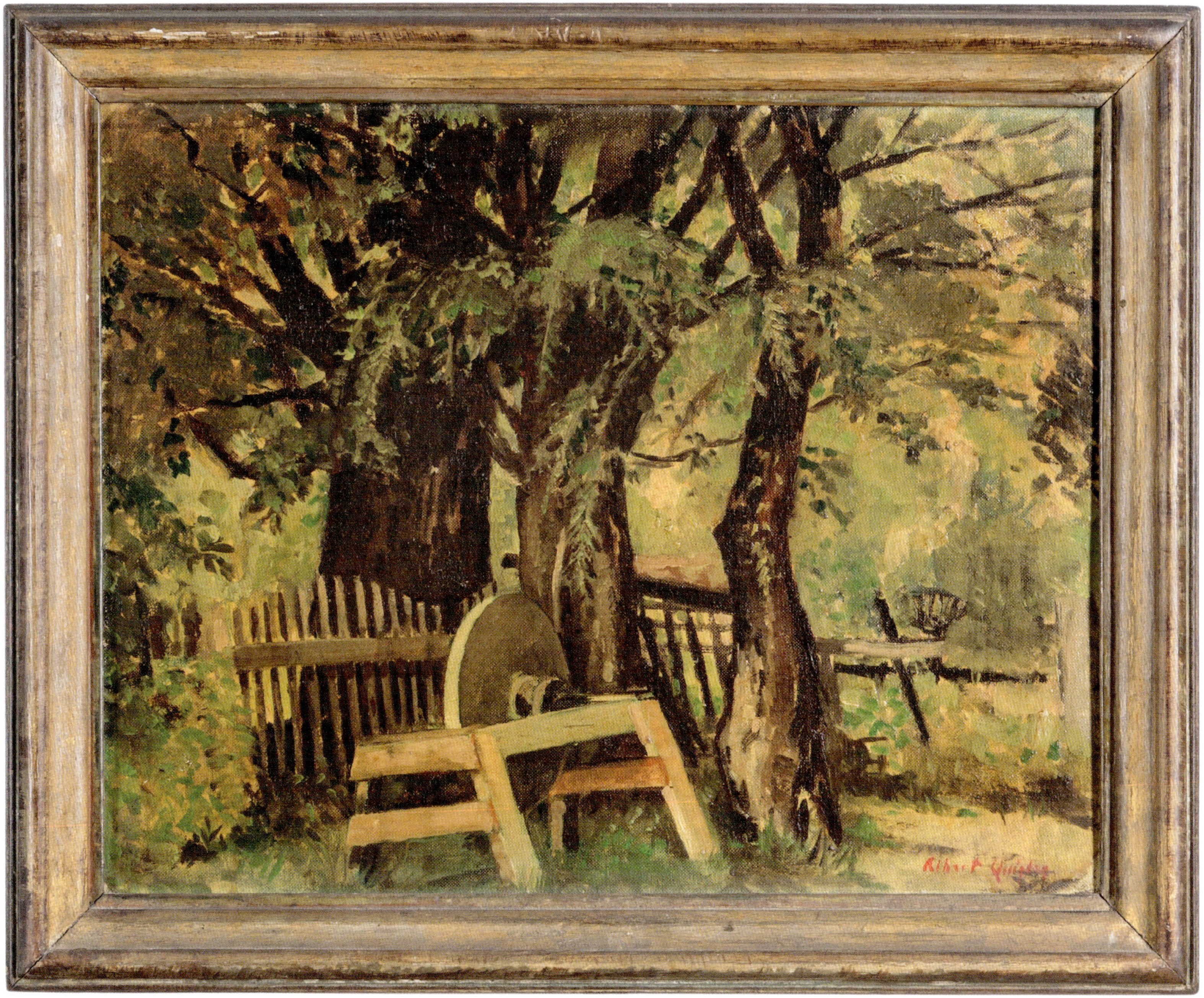

SHARPENING GRINDSTONE

Oil on canvas, Quigley frame, 17 x 21 in.

Private collection

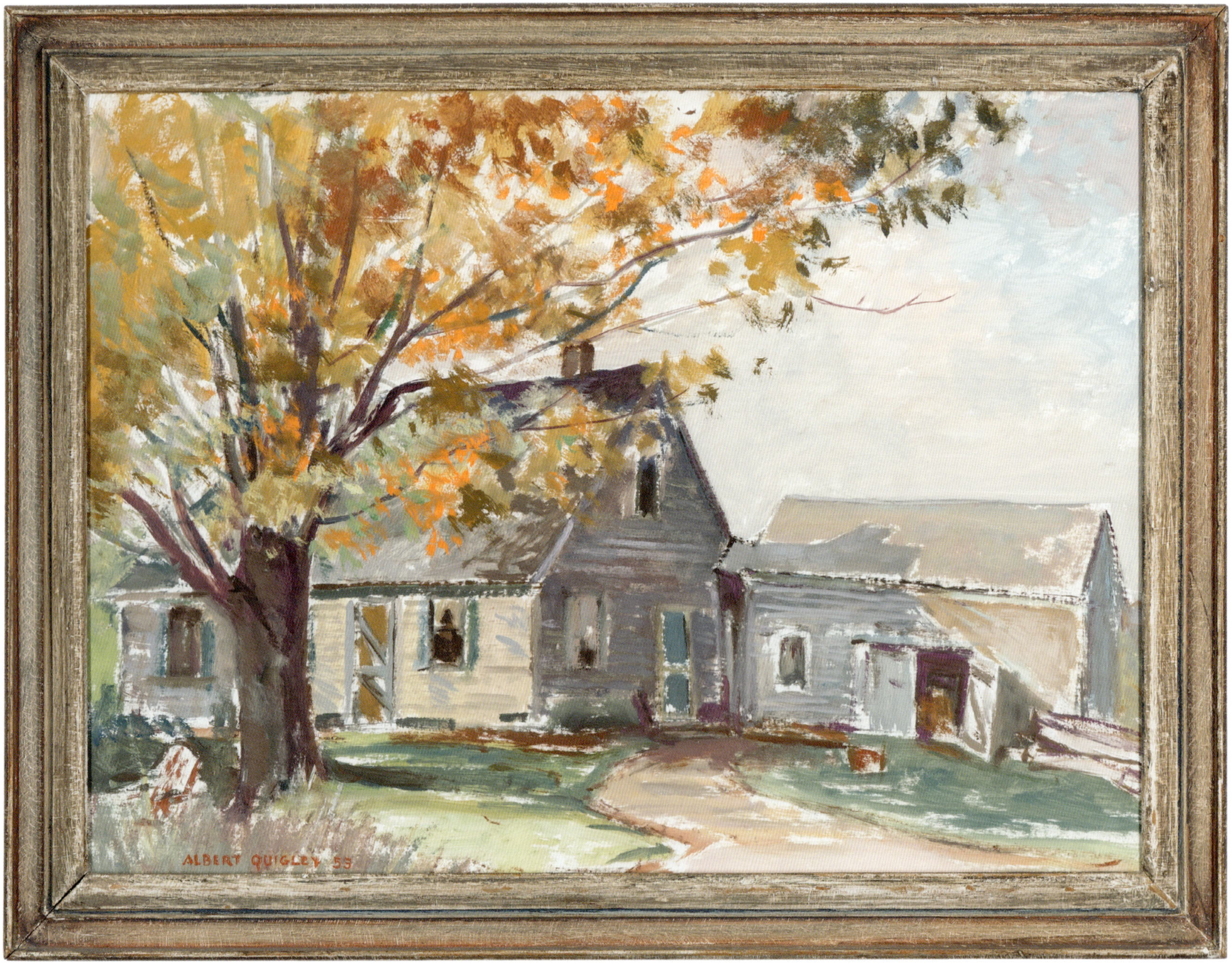

PERCY FLOOD HOUSE, NELSON, NEW HAMPSHIRE (1953)
Oil on board, Quigley frame, 21 x 28 in.
Private collection

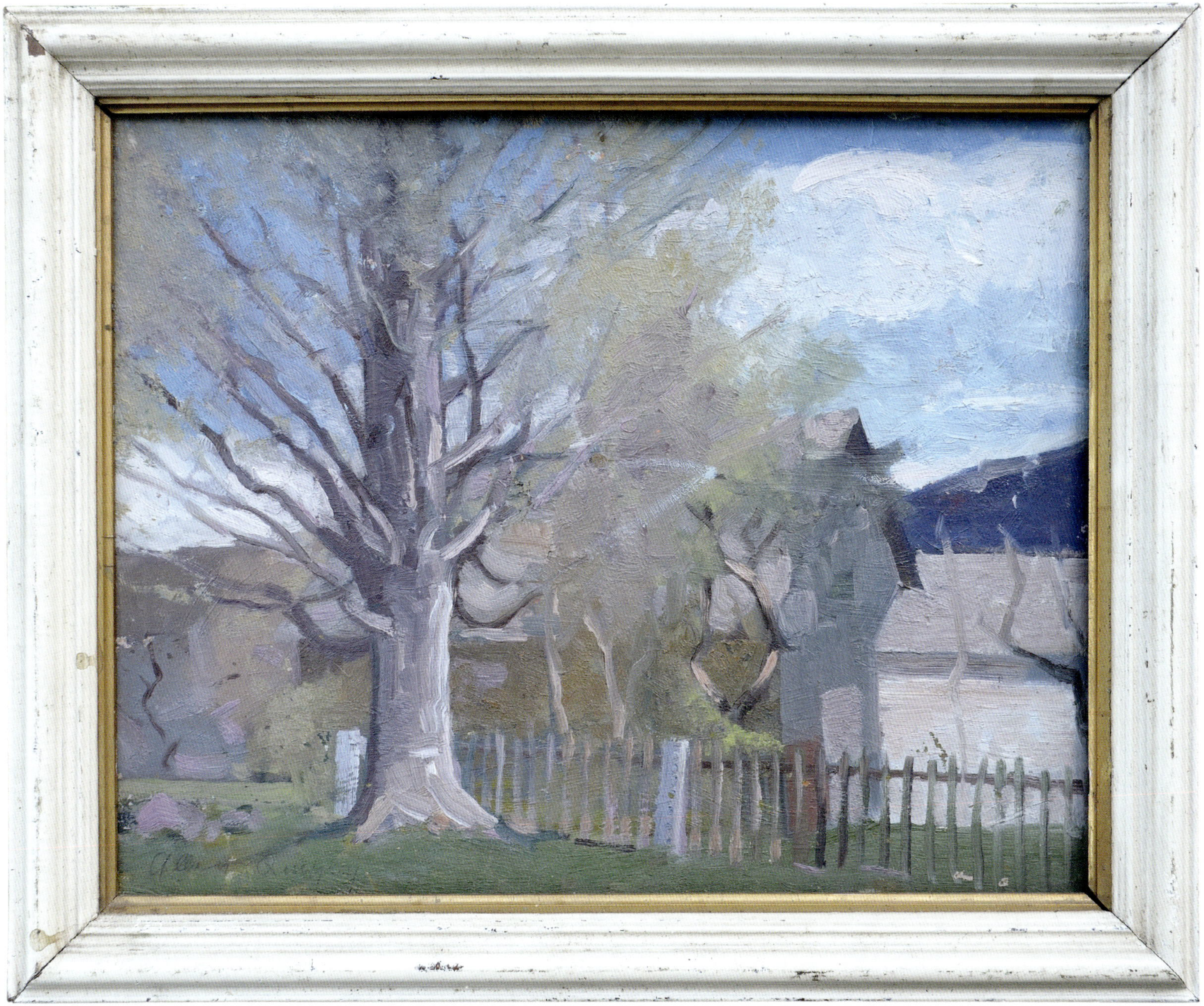

UNTITLED
Oil on board, 14 x 18 in.,
Mark Quigley
Lisa Quigley Valliere, photographer

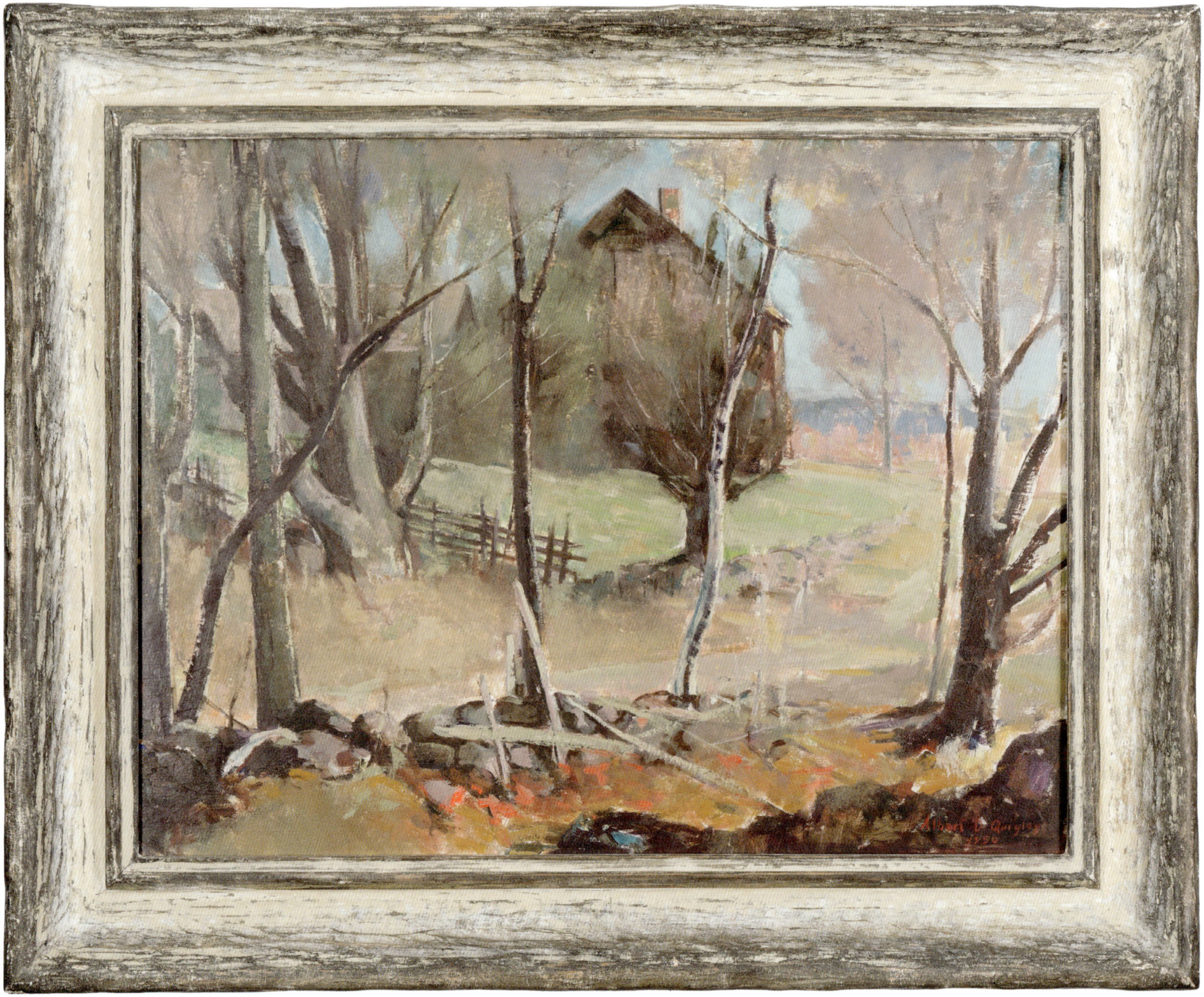

WILDER FARM, EAST SULLIVAN, NEW HAMPSHIRE (1950)
Oil on board, Quigley frame, 24 x 30 in.
Private collection

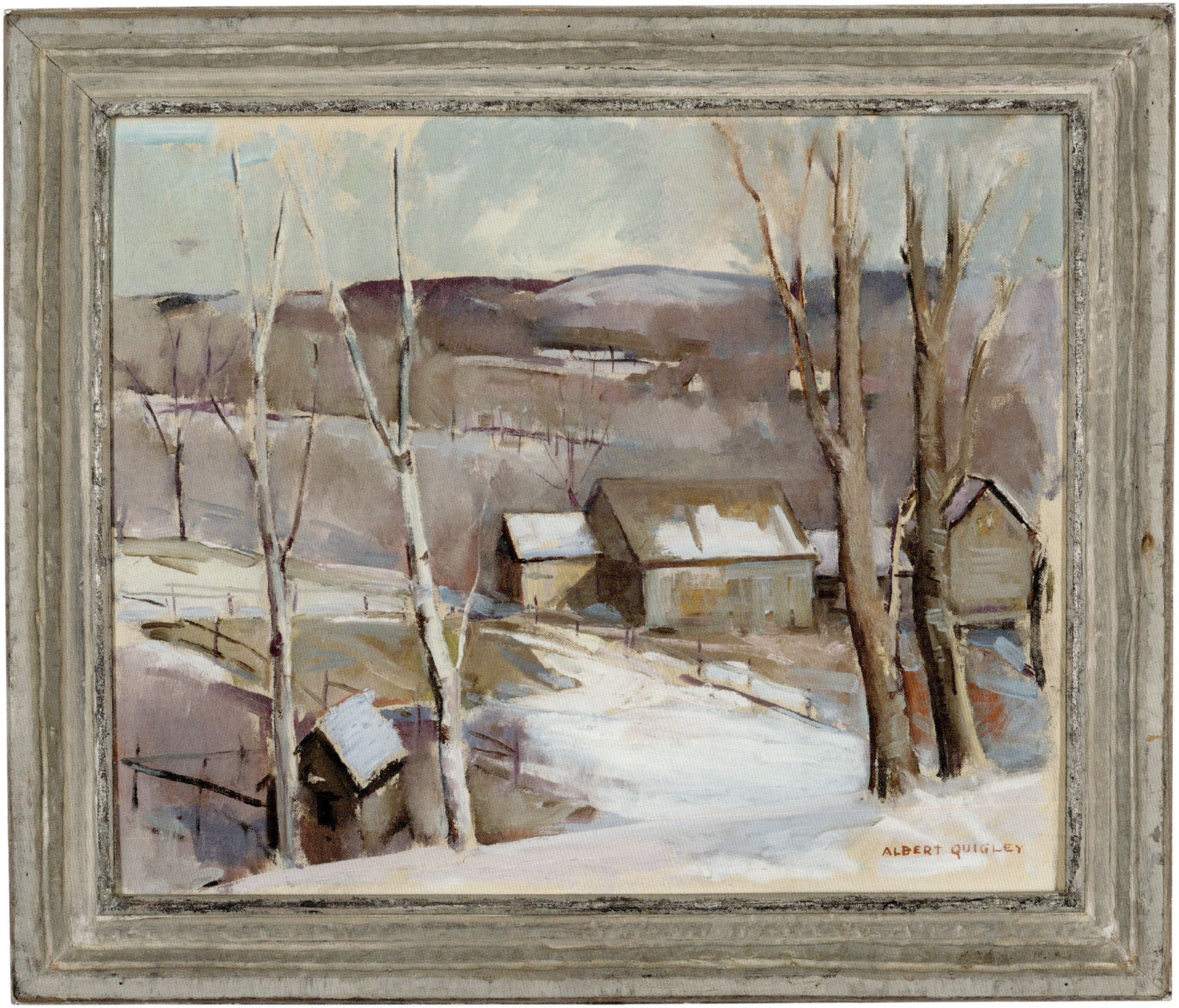

UNTITLED

Oil on canvas, Quigley frame, 20 x 26 in.

Camp Glen Brook

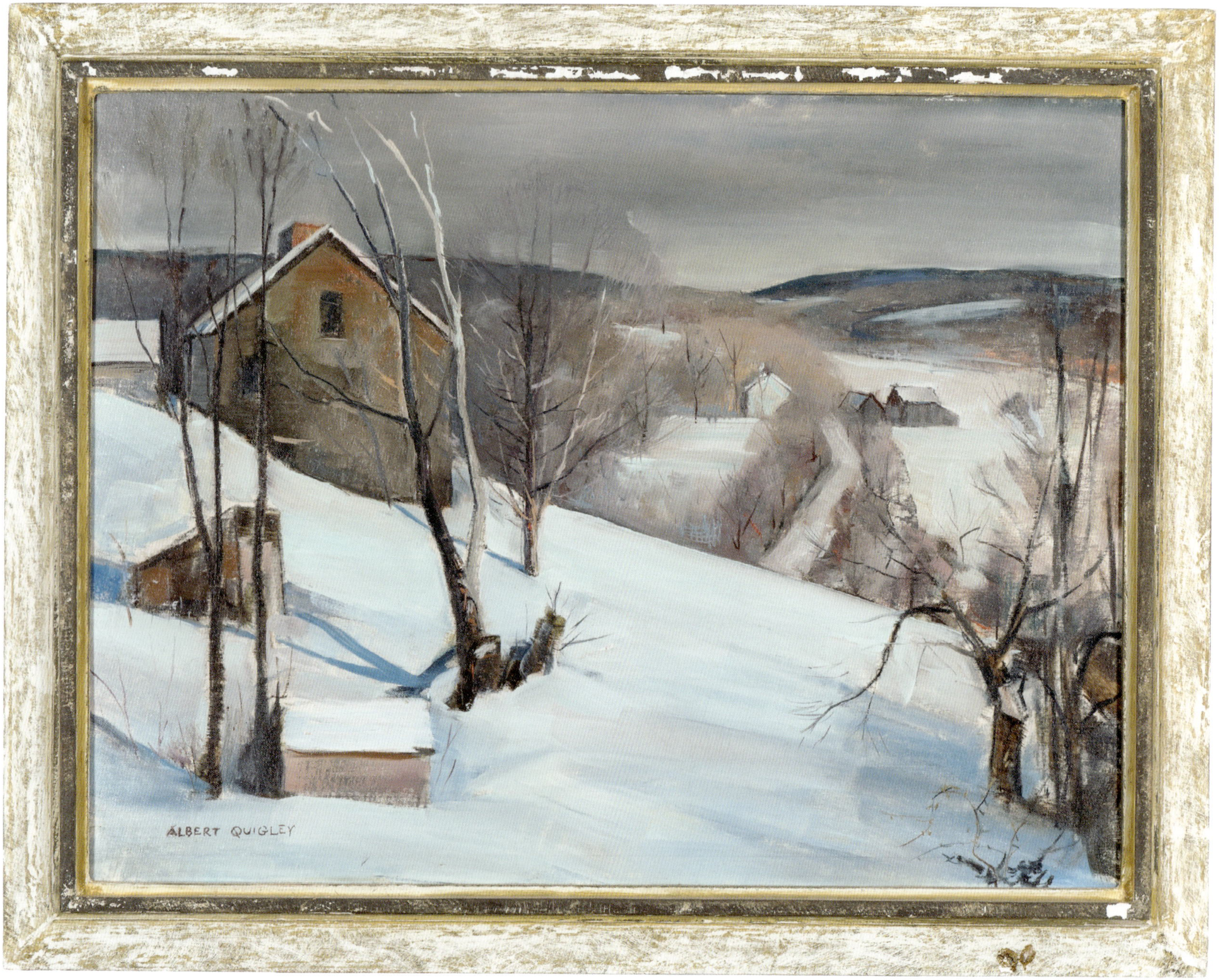

UNTITLED

Oil on board, Quigley frame, 22 x 28 in., private collection

House in Sullivan, New Hampshire, looking toward Apple Hill and other buildings

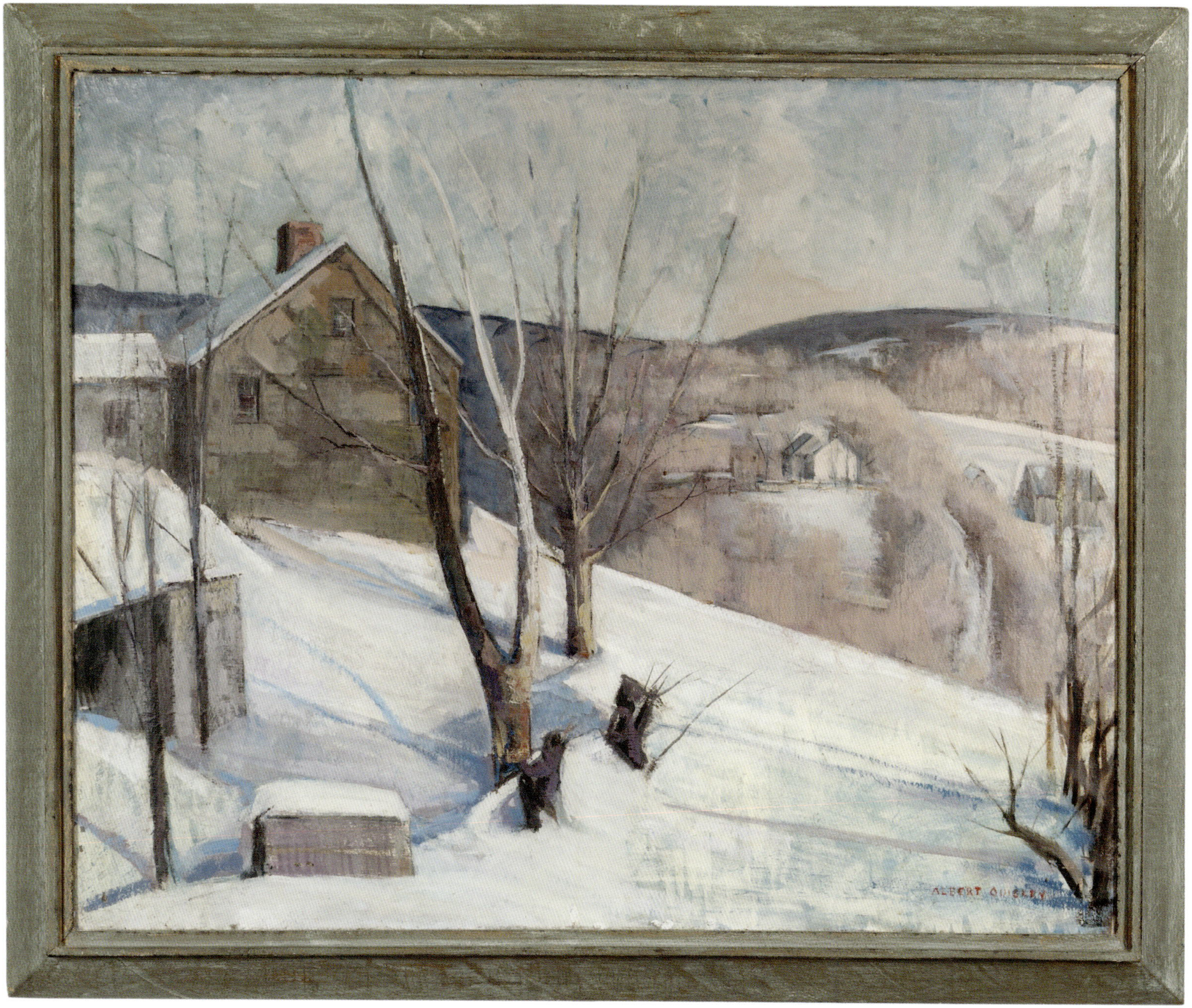

UNTITLED

Oil on canvas, Quigley frame, 34 x 41 in., private collection

House in Sullivan, New Hampshire, looking toward Apple Hill and other buildings

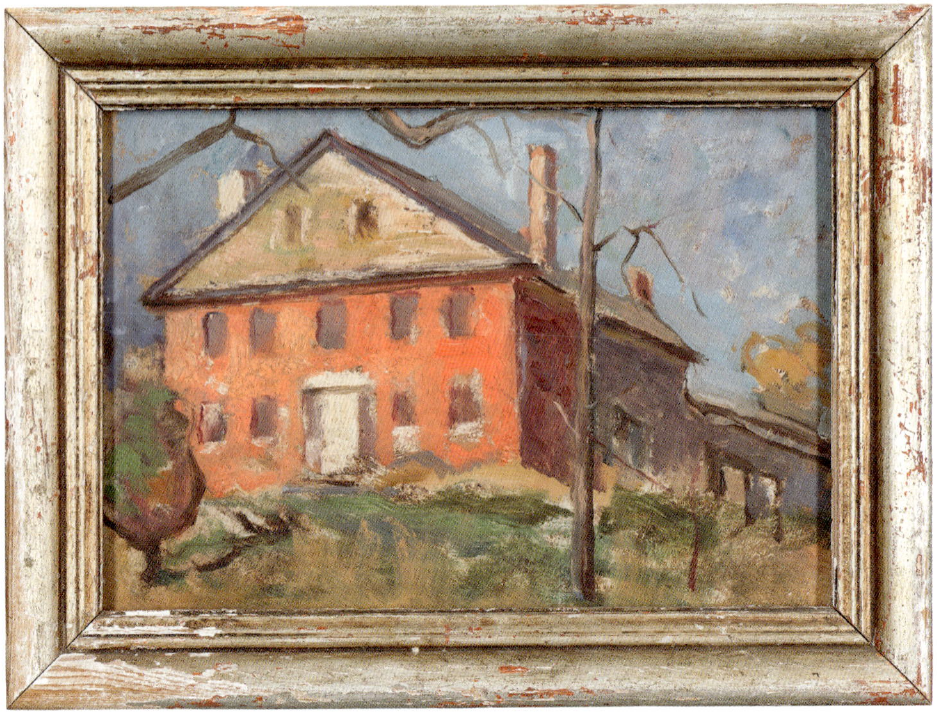

ABOVE **WELLINGTON HOUSE**
Oil on board
Quigley frame
10 x 14 in.
Private collection

RIGHT **WELLINGTON HOUSE**
Oil on board
unframed
16 x 20 in.
Brian and Jessie Quigley

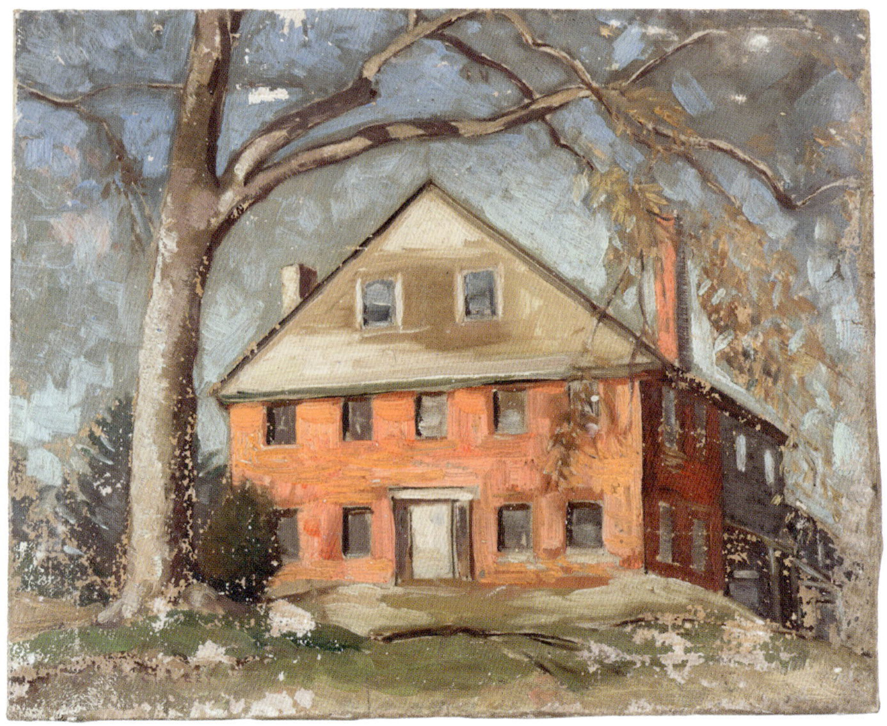

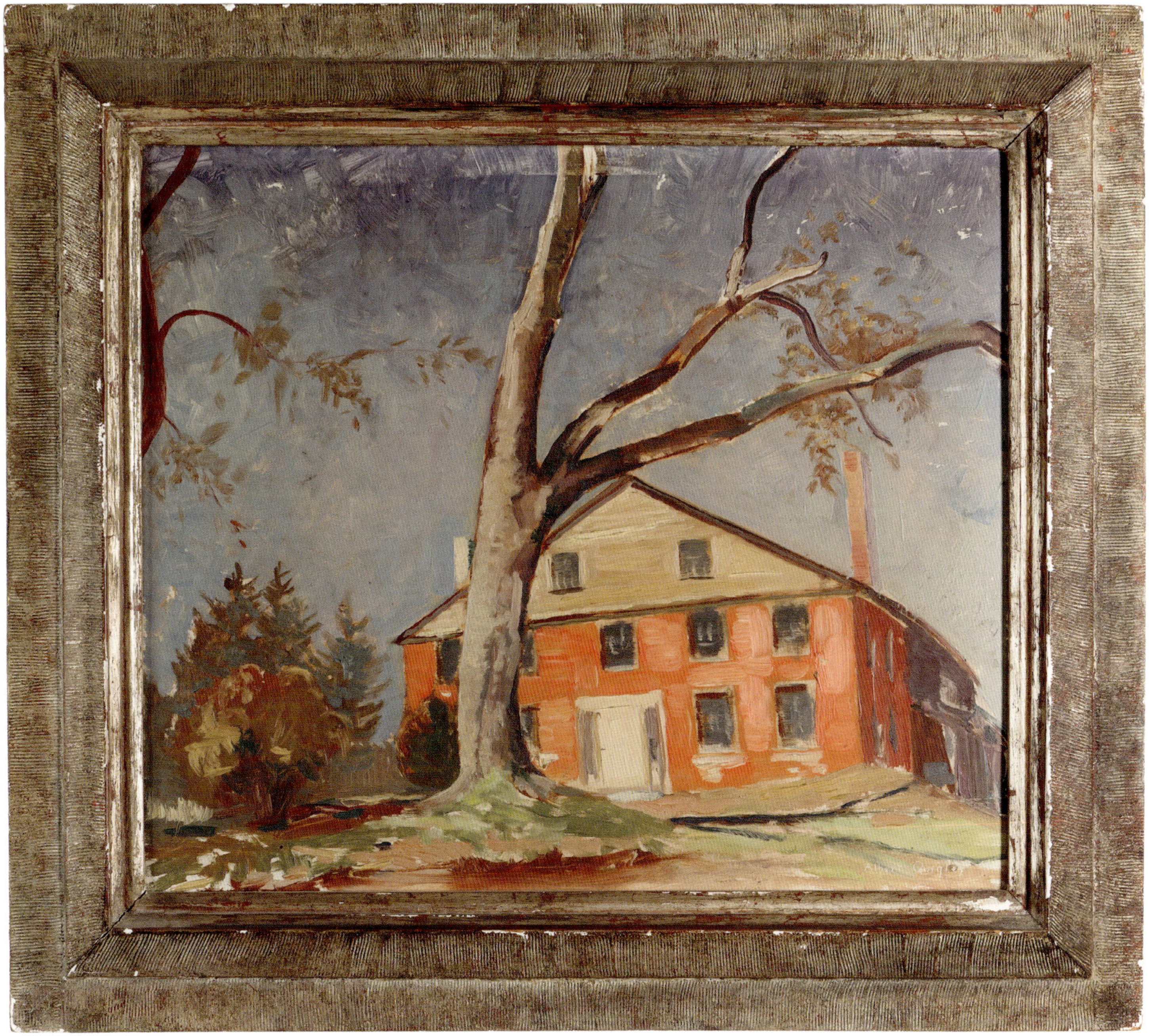

WELLINGTON HOUSE
Oil on board, Quigley frame, 24 x 28 in.
Private collection

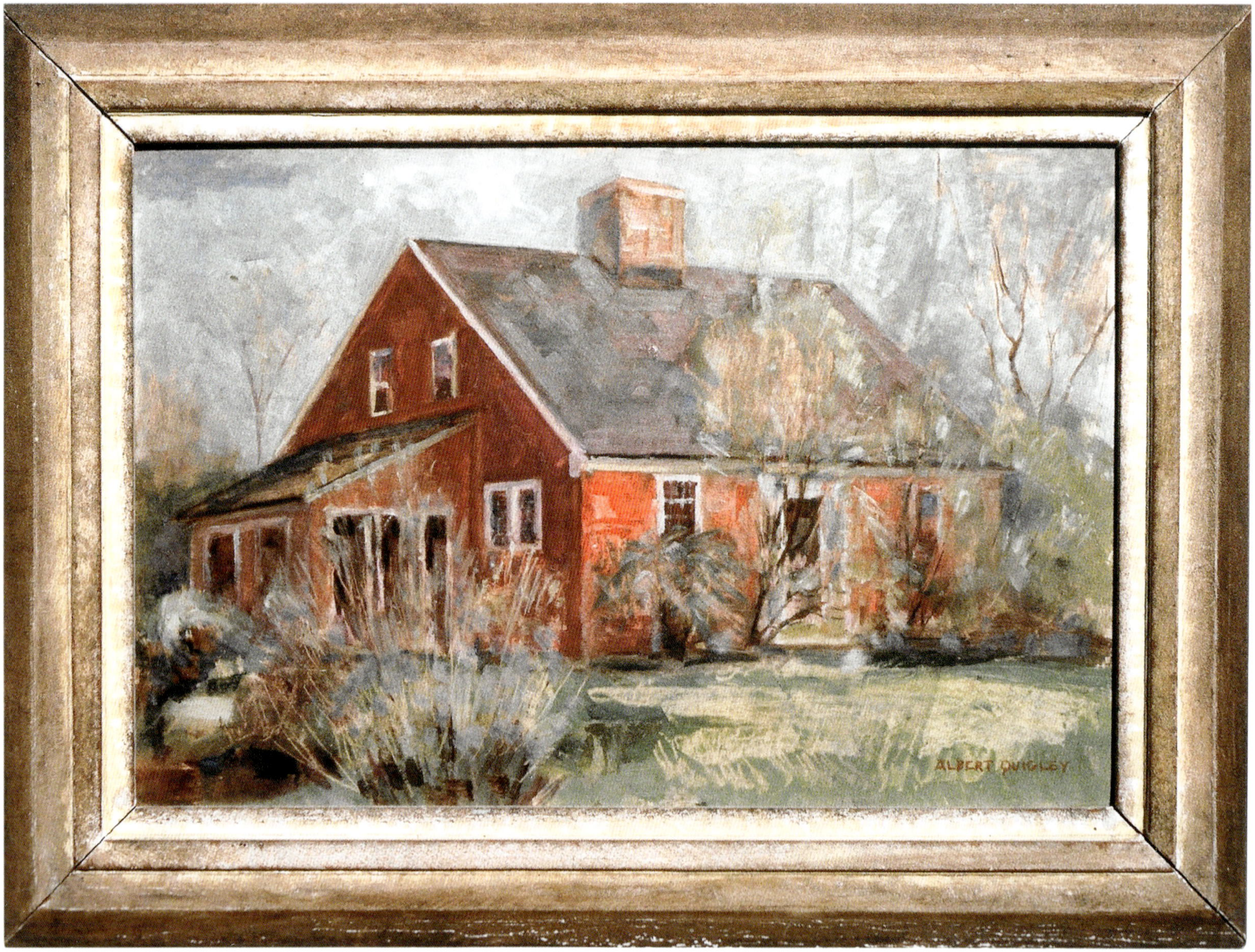

MAYFAIR FARM (1954)
Oil on board, Quigley frame
John M. Guilbert
Commissioned by Florence B. Tolman as a wedding present for Mary C. and John M. Guilbert
Courtesy photograph

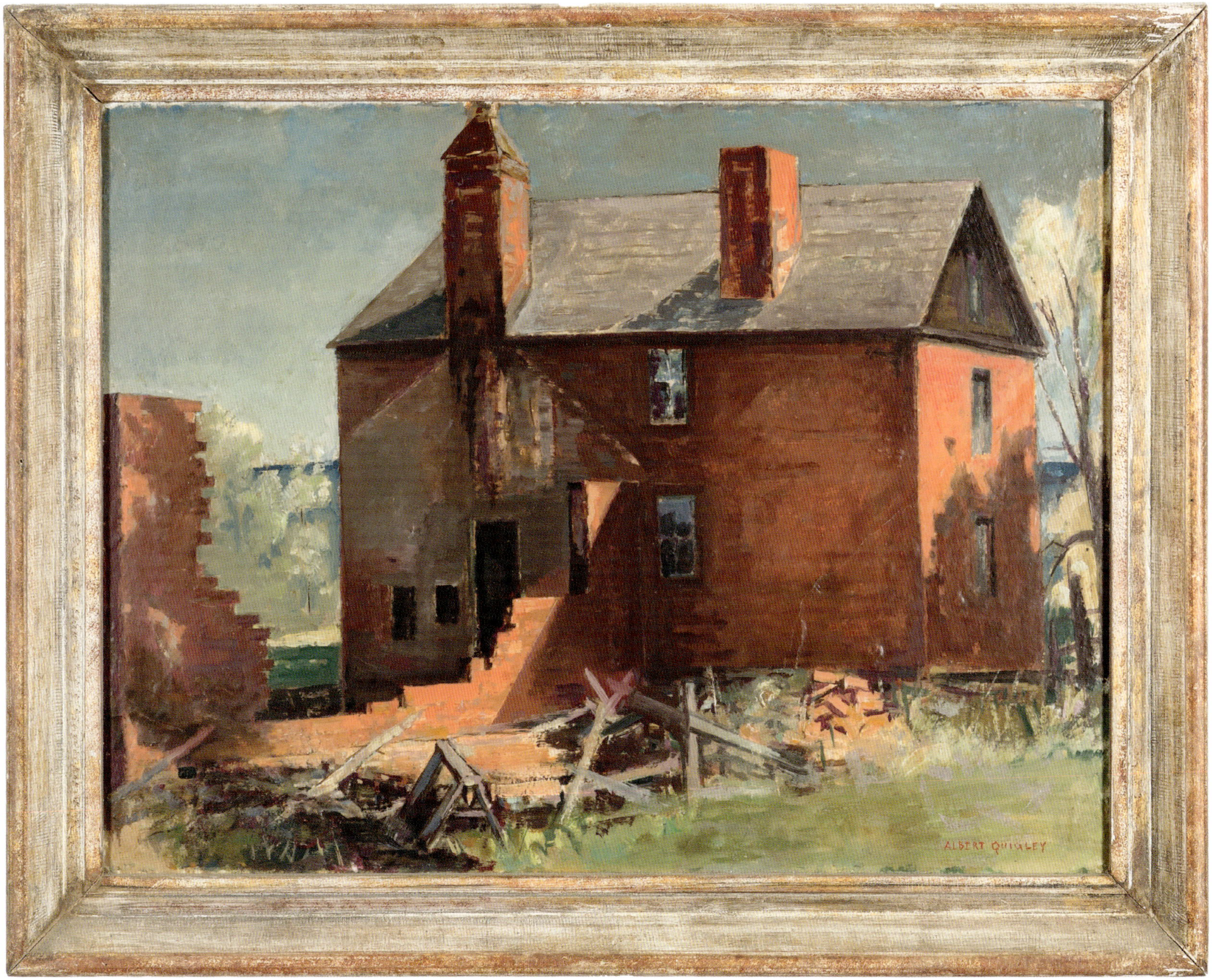

OSGOOD HOUSE, NELSON, NEW HAMPSHIRE

Oil on board, Quigley frame, 22 x 28 in.

Private collection

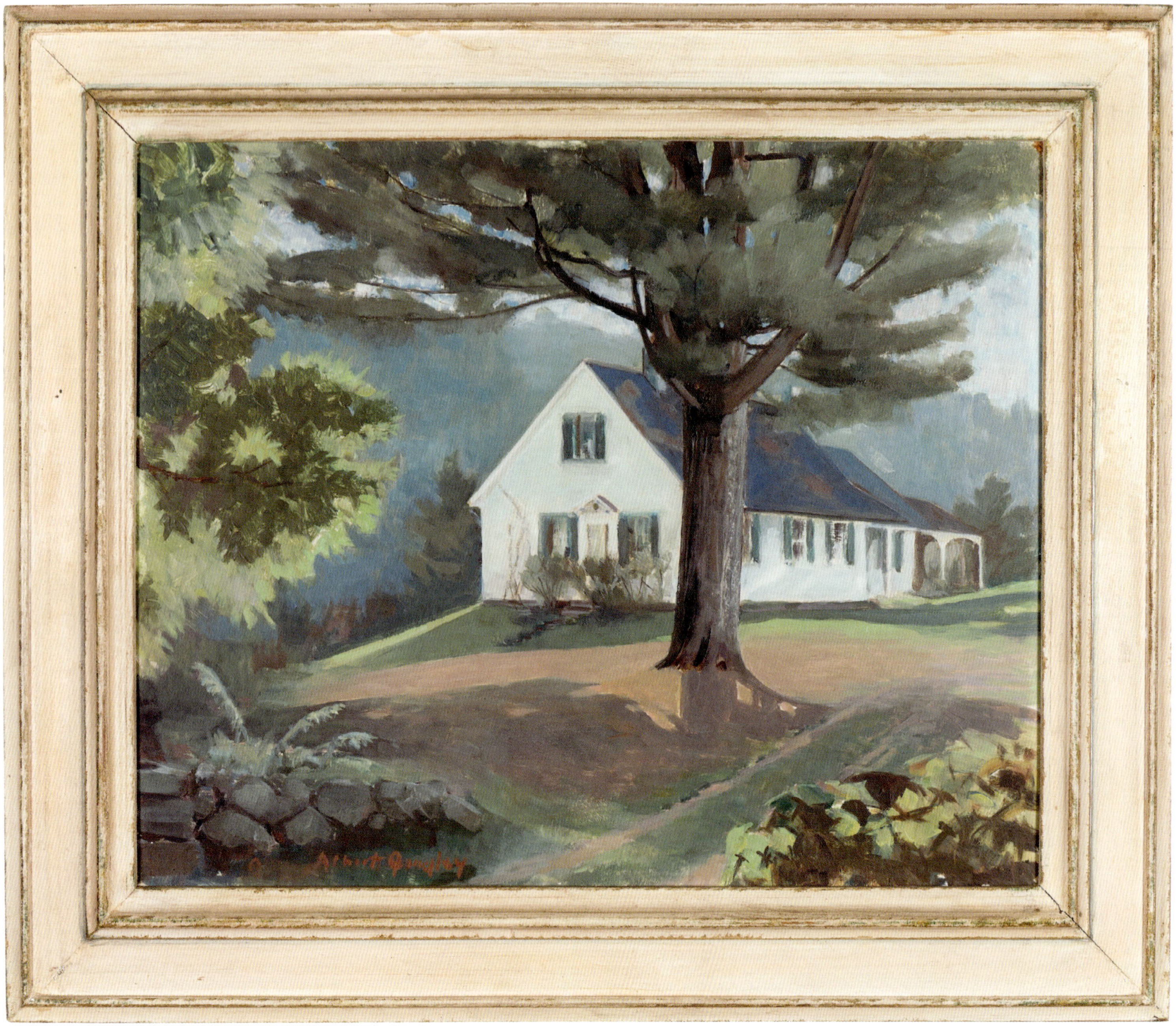

HOUSE AT OTTER BROOK
Oil on board, Quigley frame, 22 x 26 in.
Private collection

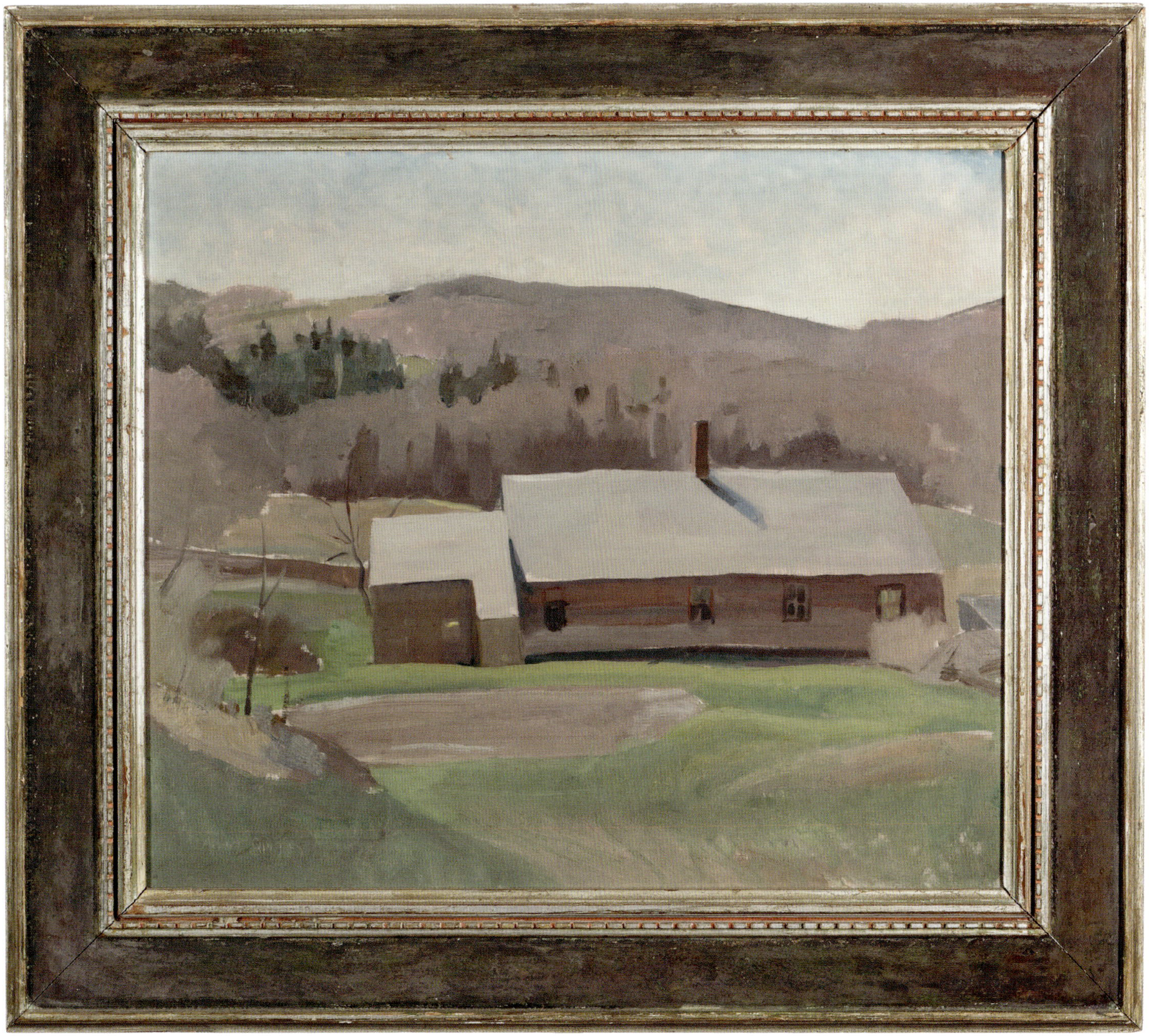

Untitled
Oil on board, Quigley frame, 28 x 32 in.
Private collection

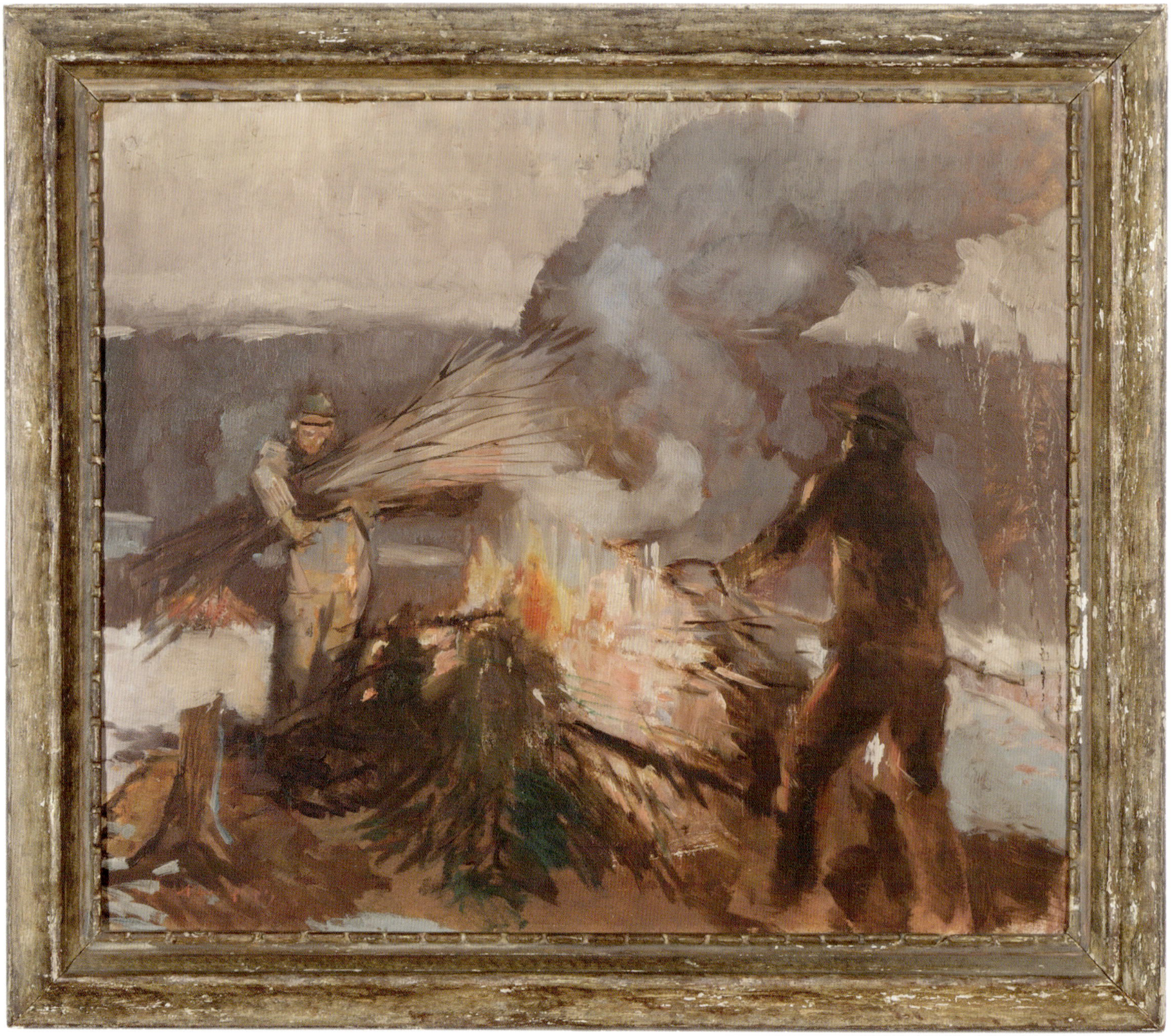

BRUSH BURNERS

Oil on board, Quigley frame, 22 x 25 in.

Private collection

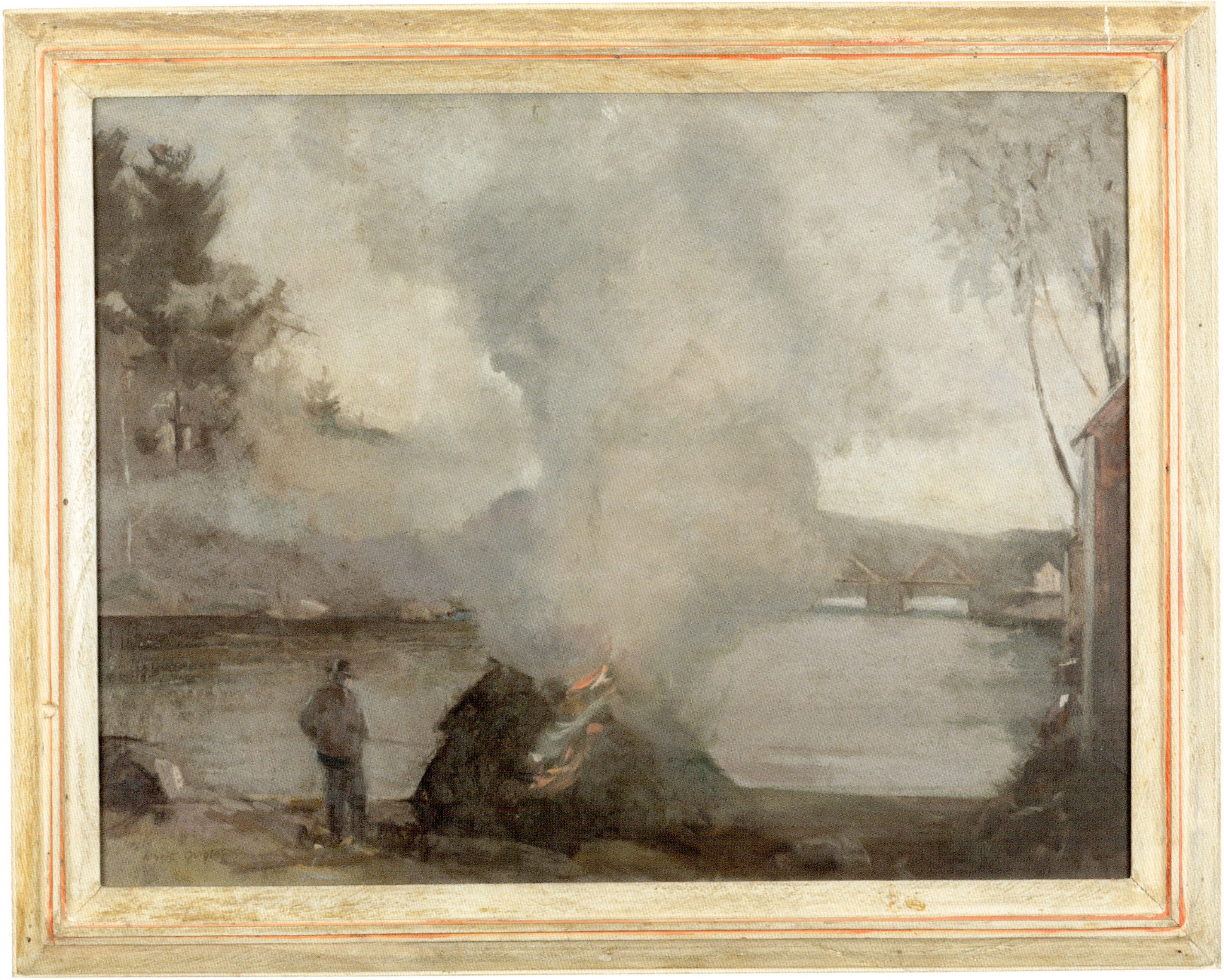

BRUSH BURNERS, FRANKFORT, MAINE
Oil on panel, Quigley frame, 21 x 27 in.
Private collection
Arnold Adler, photographer

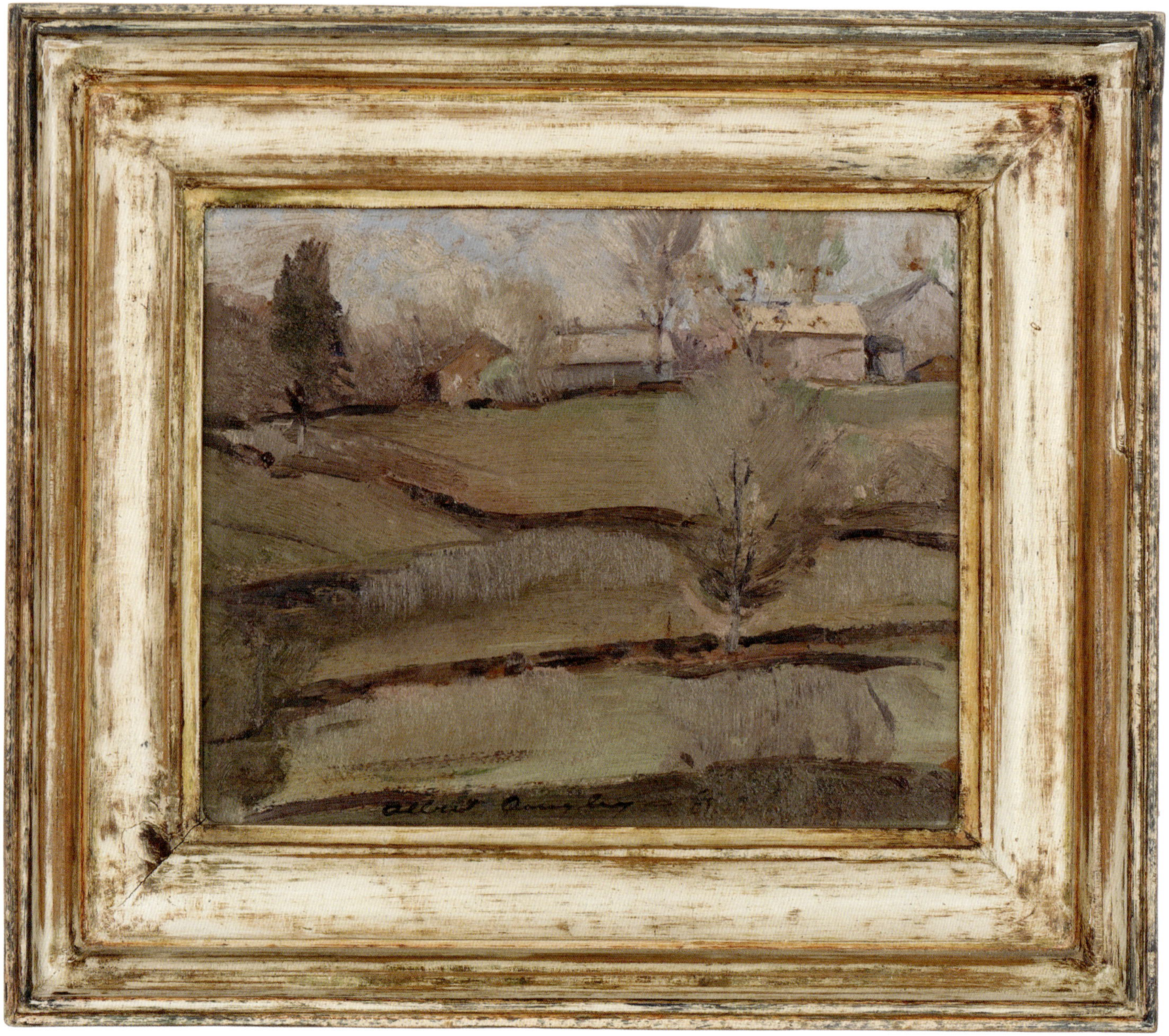

ANSON WILDER FARM, EAST SULLIVAN, NEW HAMPSHIRE

Oil on board, Quigley frame, 12 x 15 in.

Private collection

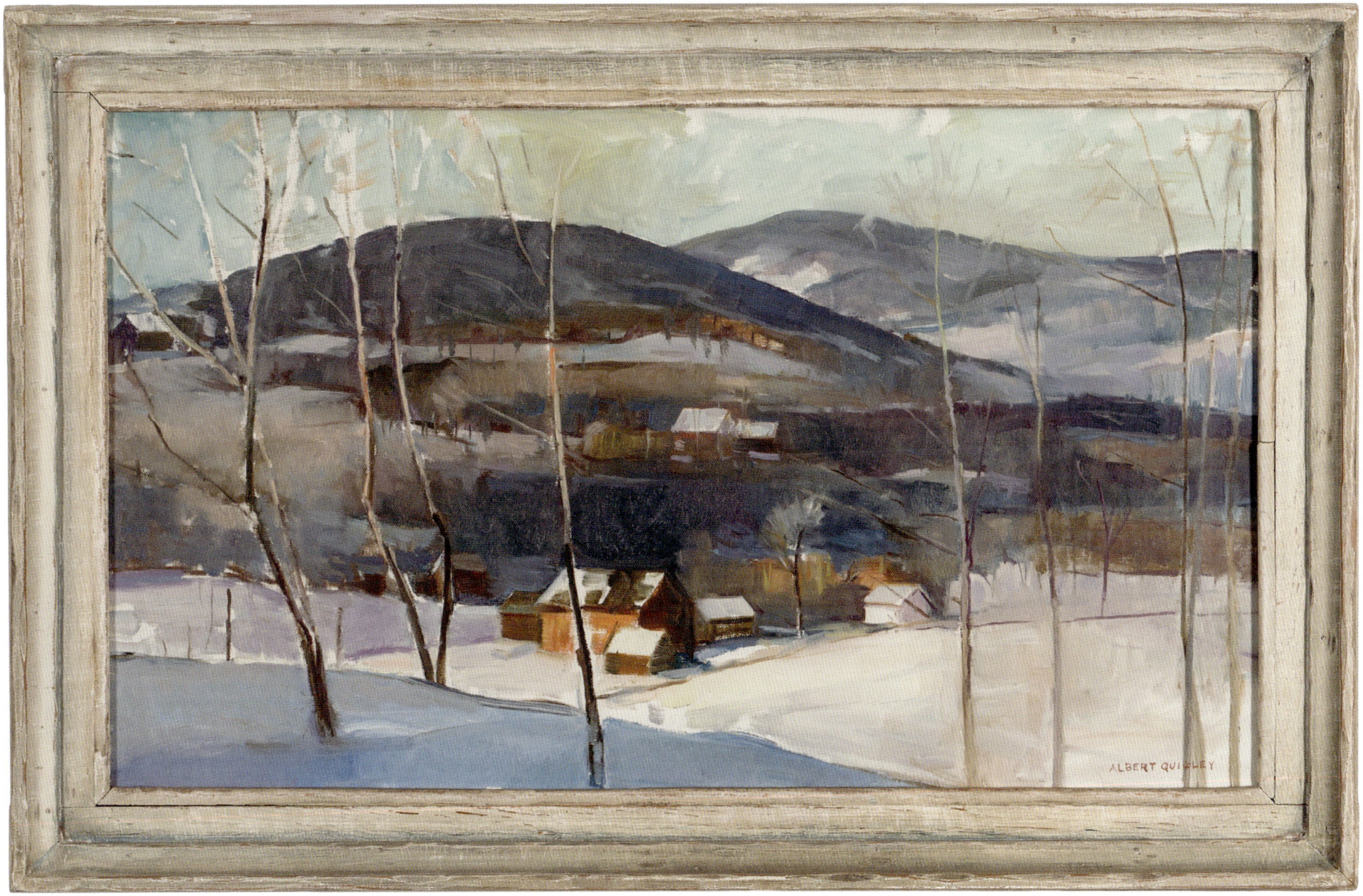

UNTITLED

Oil on canvas, Quigley frame, 18 x 28 in.

Private collection

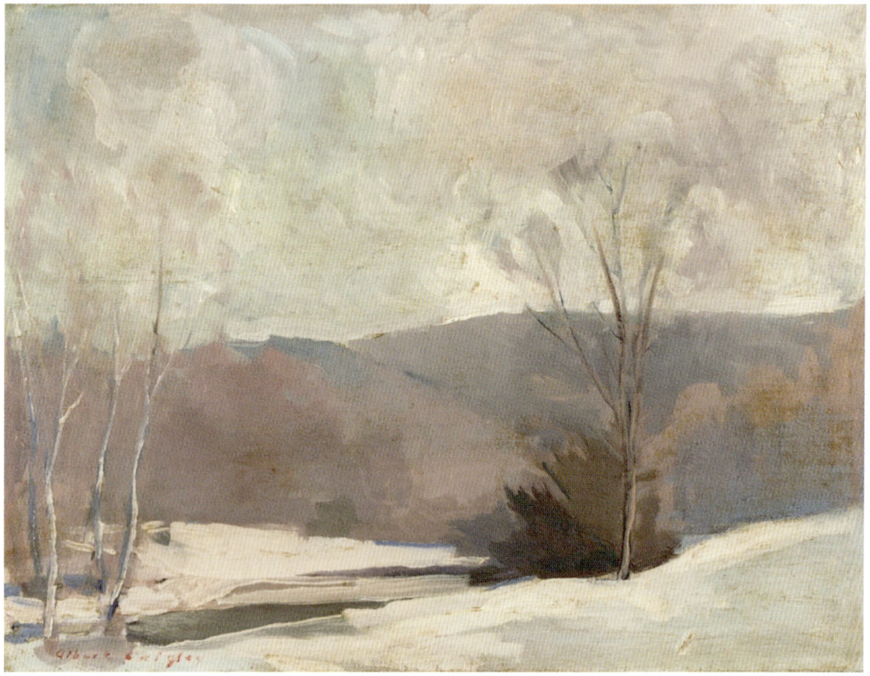

UNTITLED

Oil on board, Quigley frame, 15 x 19 in.

Private collection

The Cold Stillness of Winter

It is always a celebration when a body of work can be seen at one time. It accelerates the senses. In a real way, these images are full and uplifting. I see years of training in astute observation. I see texture and color brought to completion with the solid patience of the master—the artist and craftsman; stone carver, painter, draftsman, musician and woodworker. I see forms of structure and illusion, as well as pattern of stroke with brush and chisel. I see somber northern light as well as playful sunlit impressions; the cold stillness of winter and the steamy warmth of summer. I feel atmosphere. I see intensity and subtlety. Albert Quigley was a maker of wonderful images in sound, song, sight and touch. It is no surprise that his work is important.

—Joey de Martelly, Nelson artist
co-curator of The Paintings of Albert Quigley: The Nelson Years, 1934–1961, *a 1995 exhibit at the Nelson Town Hall*

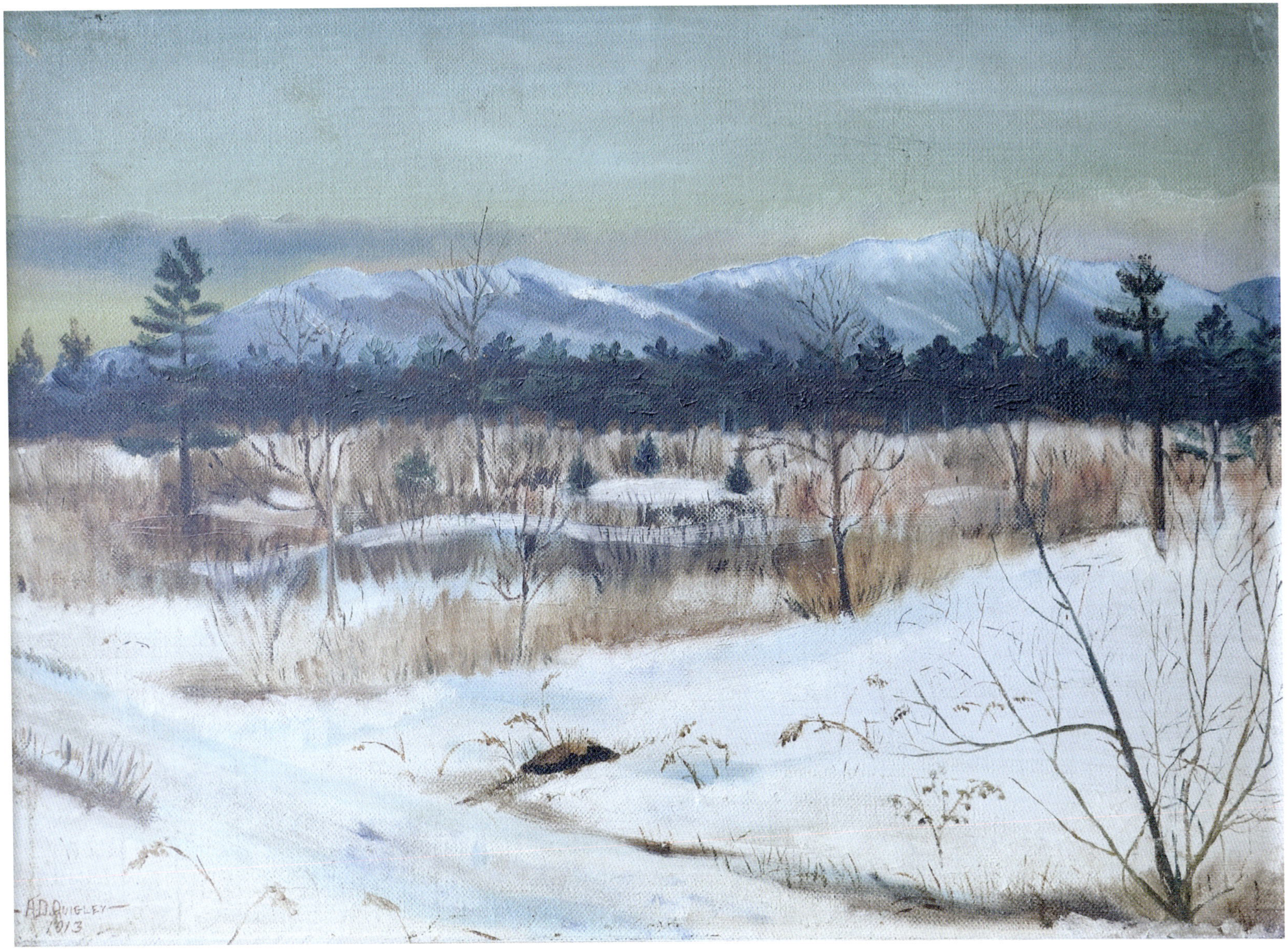

UNTITLED (1913)
Oil on canvas, Quigley frame, 16 x 24 in.
Mark Quigley
Lisa Quigley Valliere, photographer

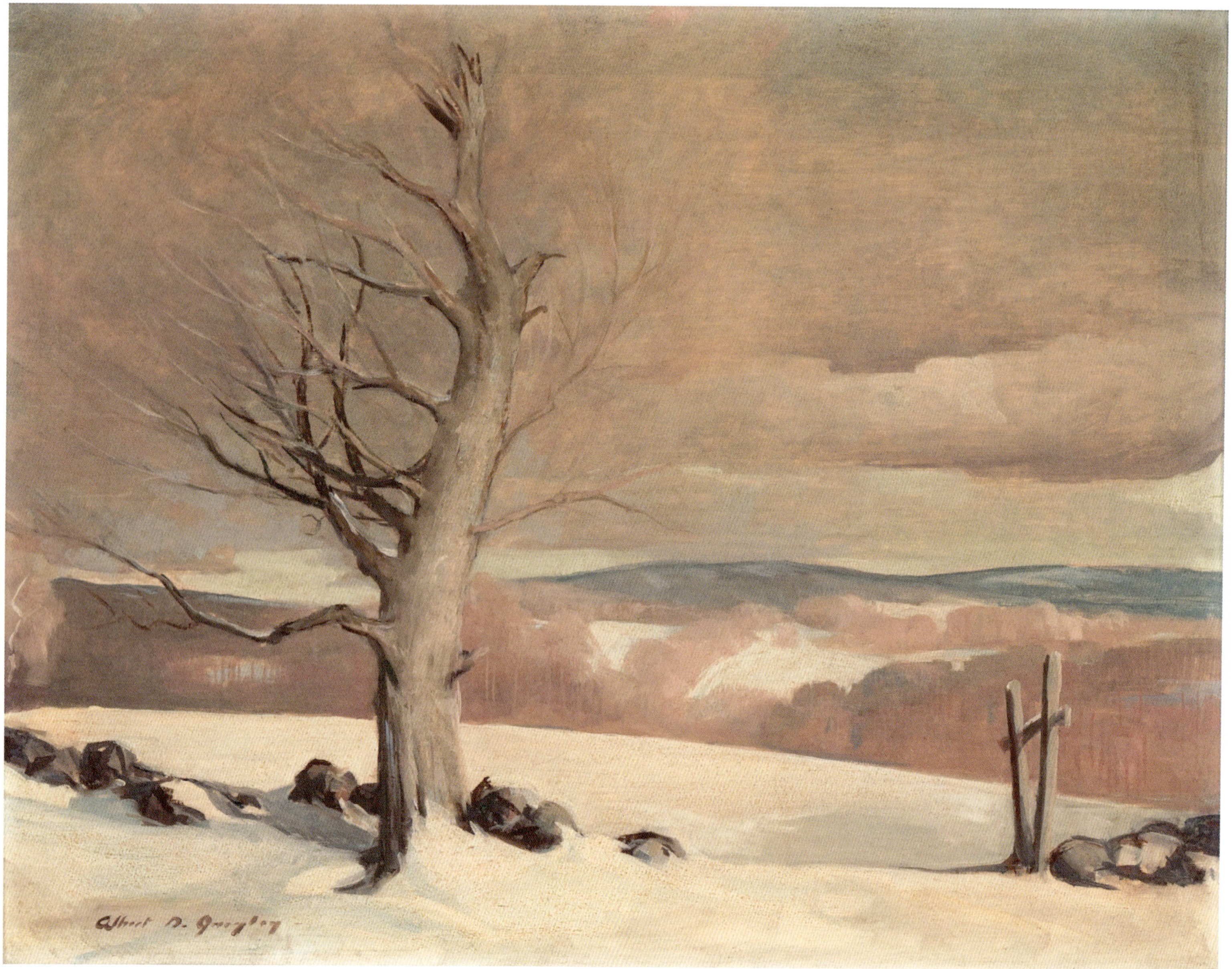

UNTITLED

Oil on canvas, 20 x 26 in.

Private collection

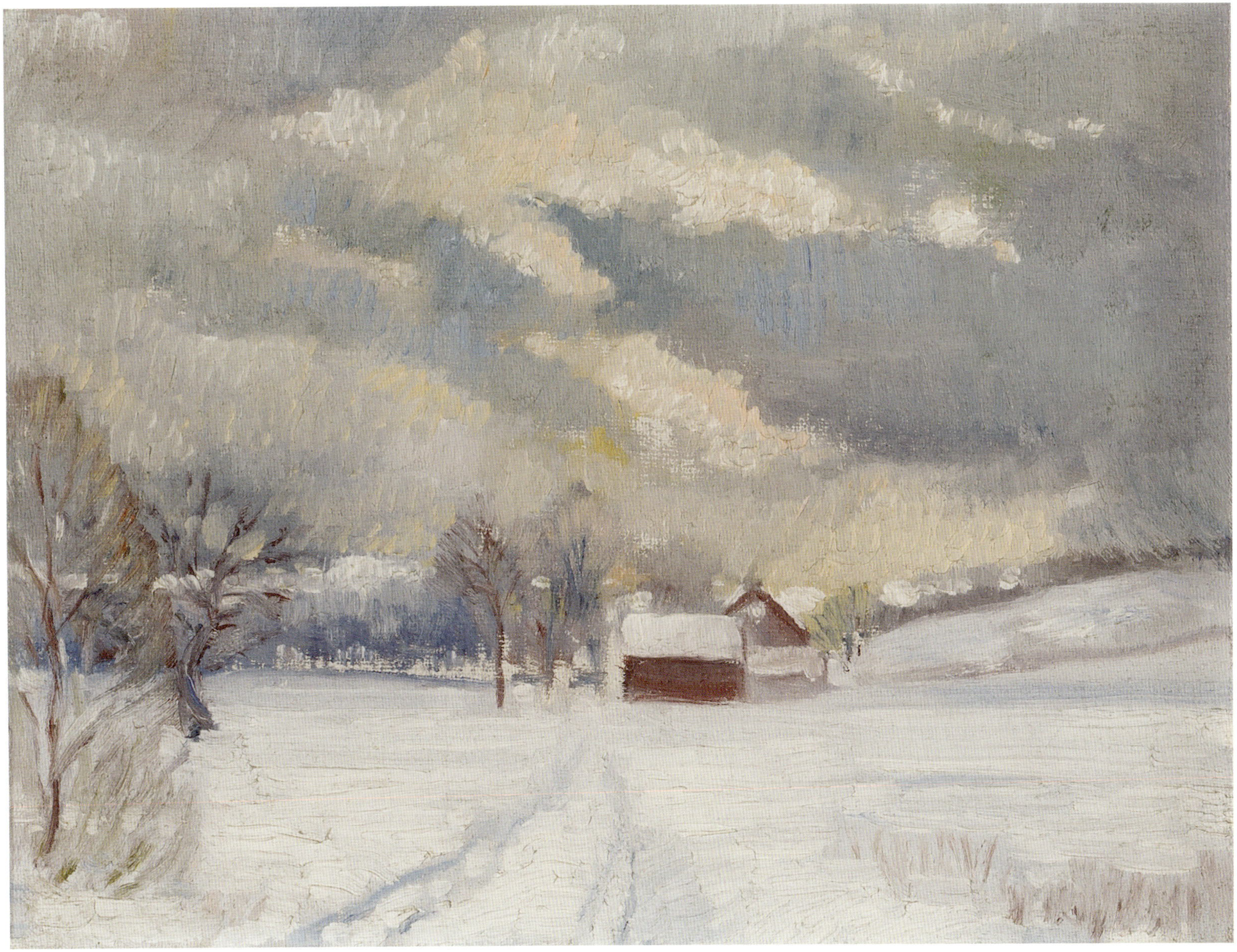

WOODWARD FARM, WEST KEENE, NEW HAMPSHIRE

Oil on board, 11 x 14 in.

Alston W. Barrett

Later called Hill Farm; buildings moved and later dismantled

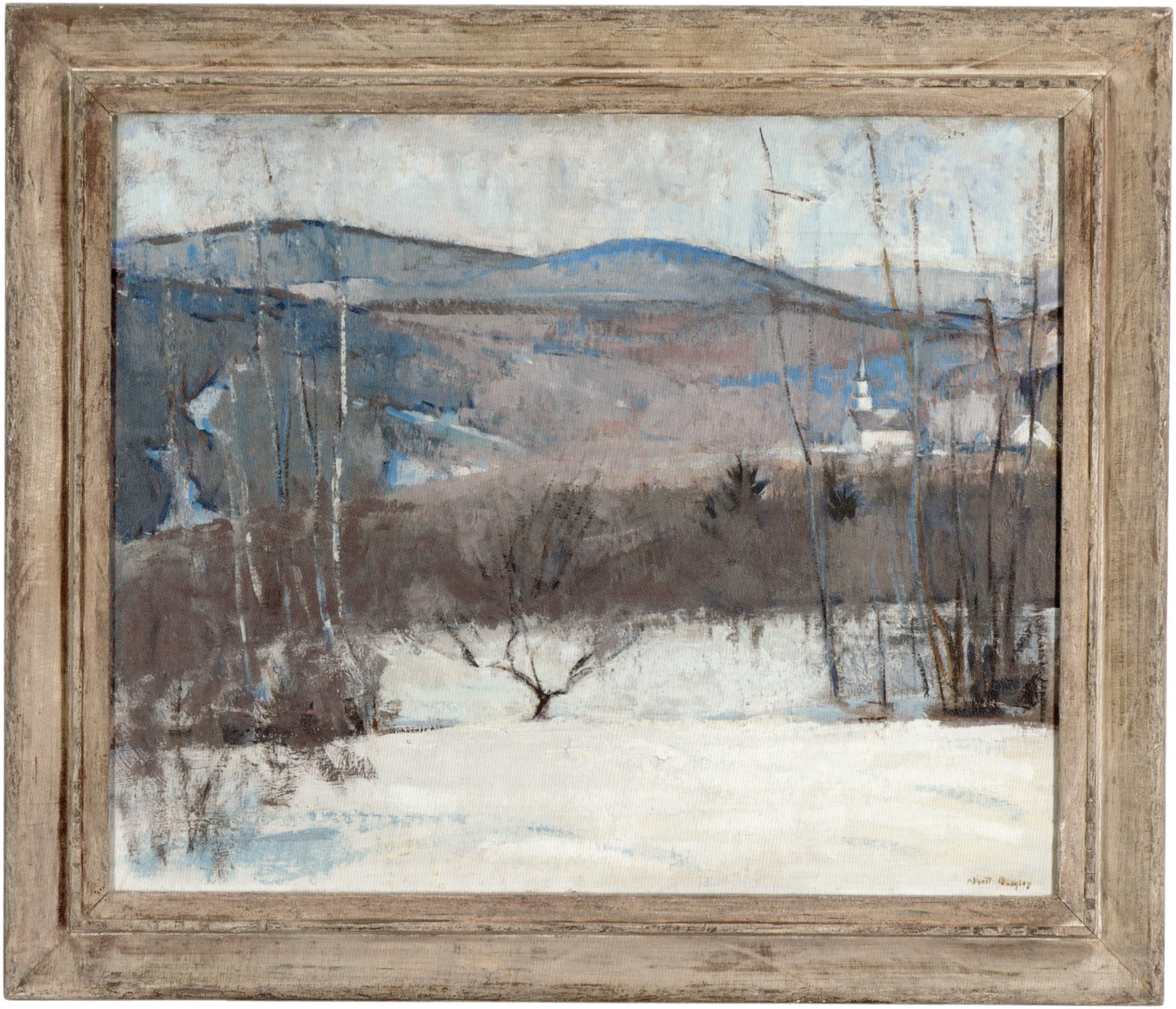

NELSON CHURCH FROM DIXON HILL

Oil on board, Quigley frame, 20 x 24 in., private collection

A farm scene is painted on the back

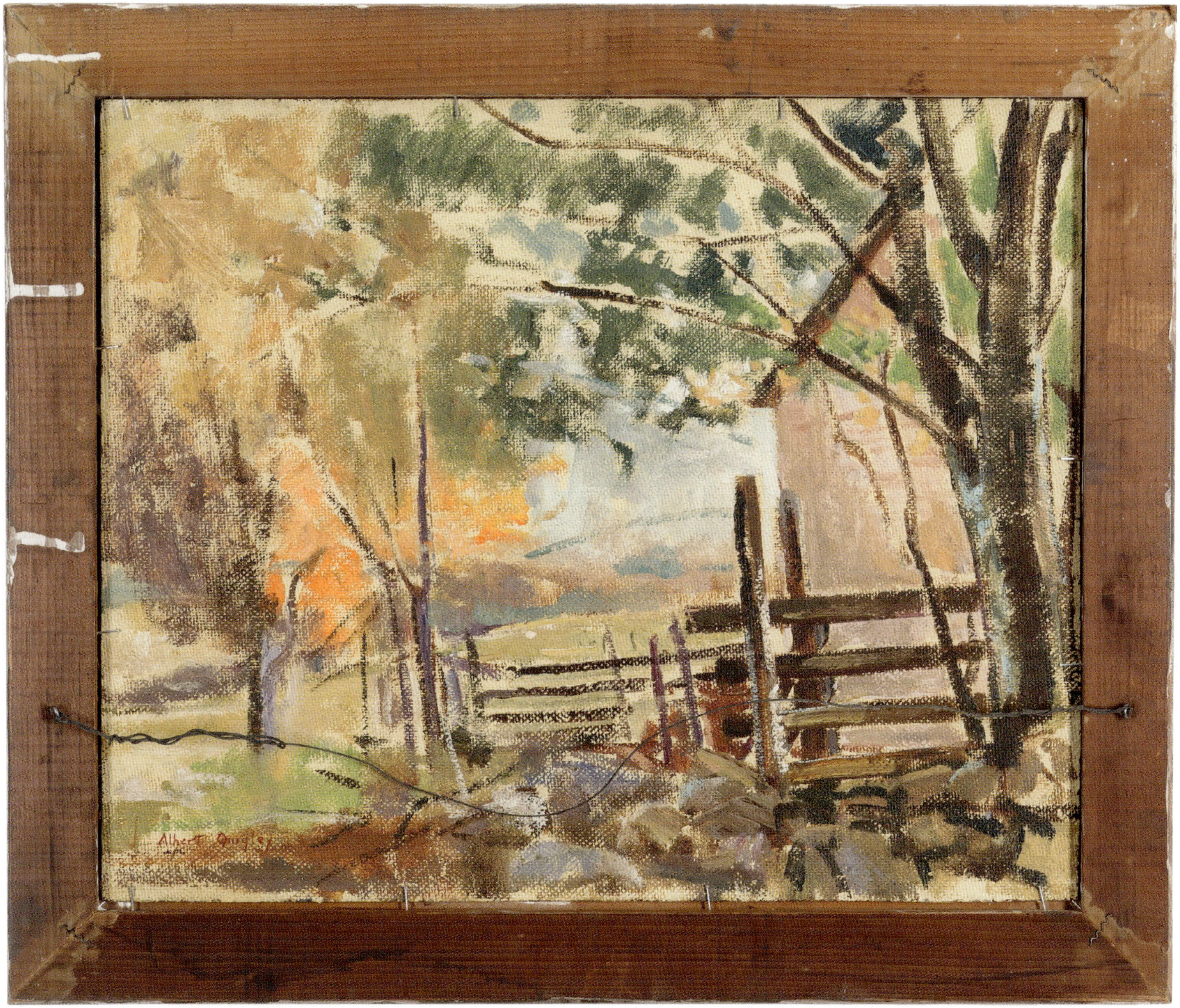

UNTITLED

Painted on the back of painting to the left

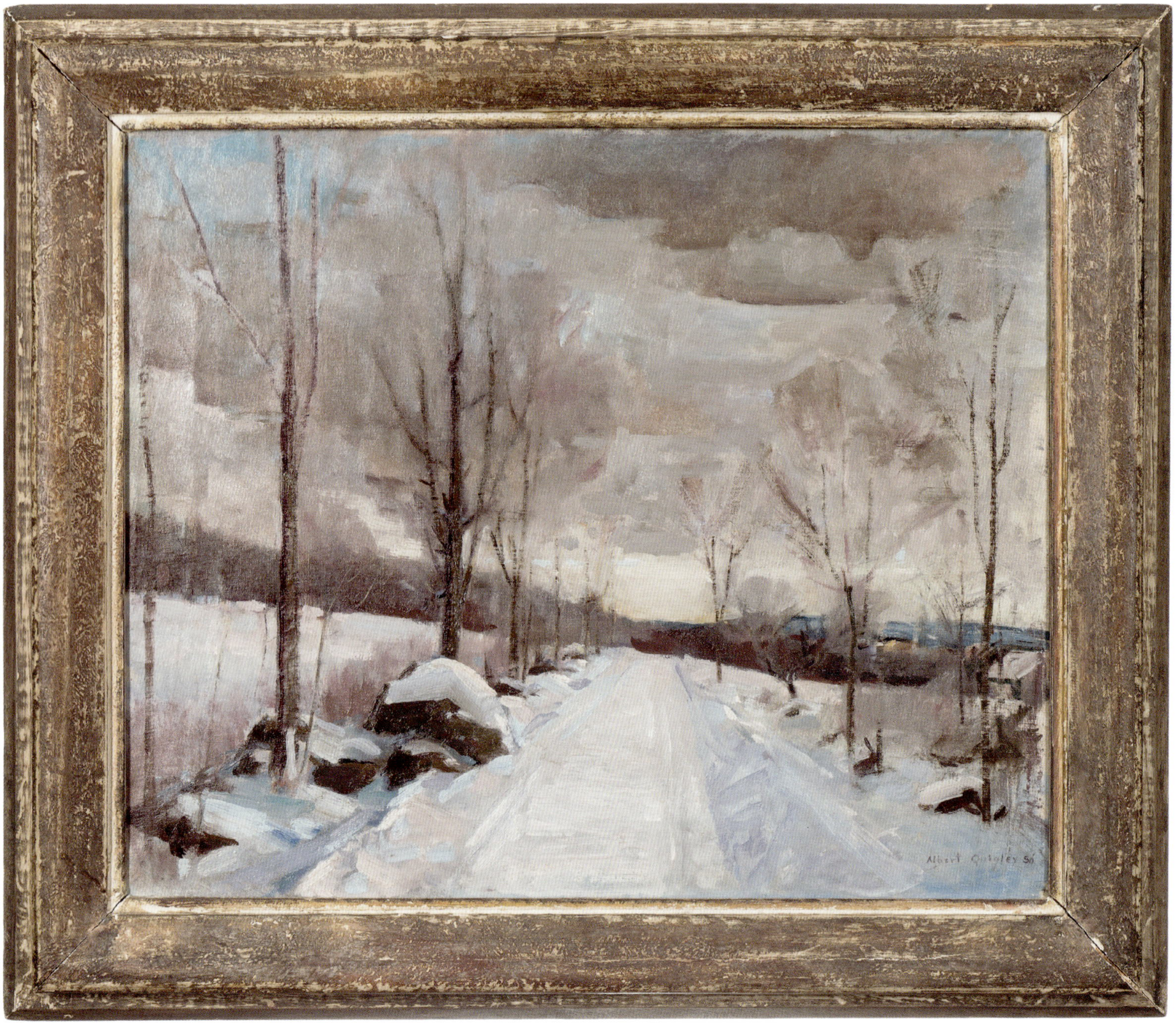

UNTITLED (1950)
Oil on canvas, Quigley frame, 23 x 27 in.
Private collection

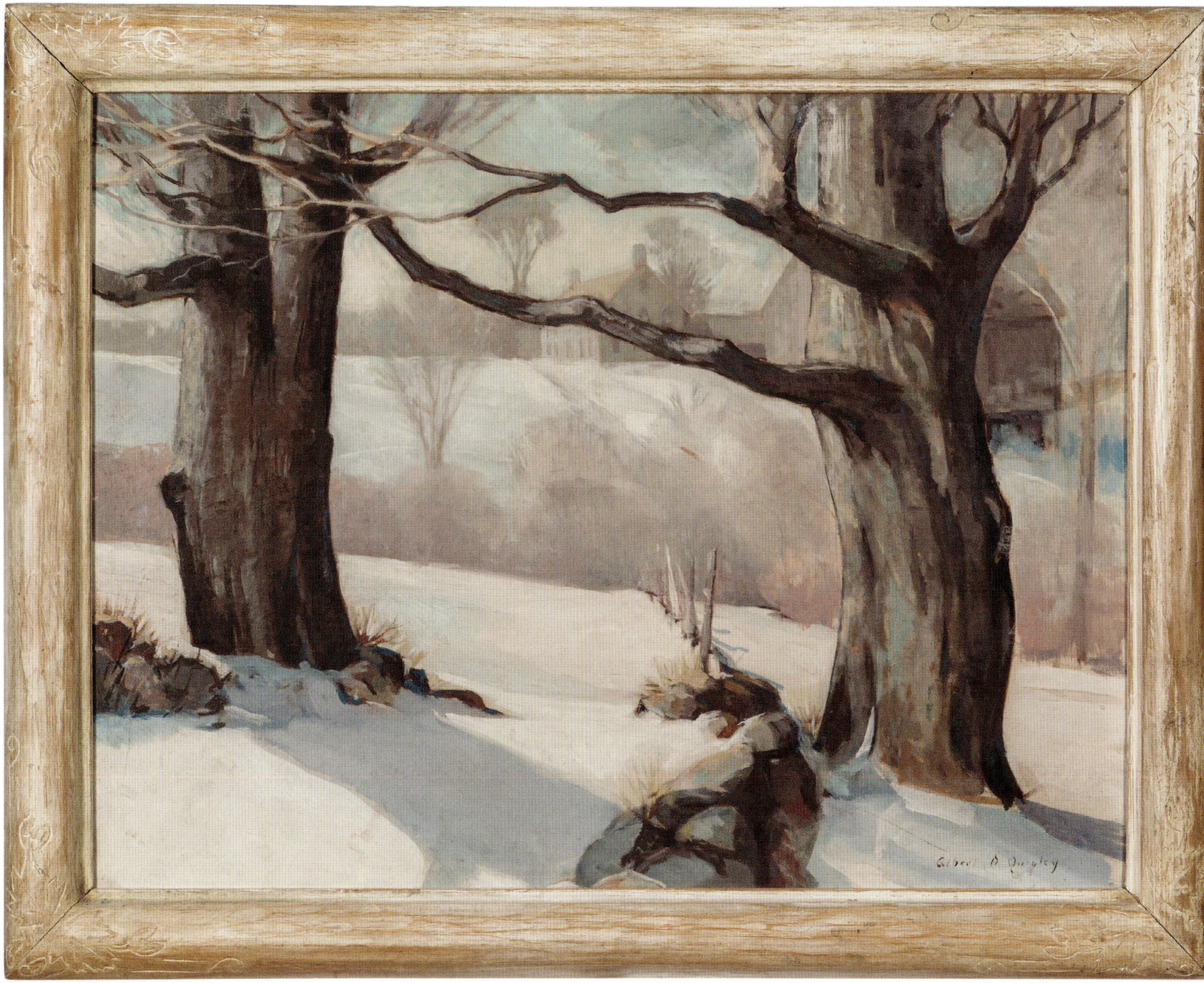

UNTITLED

Oil on board, Quigley frame, 22 x 28 in.

Private collection

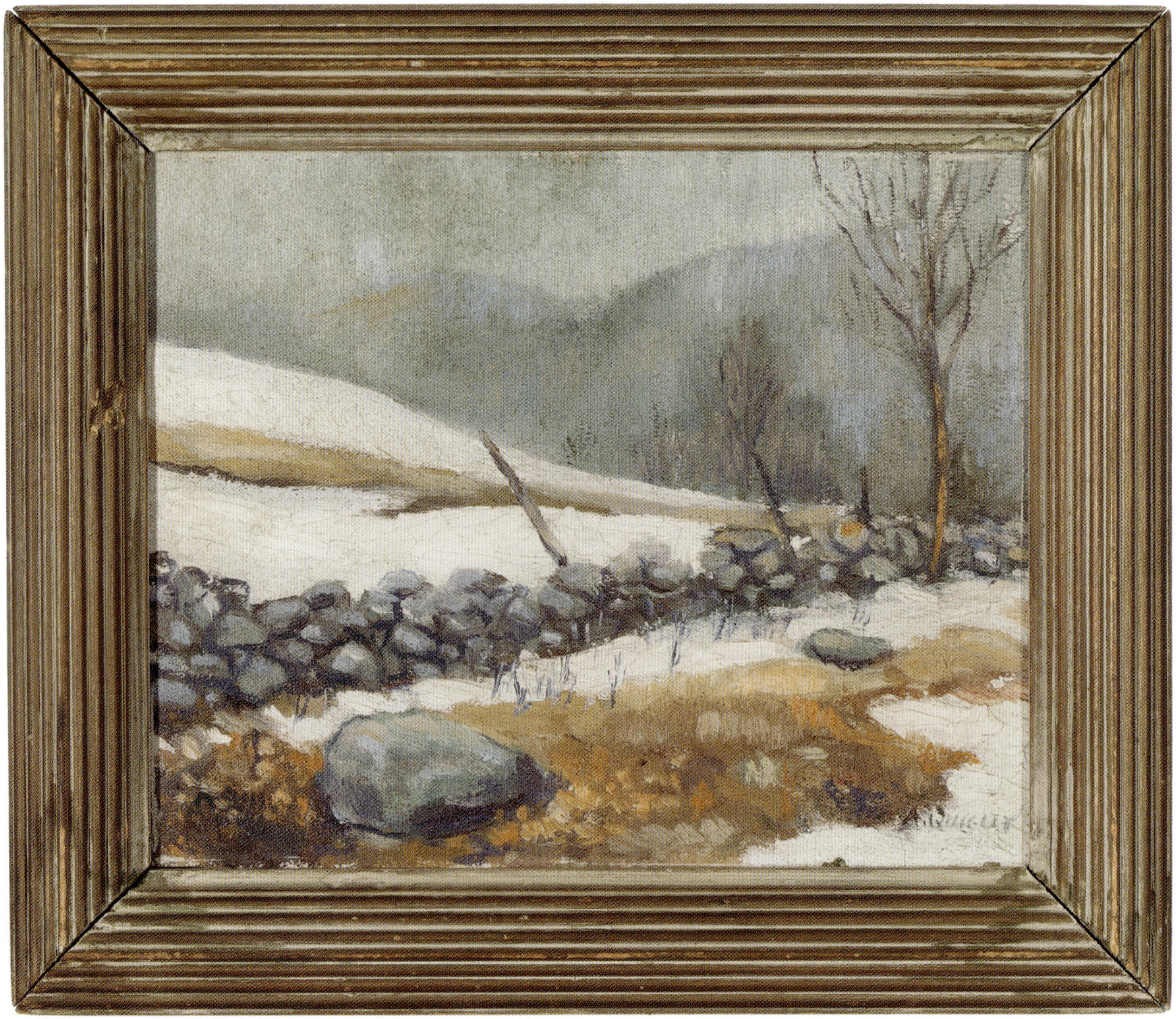

UNTITLED (1925)
Oil on board, 13 x 15 in.
Alston W. Barrett
Winter scene on the road to Gilsum Boulder

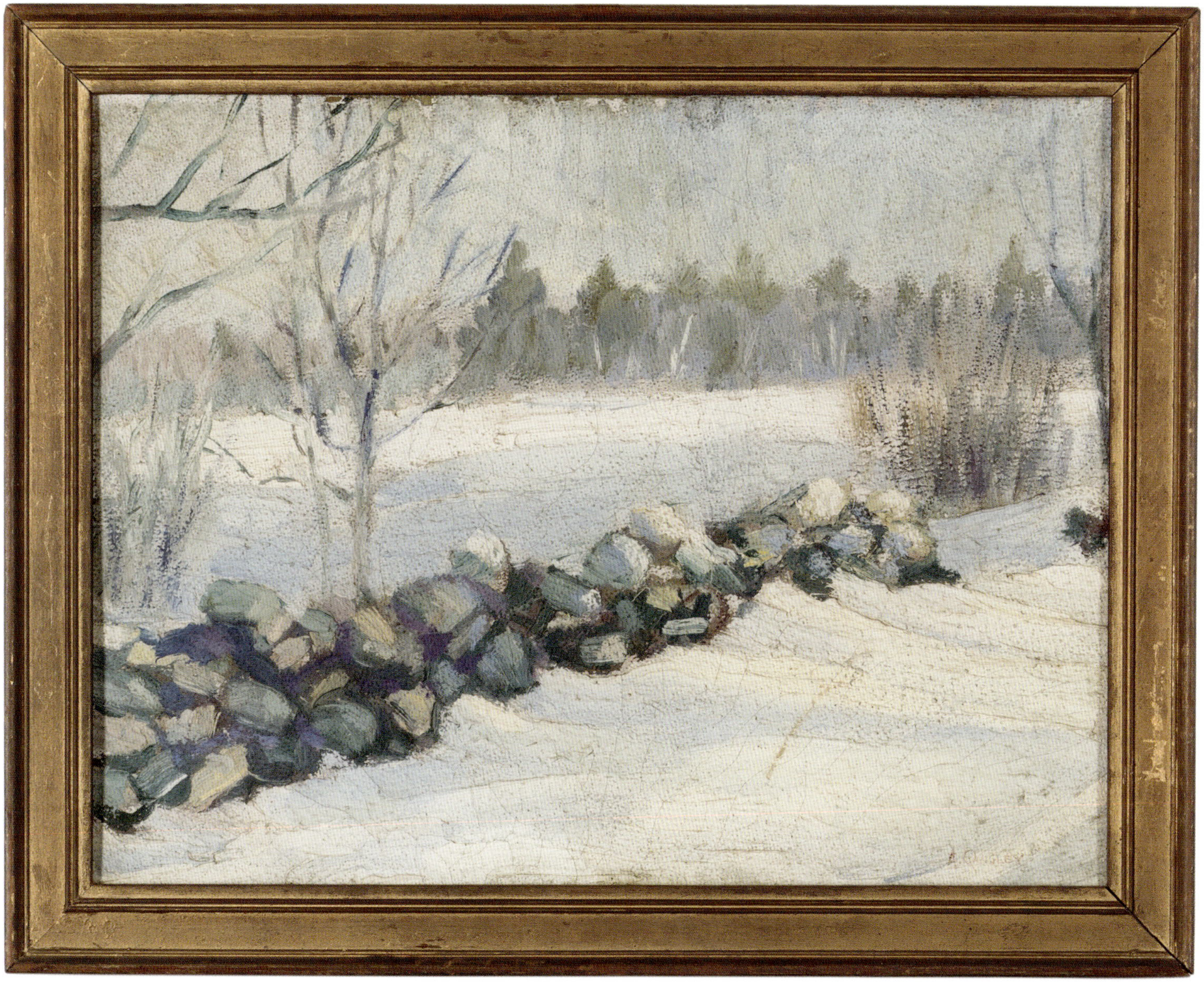

UNTITLED (1925)
Oil on board, 11 x 14 in.
Alston W. Barrett
Inscribed on back: "Gift to Louis G. Barrett Feb. 1925."

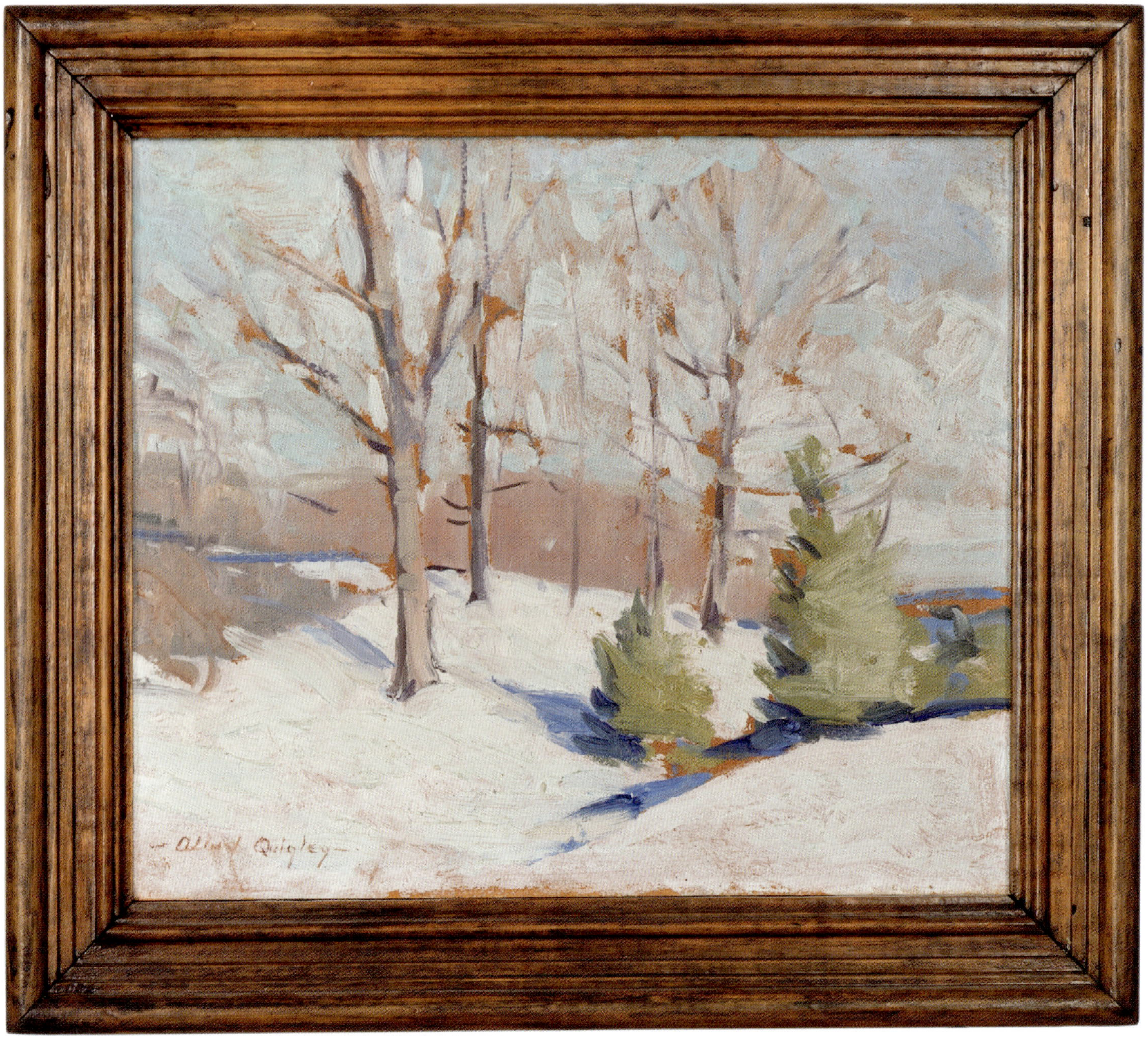

UNTITLED

Oil on board, 15 x 17 in.

Private collection

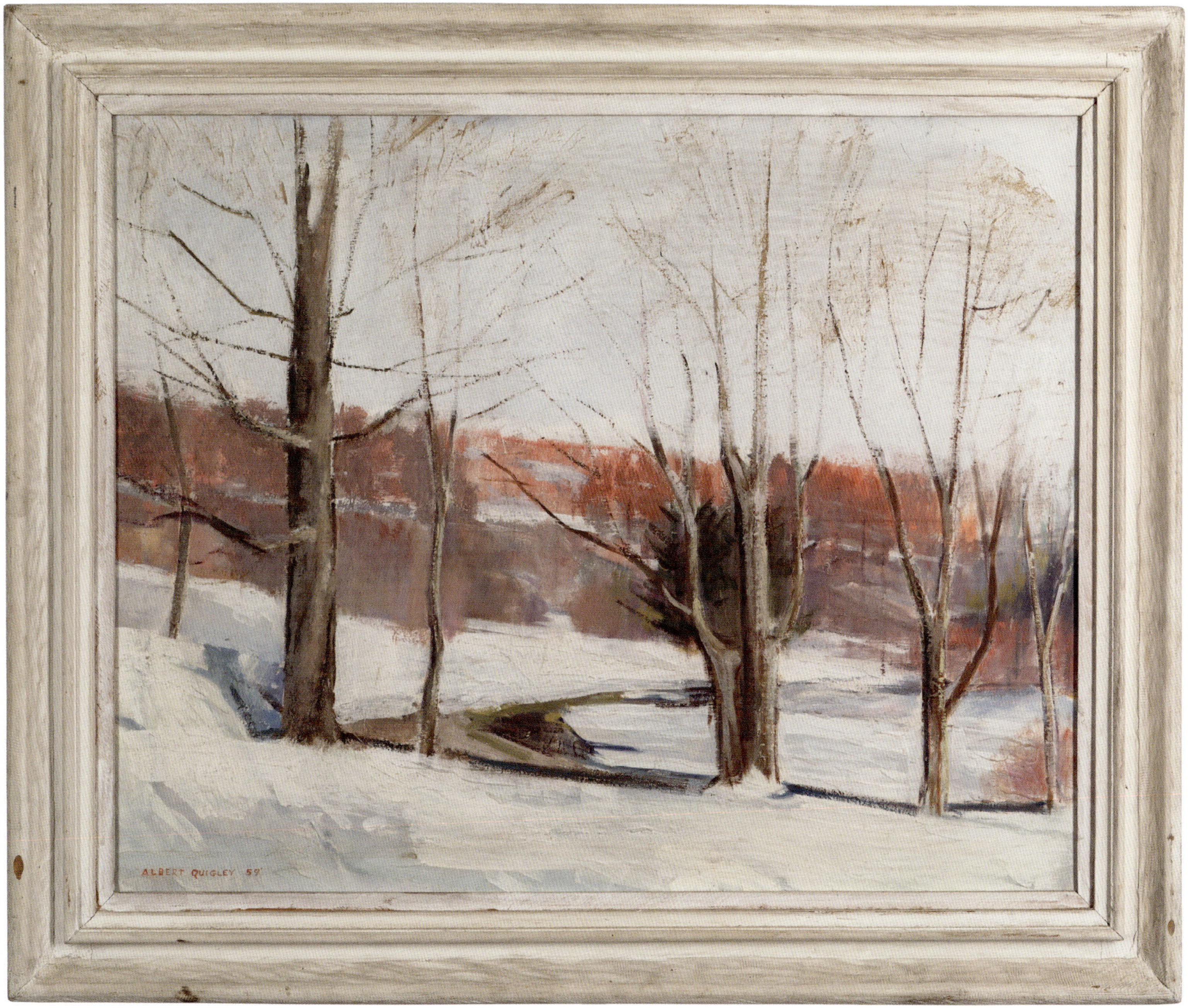

UNTITLED (1959)
Oil on canvas, Quigley frame, 29 x 36 in.
Private collection

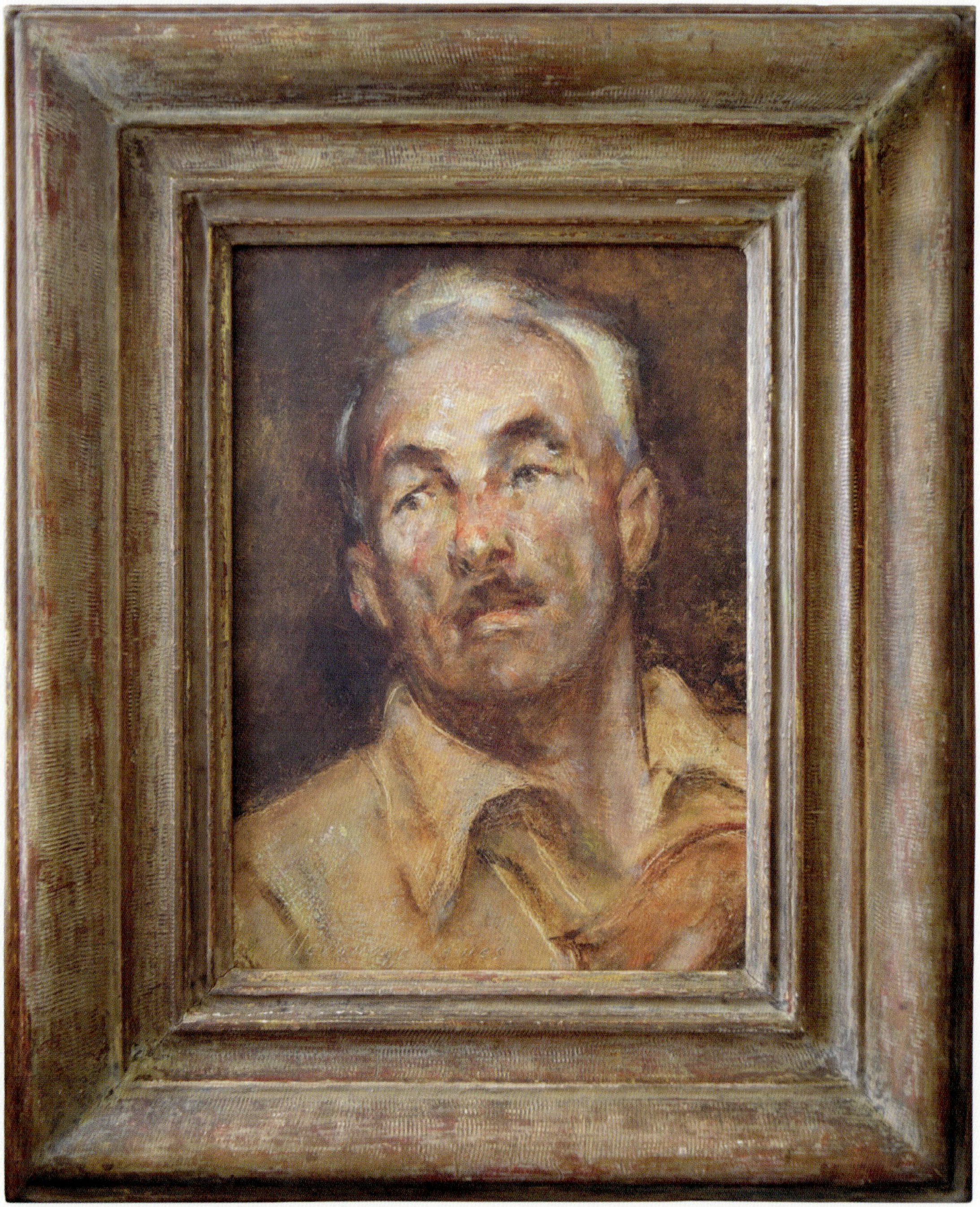

ALBERT D. QUIGLEY
(ca. 1940)
by Alexander James
Oil on board
19 x 16 in.
Quigley frame
Private collection
Peter McDonald,
photographer

Three Letters

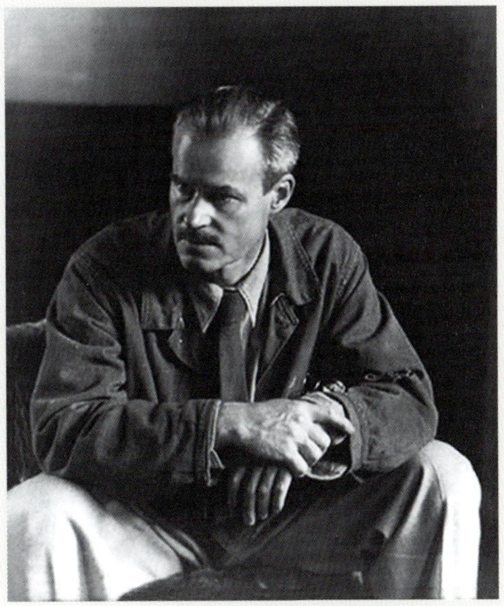

Alexander James in 1938
Peter A. Juley & Son, photographer

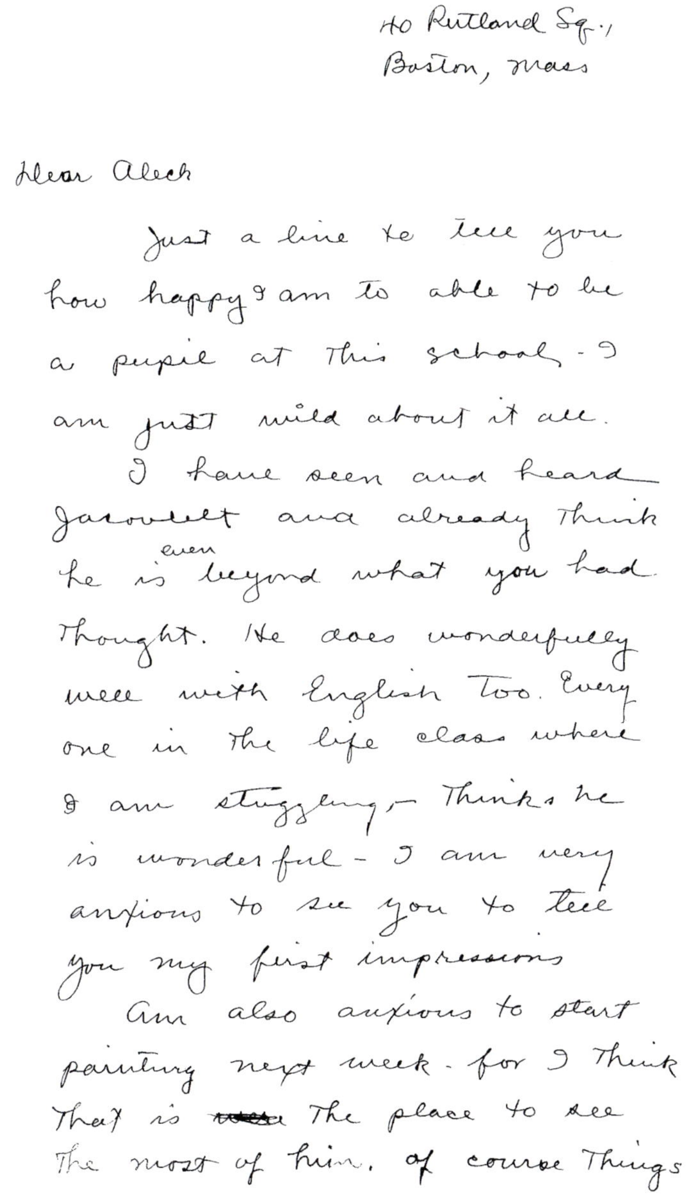

40 Rutland Sq.,
Boston, Mass

Dear Aleck

Just a line to tell you how happy I am to able to be a pupil at this school. - I am just wild about it all.

I have seen and heard Jacovleff and already think he is even beyond what you had thought. He does wonderfully well with English too. Every one in the life class where I am struggling - thinks he is wonderful - I am very anxious to see you to tell you my first impressions

Am also anxious to start painting next week - for I think that is [illegible] the place to see the most of him. of course things

First page of the first letter from Quigley to Alec James (1934) while Quig was a Bartol Scholar at the School of the Museum of Fine Arts (SMFA) in Boston, where he was taught by Russian artist Alexandre Jacovleff. Courtesy of the Quigley family

are a little unsettled yet but I am learning how to take care of myself very rapidly. I think this must be just about the best Art School in the country

Young Bill made himself known to me first day - very much impressed - nice kid too.

Met my friend Harris - with the result that he and Mrs Harris insists that I stay with them in Winchester with only car fare to pay - which will be three dollars per week, you can readily see it going work out fine - My room at my present address cost $4.00 and none to good at that but would do nicely otherwise.

Had dinner with Mrs Wilber last night. She has that work still open to me. Would like to talk it over with you if you are to be at Dublin this week end.

I have a feeling that I am going to get a lot out of this school business.

Sincerely yours in everything - Quig

First letter, page two

Wednesday night

Dear Aleck,

You must think me a terrible piker by this time - for I really meant to send you a word long before this - I guess I kind of expected to see you once in a while on a Sunday in Nelson. Anyway I have not forgotten you and am looking forward to our next meeting. I hope things are going well with you. I met Mrs Schaff in Keene last Sat. she told me you were at work on Rod's portrait.

Second letter from Quig to Alec James while at SMFA, page one

Courtesy of the Quigley family

I hope you are having a great time and that it is coming along good. He must be a very interesting person to paint. Your brother Bill told me that the Boston Museum had bought the other Cabot picture – perhaps he said that he understood that this was so. God – I hope so. How wonderfully well you deserve it two. Here is my very best on that.

Your brother Bill has been very kind and friendly to me and I feel that I gained much from his friendship. He was in the same life class with me for about two weeks.

We had some great old discussions etc. He had me out to Cambridge one night and we made one trip to the Fogg Museum together.

Aleck I wish I could tell you what these three months have meant to me – but I guess you have some idea I come home Sat with a wealth of good sound understanding of things – that I mean to work on this winter. Also with orders for frames that Jacovleff gave me – not print frames but for paintings. and am I happy?

Here's hoping I see you very soon and until then – Heres luck

Your grateful friend

Quig

Second letter while at SMFA, pages two and three

March 18,
1933.

95, IRVING STREET,
CAMBRIDGE.

Dear Mr Quigley -

I liked the 28-36 frame which you made for me very much but on unboxing it in N.Y. it fell into 4 pieces. There was no evidence of its having had rough treatment in transit and I think the trouble was due to the glue you had used for the corners being in some way defective. My bill for having it re-glued was $5 which I am subtracting from your bill which Aleck tells me was $52. Is that satisfactory to you?

It is possible that another method of dowelling the corners would be an improvement. Your tooling of frames is so good that it is a pity to have any defect in their structure.

I shall certainly come to you for my next frame.

Yours sincerely
William James.

Letter from William (Bill) James to Quigley, 1933
Courtesy of the Quigley family

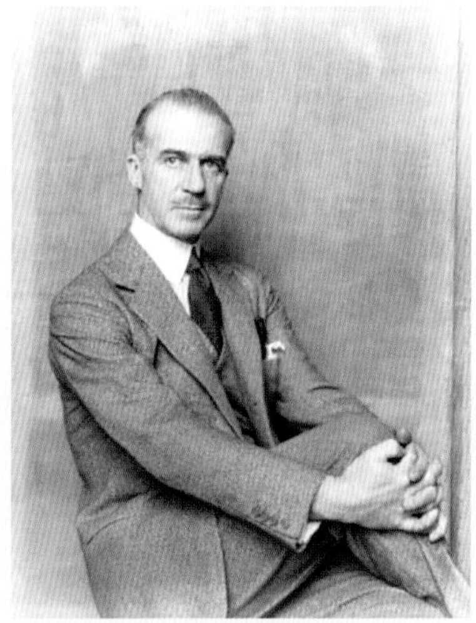

Alec James' older brother, Bill, ca. 1940, who also painted and attended the School of the Museum of Fine Arts while Quig was there in 1934.
Peter A. Juley & Son, photographer

AFTERWORD

The committee responsible for this catalogue began its work in February 2014 under the leadership of Theresa Upton. It was Teri who first suggested a catalogue that would acknowledge the importance of Albert Duvall Quigley's art and his many contributions to the town of Nelson. It was Teri who brought together our small group of people with an interest in the town's history and its reputation as a small, rural community where an unusual number of artists, writers and musicians have made their homes. Without her, this project could never have come to fruition.

We began by discussing the possibility of an exhibition of Quigley's art in conjunction with the 2017 celebration of the town's 250th anniversary. The reasons for choosing him were persuasive. His work had much to say about life in rural New England, and he was an artist who had slipped into obscurity but deserved wider recognition. Furthermore, he had lived in Nelson for over thirty years, he and his family were very much a part of the town's life, and older residents remembered them. His surviving child, Barney, had long been a summer resident and was willing to share his memories of his father and of growing up here.

Our modest project grew when we learned that the Historical Society of Cheshire County in nearby Keene was itself planning a Quigley exhibit. They offered their resources, including the Society's gallery spaces. We readily joined forces and were off and running. It quickly became clear that there were far more paintings—as well as examples of Quigley's commercial art, his framemaking, and his music—than we had ever anticipated. We became fundraisers and secured grants and private donations for this comprehensive catalogue. With roughly a hundred and fifty paintings to include, we arranged for professional photography. We searched for articles and essays that included Quigley and his times, and coaxed reminiscences from people who had known him.

In short, it has been quite an adventure, and we hope it isn't over yet. And that is where readers of this catalogue come in. Because the art reproduced here represents only a fraction of Albert Quigley's hundreds of paintings, we plan to continue searching, and we hope that anyone who knows of more Quigley art, or music, or who has more information about the man and his life will contact us as we expand our Quigley archive. We thank you in advance for helping us to fill in the missing pieces in the story of a remarkable artist.

—The Albert D. Quigley Exhibit Committee

Mary Cornog
Michael Cornog
Johanne de Martelly
Robert Germeroth
Sienna Giffin
Susan Kingsbury
Edith Notman
Barnabas Quigley
Darcy Quigley
Nancy Quigley
Alan Rumrill
Betsy Street
Frankie Tolman
Harvey Tolman
Karen Tolman
Lance Tucker
Sheila Tucker
Theresa Upton, chair

DONORS

INDIVIDUAL DONORS

John and Ann Bunce
Elizabeth and Dix Campbell
Chris Chesney and Sarah Cornog
John and Ann Clarkeson
Michael and Mary Cornog
William Coughlin
Martha Craig
John A.Cuthbert
Lucy Daniels
Marylou DiPietro and Andrew Maneval
Lynn C. Elder
Marilyn B. and E. Gordon Ellicott, Jr.
Michael and Gretchen Ezell
Charles Felix
Sylvia Felix
Charles and Shirley Fiderio
Harry and Anita Flanagan
Jan Forney
William Francis
Barbara Fraser and Greg Fraser
Marion Frazier
Robert Germeroth
John H. Giffin, Jr., 1999 Trust
Jane Gill-Shaler
Gail Googins
Shane Hanchett
Susan Hansel
Frances A. Heaney
Karen Hersey
Katherine Hyman
Michael and Alouette Iselin
Peter and Beverly Kerber
Donna Kidd
Wendy Klemperer
Paul Landry and Joy Perry
Leslie Lawrence
Ruth Lemay and Bruce McSheehy
Daniel Lyon
Kip and Sandy Mackenzie
Judith Maule and Jeffrey Taylor
Stephen McGovern and Lisa Baglione
S. Neil and Melanie McKnight
Clark and Jane Moeller
Tom Murray and Linda Cates
James E. Newcombe
Thomas and Carol Newcombe
Edith Notman
Max Nunnemaker and Lisa Sieverts
Samuel and Julie Osherson
Gordon and Susan Peery
Judith Putzel
Darcy Quigley
Nancy Quigley
Richard Ragin and Marcia Smith
William and Carolyn Rainer
Lorenz and Maria Rhomberg
Harold and Eva M.Roeder, III
Greg Rothman and Linda Singer
Lynne Russell-Johnson
Ed and Rita Schillemat
Bronson and Mary Shonk
Jonathan Smith and Laurie Redfern-Smith
Fernando Sousa and Carol Gerbis
Charles and Sandra Tatham
Barry and Karen Tolman
Frankie and Harvey Tolman
Lance and Sheila Tucker
Louis Tucker and Lance Tucker
David and Theresa Upton
Kathleen Vetter and John Zurich
Priscilla Walter
William and Judith Waterston
John Wengler and Dragana Pilipovic
Amy Whitney and Gary Robinson
Woody and Elise Widlund
Hilda and Tom Wiggin
Priscilla Williams
Roberta J. Wingerson

CORPORATE SPONSORS

The Bean Foundation
The Gilbert Verney Foundation
The Kingsbury Fund
Monadnock Paper, Inc.
New Hampshire State Council on the Arts
The Putnam Foundation

MEMORIAL GIFTS IN HONOR OF BARNEY QUIGLEY

Charles and June Camp
Zoe and Nikolaos Charitos
Mabel Cohen
Maury and Martha Collins
Mortimer and Carol Frank
Jay Joan Gerbis
Carolyn and John Greiner
Karen Hersey
Carolee Iltis
Ruth Kurtz
Leslie Leubkeman
Lisa Marum
Margo Miller
Edward and Virginia Mills
Aida Notides
Christopher and Catherine Oliva
Jean Pearce
Beth and Dan Prawdzik
Riverdale Art Association
Alan and Kim Rumrill
Lance and Sheila Tucker
Ronald and Catherine Whitlach

MEMORIAL GIFTS IN HONOR OF RENN TOLMAN

Barry and Karen Tolman
Betsy Street

ACKNOWLEDGMENTS

Many people contributed to the success of this project. The Albert D. Quigley Committee would especially like to thank Dave Birchenough; Ellen Bowman; Edie Clark; Alex Cucchi; John Cucchi; Beth Draper; Eleanor Drury/Drury Associates; The Dublin Historical Society; Janet Egan; Candyce Fulford; Martha Goble; Ted Goble; Lumina Greenway; Karen Hersey; The Historical Society of Cheshire County; Lee Germeroth Photography; The Olivia Rodham Memorial Library; Michael Lovell; Gordon Peery; Allison and Hunt Smith; Lance and Sheila Tucker; Lisa Quigley Valliere; Harriett Wise; and the team at Bauhan Publishing: Sarah Bauhan, Henry James (grandson of Quig's friend Alexander James), and Mary Ann Faughnan. We would also like to thank all those, too many to name, who gave permission to share stories, writings, photographs, and images of privately held artwork for inclusion in this catalogue, and the impressive number of donors who supported our work. This project would not have been possible without all of you.

SOURCES BY PAGE NUMBER

p. 9: Sarton, May. *A World of Light: Portraits and Celebrations*. New York: W. W. Norton & Company, Inc., 1976. Used by permission.

p. 11: Charleston Renaissance Gallery. "W. Lester Stevens (1888–1969)." From the website Ask Art, s.v. "William Lester Stevens," http://www.askart.com.

p. 13: Sarton, May. *Plant Dreaming Deep*. New York: W. W. Norton and Company, Inc., 1968. Used by permission.
Clark, Edie. "Albert Duvall Quigley—Village Painter (1891–1961)," 2008. Taken from the biographical essay on the website of the Friends of the Dublin Art Colony, s.v. "Historic Artists," http://www.monadnockart.org. Used by permission.

p. 23: Sarton, May. *A World of Light: Portraits and Celebrations*.

p. 35: Clark, Edie. "Albert Duvall Quigley—Village Painter (1891–1961)."

p. 59: (Melville sources) Fuller, Henry Melville. *Henry Melville 1858–1930*. Nelson, New Hampshire: Trustees of the Olivia Rodham Memorial Library, 1967. *The National Cyclopedia of American Biography*. New York: James T. White Co., 1891.

p. 60: (Shedd sources) Peery, Susan. "Getting Out of the Office," Keene State Today, XXII, no. 2 (Winter 2007).
Keene History Committee, The. Upper Ashuelot: A History of Keene, New Hampshire. Keene, New Hampshire: The City of Keene, New Hampshire, 1968.
Bright, Jonathan Brown, and Henry Bright, Jr. "The Bright Legacy," in *One Thousand New Hampshire Notables: Brief Biographical Sketches of New Hampshire Men and Women, Native or Resident, Prominent in Public, Professional, Business, Educational, Fraternal or Benevolent Work*. Edited and compiled by Henry Harrison Metcalf and Frances M. Abbott. Concord, New Hampshire: The Rumford Printing Company, 1919.

p. 63: (Mason sources) Keene History Committee, *The Upper Ashuelot: A History of Keene, New Hampshire*. Keene, New Hampshire: The City of Keene, New Hampshire, 1968.
Smart, James G. *Striving: Keene State College 1909/1984—The History of a Small Public Institution*. Sugar Hill, New Hampshire: Phoenix Publishing, 1984.
Wikipedia, s.v. "Keene State College," http://en.wikipedia.org.

p. 68: Batchelder Violins website, s.v. "biographies," http://www.batchelderviolins.com.

p. 76: Tolman, Renn. *Newt Tolman and the Haynes Flute*. Homer, AK: Kamishak Publishing, 2013. Used by permission.

p. 77: Tolman, Beth, and Ralph Page, *The Country Dance Book: The Best of the Square and Contra Dances and All About Them*. Weston, Vermont: The Countryman Press, Inc., 1937.

p. 80: "Square Dancing Had Ups and Downs, Say Fiddlers," *The Keene Sentinel*, Keene, New Hampshire, August 8, 1947. Used by permission.

p. 81: Clark, Edie. *Monadnock Tales*. Peterborough, New Hampshire: The Brown Rabbit Press, 2002. Used by permission.

p. 83: Bauhan, William L. Written for the 1995 exhibit at the Nelson Town Hall, "The Paintings of Albert Quigley: The Nelson Years, 1934–1961." Used by permission.

p. 95: Clark, Edie. "Albert Duvall Quigley—Village Painter (1891–1961)."

p. 101: Ibid.

p. 107: Riley, Bonnie A. Written for the 1995 exhibit at the Nelson Town Hall, "The Paintings of Albert Quigley: The Nelson Years, 1934–1961." Used by permission.
Bemis, Schuyler. Written for the 1980 exhibit at the Thorne-Sagendorph Art Gallery, Keene State College, Keene, New Hampshire. Used by permission.

p. 132: Hyman, Tom. *Village on a Hill: A History of Dublin, New Hampshire, 1752–2000*. Portsmouth, New Hampshire: Peter E. Randall Publisher, 2002.

p. 164: de Martelly, Joey. Written for the 1995 exhibit at the Nelson Town Hall, "The Paintings of Albert Quigley: The Nelson Years, 1934–1961." Used by permission.

CHRONOLOGY

1891	Albert Duvall Quigley born in Frankfort, Maine, on April 23, 1891
1917	Drafted into the US Army
1919	Awarded an American Expeditionary Forces scholarship to study painting at the Isadora Duncan Pavilion in Bellevue, France, outside Paris
1920	Resettled in Keene, New Hampshire
1925	Married Mildred Gilmore on October 5, 1925
1931	Terrence (Terry) Quigley born on October 21, 1931
1934	Moved to Nelson, New Hampshire
1934	Became a Bartol Scholar at the School of the Museum of Fine Arts (SMFA)
1936	Barnabas (Barney) Quigley born on June 3, 1936
1938	Thomasa (Tami) Quigley born on December 13, 1938
ca.1940	Purchased the Nelson house and property (probably late '30s or early '40s)
1946	Solo exhibit at the Rodman Gallery, Fitzwilliam, New Hampshire
1961	Albert Quigley succumbed to cancer, age 69, January 23, 1961
1961	Solo exhibit organized by Frederika James, widow of Alexander James. Held at the James studio in Dublin, New Hampshire, where Quigley and James had worked together, July 22–July 26, 1961
1980	Solo exhibit, *Albert Quigley 1891-1961*, curated by Schuyler Bemis (now Schuyler Gerstenzang), at the Thorne-Sagendorph Art Gallery at Keene State College, Keene, New Hampshire, August 31–September 28, 1980
1991	Solo exhibit presented at the Community Church of Chesham and Harrisville, Chesham, New Hampshire, curated by Edie Clark
1995	Solo exhibit, *Paintings by Albert Quigley: The Nelson Years, 1934–1961*, held at the Nelson Town Hall. Curated by Bonnie Riley and Joey de Martelly, July 4, 1995. Included a combination of paintings, photographs, and texts about Quig's presence in Nelson
2017	Publication of *Albert Duvall Quigley 1891–1961: Artist, Musician, Framemaker*, the first comprehensive color catalogue of Quigley's art, by The Albert D. Quigley Exhibit Committee, May 2017
2017	Solo exhibit, *Albert Duvall Quigley 1891–1961, Artist, Musician, Framemaker*, held at the Historical Society of Cheshire County, Keene, New Hampshire, May 5–September 8, 2017; curated jointly by The Albert D. Quigley Exhibit Committee and the Historical Society of Cheshire County

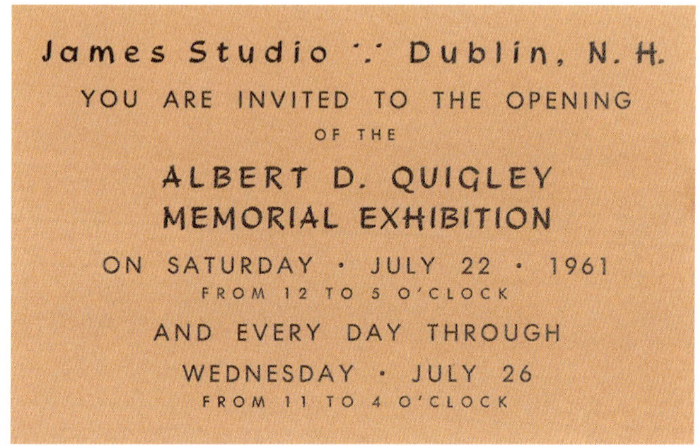
James Studio ∴ Dublin, N. H.
YOU ARE INVITED TO THE OPENING
OF THE
ALBERT D. QUIGLEY
MEMORIAL EXHIBITION
ON SATURDAY • JULY 22 • 1961
FROM 12 TO 5 O'CLOCK
AND EVERY DAY THROUGH
WEDNESDAY • JULY 26
FROM 11 TO 4 O'CLOCK